CONSOLATION FOR THE TRIBULATIONS OF ISRAEL

JUDAICA

Texts & Translations

❧

Second Series

NUMBER ONE

samuel usque's

CONSOLATION

FOR THE

TRIBULATIONS

OF

ISRAEL

(CONSOLAÇAM AS TRIBULAÇOENS DE ISRAEL)

Translated from the Portuguese by

MARTIN A. COHEN

THE JEWISH PUBLICATION SOCIETY OF AMERICA

PHILADELPHIA

5737 – 1977

TO

THE MEMORY OF MY PARENTS

ADA COHEN

&

JOSEPH J. COHEN

FOREWORD

JACOB RADER MARCUS

Many centuries ago a thoughtful and scholarly Jew asked the question: Why do the righteous suffer? Long before Job posed that problem to his generation, however, prophetic writers had asked a somewhat similar question: Why has the Jewish State been destroyed? Why has God brought the calamity of foreign conquest upon us; why has He rejected us? The prophetic passages of consolation and restoration were the answer to that anguished cry. And hundreds of years later, when the Second Commonwealth died on the walls of Jerusalem and high on the crags of Masada, a new generation of visionaries dreamt dreams of a great day yet to come when the God of their fathers would redeem those who had been crushed under the heel of the ruthless and implacable Roman tyrant.

The Diaspora followed with its wanderings from Palestine to Mesopotamia and finally to the West—to Moslem Spain, where a new Golden Age was to shine in resplendent glory, illuminating the centuries between antiquity and modernity. But the decline of the Moslems and the emergence of a new crusading Christian Spain meant that the magnificent Iberian Jewish commonwealth of the spirit would go down to extinction in the fires of the Inquisition. In 1492, royal fiat decreed an end to Spanish Jewry, the greatest Jewry the world had yet known. Thousands of Spanish Jews departed overseas, ultimately to disappear as a cultural force of any significance. Other thousands became Marranos, saving themselves from expulsion by accepting baptism, but living, in numerous instances, as crypto-Jews bound only by lip service to a Christianity which offered them neither faith, nor hope, nor charity. Thousands more, who fled to Portugal, found themselves compelled there to endure a governmentally imposed conversion and to suffer contempt as a breed of New Christians.

That generation of the 1490's knew that it had been cast into a fiery furnace from which many of its members would never escape. Like their ancestors in the days of the Babylonian Exile, and like their forefathers who saw huge numbers of Jews crucified on the Roman roads, they, too, asked: Why did this happen to us? And they asked: Are the Christians right? Are we being punished because we have rejected their Christ?

Is there no hope for the Marranos of Spain, for the New Christians of Portugal, for the scattered Sephardic refugees of the Mediterranean world?

Every persecuted, tormented age must evoke an answer or die in despair. What the prophets and the apocalyptists had attempted for their times, Samuel Usque, a Portuguese Jew, now sought to do for his people in the sixteenth century. As he saw his fellow Jews beaten, dispersed, and spiritually cowed, he wrote a religious tract for the times: God has not rejected his chosen people; they still stand proudly, refuting by their very existence all calumnies. A great future—a messianic millennial deliverance—lies in store for them, for they are the Children of a God who will never abandon them. Take hope—said Usque to his brethren—the dawn of a new and better day is about to burst forth in golden light over the pale horizon. It was Usque's way of bringing Consolation for the Tribulations of Israel.

Is our own generation any different? Six million of our brethren, men, women, and children, went to their death in the fiery ovens of Germany. A country calling itself the most civilized in the world saw fit, in our own day, to destroy a Golden Age that had given birth to a magnificent synthesis of Judaism and Western culture. What, then, is *our* Consolation for the Tribulations of Israel? What is the answer for the thoughtful and the disconsolate among us today? Anxious to help us reach out for an answer, a brilliant young scholar, Martin A. Cohen, has prepared a translation of Usque's probings, and we can but hope that the reading of this scroll, which Dr. Cohen has unrolled before us, will help give us insight and understanding so that we, too, may regain strength and faith to face the world of tomorrow.

American Jewish Archives
Cincinnati, Ohio
November 16, 1964

PREFACE TO
THE SECOND EDITION

Twelve years have elapsed since the first publication of this translation. During this time Samuel Usque's sixteenth-century New Christian audience has become the focus of considerable scholarly attention. Countless documents touching their lives have been explored, among them tens of thousands of pages from the trial records of the Spanish and Portuguese Inquisitions. The studies in which these explorations have been reported illumine numerous facets of the life of the New Christians. With increasing cogency they show that the people for whom Usque felt it necessary to compose his work were far more complex than had previously been realized.

One of the areas that has been flooded with new light is the religious life of the New Christians. In the prologue to the first edition of the translation of the *Consolaçam às tribulaçoens de Israel* I wrote: "Suddenly, in the middle of the fifteenth century, the New Christians as a group were accused of being heretics, of practicing in secret the religion of their fathers which they had publicly repudiated by their willing conversion to Christianity. The charge was false: the Old Christians had contrived the canard to fan popular hatred against their adversaries and to provide a justifiable religious ideology for their liquidation" (p. 4). The canard, of course, became the propaganda mainstay of the proponents and defenders of the Inquisition from the fifteenth century on. Curiously, beginning with the nineteenth century, it has been adopted by various Jewish writers who have been as desirous as the partisans of the Inquisition to demonstrate that Jews are irremediably recalcitrant or even congenitally indisposed to assimilation.

Various studies in the past twelve years support my analysis entirely. Of the numerous challenging books reaching this conclusion two are worthy of particular mention. They are Henry Kamen's *The Spanish Inquisition* (London, 1965) and António José Saraiva's *Inquisição e Cristãos-Novos* (Porto, 1969). To these there should now be added perceptive shorter studies like Francisco Márquez Villanueva's "The Converso Problem: An Assessment" and Antonio Domínguez Ortiz's "Historical Research on Spanish Conversos in the Last Fifteen Years," both published in *Col-*

lected *Studies in Honor of Americo Castro's Eightieth Year* (ed. M. P. Hornik, Oxford, 1965), as well as Stephen H. Haliczer's "The Castilian Urban Patriciate and the Jewish Expulsions of 1480–1492," *American Historical Review* 78 (1973), pp. 35–58. Ellis Rivkin's pioneering study was available when this translation was prepared and is therefore duly registered in the bibliography. I myself have continued my exploration in this area in various studies pertaining especially to Latin America, including "Some Misconceptions About the Crypto-Jews in Colonial Mexico," *American Jewish Historical Quarterly* 61 (1972), pp. 277–93, and my book *The Martyr* (Jewish Publication Society, 1973).

Although Usque doctrinairely declares that the New Christians "never exchanged the secret of their souls" (p. 206), other statements of his (for example, p. 209) and the very presence of his work suggest a contrary reality. Addressed to New Christian expatriates who hesitated or refused to embrace Judaism once they landed in countries where its open practice was permitted, it reveals a sufficiently large and troubling number of such people to have warranted the composition of the *Consolaçam'as tribulaçoens de Israel* and the support of a Maecenas like the redoubtable Doña Gracia Nasi.

The recent challenges to the inquisitorial posture on the New Christians have provoked interesting debates on the extent of the New Christians' Jewish identity, the credibility of inquisitorial records, and the role of both the Inquisition and the New Christians in the Iberian world. Of particular significance has been the torrid literary confrontation between the late I. S. Révah, of the Sorbonne, and António José Saraiva, then of the University of Amsterdam. Ironically, in this debate Révah, the Jew, defended the integrity of the Inquisition's ideology, while Saraiva, the Catholic, attacked it. This debate was deemed of sufficient popular interest in Portugal to be published serially by the prestigious *Diário de Lisboa* from May to September 1971.

In some of his less felicitous argumentation Révah attempts to discredit Saraiva by pointing to the fact that Saraiva had not read inquisitorial dossiers firsthand. Far from denying this, Saraiva had admitted it with an occasional boast. He has worked by relying on published records and exposing the inconsistencies revealed in the works of his opponents. That he had done a masterly job is corroborated by the findings of other scholars who have reached similar conclusions after years of archival burrowing.

Perhaps in extrapolation from their own general ideological unity, the defenders of the inquisitorial position have regularly assumed their opponents to possess a theoretical unity which simply does not exist. The challengers agree on three broad planks: first, that the New Christian issue was certainly not solely, and perhaps not primarily, a religious issue; second, that the Inquisition in Spain, Portugal, and their respective satellites was not solely, or even primarily, a religious institution; and third, that recourse to the social, political, and economic factors along with the religious is essential for an understanding of both the Inquisition and the New Christians. Within these generalities, the opponents of the Inquisition's ideology differ markedly from one another.

The idea that the bond uniting New Christians transcended religion is of utmost significance. As long as scholarship was generally persuaded that a devotion to Judaism was their unifying factor, the New Christians and the Inquisition could be regarded as vestiges of the medieval world extending into the nineteenth century. New research strongly supports the contention that instead of being a coda to the medieval world, the New Christians and the Inquisition were early products of a modern world whose presence in Spain and Portugal is otherwise evidenced during those centuries. The Inquisition, with its doctrinaire indictment of an entire group as "the enemy" and its terrifying methods of apprehending, trying, and punishing its "criminals," appears to furnish a precursory instance of conformity-insuring institutions in modern totalitarian societies. The New Christians, on the other hand, become the forerunners of the Jews of the early Enlightenment. Like the later Enlightenment Jews, although not in the same way of course, the New Christians were separated from the organic Jewish community; they were given rights in the general society; they rose to positions of importance; they began to assimilate. Before long, however, they found themselves stultified by exclusionist ideologies based on mythical concepts of nationality and race.

The full implications of the new challenges must yet be comprehensively studied. But they have already accomplished much by reopening Samuel Usque's world for further exploration.

Whatever the future direction of such explorations may be, we can be sure that Samuel Usque's eloquent and impassioned testimony to the conditions of his day will continue to serve as an indispensable landmark.

Martin A. Cohen

New York City
22 Shevat 5737
February 10, 1977

PREFACE

Since the days of my graduate studies in Romance Languages and Literature at the University of Pennsylvania, I have been interested in the Inquisition and its attitude toward the Spanish and Portuguese converts from Judaism who were opprobriously dubbed Marranos. Our information about these hapless creatures comes almost exclusively from non-Jewish sources that more often than not manifest a virulence toward the seed of Abraham. Marrano refugees from the Iberian Peninsula have left us glimpses of their life under the Inquisition, but these are infrequent and sporadic, and appear mostly as *obiter dicta* in responsa dealing with legal problems engendered by the Marranos' religious status.

It was therefore a momentous personal discovery when I learned that the library of the Hebrew Union College-Jewish Institute of Religion contained copies of all three editions of the exceedingly rare *Consolaçam as tribulaçoens de Israel,* a history of the Jews written by a Portuguese Marrano who had witnessed the tragic events that befell his people in Portugal in the first half of the sixteenth century.

I learned to my surprise that although several attempts had been made to translate the *Consolaçam* into a language more accessible to modern Jewish scholarship, no full translation of the work as yet existed in any language. I therefore undertook this task and completed the translation nearly five years ago. I proceeded to write a book-length study on the work, which revealed the context of the times in which it was written, and the life, methodology and sources of its author. In preparing the translation for publication, I decided to condense this lengthy study so that it would fit into the confines of the present introduction.

The *Consolaçam* is not an easy work to translate. Its shoals and reefs are difficult to navigate. Its excursive and florid style, its intricate syntax, its lengthy periods, its flexible, almost fickle vocabulary and its abundant Hispanicisms and neologisms all make inordinate demands upon the translator. Its often elusive references to the Bible and to rabbinic and secular literature force him to painstaking research to insure that measure of comprehension which makes possible the translation of the author's intent. Besides, the two sixteenth-century editions and the twentieth-century edition which is based on them are not free of serious textual errors, such as misspellings, incorrect punctuation, word omissions and faulty word divisions. The difficulties involved in the preparation of a translation of the *Consolaçam* have, not without good reason, long been recognized as formidable.

In my translation I have sought to communicate the *Consolaçam's* flavor and variegated style in a lucid and modern English. To accomplish this I have divided Usque's long periods into shorter components, with corresponding adjustments in the various parts of speech affected. I have omitted many of the redundant expressions which characterize Usque's style, but which are not palatable in modern English. I have paraphrased obscure allusions and complex metaphors. In cases of textual error I have, with conservative caution, tried to reconstruct and translate the correct original. For the sake of readability, I have omitted the scholarly brackets or parentheses for such alterations in all but a few of the most important instances, where confusion might otherwise result.

In the translation of Usque's biblical quotations, I have been guided by the translation of *The Holy Scriptures* published in 1917 by the Jewish Publication Society of America.

My translation is based largely upon the modern edition of the *Consolaçam,* published in three parts by Joaquim Mendes dos Remedios in Coimbra, Portugal, between 1906 and 1908.

Considerations of space have limited the length and nature of my notes to each Dialogue of the *Consolaçam*. A detailed commentary to Usque's work, pointing out the numerous historical inaccuracies which it contains, would not have been without value. Most of these errors, however, were not committed by Usque; they belong to the sources which he uncritically accepted and from which he usually borrowed verbatim. It was therefore decided to use the notes to refer the reader to Usque's sources, to call attention to the major changes for which Usque himself is responsible and to elucidate unusual details. In the case of Dialogue II, where Usque copied slavishly from the medieval Pseudo-Josephus (the *Yosippon*) I have, wherever applicable, cited as well the corresponding passages from the works of Josephus. By consulting Josephus, the reader can appreciate the extent to which the Yosippon distorted historical facts and embellished them with legend.

Dialogue III, based on sources not readily available to the reader, contains more detailed footnotes. This is especially true of the last thirteen historical chapters in this Dialogue, which constitute Usque's only original historical contribution in the *Consolaçam*.

The study and translation which follow could not have been achieved without the encouragement of my revered teachers, Professor Jacob Rader Marcus and Professor Ellis Rivkin, of the Hebrew Union College-Jewish Institute of Religion, who have given me of their knowledge, their counsel and their inspiration. Words adequate to express my debt of gratitude to them cannot be found.

I also express my deep appreciation to Dr. Solomon Grayzel, editor of The Jewish Publication Society of America, for his devotion in guiding the manuscript of this book to publication; and to his assistant, Mrs. Evelyn Weiman, for her patient study of the manuscript and her invaluable suggestions for the enhancement of its literary quality.

To the president of the Hebrew Union College-Jewish Institute of Religion, Dr. Nelson Glueck, for his unfailing support of this project; to my colleagues, Drs. Stanley F. Chyet, I. Edward Kiev and Julius Kravetz, for their gracious suggestions and help; to my student, Mr. Leonard Zoll, for assisting me in the preparation of the indices; and to my wife, Shelby Ruth, who helped in the preparation of every phase of the work, go forth my heartfelt thanks.

MARTIN A. COHEN

May 1, 1964

CONTENTS

CONSOLATION FOR THE TRIBULATIONS OF ISRAEL

INTRODUCTION

THE DOUBTING REMNANT

In the middle of the sixteenth century the Portuguese coast swarmed with incessant activity. By day majestic caravels, their hulls bulging with the luxuries of the East, sailed proudly into its harbors. Seamen spoke of exotic lands that formed the outposts of Portugal's growing commercial empire, and writers like Camoens and De Barros captured their excite- ment in poetry and prose. With wealth pouring into its narrow confines, tiny Lusitania began to bask in the sunshine of fortune.[1]

Yet not all its citizens enjoyed this happy estate. While the treasure ships slept in their quays by night, other boats stole surreptitiously out of the land, laden not with regal fare, but with wretched human beings who had strained their last resources to escape from Portugal. Their capture meant certain death for them and eternal obloquy for their families. Their escape opened the possibility for a life of freedom to which they could no longer aspire in the Iberian Peninsula.

These hapless men and women were *conversos*, or New Christians, as they were officially called, though they were less generously and more customarily referred to as *marranos*, or pigs.[2] They were the descendants of recent converts from Judaism in Portugal. Their ancestors had not sought conversion; indeed they had steadfastly resisted the lures and cozening of priests and kings alike until they were forcibly baptized into the Christian faith. Involuntary conversion did not, however, shake the determination of the majority of these people to remain Jews. They feigned Christianity in public, while they continued to teach and prac- tice Judaism in their homes and to meet clandestinely for worship with their fellow New Christians. The Old Christians chafed at reports of these heresies and the king eventually called for an Inquisition to uproot them. An Inquisition, though officially powerless against Jews, could punish heretical converts with fines, imprisonment, degradation and even death.

The New Christians of Portugal who remained constant to Judaism were neither purblind fanatics nor doctrinaire heroes of their ancestral faith. They were not without their moments of doubt and despair. They were warm and tender-hearted people, who desired nothing more than a life of peace for themselves and security for their children. It was not ambition or fanaticism that turned them into heroes. It was rather the forces of history which shaped their destiny in a heroic mold.

Most of the Portuguese New Christians were the descendants of Spanish Jews who had learned through bitter experience that conversion to Christianity did not solve the problems they faced as Jews. In 1391 anti-Jewish feelings had erupted into violent massacres throughout Spain and the Balearic Isles, and in their wake numerous Jewish families had sought protection for their lives and property in the bosom of the Church.[3] For a while they believed that they had found it, for within two generations these New Christians had risen to social and political heights which they could never have hoped to scale as Jews. They had married into the noblest of Old Christian families. They had achieved prominence in positions previously closed to them. They had even attained rank in the hierarchy of the Church.[4]

The waxing wealth and influence of the Spanish New Christians proved to be their undoing. The moment the Old Christian aristocracy felt itself threatened by these parvenus, it turned against the converts with the same spleen it had vented against their Jewish fathers and grandfathers a half century before.[5] Suddenly, in the middle of the fifteenth century, the New Christians as a group were accused of being heretics, of practicing in secret the religion of their fathers which they had publicly repudiated by their willing conversion to Christianity. The charge was false: the Old Christians had contrived the canard to fan popular hatred against their adversaries and to provide a justifiable religious ideology for their liquidation.[6] Some Old Christians rushed to the converts' defense, but their efforts proved unavailing.[7] The Old Christians in government did not hesitate to have Jews appointed to positions of influence in order to offset the New Christians' power, thus manifesting that they were less concerned with the open practice of a despised religion than with the destruction of envied competitors.[8]

To the Jews and the New Christians alike, who knew only too well how sincere the vast majority of converts had been in their new faith, the shocking truth revealed itself that an apostate was as vulnerable to persecution as a Jew who had not converted. As the attacks on the New Christians mounted in intensity, many of them, burdened by feelings of guilt for their conversion and viewing their predicament as a divine visitation for their apostasy, began secretly to return to Judaism. They even sought religious instruction from the Jews who had not wavered in their faith. The Old Christians' charge of heresy was no longer a fraud.[9]

Time was to prove that the position of the New Christians was more precarious than that of the Jews. In 1481 the Catholic Sovereigns, to combat the now patent Judaizing which the Old Christians' propaganda had helped foster and intensify, established an Inquisition to ferret out the heretics, sequester their possessions and punish their persons.[10] The

Inquisition did its work admirably. Its leadership was composed for the most part of sincere and dedicated Christians, as were doubtlessly the majority of Spaniards who favored and supported it. Yet the undeniable fact remains that the Inquisition's net caught many of the wealthiest and most powerful New Christians, and its definition of heresy was sufficiently flexible to encompass many impeccable Old Christians with coveted estates. Within a few short years the Inquisition, imprisoning and torturing hundreds of converts and destroying not a few who were among the country's leading citizens, had engendered a mortal terror in the hearts of all the New Christians of Spain.

In the religiously oriented atmosphere of the time, those who had remained Jews turned to the God of their fathers and thanked Him for strengthening their resolve and sparing them such a fate. Though exposed to oppression and persecution, they felt that their constancy to the Law of Moses would forever shield them against the terrors of the Inquisition, which was officially powerless against unconverted Jews.[11] It is thus not surprising that when the Catholic Sovereigns in 1492 offered the Jews the alternatives of expulsion from Spain or conversion to Christianity, few chose the latter, though it would have meant the preservation of their property and their accustomed mode of life. The fate of their New Christian brethren had in their estimation left them no choice but to take up the wanderer's crook.

Though many of the exiles fled to Africa, Italy and the Ottoman Empire, others preferred to cross Spain's western border into Portugal, attracted by its proximity, its familiar culture and the placid history of the Portuguese Jews. Little did they realize that almost from the moment of their entry this history would change and that the throne of Portugal would embark upon a relentless drive to convert all its Jews to Christianity.[12]

The conditioning of these Jews in Spain had doomed all royal efforts to failure. King John II, who admitted few of the Spanish refugees as permanent residents and gave most of them permission to remain in Portugal for a period of eight months, was loath to let them leave when the term expired. He respected their skills and planned for them to play a vital role in building his domestic economy and providing funds for his military campaigns. He therefore allowed them to stay but spared no effort to induce them to abandon their religion. He first subjected them to conversionist sermons. When he failed to make any headway among them, he tore young Jewish children away from their parents and sent them to be reared as Christians in the insalubrious land of São Thomé, off the African coast. He promised the parents that they would not see their offspring again unless they converted. Again he failed. His efforts were continued by his cousin and successor, Emanuel III (1495-1521), but with the same disappointing results. To please the Catholic Sovereigns of Spain and to pave the way for their daughter's hand in marriage, Emanuel reluctantly issued a decree in December, 1496, expelling all Jews from his dominions. It was, as one historian has stated with poignant irony, the only case of Jewish persecution that has been motivated by love.[13] But Emanuel found it impossible to part with so vital a source of his country's productivity and wealth. After further desperate efforts to convert the Jews had failed, he assembled them in Lisbon on the pretext that he would there provide them with ships for their exile; but when he herded them together, he starved them, sub-jected them to conversionist sermons, and dragged them to the churches. Here he had water sprinkled upon them which baptized them against their will in the faith of Christianity. Soon thereafter he closed the borders of his country to prevent the flight of the panic-stricken Mar-ranos of Portugal.

Emanuel sought to remove all legal distinctions between the New and the Old Christians, but the distinctions persisted in fact, and tensions soon flared between them. The Inquisition across the border, the im-passioned sermons of venomous clerics, and the unconcealed hatred of Emanuel's fanatical queen fanned popular hatred against the erstwhile Jews almost from the beginning of their forced conversion. In panic, many of the new Marranos sought safety in flight, but Emanuel was quick to close the borders to the sources of his wealth. The cowering Marranos began to steal away from Portugal. They were aided often by sympathetic Old Christians, who risked perpetual slavery and death if they were discovered, but who could not tolerate the injustice of the Marranos' plight.

In 1503 the Marranos were blamed for a devastating famine. In the following year an altercation of little moment between some youths of Old and New Christian stock raised tensions to a new pitch. And in the plagued and famine-ridden city of Lisbon, on Easter Sunday, 1506, a Marrano's remark that the sudden glow on a statue of Jesus in the cathedral was no miracle, but the natural reflection of a nearby candle, kindled a frightful massacre: for two days a crazed and bloodthirsty mob ransacked homes, violated women, impaled children on lances and heaped scores of men and women on bonfires. Among the rioters milled many who wore the cloth.

After this incident, tempers cooled. Emanuel severely punished the instigators of the massacre. He opened the doors of Portugal to the New Christians and promised them that no inquiry as to the sincerity of their faith would be made if they opted to remain in his realm. Their Judaizing thus assured, most Marranos stayed in Portugal and, until well into the reign of John III, Emanuel's son and successor, their security was not seriously challenged again. Indeed, many Marranos began to lead the lives of good Christians, at least outwardly, and to reap the benefits which religious conformity made available to the Christians. By the end of Emanuel's reign the New Christians had attained the highest social, political and economic prominence in the land and virtually monopolized medicine, trade and government administration.

This comparatively idyllic state was ephemeral. Had the New Christians, engrossed in the quest for status and wealth, not been blinded to the empirical realities of Portuguese life, they would have perceived the approaching storm clouds that boded ill for their future. The masses' ineradicable antipathy toward the seed of Abraham, the repressed hatred of Marranos for the punishments meted out to Old Christians after the riots of 1506, the increasing jealousy of the Marranos' wealth and favor at the court, and the steady erosion of the social and economic foundations of Portuguese life combined to make the New Christians an easy target for persecution.

The storm broke with sudden fury in the reign of Emanuel's successor, John III (1521-57). Responding to a crescendo of demands for action against the notoriously heretical Marranos, King John, who recalled that in 1515 his father had secretly asked Rome for permission to introduce an Inquisition into Portugal, began considering applying pressure to obtain one.

The Marranos knew well what an Inquisition meant—unrelenting pursuit, excruciating torture, secret denunciations of family and friends, and a haunting fear hovering near them every hour of the day. The Marranos had not wanted to become Christians, but Christians they were and as such the Inquisition had jurisdiction over them. They could plead no innocence: their Judaizing was notorious. All they could hope to do was to marshal all forces at their disposal and prevent the entry of an Inquisition into Portugal.

This they did for a while. They made available large sums of money to fight the Inquisition, suborned highly placed government and ecclesiastical officials to aid them, and maintained skillful lobbyists in the Vatican to plead their cause. To their good fortune, their fear of an Inquisition was shared by both the Pope and a large segment of the Portuguese nobility. The Holy See mistrusted John and felt that the monarch was motivated as much by a lust for gold and power as he was by a love for the purity of the Christian faith. Many Portuguese nobles feared that the Inquisition would lead to a greater concentration of royal power at their expense. These unusual bedfellows of the Marranos helped them delay the entry of the Inquisition, but not to repel it completely.

In the meantime, John had not been idle. He had rallied the restive masses and the fanatics among the Portuguese clergy behind his anti-Marrano policies. Marranos were blamed for crop failures and the rampant inflation that plagued the land. Their physicians and apothecaries were charged with plotting the extermination of Old Christians. Spies were sent out among them to report on their Judaizing activities and their squeamish abstention from Christian practices. The seed of propaganda which John had carefully sown soon reaped the desired harvest of violence. In the late 1520's Marranos were butchered and burned in Gouvea, Alemtejo and other cities and towns throughout the land. An earthquake which struck Lisbon and leveled the city of San-tarem in 1531 was interpreted by the clergy as a divine visitation for the toleration of Judaizers in the land. The defense of the Marranos by prominent clerics and laymen, like the great poet and playwright Gil Vicente, went unheeded. Instead, John used these events and disturb-ances to press for and obtain the introduction of the Inquisition.

It was a crushing defeat for the Marranos. By the thousands they began to flee from Portugal, but a royal decree soon closed the borders again. Countless numbers, however, defied the order and risked their lives in attempts to escape, while those who remained behind worked sedulously for the revocation of the Inquisition. In 1533 the Marranos won from Pope Clement VII a general pardon, which also permitted their unhindered egress from the land. John, however, fought the papal bull and a year later influenced the succeeding pope, Paul III, to rescind it. In 1535 Marrano gold won the reinstatement of the bull, but it was again revoked in 1536. In that year the Inquisition was firmly established.

The Marranos continued to fight in an attempt to limit the power of the Holy Office. In 1539, however, when anti-Christian placards dis-covered on Lisbon's cathedral and parish churches were traced to the Marranos, the Marranos were subjected to the most severe physical violence and legal restriction. A further bull modifying Inquisitional procedure went unheeded, and tribunals of the Inquisition were set up throughout the land. The Marranos continued to fight. They won a reprieve when the Holy Office was suspended in 1544, but the bull *Meditatio Cordis* (July, 1547) reinstituted the Inquisition and bestowed upon it a power and supremacy that were to remain without effective challenge for more than two centuries.[14]

The battle was over. It was not a total defeat. The Marranos' valiant struggle had permitted numerous of their brethren to escape from Portu-gal. Yet the price that the Marranos paid was dear. Unwillingly caught in the web of a religion they did not want and then persecuted for re-jecting it, the Portuguese Marranos, who had been taught to regard their constancy to Judaism as the talisman which would extricate them from all evil, now groped for an answer to the perplexing question: Why had all this happened to them?

For many of the Marranos, the traditions of their fathers provided an answer. Throughout the history of Judaism, whenever the burdens of life seemed unbearable and the sufferings inexplicable, the faithful be-lieved that the days of the Messiah were approaching.[15] It is not sur-prising that from the mid-1520's a Messianic fever gripped many Marranos. Around that time a quixotic impostor named David Reubeni came to Portugal, posing as the ambassador of his brother Joseph, king of the lost tribe of Reuben in the regions of Tatary. He was immediately hailed as the Messiah and thronged by faithful believers among whom was the tragic figure of Diogo Pires (Shelomo Molkho).[16] Little more than a decade later a new Messianic fervor swept over the New Christians, this time centered around a humble tailor named Luis Dias de Setubal.[17]

Others, while not claiming the Messiahship, regarded themselves as his precursors. The romantic physician known as Master Gabriel went from house to house winning converts to Judaism.[18] Many Old Christians, like the government official Gil Vaz Bugalho, converted to Judaism and spread the contagion of Messianic expectancy.[19] Another erstwhile Old Christian in Coimbra gathered a large flock of believers and even opened a school for the teaching of Hebrew.[20]

For those New Christians who had not harbored Messianic hopes, as well as for those whose dreams of the coming of the Messiah were disillusioned, the faith which had impelled their forebears to leave Spain had now begun to ebb. Faithfulness had not brought its reward. Try as they might, the New Christians of Portugal could not close their ears to the claims of the Old Christian preachers and apologists who said that God had abandoned the Jews when they rejected Jesus, and that their dispersion and suffering attested to the truth of the Christian faith.[21] These assertions, relatively rare in Portugal during the fifteenth century,[22] became frequent in the sixteenth century as polemical books and ideas were imported from Spain. Native writers of stature, like Francisco Machado (in his *Espelho de christãos novos e convertidos*) and João de Barros (in his *Rópica Pnefma* and the *Diálogo evangélico sobre os artigos da fe contra o Talmud dos Judeos*) began to turn to the vernacular instead of the customary Latin to express their antipathy toward the Jews.[23] And to incite hatred in the masses, preachers and writers began to appropriate the contents of Alfonso de Spina's *Fortali-tium Fidei*.[24] This was a hate-monger's *vade mecum*, written in Spain at the time the New Christians there were first charged with heresy, and containing, among other things, a refutation of Jewish objections to Christianity and an anthology of the most preposterous and vicious libels concocted about the Jews throughout the Middle Ages.[25]

Such writings and preachments, which went unanswered because no New Christian dared defend Judaism without exposing himself as a heretic, drove the Portuguese Marranos to the brink of despair. Some sought to avoid their problem by turning sincerely to Christianity; others developed an apathy to all religion, while those who could not sever their ties with Judaism were racked with exquisite pain.[26] Many New Christians of all shades of religious opinion recognized that their only security lay in flight from Portugal, and they fled, riddled with con-fusion and doubt about their religion, about God, about the meaning and purpose of their lives. Even when they had found a haven of refuge, many hesitated to embrace Judaism openly. Despite the passionate pleas of some former New Christians for their reconversion, many chose to live as at least titular Christians, and some even returned to Portugal for a reconciliation with the Church. The New Christian refugees from Lusitania were not a saving remnant of the Jewish faith. Indeed, for a long time there was a question as to whether much of this remnant could itself be saved for Judaism.

One of the exiles, Samuel Usque, was convinced that it could. He believed that the New Christians' sufferings would be the last in Jewish history. To his fellow "gentlemen of the Diaspora of Portugal"[27] he addressed a stirring message in which he sought to refute the Christian explanation of Jewish suffering and to prove from history that a better world was dawning for all Jews. Writing in Portuguese, he entitled his work *Consolaçam 'as tribulaçoens de Israel, A Consolation for Israel's Tribulations.*

Though a history, the *Consolaçam 'as tribulaçoens de Israel* is written in the form of a pastoral dialogue. Three shepherds, Ycabo, Numeo and Zicareo, their pastoral names thinly veiling the biblical figures of Jacob, Nahum and Zechariah, discuss the history of the Jews. The patriarch Jacob, speaking alternately as progenitor and personification of his people, dolefully narrates his history, while Nahum "The Comforter" and Zechariah "The Remembrancer" console him by calling his attention to its brighter implications. The book is divided into three sections called "dialogues," each dealing with a different phase of Jewish history—the period of the Bible, the Second Commonwealth and the medieval and contemporary history of the Jews. The entire work is encased in a theological frame which contains the message of consolation implied in the title of the book.

The choice of the pastoral genre, the dialogue form and the discipline of history for his polemic were not made fortuitously by Samuel Usque. Pastoral poetry and prose were the delight of the cultured classes of the Renaissance,[28] to which most of Usque's audience belonged. This was particularly true in Italy, where Usque wrote, and Usque was sensitive to the importance of using a fashionable literary form for his message. The dialogue form was greatly in vogue in the Renaissance;[29] in addition, it was a traditional device in Christian polemical works against the Jews.

During the Renaissance also history was becoming the battleground for religious polemics.[30] The Protestant Reformation had turned to history to validate its theological claims. Calvin, Zwingli and Peter Martyr availed themselves of historical arguments. Luther was an avid student of history and the author of various historical treatises. He commended the study of history as a valuable tool for life, and in words which foreshadow Usque's, called it a mirror in which to recognize the meaning of contemporary life.[31] In this sense Luther can be said to have inspired works like Sleidan's *Commentary,* Carion's *Chronicle,* the *Magdeburg Centuries* and Melancthon's *Loci Centuriae,* the latter of especial interest because of its structural affinity to the *Consolaçam.*[32] Later writers of the Catholic Reformation like Baronius, Pallavicino and the historians of the Council of Trent, felt compelled to counter their opponents' arguments by appeals to history.[33] Usque, living in the heyday of Protestant historical productivity, was probably greatly influenced by its spirit and particularly by its hopes for the dissolution of the Church of Rome, which for him rang with the sweet overtone that the oppression of his people might soon come to an end.

Usque's choice of Portuguese as the medium of his literary expression is tinged with the heroic. Hebrew, of course, was out of the question, since few New Christians now had the opportunity to learn it well.[34] Usque's friends had attempted to persuade him to write his book in Spanish, then the *lingua franca* of Europe. Had he heeded this advice, Usque might have reached a larger audience and his fame would have been more widespread. Though fluent in Spanish and doubtlessly fully aware that he was restricting the circle of his readers, he decided not "to seek a borrowed tongue."[35] Instead he chose to mold his native Portuguese, which many Lusitanian writers shunned in favor of Latin or Spanish,[36] into a beautiful lyrical prose which stands out today as a monumental contribution to Portuguese literature. Ironically, Usque, an apologete for the Jews living outside his native land, tapped the inherent beauty of the Portuguese language at the very time it was being used to persecute and degrade the children of his people.

ONE OF HIS PEOPLE

Of the life of Samuel Usque little is known. His one work yields few biographical details, and these are insufficient to distinguish him sharply from countless others of his Marrano brethren with parallel histories and similar fates. The lack of precise data about his life turns Usque as it were into a symbol of the composite personality of the Portuguese Marrano and his biography into the epic of his suffering people.

Even Usque's real name may be unknown. He certainly possessed a Christian name, but this has not been preserved. The name Usque, suggesting as it does some tie to the city of Huesca which figures so prominently in the history of the Jews of Aragon, appeared only after he had fled the Inquisition, and may have been a pseudonym, adopted to protect dear ones left behind in Portugal.[1]

His ancestors, Samuel tells us in a rare autobiographical aside, had belonged to the vast "Diaspora of Castile"[2] which had crossed into Portugal in 1492 and was forcibly baptized five years later. Samuel was born around the time of the forced baptism, perhaps shortly thereafter.[3] He speaks of Portuguese as his mother tongue, and of the Portuguese New Christians as his countrymen.[4] His work reveals the profound knowledge of religious and classical disciplines which characterized the well-bred man in the Iberian Peninsula in the middle years of the six-teenth century. He had mastered the Bible and the Apocrypha. He quoted classical authors like Plato, Ovid and Lucan. He seems to have studied Josephus. He possessed a first-hand acquaintance with the *Yosippon*, which he used extensively in the *Consolaçam*. He was aware of the main currents of Christian apologetics. He was at home in the literature of the Jewish mystics. He could cite the Talmud, the Midrash and Maimonides. He displayed a keen interest in geography, and, as we have seen, in pastoral literature. He had mastered many languages. In addition to Portuguese and Spanish, he was proficient in Latin, Greek and Hebrew, and could hardly have failed to know both Italian and French.[5]

Where Usque acquired such an extensive knowledge, particularly of Hebrew, is mystifying. The learned Immanuel Aboab, writing in

1624, called him a rabbi, which he could hardly have become in Portu-gal.[6] After 1497 rabbinical academies were officially obsolete in Portugal. A royal edict that year even forbade the erstwhile Jews to possess or read any Hebrew except in medical books.[7] Numerous sources attest to the New Christians' dread of owning books in the sacred tongue and to the general decline of traditional Jewish knowledge in Portugal in the sixteenth century.[8] Still, many New Christians might have retained their Hebrew tomes for clandestine study. It is thus possible, as one scholar says, that Usque "early in life and at great risk . . . was taught to recite Hebrew prayers and to read the Bible in the sacred tongue."[9]

This, however, cannot account for the range of Usque's learning, which rather suggests a regimen of studies at a university. It may be that Usque attended Portugal's renowned university, located at Coimbra after its transfer from Lisbon in the late 1530's.[10] The tantalizing possibility insinuates itself that Usque was sent to the university to pursue the only career open to a noble Marrano youth who sought a broad humanistic education and a proximity to the Bible and Hebrew—the career of the priesthood![11] This, of course, is conjecture, but it would help explain Usque's wide knowledge, his religious sensitivity and the feelings of guilt for which the Consolaçam appears to be, at least in part, a compensation.

The historical highlights of Usque's formative years—John's deporta-tion of Jewish children to São Thomé; Emanuel's forced conversion of the Jews; the massacre of 1506 and the introduction of the Portuguese Inquisition—are described by Usque with a vividness and an emotional involvement that ring with autobiographical authenticity. Indeed, the last eleven historical chapters of the third Dialogue of the Consolaçam all seem to reflect Usque's personal experience and thereby yield valuable information on the course of his life.[12]

On the basis of these chapters, one can surmise that Usque left Portu-gal shortly after the Inquisition was established in 1531. He may then have pursued the path of the fugitives he traces in his book, sharing their hardships in England, France, Germany and across the Alps in Italy. In any case, he appears to have proceeded to Naples, where he began a close and warm association with the renowned Samuel Abravanel and his wife, Benvenida. In 1532 the Abravanels left Naples in protest against the Emperor's decree requiring its Jews to wear a badge, and established their residence in Ferrara,[13] where a decade later we find Usque with them again.

If the concluding chapters of the historical section in Dialogue III reveal Usque's itinerary, we can follow him from Naples to Constanti-nople and then to Salonika,[14] the latter now a major center of Judaism which welcomed the Marranos fleeing Spain and Portugal "as if she were Jerusalem, that old and ever pious mother of ours."[15] Could Usque have been sent to Salonika by Samuel Abravanel, to study perhaps at the academy where Abravanel himself had been taught? No one knows.

What is clear, however, is that during his travels in the Ottoman Empire, Usque visited the Holy Land. He sojourned in Safed, where Jewish mystics and Messianic speculators were actively engaged in preparing for the millennium.[16] A curious account by the bibliophile Isaac Akrish in 1577 speaks of Usque as being among those who were preaching the doctrine of the imminent return of the Ten Lost Tribes around the year 1550. Akrish, who harbored no love for the Jewish chiliasts, calls Usque a scoffer and a rascal.[17]

From the Ottoman Empire Usque returned to Europe, passing through Bohemia, where he heard of the Prague blood libel of 1546, and then going to Italy, where we find him established in 1551 in Ferrara, "the safest port" of the Peninsula.[18]

In the middle of the sixteenth century two other distinguished ex-Marranos named Usque resided in Ferrara. One was the printer, Abraham Usque, who published numerous liturgical works in Hebrew and in the vernacular, and from whose press issued classics like the Ferrara Bible, the *Consolaçam 'as tribulaçoens de Israel*, and anomalously, it would seem, Bernaldim Ribeiro's pastoral novel, *Menina e Moça*.[19] The other was the poet-playwright, Solomon Usque, known also as Salusque Lusitano, who wrote in Italian and Spanish. He gained renown for his translations of Petrarch into Spanish and for his co-authorship with Lorenzo Gracián of a popular Spanish drama, *Esther*.[20]

The simultaneous appearance of three men with the same unusual name in Ferrara has led to a gamut of conjectures regarding their relationship. Some are content to consider them related without further specification, but others cannot leave the matter without speculating on the degree of their relatedness.[21] Thus we find that Abraham and Samuel are often referred to as brothers,[22] and Samuel is pictured as fraternally assisting Abraham in the operation of his press.[23] Abraham Usque is occasionally represented as the father of Samuel and Solomon,[24] and Solomon as Samuel's father.[25] In addition, Samuel has been confused with both Abraham[26] and Solomon.[27] Though in itself innocuous, the attempt to determine Samuel's kinship to Abraham and Solomon Usque has tended to obscure the more significant relationships Samuel is known to have enjoyed in Ferrara. These were his friendships with Doña Gracia Nasi and the family of Samuel Abravanel.

Doña Gracia Nasi, herself a Portuguese New Christian, had been residing in Ferrara since 1549. She had fled there from Venice, where she had been accused of Judaizing.[28] She had already achieved fame for her masculine management of her family's commercial empire and the utilization of its vast resources in aiding her fellow Marranos. She provided ships to transport refugees from Portugal to Northern Europe and then directed them across Europe to safety in the Ottoman Empire. She suggested to them the best routes for travel and even the inns safest for their lodging on their perilous journey eastward. In later years, when she was more happily settled in Constantinople, she founded schools and synagogues and continued unfailingly to provide for the material and spiritual needs of her fellow Jews.[29]

Nowhere is there found a more beautiful literary portrait of this grand lady than in the *Consolaçam*. Here Usque says that in Gracia there coalesced "Miriam's innate compassion; Deborah's remarkable prudence; Esther's boundless virtue and surpassing piety; and the true-hearted courage of the chaste and generous widow Judith."[30]

There was to be sure more than a kernel of truth in this encomium, but it was not without its practical reason as well. In Italy Doña Gracia, following the example of other Italian noblemen and their ladies, became a Maecenas of literature and supported what she considered to be worthy creations of the erstwhile Marranos.[31] Significantly, all three Usques were indebted to her. All three received of her munificence and two honored her with notable dedications, Abraham in the Jewish edition of the Ferrara Bible,[32] and Samuel in his *Consolaçam ʾas tribulaçoens de Israel*.

In his dedication, Samuel calls Doña Gracia "the heart in the body of our people" and exalts her excellence above that of the sun for "bringing forth into the light the fruit of the plants (i.e., the Marranos) that lie buried in its darkness"[33] (i.e., in the Iberian Peninsula). This dedication and the paean on Doña Gracia in the body of the *Consolaçam* suggest that her funds made the publication of Usque's book possible and provided him with sustenance in the years of its composition.[34] The practical purpose of the *Consolaçam* could well have induced Doña Gracia's support. Though a patron of art, her interests transcended art for art's sake. In literature, as in other realms of life, she supported activities that would return the New Christians to Judaism and to a useful and productive life.

Of perhaps even greater significance for the *Consolaçam* was Usque's friendship with Samuel and Benvenida Abravanel. Samuel, Usque correctly reports, was "a venerable individual, a dignified elder of the Spanish Jews, the chief and most distinguished person among them, whose merit was sufficiently great for him to be called 'Trismegistus,' three times great, as the Greeks say. He was a great sage in the Law, eminent in noble society and philanthropic with his wealth, which he generously used to alleviate the tribulations of his brethren."[35] Usque summarizes his activities by stating that "he provided for the marriage of countless orphan girls, maintained many needy people and distinguished himself pre-eminently in the freeing of captives. He gave his help so extensively that all the qualities needed to receive prophecy were present in him."

Doña Benvenida, Samuel's cousin and second wife, was a typical grand dame of the Italian Renaissance, cultured, gracious, and beloved by Jew and non-Jew alike. The viceroy felt secure in entrusting to her the education of his daughter, later the Duchess of Tuscany.[36] Her home, both in Naples and Ferrara, became the center of a circle of Italy's intellectual elite. Learned Jewish and Christian aristocrats flocked thither to discuss the arts and philosophy and even to delve into the mysteries of the Kabbalah.[37]

Usque calls Doña Benvenida her husband's "peer in all virtues," and describes her in terms as glowing as those used to depict Don Samuel.[38] Significantly, the descriptions of Doña Gracia and those of the Abravanels are the only such tributes to Jews found in the *Consolaçam*. The only other such encomium is reserved for the Duke of Ferrara, Hercules of Este.

The exact relationship of the Abravanels to Usque and to his work can only be conjectured, but there can be no doubt of the existence of such a relationship. The *Consolaçam* reveals Usque's striking dependence on the writings of Samuel Abravanel's father, the princely Isaac Abravanel. Isaac's mystical works are echoed in the *Consolaçam*, and his no longer extant historical work, the *Yemot Olam*, may well have provided Usque with his major literary source for the historical chapters of Dialogue III.[39] Of Isaac's sons, the only one living in 1540 and therefore the only one in possession of his father's library, was Samuel. It would be natural to assume that Samuel opened his father's library for Usque, whetted his appetite for Jewish history and mysticism, possibly encouraged him to travel eastward to visit and perhaps study in the great cultural centers of Judaism, and introduced him both in Naples and in Ferrara to the intellectual circles that provided the ideological stimulus for his work. Samuel died in 1547, and there is every reason to suppose that Doña Benvenida, who continued her husband's business and communal policies, continued this practice as well. Only a conjecture of this magnitude could explain the dependence of Samuel Usque on the works of Isaac Abravanel or his panegyric upon Samuel and Benvenida.

The twilight of Usque's life, like his birth, is cloaked in the veil of mystery. The thirty-sixth chapter of the third Dialogue, which seems to locate him in Ferrara, is not the last of the series of historical narratives. The subsequent and final account, dated 1553 and probably the last page of the *Consolaçam* that was written, deals with Pesaro and the desecration of two of its synagogues early that year. Was Usque an eye witness to these events? Had he gone to Pesaro in 1551 after the general banishment of the Jews from Ferrara?[40] It is impossible to answer these questions. It is, however, safe to surmise that he was back in Ferrara in 1553 for the publication of his work.

After 1553 only Akrish, in 1577, mentions Usque, and he speaks of him as dead, perhaps long dead. Some would like to understand Akrish's account to mean that Usque visited the Holy Land after his residence at Ferrara, and therefore, by implication, after the appearance of his book.[41] It would seem more reasonable to assume that the mystic overtones of the *Consolaçam* reflect rather than foreshadow Usque's Safed experience. Yet a later trip, even a second trip, by Usque to the Holy

Land cannot be ruled out of the realm of possibility. Indeed, it might be satisfying to imagine Usque spending the sunset years of his life in the congenial atmosphere of Galilee or perhaps in the City of David, or even dying under the hoofs of a hostile horseman, as legend tells of Jehuda Halevi, another sweet singer of Zion. Usque's burial place, like the site of his birth, is unknown. He has no monument except the work which helped to bring life of the spirit to many a dejected New Christian of his own and of a later generation.

THE MESSAGE OF THE CONSOLAÇAM

If the casual reader, who cannot share the Marranos' sensitivity, finds the *Consolaçam* to be the work of an ingenuous soul who views life with the naïve piety usually associated with the medieval mind, then he is receiving the impression which Usque intentionally sought to impart. The very prologue of the *Consolaçam* conveys this tone. There Usque tells his readers that he will narrate Israel's past misfortunes in the hope that their reading may mitigate the Marranos' present anguish. He tells them that at the end of each section of narrative he appends verses culled from the biblical prophets, not that he sees any necessary relation between prophecy and event, but merely as a gesture of piety. And he apologizes for the long concluding section of the *Consolaçam*, where he summons the New Christians to prepare for the millennium, by calling all of it an after-thought to insure a balmy conclusion for a history so heartrending, with "wounds raw and open."[1]

The incisive reader will soon discover that Usque's intention contradicts these words. It will become evident that Usque narrated Israel's misfortunes because he was convinced they were about to end. He cited prophetic verses because he believed they were specifically fulfilled by the accompanying events. He did not hesitate to alter a biblical quotation to make sure his reader grasped its contemporary significance.[2] He regarded the heralding of the millennium as the very climax of his work. His façade of naïveté was intentionally created in order to camouflage the daring message his work contained, to distract his enemies and to guard against the haunting threat of the confiscation of his book, which would prevent his message from reaching his readers. He constructed this façade from the biblical narrative and the traditional histories his people knew so well. By imbedding his message in a context of antiquity, by skillfully selecting from history incidents that reflected the life situation of the Marranos, by insinuating allusions that only they were certain to grasp, Usque hoped to elude the casual and unconcerned reader while he struck the Marranos with the compelling pertinence of his message to their lives. Ironically, Usque succeeded less in concealing his message from the Inquisition, at whose doorstep we must lay the responsibility for the rarity of his book, than with his fellow Jews elsewhere in the world. Among them his message has remained undiscovered.

Jews who have become acquainted with the *Consolaçam* have for the most part believed it to be a martyrology. They have generally depreciated the first two Dialogues, which seem to do little more than précis the history of the Bible and the *Yosippon*. They have declared Usque's contribution to lie in the historical chapters of Dialogue III, the first twenty-four dealing with the Middle Ages, and the last thirteen, for them the most important, containing the record of Usque's own experiences or those of his Marrano contemporaries. This appraisal overlooks the fact that the *Consolaçam*, as its title indicates, was not intended as a martyrology, and further, that Usque was not primarily interested in contributing primary source material to future scholars. He was not concerned with accuracy of detail. He exaggerated constantly. He uncritically accepted any source that furthered his thesis and indiscriminately blended the legends and facts within it. He planned and wrote the *Consolaçam* not as a disjointed chronicle but as a unified apologium for Judaism. The first and second Dialogues and the long theological conclusion of the book are as important as the historical chapters of the third Dialogue, and in a sense more vital to the message Usque was seeking to impart.

The key to understanding Usque lies in the personage of Ycabo, the eponym of the people Israel. Though Ycabo narrates the past history of his people, he stands in the present as a contemporary of Samuel Usque: he sees in the past not the dead relics of bygone generations but his own reflection and the reflection of his people's life. When Ycabo bemoans his fate, when he raises questions or voices doubts, he does so from his vantage point in the present, fully aware that the entire sweep of his history has failed to provide him with satisfactory answers. Through Ycabo, Usque is enabled to confront his readers repeatedly with the parallel between their history and their lives. This is already evident in the *Consolaçam's* pastoral introduction, where Ycabo raises the questions that beset Usque's Marrano brethren and thereby sets the stage for the message of the work:

When will I see the end to wrongs and offenses against me, to my longings and agonies, to my bruises and the wounds in my soul? When will my happiness not be confined to dreams and my misfortunes not be real? When will my ever-present ills be removed and the fulfillment of my wearied hopes not seem a distant reverie? And when will peace come to my battered body, or to the fears, suspicions and apprehensions of my spirit? How long must I moan and sigh and slake my thirst with my tears?[3]

These questions, it will be recalled, had already been answered by Christian polemics, and the answers rang disconcertingly in the Marranos' ears: The Jews' tribulations will never cease, for the Jews have been eternally condemned by God for the sin of rejecting the Messiah Jesus. As a result their Temple in Jerusalem—the Second Temple, which the Christians naturally regarded as the one prophesied for Messianic times—was destroyed, and the Jews were destined to roam the earth in misery and hardship as an atonement for their sin and as a living warning to the nations. What hope have the Jews? None, said their adversaries, none save sincere conversion.

To confute these arguments, Usque turned primarily to the Bible. Like his Christian opponents, Usque believed in the literal revelation of Scripture, in the validity of its prophecy and in the divine guidance of history. The Bible compelled Usque to agree with his opponents on two fundamental points—first, that Israel had once basked in divine favor, and second, that it was later catapulted into an abjectness from which it had as yet failed to emerge. Since God would not have punished Israel without reason, its downfall must have been occasioned by a grievous sin on Israel's part. Ycabo admits, "Because I was disobedient, like Adam in the terrestrial paradise, I abandoned the Lord, the fountain of living waters."[4]

It was on the identification of this sin that Usque parted company with his Christian opponents. Usque turned to the Bible to demonstrate that Israel's sin—which meant the Marranos' as well—reached back to the days of the Hebrews' entry into Canaan and persisted to Usque's own. It was the sin of assimilation to gentile peoples, leading Israel to apostasy, idolatry and marriage with nonJews. By this sin Israel broke its covenant with God and provoked the divine punishments recorded in the Bible.

This theme is stressed again and again throughout Dialogue I. Since Usque's narrative relies heavily on the books of the Bible written in the Deuteronomic spirit which dwell on this sin in ancient Israel, the reader may be unaware that he is dealing with the identical problem in his own day until the force of his repetition makes this increasingly evident. The Marranos could not have failed to grasp Usque's cautious allusions to their lives. When they read his denunciation of the ancient Hebrews for following the ways of Ishmael and Esau, whom later Jews identified respectively with the Moslems and the Christians,[5] or when they saw Usque's lengthy account of the mixedbreed Samaritans who were neither Jews nor Gentiles "and until this day have remained in this confusion, for now they neither fear the Lord nor do they keep their ancient ceremonies,"[6] they could not have helped but identify with New Christians past and present exactly as Usque wished them to do.

Ironically, Usque demonstrates, whenever Israel sinned, her punishment was identical: she was enslaved by the very peoples she sought to imitate. Her punishments, revealed by the prophets in an attempt to dissuade her from sin, had been prepared in advance by God. They were automatically executed whenever Israel's sin reached a gravity that made repentance unlikely and outbalanced the merit of her righteous men.

Usque insists that God did not want to punish Israel; that He warned her repeatedly before her transgressions; that He punished her less severely than her transgressions required; that even after she sinned He tried to woo her back with favors and miracles, and when she did repent, He immediately restored her to divine favor. Only her addiction to idolatry occasioned her ruin. Israel therefore had no one to blame but herself. Ycabo is compelled to "acknowledge that my wickedness prepared the trap for me and my rebelliousness snared me in it."[7]

Whatever uncertainty might have remained in the New Christians' minds about the intentional parallel of this dialogue to their own lives is removed by Ycabo's questions and doubts. Perhaps the most important of these are voiced immediately after he has recounted the captivity of the Ten Tribes:

I fear above all that the Lord, so provoked and offended, has now rejected me as His people. And then I fear lest He has gone over to another people, after seeing how little effect His remedies and punishments have had on me. And if He has left me, I dread still a third evil, namely, that being thus deprived and absent from His favor, my memory may end and be consumed in the paws and teeth of the animals of this world, this frightening desert through which I travel.[8]

Usque obliges his readers with a dual answer to these questions. The first is a "divine consolation": Just as the prophets' promises of doom and punishment were realized, so will their predictions of Israel's happiness be fulfilled. The Ten Tribes, though indistinguishable from their neighbors (were the Marranos not often in this condition?), will be reassembled and Israel restored to favor. The second is a more convincing "earthly remedy to satisfy you further and to reassure your timorous spirit."[9] Here Usque briefly summarizes the "Origin of Idolatry" to demonstrate that though ancient Israel was steeped in idolatry, all other earlier and contemporary peoples were more idolatrous. How could any of them therefore have been more worthy of God's blessing than Israel? "If, indeed, He had desired to exchange you," argues Usque, "He could have chosen another, better people than the one He was leaving."[10] And to make certain that his reader draws the parallel for his own life and understands that God has not exchanged Israel for the religion of his Inquisitional oppressors, Usque continues:

And since I have clearly proven to you here that there was no better people at the time, and the force of the ancient error in worshiping mortal men went on to affect modern peoples—and the rest I shall tell you in your ear—do not fear, because the Lord, the God of your righteous fathers, is with you.[11]

The Marranos therefore have not been abandoned. Yet, objects Ycabo, how can they ever hope to be reconciled with God in view of the ineradicability of their inclination to idolatry? Like Job, Ycabo laments to God:

You have placed me in a frame made of clay and adobe, subject to temptation's unabating winds and storms; how can that which is infirm by its very nature sustain itself when it is buffeted to and fro?[12]

Usque responds by reassuring the Marranos that "the force of divine mercy toward you has not diminished, nor does the pardon of your children and the healing of your wounds depend upon your good or evil deeds alone. Many and incomprehensible are the ways by which the Lord performs lofty actions and marvels."[13] Usque proceeds to demon-strate how God, despite Israel's idolatries, showered her with favors at a time when all hope seemed lost—a time so parallel to Usque's own— and when "because of their abominable sins they deserved to be pun-ished with a thousand kinds of death."[14] The Marranos are therefore urged to hope, for "hope . . . is one of the chief gates by which God's compassion comes forth to visit the world."[15]

Yet if God had not abandoned His people, would not the merit of the eight righteous kings of Judah have obviated the destruction of the Temple and the Babylonian captivity? Usque insists that God did weigh their righteousness but that Judah's sin was beyond repair. Righteousness is certainly rewarded. "The compassion of the heavens is prepared to give infinitely as long as there is room for it in the recipient."[16] The implication is clear that righteousness on the Marranos' part can restore them to God's mercy, and "this mercy would still be protecting you if you did not choose to go to the extreme with your wicked deeds."[17]

As the first Dialogue concludes, the parallel between Israel's early history and the Marranos' lives is evident. Reflecting their problems in a context they can view with detachment, Usque lays the responsibility for the Marranos' plight on their doorstep alone. The prophet Ezekiel had spoken analogously to the Judeans after the destruction of the Temple in 586 B.C.E. Like Ezekiel's, Usque's purpose in so doing was to assure his people that by removing the cause of their troubles they could become reconciled to a God whose love for them had not abated.

Indeed all that Usque felt was required of the Marranos was faith-fulness to their religion and a trust in God's continued concern for them, and he turns to a consideration of these elements in Dialogue II. After he describes how God favored his people by restoring their Temple, he studies the persecution of the Jews by Antiochus Epiphanes. Like the Portuguese monarchs of Usque's day, Antiochus punished all people of Jewish origin who observed the rituals or festivals of their ancestral faith. This persecution gives Usque the opportunity to discuss at length two examples of constancy to Judaism, "because they are so exemplary and of such great importance. . . ."[18] Neither could have failed to remind the Marranos of the Inquisition. The first narrates the

22

martyrdom of the aged priest Eleazar, who suffers death in the torture rack (!) rather than feign the breaking of the Jewish law. The other recounts in detail the martyrdom of Hannah and her seven sons, who all march resolutely to gruesome deaths by fire (!) rather than relinquish the religion of their fathers. If martyrdom under duress was preferable to sincere or even feigned conversion, would it not follow that in lands of freedom, such as those which the Marranos found when they escaped from the Inquisition, the failure to doff the cloak of conversion ranked among the most unconscionable of sins?

Usque now turns to the second major theme of the dialogue, the refutation of the claim made by Christian polemics that the Second Temple was the shrine promised the Jews for Messianic times. At the beginning of the dialogue Usque emphasized that the Second Temple was inferior to the First, and now he proceeds to demonstrate this by reviewing the history of the Jews in the period in which it stood. He shows that this history was one of interminable internecine strife that was ended only by the Roman subjugation of Judea. It is difficult to tell whether through this narration Usque wanted to conjure up in his readers' minds pictures of the fratricidal struggles among the Jews and Marranos of the Iberian Peninsula, or of the hated informers who de-nounced their own brethren to the Inquisition, or of the violence of New Christian churchmen toward their own Jewish blood. But cer-tainly his readers could infer that the period of the Second Temple was not the era of peace and well-being for the Jews forecast for Messianic times, and that therefore these times had as yet not arrived.

As in the first Dialogue, Usque's argument raises a question in the Marranos' minds. Why, asks Ycabo, did God erect the Second Temple if He was determined to destroy it?[19]

"If your flesh has suffered," Usque cautions his readers, "its pain should not have blinded your understanding."[20] God did not predestine the destruction of the Temple, but hoped that it might become the Messianic shrine. Throughout its existence God was concerned for Israel. He admonished her repeatedly to be faithful, punished her mercifully when she was not, and showered favors upon her despite her persistent sinfulness. Usque narrates fourteen miracles on Israel's behalf to convince his readers that the God who performed them could not have wanted the Temple razed or His people led into captivity. As with previous disasters, it was not God who abandoned Israel, but Israel who abandoned God.

But has not God's favor been severed from Israel as a result of her sins? In Dialogue I Usque answered the question with logic: How could God have abandoned Israel for its idolatry if all other nations past and present have been more grievous offenders than she? Now he answers through history, as he rhetorically bids his readers tell him what has happened to all other nations. Egypt, Babylonia, Persia and Greece all ruled their world, but where are they now?[21] Each in turn was devoured by the next, and the last by the frightful Romans. And the Roman might and glory proved no less illusory or vain. Rome was decimated by civil strife and finally humiliated by the Goths.

Thus all nations that had oppressed Jacob vanished from the scene. Yet Israel, though bruised and battered, was still alive. What better proof could there be that God had not abandoned it? Applying Isaiah's thought, Usque explains that Israel's oppressors were all instruments of God's wrath, sent to punish Israel, but then destroyed for attributing their success to their own might and gloating in Israel's suffering. Early in Dialogue II, when speaking of the destruction of the Babylonians, Usque relied on the biblical verse when he concluded "for this is always the portion of those that spoil you and the lot of those that destroy you, O Israel."[22] Now, to insure that his readers will apply this idea to their contemporary oppressors, he affirms:

> Certainly with only these proofs you can regard yourself as the happiest of all creatures, for you will find that He has not employed any of these means with any other people that was or is yet to be punished. (Emphasis mine.)[23]

Lowly and degraded though it may presently be, Israel has not been rejected by God!

Fortified with this analysis of Israel's past, Usque can turn in Dialogue III to the medieval and contemporary history of his people in order to demonstrate the continuation of the patterns he has so convincingly presented in the preceding sections of his work. The thirty-seven historical chapters in Dialogue III show that Israel's sin of apostasy and assimilation did not change and her punishment by the nations inexorably followed. Israel's sufferings throughout the Middle Ages and their amazingly similar counterpart in Usque's own day were the fruit of her faithlessness to the covenant. They had long before been predicted by the prophets, as is manifested by the verses from their writings which Usque appends to the end of each chapter. As before, the nations that punished Israel were instruments of God's wrath and each charge they trumped up as a pretext for persecution was "a scourge with which the Lord chastises them (the Jews), payment in kind for the commandment of blood which they and their fathers willfully broke," and "God's justice wishes them to be punished through a lie."[24]

Yet the fulfillment of the prophecies of doom for Israel's infraction of her covenant with God implied its continued existence and even the possibility of Israel's eventual restoration to divine favor. Indeed, Usque believed that this possibility would soon become a reality. He was convinced that with the suffering of the New Christians in Spain and Portugal, all the punishments predicted in the Bible had been meted out to the children of Israel.[25] The quiver of prophetic arrows was now empty; God's mercy could heal undisturbed. At the end of the final historical chapter, dealing with the defilement of the Pesaro synagogue and recalling in a minor key the theme of the destruction of the Temples with which the previous dialogues had ended, Usque urges God that the time for the new theophany is at hand.[26]

It was not without good reason that Usque could think that "the dawn will break and the longed-for morning after winter's stormy night will graciously appear to us,"[27] for he had already seen this dawn break in the East. The Ottoman Empire was on the ascendant, favoring the Jews with its "gates of liberty . . . wide open . . . that you may fully practice your Judaism,"[28] and poising its armies at Europe's door to humble the Jews' inveterate oppressors. The foundations of Europe were quaking from internal spasms as well. Christianity had split and splintered it into warring religious camps, and the sack of the Eternal City in 1527 had dealt it a humiliating blow. Furthermore, Europe's centrality was threatened by the discovery of new continents bulging with wealth and possibility. All of this reinforced Usque's intuition of millennial imminence.[29] If his analysis of Israel's history was accurate and Israel, because of her sins, had to traverse the sea of suffering in accordance with divine fiat, could she not now observe the shoreline of a new era welcoming her with the felicity of rest?

Such reasoning provided the enthusiasm for Usque's lengthy concluding section of consolation. Its exquisitely lyrical pages contain a systematic presentation of Usque's polemic, in which he meticulously resumes his major arguments and reiterates his daring conclusions.

He begins with a "Final Lament over All Israel's Misfortunes Past and Present." Here Ycabo recapitulates the seemingly endless chain of Jewish suffering and queries why Israel has been chosen as an example of God's wrath. He recalls the idolatries of Israel's ancient oppressors and bids God observe "the works of the contemporary peoples into whose power You have delivered Your world," to determine "whether they have left the errant way which their forebears followed."[30] Though he is clearly referring to the European nations, Usque discreetly proceeds to narrate the idolatries of the Asians and the Africans, with none of whom the Marranos had any appreciable contact. But to ascertain that his readers understand his true intent, he concludes:

> But why O Lord must I dwell on what You can know so intimately of the religions and practices contrary to Your pleasure, not only of these people in Africa, but also in other kingdoms of the world?[31]

In any case, Ycabo contends, the Jews now clearly "have suffered the fulfillment of all the judgments which You pronounced against us."[32] The time has therefore come for Israel's fortunes to change. Yet they have not changed! "We see clearly," Ycabo realizes, "that the multitude of our sins have delivered us into the power of Your wrath, and that we have persisted in these same iniquities, for if it were not so, our affairs would have a happier and more favorable end."[33]

Numeo and Zicareo systematically answer Ycabo's complaints in a

"Human Consolation for the Tribulations of Israel." Israel's punishment, Usque explains, was really a blessing, for it purged her of sin and prepared her for eventual reconciliation with God. Besides, Israel was punished only physically, in the body of her people; her spiritual bond with God remained inviolate. To this day, says Usque, Israel retains her status as God's holy people, preferred by Him to all others.

Indeed, the very methods by which God inflicted punishment upon Israel manifested His love. He did not wait for her misdeeds to accumulate to the point where condign punishment would destroy her completely, but chose to punish her for part of her iniquities at a time, that she might recover and repent. Even the Jews' dispersion was an act of divine benevolence, insuring their survival in one land when Jews in another were destroyed. No other people on earth ever merited such consideration, but all other sinful nations were annihilated "once and for all." And, Usque declares:

And you may infer that He will do the same to the peoples who rule at the present time, and whom you mentioned in your lament.[34]

Usque recalls God's vengeances on Israel's behalf against Sisebut of Spain, Philip of France and John II of Portugal, but refuses to proceed to the contemporary scene in order "not to weary you with such details."[35] Rather he goes on to say generally,

. . . among all your abusers, though they were brethren of one and the same religion and faith, such an accursed strife has arisen and continued to this day that great torrents of Latin blood have run throughout their lands and abroad. We can thus say of Spain that Italy is its grave; of France, that Spain is the means of its consumption; of Germany, that all of its neighbors, including the Turk, are its executioners, who set up the wall where their artillery strikes; and of England, that continual pestilence and hostile Scotland are its scourge.[36]

In addition to these vengeances, God favored His people with numerous blessings in the darkest days of their persecution. Not the least among these was the destruction of many New Christians in Spain and Portugal(!): "Since you had forgotten your ancient Law, and feigned Christianity with all your might solely to save your life and property, without realizing that you were jeopardizing your soul, it was proper that in such a perilous and mortal illness the Lord should not be apprehensive about applying the cautery to you. Because when a person's limbs are being devoured by herpes, it is best to cut them off with a knife or the fire so as to prevent the spread of the disease and save the rest of the body."[37]

Other blessings included the leadership of Doña Gracia Nasi, the friendship of the Ferrara duke, Hercules of Este, and above all the hospitality of "the great nation of Turkey." Usque says, "this country is like a broad and expansive sea which our Lord has opened with the rod

26

of His mercy, as Moses did for you in the Exodus from Egypt, so that the swells of your present misfortunes, which relentlessly pursue you in all kingdoms of Europe like the infinite multitude of Egyptians, might cease and be consumed in it."[38] In addition, Usque continues, God has sent many consolations to His people "which you cannot understand, for since your merit is little, He communicates His secrets to you in obscure terms."[39] By "secret consolations" Usque had in mind the religious discord in Christianity, which he regarded as spurred by forced converts, and two beliefs current in the Kabbalistic circles of Safed—the belief in the imminent return of the Ten Tribes and the belief in metempsychosis, or the transmigration of souls.

Arguments such as these compel Ycabo to acknowledge "with what ingratitude we have requited the Lord. We have dwelt on the travails we suffer and disregarded and overlooked the benefits which we receive."[40] Yet Ycabo's fears are not fully allayed, and he poses one of the questions foremost in the Marranos' minds: When will his people's suffering come to an end?

Usque answers that the happy hour is coming. With the suffering in Spain and Portugal "you have run the entire gauntlet of misfortunes and have reached the end of your tribulations." Indeed, as predicted by biblical prophecy, the seed of Abraham can already be seen returning to the Holy Land. "The ancients," Usque proudly contends, "were unable to attain this proof as were we, for we find ourselves living it in experience, which is the mirror where truths are clearly seen."[41]

The prophets had predicted the coming of this glory, and with the help of their writings Usque proceeds to depict it in rapturous tones in the "Final and Divine Consolation." Here Numeo and Zicareo reveal their identity: they are celestial couriers dispatched to earth to proclaim the cessation of Jewish suffering and the inception of the Sixth or Millennial Age.[42] God himself will inaugurate this era with a vengeance against Israel's foes. Then He will fulfill all the promises uttered by the prophets. He will restore constancy to His fickle people and fruitfulness to the Holy Land, "now so poor that your children do not wish to live there because of its wretchedness which is greater than that of all the other lands in the world."[43] There He will assemble the dispersed children of Israel, implanting within them a new spirit and a soul athirst for the Law. Israel's lost tribes will be found, her dead resurrected, her unity restored under a Davidic king and her enemies destroyed in the war between Gog and Magog, which Usque doubtlessly understood to be the impending struggle for survival between the Ottoman Empire and Christian Europe.

As is evidenced by the contemporary allusions he inserts into their speech, Usque was certain that the prophets spoke these words of consolation for his time alone and that the Marranos who reconverted to Judaism were truly of the generation that the Lord had chosen.[44]

It was therefore to the Marranos who vacillated between Judaism and

Christianity that he addressed his ardent message. In his mind the grief for those "who abandoned their most holy Law to save their lives, and have to this day persevered in their error; like rebellious limbs, they refuse to attach themselves to the body of Israel, continuing to wander among the deceitful pleasures of the nations . . . exceeds all the others combined as much as the divine soul surpasses the earthly body."[45] Usque exhorts these Marranos to declare themselves openly as Jews and to prepare for their approaching good fortune. He assures them that now that they have been purged in the fire of the world, they will remain alive by cleaving to God. At the same time he urges constancy to the God of their fathers and even martyrdom upon those New Christians remaining behind in Spain and Portugal:

. . . let not your flesh feel the cruel fire where it is cast, or the sword with which your enemies punish you; hope for a blessing as great as the one you are destined to enjoy when you leave this life.[46]

To his brethren wherever they are he urges a greater reliance upon God:

Rely upon the Lord more than you have done in the past and endeavor earnestly to do what is right. And fear not . . .[47]

But above all, what Usque wants the Marranos to do is to abjure the Christian faith:

Break forth the words which you have held back in your breast out of fear of the nations in praise of your Redeemer.[48]

"At least," he urges, echoing the prophet Hosea, "take words with you and with them convert to the Lord."[49] Israel's history has taught her that her hope "must be separated from all earthly hopes," that she is to be dependent on God alone.[50] God alone is the true hope of Israel.[51]

In the closing pages of the Consolaçam Usque repeats these ideas with an even greater sense of urgency. He exhorts the Marranos who have fled to freedom, or, as he calls them, "you children of Israel who have escaped from the nations," to look to God for salvation.[52] Why do they persist in ignoring the Lord out of fear of mortal man?[53] They must not deceive themselves, for the tyranny of mortals will not endlessly endure, and their oppressors will soon be destroyed.[54] Israel must patiently await her blessing,[55] but it will not be long in coming. God's salvation for her has already gone forth.[56] Israel should therefore take courage "and let not your spirit be dismayed because of their reproaches and persecutions."[57] In times like these, the call is for steadfastness in faith, and Usque counsels his brethren: "Until your salvation comes, travails may effect a change in you and alter this divine disposition at which you have now arrived."[58] But he urges them to battle dejection and despair, with the assurance that "those who ridicule your hopes shall find themselves confused and ridiculed."[59]

Thus concludes Usque's message in the *Consolaçam*. Yet the book does not end without a significant reply from Ycabo. Throughout the book he had represented the perplexed, skeptical and even cynical Marrano. Now, at the end, he is transformed into an inspired and devoted Jew. In ecstatic speech borrowed from the prophets and adapted to the context of the Marranos' lives, Ycabo utters the words that Usque would have wanted to hear from the lips of all his brethren:

I will wait for the Lord. I will trust in the God of my salvation. He will hear me. Rejoice not against me, you, my enemy Bozrah because I have fallen, for I will arise with the Lord's favor, and though I sit in darkness, He will give me light there, for He is my light. I will bear His indignation with patience, for I have erred against Him, until He renders a favorable decision in my case and judges my cause, and brings me forth to the light from the darkness where I am at present, and then I shall behold His righteousness. I shall also see my enemy Bozrah covered with dishonor and shame, she who now asks me mockingly: 'Where is your God? Why does He not save you from your perils and from my hands?' But I trust in the Lord of hosts, that my eyes shall see her trodden down as the mire in the streets.[60]

THE FATE OF THE CONSOLAÇAM

To measure the greatness of the *Consolaçam* by the influence it exerted upon Usque's contemporaries and later generations would be unjust. Usque had every reason to hope that his "small book" would inspire other Portuguese Marranos "to say more fully and felicitously what I am attempting in this small volume."[1] It was Usque's misfortune that no Marrano arose to continue his efforts and that Portuguese gradually lost its position as a major language in the culture of the Jews. The *Consolaçam* was rendered even more inaccessible by the rarity of the copies of its two sixteenth-century editions.[2] Few Jews and even fewer non-Jews were aware of Usque's book, and in Jewish literature it was known chiefly through references in Joseph ha-Cohen's *Vale of Weeping* (*Emek ha-Bakha*) and Gedaliah ibn Yahia's *Chain of Tradition* (*Shalshelet ha-Kabbalah*).

It was the first edition of the *Consolaçam*, which left Abraham Usque's press in Ferrara on September 7 of the Hebrew year 5313 (that is, 1553)[3] that Joseph ha-Cohen and Gedaliah ibn Yahia used.[4] Both copied or paraphrased a significant amount of Usque's material and did not hesitate to mention Usque as their source.

Not long after its publication in Italy, the *Consolaçam* was being circulated in England both in printed form and in manuscript copies prepared from the Ferrara text. Its readers were Portuguese Marranos who had entered England in the guise of devout Christians, but who in the secrecy of their homes read Jewish books, followed the Jewish calendar and convened to celebrate the Passover. This fascinating information is bequeathed to us in a number of documents stemming from the Lisbon Inquisition. The documents relate to the trial of a certain New Christian named Thomas Fernandes, who in 1556 was accused of having observed Jewish practices in Bristol, England, several years before.[5]

In one of his confessions, dated February 9, 1558, Fernandes recalled a book of prophecies and consolations written in Portuguese that circulated among his fellow Marranos in England "three or four years ago." The description of its contents leaves no doubt that the book in question was the *Consolaçam*:

. . . he remembers, that about three or four years ago this confessant, being in the city of Bristol, in the kingdom of England, one Simão Roiz, surgeon, new Christian, resident of London, of whom confessant has spoken in former confessions, sent a printed book of prophecies to Anrique Nuñes and his wife, confessant's uncle and aunt, the which book spoke of the troubles which the sons of Isaac suffered scattered over the kingdoms and cities where they wandered, but that they must not lose confidence nor be discouraged for Our Lord would deliver them, and send the Messiah to them, and they must live in that hope; and confessant believes that the book was sent from Italy to those ports of England, and it was entitled, "To Beatriz de Luna, wife of Diogo Mendez." . . .[6]

As Cecil Roth, who published this curious account observes, there are several inaccuracies in Fernandes' report. To begin with, the name Beatriz de Luna is not to be found in the *Consolaçam*. Beatriz de Luna was the Christian name of Doña Gracia Nasi, but the *Consolaçam* uses only the Jewish name of the grand lady. Furthermore, it is not the title but the dedication that bears her name. Yet these and other minor inconsistencies in Fernandes' testimony, understandable in the light of the pressure upon him and the length of time which had elapsed since he saw the book, in no way impair an identification of the book he mentioned with the *Consolaçam*.[7]

Aside from these few and faint echoes, little is heard about the first edition of the *Consolaçam*. The book soon became scarce. Perhaps the Papal Inquisition, which had begun to burn books in Italy on Rosh Hashanah day, 1553, destroyed its copies before the ink on its pages was dry.[8] Perhaps to avoid the Inquisition's scrutiny most of its copies were concealed and forever buried by its first Marrano readers. The fact that neither the *Consolaçam* nor its author appear on any of the great Inquisitorial indices of the sixteenth century only adds to the mystery of its fate.[9]

By the end of the sixteenth century, Usque's generation of Marranos had passed away. But Marranos were still fleeing the Iberian Peninsula as perplexed and doubt-ridden as those for whom the *Consolaçam* was written. The Marranos no longer wandered to the Ottoman Empire, which was now declining, but to the new refuge to the North, in the United Provinces of the Netherlands.[10] From the time of their independence from Spain in 1581, the Netherlands welcomed Marranos. The Marranos came in increasing numbers and they reciprocated by developing the city of Amsterdam into the "Venice of the North," Europe's commercial center in the seventeenth century.[11]

As was the case with the Marranos in Italy, not all the New Christians in the Netherlands abjured their Catholicism when the opportunity presented itself; this despite the fact that the Netherlands was a Protestant country with vehement anti-Catholic sentiments. Whether the Marranos remained Christians for business or social reasons, or because they feared an imminent Spanish reconquest,[12] or because they had become apathetic to all religion, they found themselves in circumstances analogous to those which had led Usque to compose his work.

It was in the Netherlands, and most likely in Amsterdam, that the second edition of the *Consolaçam* saw the light of day. It is a curious volume and can easily be mistaken for the first edition.[13] Its title page lists Ferrara as the site of publication, 5313 (1553) as the year, and September 27 (!) as the date.[14] Its text is identical with that of the first edition, except for a large number of errors, which frequently obscure its meaning. The size of the volume is exactly the same as that of the Ferrara edition,[15] and though the print is different, this could easily escape the notice of someone who did not have the two editions before him.[16] Could the second edition have been intended as a counterfeit of the first, as has been claimed?[17] Hardly, because right at the point of Usque's Prologue where he speaks of his contemporary Portuguese New Christians, the date 5359 (1599) appears in the margin, as if to announce to the world that the editors, far from perpetrating a fraud, were actually seeking to preserve the integrity of a text that still spoke with contemporaneity nearly a half century after it was written.[18]

The Amsterdam *Consolaçam* marks the beginning of Sephardic literature in the Netherlands. Isaac Aboab in his *Nomology, or Legal Discourses* (*Nomologia, o Discursos Legales*, 1629) and Isaac Fernando Cardoso in his *The Merits of the Hebrews* (*Las excelencias de los hebreos*, 1679) reveal their acquaintance with Usque, while David Abenatar Melo's paraphrase of the Psalms (1612) and Diego Enríquez Basurto's *Triumph of Virtue and Patience of Job* (*El triunfo de la virtud y paciencia de Job*, 1626) utilize Usque's method of imbedding attacks on the Inquisition in the innocuous context of the Bible. The exact influence of Usque's work on rich Sephardic literature of Amsterdam is difficult to trace. His primacy, however, is beyond question.[19]

It was doubtlessly the second edition to which the Spanish Inquisitor, Sotomayor, referred in his Expurgatorial Index, which was published in Madrid in 1640.[20] There Sotomayor specifically forbade the reading of the *Consolaçam* "in Spanish, Portuguese, or in any other tongue." What did this phrase mean? Was it a protective formula used by the censors for many texts and intended to prevent the circumvention of the interdict through the reading of a work in translation? Or did it mean that the *Consolaçam* had actually been translated?[21] While the former explanation is the more likely, some scholars have conjectured that translations actually existed, especially in Spanish and in Hebrew. One scholar, Joseph Rodríguez de Castro, in his literary catalogue entitled *Biblioteca española*, even provided a Hebrew title for the book נחום ישראל (*Nahum*, perhaps for *Nihume* "the consolations of" *Israel*).[22] Another scholar, José Benoliel, picked up where Rodríguez de Castro left off. He claimed that the original title of the book was נחום ישראל וזכריה (*Nahum, Israel* [i.e. Jacob] *and Zechariah*), and

32

that furthermore, if the letters of the three words were rearranged, they would read ר' שמואל וזכי הירחון, R(abbi) Samuel Usque de Luna. He also says that the numerical value of the letters of the last two words totals 5311, the approximate year of the composition of the *Consolaçam.*[23]

Equally imaginative theories have attempted to identify Samuel Usque with the Portuguese belletrist, Bernaldim Ribeiro, author of the pastoral novel, *Young and Tender Maiden (Menina e Moça),*[24] which left the press of Abraham Usque in 1554. There have been further attempts to find a link between the style of the *Consolaçam* and the great epic of Portuguese literature, the *Lusiads* of Camoens. However, the influence of Usque on the literature of Portugal is as difficult to establish as his influence on the literature of Amsterdam. One work, however, clearly reflects Usque's style and approach. It is João Baptista d'Este's *Christian Consolation and Light for the Hebrew People (Consolação christãa, e Luz para o povo hebreo).*[25] Published in 1616, it represents a valetudinarian attempt to employ Usque's method to counteract his purpose of bringing the seed of Abraham in Portugal back to the Judaism of their forefathers.

At the beginning of the present century, the *Consolaçam as tribulaçoens de Israel* was republished in Portugal (Coimbra, 1906-1908).[26] Carefully edited by the eminent Joaquim Mendes dos Remedios and published under Portuguese auspices, the modern edition testifies to the fact that Usque's masterpiece has at last won its place among the classics of Portuguese literature. And though the Coimbra edition itself soon became scarce, the noble motives which inspired its publication and the impact of Mendes dos Remedios' sober and sympathetic appraisal were carried over into the histories of Portuguese literature and thence to the classroom. Almost all these histories echo the classic appraisal of Fidelino Figueiredo, who said, "*E uma obra nobilissima, que honra a lingua portuguesa.*" ("It is an eminent achievement and brings honor to the Portuguese language.")[27]

The *Consolaçam as tribulaçoens de Israel* also honors the Jewish faith, which inspired it, and the Jewish people, for whose survival it was written. The sufferings which its pages narrate have been dwarfed by the incredible tribulations of Jews in modern times. Usque's vision of the approaching millennium proved only an hallucination bred by fervid hopes and smarting pain. Yet his *Consolaçam* remains an example of the call for faith in adversity, the trust in the survival of the Jew, and the belief in the providential guidance of human history which have been hallmarks of the religious Jew throughout the ages.

It is noteworthy that in our times Jew and Christian alike can admire the literary beauty of the *Consolaçam* while viewing its polemic with historical detachment. In the minds of intelligent men of good will in all creeds the suspicions and antagonisms of the past have begun to yield to mutual understanding and appreciation. Like their forebears, they, too, may feel that the age of righteousness, brotherhood and abundance is now dawning. But unlike them they know that when it comes it will vindicate not the men of one faith alone, but all men of faith who can forget the tribulations caused them by their neighbors in the past and be consoled by the love they offer them in the present.

samuel usque's

CONSOLATION FOR THE TRIBULATIONS OF ISRAEL

CONSOLACAM AS TRI-
BVLACOENS DE
ISRAEL.

COMPOSTO POR SA-
MVEL VS-
QVE.

Empreſſo en Ferrara en caſa de Abraham aben
Vſque 5313 Da cria¸dm.d 7 de Setembro

FRONTISPIECE FROM ORIGINAL EDITION IN 1553

DEDICATION

TO
THE VERY ILLUSTRIOUS LADY,
DOÑA GRACIA NASI

The heart is prized as the human body's noblest and most important organ, for it is the first to feel the pain which any other part of the body suffers. Indeed, it must be kept content for all the others to be at ease.

Since my prime purpose is to serve our Portuguese nation[1] with this small branch bearing new fruit,[2] it is proper to offer it to your Excellency, for you are the heart in the body of our people: in the remedies you have offered you have always shown that you feel our people's sufferings more poignantly than anyone else.

I say this not out of blind devotion, though I am your protégé, most illustrious lady, and desire to satisfy you through works, writings and deeds and to show myself in some small way grateful for the largesse I have received from your generous hand. Since you began to reveal your light, even our sucklings have imbibed this truth at their mothers' breasts, and your name and the memory of your goodness will forever be a part of the marrow of their bones.[3]

Besides, if the sun is superior to all other planets, it is because its powers bring greater benefits to all that grows on our earth. Which of the lofty luminaries of our people can deny similar superiority to you, most illustrious lady? Though their powers have been trained on the farthest province of the earth,[4] you have done more than all of them to bring forth into the light the fruit of the plants that lie buried in its darkness.[5]

Wherefore I beg you, since you are wont to be gracious to me, kindly to accept this small token of service, so that the protection of your favor may give it the authority and respect that everything attains which draws nigh to your Excellency. May our Lord prolong and prosper your life and estate, and that of your eminent daughter[6] for many years to come.

SAMUEL USQUE

PROLOGUE

For troubled spirits the recollection of past misfortunes will somewhat diminish the suffering from present ones, especially if those gone by have been more intense. And although one misfortune is hardly cured by another, this form of medicine was approved by the great worthies, whose broad knowledge has left us remedies for the soul's afflictions and who have counseled people how to endure the sufferings to which this wretched life of ours is so subject and subjected. Take Socrates, the mirror and lodestar who guided not only the Athenians, the inventors of every branch of knowledge, but the rest of the pagan world, the possessors of classical culture. He said that when people found themselves in trouble, they should compare the misfortunes they had survived in the past with their present ones, and they would easily find consolation: for no past misfortune would prove to have been so small that it would not turn out to be much greater than the present one.[7]

Indeed, if we wished to examine things closely and not allow ourselves to be overcome by emotion, there is no affliction, however great, whose might is now buffeting us, that past generations have not seen and suffered greater. And if there be any people that can exemplify and demonstrate this experience, surely it is our own toilworn and harassed nation. Though our people has been suffering grave tribulations in our days, the tribulations which beset it in ancient times were yet much greater, and compared to them today's troubles can be considered small. In my judgment, this can easily be believed, not only because our people is so reduced in numbers that the misfortunes, great as they are, cannot find a large enough target on which to spend their strength; but also because, as I believe and trust, after this storm which has pursued us until this day, the dawn will break and the longed-for morning after winter's stormy night will graciously appear to us. Indeed, since all things are perfectly governed by the infinite Creator and composed without blemish, I cannot help but believe that, just as they had a beginning, they will not lack an end, for He alone is without end and without beginning. Thus, since our sufferings are obviously so many and of such long duration and since their intensity has increased, it is certain that unless our sins provide nourishment to sustain them, they will speedily come to an end and the fair weather we look for will begin to appear.

I have been moved by this consideration to write my book. I have seen members of our nation recently pursued and routed from the realms of Portugal, vacillating in their faith, resigning themselves unnecessarily and succumbing to their afflictions.[8] Some have done this out of poverty, others out of fear, but most out of the too little constancy which has resided in our spirits from the very beginning.[9] I have therefore proposed to relate the tribulations and hardships which have befallen our people and the causes which led to each disaster. I have culled them, indeed not without some toil and trouble, from various highly accredited authors, as can be seen in the margins,[10] and from the most recent works which contain the eye-witness accounts of our elder contemporaries. And because I did not think it fitting for us to be left with our wounds raw and open, I decided to close them with the consolations that our Lord offers us, thus setting forth in writing the happy ending which we expect in reality.

Each tribulation is followed by the prophecy which seems to have been fulfilled in it. In this way, we can see that just as those who prophesied our misfortunes proved to be right, so (we must believe) will our blessings come to pass, since both emanated from the same Source.[11] I do not believe that each prophecy I cite is the exact one which was enunciated for the particular misfortune it is coupled with. This secret belongs to God alone, and I am of the opinion that not even the prophet discerned in his imagination and purpose in what places each uttering was specifically to be fulfilled. But since I am narrating what happened to us, I will take each misfortune and merely compare it to what the prophecies have told us would happen. I do this without bias to the opinions of our sages, who have written that some of the prophecies did not really occur as they are described, but that they were a metaphor for something else, or a device sometimes used by the prophets to expound their teachings. It is true that those who have tried to prove by recent events that the prophecies refer to our generation have some measure of authority. Still, I would not rely on them to challenge the opinion of those divine sages who understood the prophecies differently.

For most of this work I used the following scheme:

I imagined the great patriarch Jacob as having the name Ycabo, as wearing the garb of a shepherd (which he was), and bewailing the misfortune of his children: children by blood, children in the Law, children in spirit. Often he stands for the entire body of Israel,[12] and very properly so, since he and Israel are the same.[13] He is consoled by Nahum and Zechariah, their names somewhat changed in the manner ancient writers customarily employed. Since these prophets are as excellent as their words show, they not only satisfy many doubts which Israel raises, but at last persuade him, with arguments and reliable prophecies, that his suffering is past and his longed-for felicity is at hand. And they bring many true tidings about the nature of this happiness.

Would to our Lord that I could write as well with my pen as the lofty subject of this work deserves. Yet I console myself that in grand and memorable matters, good judgments notice the language or style last, for the subject has value on its own; the words are only a device of communication, and it matters little whether they be elegant or unornate.

I was also induced to write this book by a desire to spur men of talent, of whom there are not a few in our nation, to say more fully and felicitously what I am attempting in this small volume. Indeed, my interest is so bent on my people's welfare that I would consider my work to have been well worth the effort if it were regarded as trifling and of little moment when compared to the good and laudable compositions which might succeed it.

The shepherd's names are not devoid of meaning. Ycabo, who represents our patriarch, has the same letters as Jacob.[14] Besides, "Ycabo" in the holy tongue means "gone is Israel's glory," and was the name that the daughter-in-law of Eli the priest gave the son she bore when she heard the sad news of the capture of the Ark by the Philistines.[15] Numeo is derived from Nahum, the consoler, which is the effect he has in this work; and Zicareo from Zechariah, the remembrancer, who recalls the blessings Israel received in compensation for his afflictions and the vengeances which were carried out in his behalf.

Before learning of my intention, some gentlemen felt that it would have been better for me to have written in the Castilian tongue, but I believe that I have done the right thing. My primary intention was to speak to the Portuguese [New Christians],[16] to describe the record of our Diaspora, and by many sometimes circuitous means, to seek some relief from the hardships we have been enduring. It would therefore have been inappropriate for me to shun my mother tongue and to seek a borrowed language in which to speak to my countrymen. And though at one time there were many among us from the Diaspora of Castile—my own forebears came from there—it seems more proper for me to consider the majority of our people today.[17]

FIRST

DIALOGUE

ISRAEL,

WITH THE NAME OF YCABO,

A SHEPHERD,

HAVING TAKEN REFUGE IN A PLACE

REMOVED FROM HUMAN SOCIETY,

LAMENTS HIS WOES.

HE IS DISCOVERED BY CHANCE

BY NAHUM AND ZECHARIAH,

PROPHETS IN THE GARB

AND NAME OF SHEPHERDS,

TO WHOM HE RELATES ALL HIS AFFLICTIONS,

AND THEY CONSOLE HIM.

SUBTITLES

FOR DIALOGUE I

PASTORAL LIFE
HUNT OF CONIES & HARES
HUNT OF STAGS [& HERONS]
THE ORIGIN OF ISRAEL & THE CONSTRUCTION OF THE TEMPLE
TRIBULATIONS OF ISRAEL, ABBREVIATED
THE FIRST EXPERIENCES OF ISRAEL IN THE HOLY LAND
THE LIFE OF THE WICKED, IN THE GUISE OF CONIES & HARES
KINGS
KINGS OF ISRAEL
THE HUNT OF STAGS TRANSFIGURED INTO THE LIFE OF THE WICKED
LAMENT OVER THE LOSS OF THE TEN TRIBES
CONSOLATION ON THE CAPTIVITY OF THE TEN TRIBES
ORIGIN OF IDOLATRY
HUMAN CONSOLATION FOR THE CAPTIVITY OF THE TEN TRIBES
DIVINE CONSOLATION FOR THE CAPTIVITY OF THE TEN TRIBES
CHAPTER ON THE KINGS OF JUDAH
HUNT OF HERONS, ADAPTED TO THE WICKED KINGS OF JUDAH
ISRAEL'S LAMENT ON THE LOSS OF THE FIRST TEMPLE

PASTORAL DIALOGUE
ON MATTERS OF SACRED SCRIPTURE
INTERLOCUTORS: YCABO, NUMEO & ZICAREO

YCABO: What an appropriate place this is for me to bemoan my misfortunes and for my sighs to rise to the farthest heaven! O trees and
gentle waters, you alone are disposed to hear me; hear and take pity at
my cries. O drooping spirits of mine, O limbs wearied and bruised, O
bodily burden so heavy to bear, strengthen yourselves. O eyes of mine,
tired of being an arid bed, send forth tears of blood by the thousands. O
tall and thick branches that hold back the rays of my weakened sight,
spread a little that my continuous and doleful sighs may mount higher
than the clouds, and make room for my groans to be heard in all four
corners of the earth.

O Asia, spacious, fortunate and great, sown with precious gems and
planted with rich and noble trees, you pleasantly delight your tawny
inhabitants with infinite wealth and soft and marvelous fragrances.[1]

O Africa, mountainous, rugged and scorched, pregnant with the finest
gold, cloaked with sweet and handsome palms, and sprinkled with milk
and honey, you keep your children happy with buried wealth and the
savory foods of Nature.

And Europe, bellicose, wise and fair, swelled by crafty strategems
and by proud and wondrous triumphs and converted into a terrestrial
paradise,[2] your children delicately suck your full breasts in boundless
luxury, and anyone who grows up in any of your regions finds himself
lovingly protected beneath the shadow of its wings.[3]

But you, O ancient inheritance and pious motherland of mine,[4] you
who once were mistress of the nations, and like the eagle among the
creatures of wing,[5] a princess over all the provinces, where shall I go
to seek your glories past? Your Temple mysteries have vanished.[6] Your
sublime miracles have taken refuge in the heavens.[7] Vile abominations
have adulterated your divine sacrifices. The joys of your holy festivals
have been cloaked with mourning and sadness. Instead of the softness
of the earth's marvelous abundance, you feel the harshness of cruel
peoples' captivity.[8] Instead of heaven's continual favors, you feel its ire
and its abandonment. Instead of your beloved children's sacred repose
and calmness of spirit, you see them cruelly banished from province to
province in wretched fear and continuing misery. Instead of savory
fruits, you breed poisonous vipers.[9] And the clear waters of the Jordan
and the fountain of Idumea run red with human blood.[10]

Then where in the world can I turn that I may find a remedy for my
wound, relief for my pain and consolation for such grave and pressing

ills? O afflicted body of mine, the whole earth is full of my wretchedness and suffering.[11] Among the riches and pleasures of joyous Asia I find myself a poor and wearied traveler, amidst the abundance of gold and fatness of the burning land of Africa, a wretched, famished and thirsty exile. Now Europe, O Europe, my hell on earth, what shall I say of you, since you have won most of your triumphs at the expense of my limbs?[12] O Italy, depraved and bellicose, for what shall I praise you? Famished lions have fattened themselves within your borders by tearing apart the flesh of my lambs. O France, in your luxuriant pastures my ewes have grazed poisonous herbs. O Germany, haughty, rough and mountainous, my goats were dashed to pieces as they fell from the summit of your craggy Alps. O England, my cattle drank bitter and brackish drafts from your sweet, cold waters. And Spain, hypocritical, cruel and lupine, ravenous and raging wolves have been devouring my wooly flock within you.

NUMEO: Zicareo! Either I am deceived, or someone is walking in this forest, for I hear a sound like a human voice. I beg you, wait a moment, and we shall hear it.

ZICAREO: It must be Yranio,[13] who is feeding his cattle on the other side. Perhaps his mastiffs are chasing a wolf. Let us hurry, for our flocks are moving far ahead and the passes in these parts are not very secure.

NUMEO: They are well protected by the mastiffs. Wait, because we shall not be long detained. Be attentive, for whoever he is, he is continuing his discourse.

YCABO: O world, world, since you do not permit your rational creatures to be grieved by my tribulations and miseries, if the heavens have infused some secret mode of pity in insensitive things, grant permission to the rivers, which cascade from the high mountains with a frightening rumble to break their frothy waters down below, to check their frenetic pace. Let them accompany the continuous flow of my tears with a gentle and plaintive murmur, and by their wearied course let them show a new sympathy for my long agonies.

And you, Nile, Ganges, Euphrates and Tigris, chief among them all, who detach yourselves from the terrestrial paradise[14] and come freely to give water to the thirsty Egyptians and to the soft and scented Indians; who change your course, hide in the sands for many days and then emerge and appear to the wild and dark Guineans;[15] who rise and fall through rugged and mountainous wastes on your way to greet the cruel and warlike Tartars;[16] who there commune with the longed-for messenger who was carried swiftly away to the heavens[17] in a chariot with horses of fire; I entreat you now graciously to tell me this secret:

When will my afflictions and toils have surcease? When will I see the end to wrongs and offenses against me, to my longings and agonies, to the wounds in my soul and the bruises on my body? When will my happiness not be confined to dreams and my misfortunes not be real? When will my ever-present ills be removed and the fulfillment of my wearied hopes not seem a distant reverie? And when will peace come to my battered body, or to the fears, suspicions and apprehensions of my spirit? How long must I moan and sigh and slake my thirst with my tears?

ZICAREO: You heard correctly, brother Numeo. It was a human being. But it was not Yranio, feeling our divine and indescribable absence, for I know his voice well. It is another shepherd who is lamenting in the same tones.

NUMEO: Though I run a great risk,[18] I would not lose the opportunity of finding out if this is the shepherd whom we have wanted to meet for such a long time. Upon your word, Zicareo, let us go to find out about him.

ZICAREO: Let us go.

YCABO: In order to reflect more calmly upon my troubles without the noise of shepherds disturbing me, I have withdrawn to this thick grove, which nature formed at the foot of this rough mountain. But if fortune has not deprived me of my sense of hearing, as it has stripped me of my other blessings, I perceive the steps and speech of more than one person not far from me.

NUMEO: O good shepherd, what are you doing in this strange and secluded place? And where are you from, you who show yourself so courageous by withdrawing to such a solitary and awesome spot? May good fortune gladden you with an increase of your sheep and lambs if you do not conceal your secret from us. Indeed, if some remedy for your hardships were within our power, we would very gladly offer it to you forthwith. Cheer, cheer your unhappy countenance, and raise it toward us. Let your long and wearisome sighs now cease; for I see them throbbing in your breast at times gently, at times with restless, almost live palpitations.

ZICAREO: O brother, get up from where you are. Come with us to the clear brook nearby, where you will wash your eyes that are so wet and heavy from crying. And if you should want our company further, you may return with us to our cottages. There you will rest, and we shall refresh you with some white milk and fresh cream.

YCABO: Kindly and friendly shepherds, the time of my rest has as yet not arrived, and all the contentments and pleasures I take in this world, since they are unbecoming, cannot satisfy me or even penetrate my coarse shepherd's cloak. Therefore do not try to offer me cheerful things, for they only add to a sad man's sorrows. And, though you did not mean to, you have aroused my sorrows, which were calmly reasoning with me. Turn about and I shall still them again.

ZICAREO: We will certainly not turn away, for every care is harmful. Instead, we entreat you fervently to unburden your passions before us. Without a doubt I believe you will feel some improvement in your pain, for the way to relieve misfortunes is to talk about them.

YCABO: Ah, brothers, I cannot without great anguish of spirit recall times passed or reflect how my memory of them clashes with the picture of me today. It suddenly sends a chill wind which seems almost alive through every limb of my body, and as it moves, it congeals the blood diffused through all my veins.

They say that the body's natural color is the seat of the soul's divine and precious form.[19] I have lost my natural color. So do not marvel if my face appears unnatural, my eyes dull and lightless, my hair disheveled, my hands cold, and my nails blanched. Do not wonder if my body lies unconscious on the ground, alone beneath this tree, deprived of all its instincts, including self-preservation. But if I think of those past times again, I will bleed the raw wound still more, though its condition cannot tolerate too much contact. Yet, despite the discomfort it may bring me, I do not wish to appear ill-mannered and ungrateful for your virtuous and guileless offer of friendship, which I fully appreciate, and I wish to please you. I will open my heart fully and tell you of myself and the sorrow imprinted on my soul.

PASTORAL LIFE

You probably know, brothers, that I am that shepherd from days of yore who covered his neck and hands with hair to deceive his father and succeed to the blessing.[20] And for the love of a beautiful shepherdess, I led sheep in Mesopotamia's luxuriant pastures for seven years and then another seven.[21] When I left there with a rich and beautiful flock of goats and sheep of motley spots and colors,[22] I returned to inherit the spacious fields and happy pastures of Canaan, which my fathers had possessed.[23] I received twelve robust male children[24] from God's hand, and in their company I happily rejoiced in my abundance of splendid riches.

Some of my sons took great delight in watching the innocent, graceful sheep. At the break of day, before the eastern sky was stained with ruddy hue, they would go forth with their flock. As the birds twittered sweetly, my sons roamed through the dewy grass and quietly and gently guided their flock toward some cool and pleasant meadow. Nearby, on the verdure of a hillock, they sat down to observe their drove.

The yeanlings came forth. Some fed meekly on the small, green grass in the flat meadow. Others moved up to rougher terrain and stretched to gnaw at a sapling that rose delicately from the earth. One stood on its hind legs to reach a fig-branch. Another bit the tender buds of wild vines. A third nibbled at a stalk of wild artichoke. The small and tender suckling lambs, recently dropped, rushed upon the full udders of their compassionate dams and sucked swiftly, with such gusto and relish that it seemed as if they wanted to pull off the long teats. Others had had their fill of grazing; they drank in the clear brooks and amused themselves as they gazed at their life-like image in the water. Some rams grew angry at their reflection and butted it from time to time; and when they were frustrated, they stood still, holding their drenched heads motionless, as if struck by thunder.

Thus they spent the freshness of the morning in this luxury. And when the sun's dry heat had drunk the dew in the greenery, they rose and moved on with their flock of gentle sheep to seek pleasant shades and the refreshment of a cool and temperate breeze. Soon, beyond a cheerful dale, they were welcomed by a beautiful, thickly-wooded grove, luxuriantly watered by a gay and gurgling fountain which flowed with sweet waters at the foot of a tall cypress tree. They sat down nearby in their appointed places as mealtime approached. They took their wooly shepherd's bags—made of the white hide of a tender lamb that had been torn by a wolf or the ruddy skin of an abortive calf—from off their shoulders, and each drew out some of his savory natural victuals upon the table. And they ate with relish, combining their food with the honey that dripped in thick skeins from the trees and the white milk which dropped from the fat ewes' teats as they pastured.

When their hunger had been satisfied, they felt a cool breeze softly rustling the tops of the tall poplars and the large, luxuriant ashes. Their uppermost branches swayed with such a relaxed and tender cadence that they seemed to be secretly greeting one another. And all the while the blackbirds' murmur, the nightingales' enchanting airs, and the tunes of numerous fledgelings that flew to the grove for shelter against the oppressive heat filled the entire place with melody. They answered one another in varied tones, their songs blending with the cadence of the burbling fountain. Some shepherds played softly on their flutes and rustic instruments. Others accompanied them with passionate songs to their beloved shepherdesses. Some wrestled dexterously in rustic manner and style. Others incited the strong and fearless rams against one another and watched their rough butting. Still others, vanquished by drowsiness, dozed off, sated with pleasure, near the gurgling of the clear fountain.

The sun had now completed its task in the fertile earth of the [Northern] hemisphere and hidden beneath the waters of the West. As it departed, it shot the sky with brilliant clouds, some bright yellow like the color of the pure gold of Ophir;[25] some crimson, like fine scarlet and precious rubies; a few black, jutting like long rays; many white, like snowy mountains or wool strewn over the glaucous waters of the sea; and some, long and ridgy, were ashen and bordered with gold. Then it left the high mountains and green fields in a delicious calm of cool breezes and still shadows.

The shepherds then gathered their roaming sheep that rambled and grazed throughout the grove and led them through another part of the woods to a beautiful virgin plain, which led directly to their cottages. The entire joyous company, guiding themselves with their crooks, slowly began to make their way homeward to their cots to rest. As they moved, they began to play games. They slung at targets with their pebbles, and lifted the best marksman on their shoulders with applause and huzzas. From this game they turned to jumping, pitching the bar, and wrestling. They crowned the winners with garlands of green laurel[26] and played their rustic flutes and fiddles in honor of their victories. And so they gradually approached their huts. When they arrived, full of content-ment and sated with the pleasures of the day, the frogs had begun to croak raucously in the clover-decked marshes, the crickets chirped in-cessantly in plaintive tones in the roadside ditches, and the entire coun-tryside resounded.

And when they had gathered their wooly flocks into the shelter of their folds, they took off their coarse bags, laid aside their crooks, and prepared for their longed-for supper. They sat down in their appointed places at the entrance to their bowers, built on the bank of the clear river Jordan, and ate by the light of the moon; the moon flashed in the waters and dazzled their eyes with its crystal rays. When they had finished supping with great relish, they played more games until it grew quite late, and then, on the grass outside or hither and yon within their huts, they fell asleep, drunk with joy, their faces looking upward at the calm of a star-studded sky.

HUNT OF CONIES AND HARES

This Golden Age had progressed for a while under the staff of the Supreme Shepherd, whose flocks pasture the entire universe, and other earthly shepherds, appointed by His hand, who faithfully guarded the sheep, when a group of terrible shepherds arose from among these same children of mine. Neglectful of their cattle, they let it feed on poisonous herbs and drink bitter waters, while they pursued a different way of life: the harsh and heathen chase.

In the coolness of the early morning, before the sun descended upon the dew on the rugged slopes and green hills, they would enter a dense thicket with their ferreters on leash, their crooks on their backs, their traps in their knapsacks and their dogs tied in pairs before them. They would probe in all directions until their setter caught the track of a meek coney feeding in the grass. He barked; the other dogs responded and ran furiously in swift pursuit, occasionally seeming to lose the game, but finally forcing it into the confines of a cave. And while some dogs yelped in the nearby thickets, others barked angrily, rushed to the mouth of the cave, and blocked all the escapes but two. Into one a keen ferreter was speedily unleashed, and in the other the deceitful trap was set; then the conies meekly came forth to surrender.

Nearby, the dogs pointed to some terrified rabbits that were nimbly running along the highway. With the speed of flight, the graceful and delicate greyhounds pursued them for a league and a half. Finally the

rabbits, seeing their foe approach, in sheer exhaustion and fright pitifully sought shelter along the road at the hem of a rustic woman's skirts
or at the foot of a wearied traveler.

HUNT OF STAGS (AND HERONS)

These hunters would spend the cool of the morning in this sport.
And when the sun began to rise and swell with heat, they mounted their
pampered mares and, with their long shafts in their hands, their green
hunter's caps[27] on their heads, and their bulging leathern bottles and
bags at their sides, they rode onto a beautiful spacious plain, stippled
with small stags and tender roebucks. In some places it was flat and
covered with fragrant pennyroyal, sweet honeysuckle and other wild
plants. In the foreground pleasant hillocks rose and cast shadows with a
distinctive charm. In the distance, sitting on verdant hills by the waters
of coursing brooks that spread profusely as they descended throughout
the entire landscape and preserved its green luxuriance, forty or fifty
hunters could be seen.

As they bantered with one another they loosed the game they had
readied, separated a distance, and set their gins. Then they swiftly
spurred their fleetest mare. The nimble stag leaped forward and ran
wildly with the thrust of a speeding arrow, its head high in the breeze.
The first hunter shrewdly strove to keep it in front of its pursuers and
craftily pressed it from side to side before him. Finally it reached the
post of his companion, the second hunter, who had tired of waiting and
slumped to doze at the base of a tall thicket, with his wine-bag for a
pillow and his mare's curb fastened to his sash. When his horse heard
the first signal—which it understood because it had heard such signals
often—it woke and nearly dragged the sleepy hunter into pursuit of
the furious stag. In this way, all the hunters ran their relays and followed hotly on the heels of the chase, until the last one could easily
kill the tired game. In their great joy at the victory they had won,
some spoke of the many marks found in the dead stag's flanks that came
from the bites of a mare that had thrown its hunter; others argued with
gusto about the age of the huge hart, which could be figured by the size
of its antlers and the tips of its long, hard horns. Then they remounted;
some gracefully galloped their docile mares while others promenaded
their weary jennets with a more gentle pace. Thus amidst great rejoicing
and exhilaration, they proceeded to their village or hamlet.

At this hour a temperate shade was spreading a delicious silence
over all those happy vales. Suddenly twelve or fifteen hunters appeared
from a different direction, hungry falcons in hand, knapsacks at their
sides, riding their light jennets and docile mares across a green and airy
plain. As they moved trippingly over the lovely field, in the distance
they espied an exquisite bird, a majestic heron that lightly flapped its

wings, cutting the fine, thin air in its flight. The hunters unhooded their large, swift falcon-gentle to give it a glimpse of the graceful bird. The intrepid falcon soared up toward it and pursued it impetuously for an entire league. To entrap its prey, it flew high and swept down upon it. The heron climbed higher and higher, but its ascent was so blocked by its soaring enemy that it realized the danger and hastened to defend itself in a final stand. Angrily, the delicate bird prepared itself. It turned its tender breast, hard bill and long legs upward and waited. The powerful falcon attacked it from all sides. The noble game, breaking under this furious onslaught, began to moan gently and pitifully at the first blow. It rose as high as it could in an effort to escape, but its foe kept mounting and pressing, and again wounded it gravely. In this way, by moving swiftly from one place and deftly attacking it in another, the falcon tore at it so repeatedly with its long, sharp claws that pieces often fell from the weary, vanquished heron, and its dove feathers drifted through the clear, fresh air or fell and scattered across the verdure. At this point a coarse, large kite was moved by the wounded heron's mournful cries and came to its aid, to the hunters' great delight. One of the crafty hunters then threw a bold sparrow-hawk at them, another a robust saker, a third a sharp-beaked gerfalcon and a fourth a large and handsome hobby. Both groups lustily attacked their enemies and soon were locked in fierce combat. The forces of the weaker birds were finally overcome, and they surrendered to their adversaries. And when the beautiful bird at last expired, the hunting companions divided its carcass, each carrying off his part of the prey with joyous exhilaration.

ZICAREO: From your intimations at the beginning of your discourse, we understand that you are the grand patriarch Israel. Your high ideals, your lofty contemplations and your divine works made you a beacon of light which dispelled men's ignorance and lifted the pall of darkness which prevented them from knowing the Cause of all Causes. Since your teachings were sincere, we are surprised at your children's contrary behavior; for they have shaped their lives solely by vain and mundane delights.

NUMEO: And I am even more surprised, Zicareo, for he seems to think of nothing but his children's loss. Yet he is the storehouse of discretion, and the straight path which leads unswervingly from earthly things to a sure understanding of God's higher purposes. The pleasures of his days have always been absorbed in contemplating the divine and in reflecting on life's profound mysteries.

YCABO: If you will not break the thread of my story and will listen patiently to the long account of my years, you will find the answer to your doubts and will comprehend the exact cause and source from which my lamentations arise. And so that you may know that my words have a double meaning, I will remove the veil with which I covered them, and the true image (which you have thus far not discerned) will emerge from their strange garb.

THE ORIGIN OF ISRAEL AND THE CONSTRUCTION
OF THE TEMPLE
{THE EXPLANATION OF THE METAPHOR ENTITLED
"PASTORAL LIFE"}

You should know that He whose will created and sustains the immense celestial edifice and all its hosts, as well as this world below, a mere dot and invisible speck by comparison, loved my grandfather Abraham with His infinite mercy and supreme goodness, and said to him, "I am your shield and your reward is very great" (Gen. 15.1). He therefore held back the punishment which man's abominable sins from the time of Noah until Abraham required of His divine justice as vengeance on the world.[28] He also loved my father Isaac, who was a sacrifice without blemish.[29] Isaac begat two sons, Jacob and Esau. The Lord loved me, Jacob, but He hated my brother, Esau.[30] He gave me seventy souls, begotten of my thigh, who went down with me to sojourn in Egypt.[31] There, through divine favor, these souls multiplied into a great and powerful host, but they were used as slaves because of the wickedness of the people of the land, where they were strangers.[32] Yet with signs, wonders, a strong hand and an outstretched arm, He liberated them from their captivity with everlasting freedom.[33] The Lord destroyed and drowned all the Egyptians who pursued them, and brought them safely through the midst of the Red Sea to dry land.[34] He performed countless wonders for them as they went across the desert. He sent a cloud with them by day and a pillar of fire to guide them by night.[35] He made Horeb's hard rocks run with clear waters for their thirst[36] and sent manna, the food of angels,[37] from heaven for their bread and delicious fowl for their hunger.[38] On the mountain of Sinai He gave them a divine Law as food for their souls, so that they might live for-ever in heaven above and prolong their days on earth below.[39] He warred against the enemies who blocked their advance,[40] and gave their children possession of the land flowing with milk and honey which He had promised to my fathers.[41]

And following a commandment which I received from the Lord in the awesome place where I slept—the house of the Lord and the gate of the heavens[42]—a holy city was built of such marvelous architecture and unsurpassed beauty, that it resembled the terrestrial paradise,[43] and I, Israel, inhabited it in Adam's place.[44]

There a temple to our Lord was built by Solomon, the son of David. Its frame, made of whole stones, was set on a hard hill. The stones of its foundation were forty cubits in size; the length of the frame was sixty cubits, its breadth twenty, and its height thirty.[45] It had twin galleries around it, supported on beautiful pillars twenty-five cubits high, each one fashioned from a single block of white marble.

Its doors were overlaid with gold or silver, as were its wickets and doorposts, but the Temple's main gate was of bronze from Corinth, finer than gold or silver. The beams of the house were planks made from smooth and fragrant cedar and other choice trees. The floor, the walls, and the rest of the interior were covered with bright gold, as was the Holy of Holies within and without. Sculptured in the metal were cherubim, date trees and many budding flowers.

The entrance to the innermost and holiest precinct was fashioned in the likeness of human shoulders; it had no doors, suggesting that the secrets of the heavens [were always available to man]. Above the entrance were golden vines, which supported clusters of grapes the size of a man.[46] It had a curtain fifty-five cubits long known as the Babylonian veil. It was fashioned with consummate skill from byssus, a very white linen, variegated with violet, the color of the sky, and with crimson and purple. This blending of colors was said to contain great secrets and to represent the image of all things.[47] The crimson stood for fire, the byssus for earth, the violet for air, and the purple for the sea.[48]

Nearby there was a golden candelabrum, with seven lamps which signified the seven shooting stars.[49] A golden table with twelve breads represented the twelve signs of the zodiac and the twelve months of the year.[50] A golden censer filled with thirteen kinds of incense, gathered from the impassable parts of the sea as well as uninhabitable areas of land, signified that everything belonged to the Lord and served Him.[51] No one was permitted to enter or see the innermost precinct, but there was nothing on the outside at which the soul did not marvel and the eyes did not smart, as they do from the rays of the sun, because of the splendor which radiated from the marvelous gold sculptures. The entire structure was so striking in appearance that it seemed clearly to be a copy of a celestial building which had been shown to my son Moses on the mountain of Sinai.[52]

Herod's second Temple was like Solomon's. During its existence of many ages, sacred treasures were consumed which had been sent from all over the world as gifts to the Temple. This Temple was taken as a home by the Lord, whose immensity cannot be encompassed by that of all the heavens[53] above and the earth beneath. He said, "Wherefore I have hallowed this house which you have built, to put My name there for ever; and My eyes and My heart shall be on it forever" (I Kings 9.3). And as a result of the people's holy deeds, which conformed to His holy Law and will, His glory descended thither, by degrees so to speak,[54] to converse familiarly with them as He communes with angels' spirits in His celestial court above. This was the true meaning of the vision that appeared to me. I saw a ladder standing on the ground by my pillow and touching the heavens with its top. On it angels were ascending and descending, and above it stood the Lord. Here, in the Temple, the Lord diverted misfortune from all His people and taught them through His doctrine to realize the aim of blessed souls and the rewards of those who serve Him.[55] And in order to draw and attract them into His service,

He called them His flock, and He was their shepherd.[56] He thereby gave them assurance of the love He had for them.

These are the sheep of which I spoke above, that rose in the cool of the morning and went out into the delightful pastures of the Law to be nourished on the study of divine knowledge. Here they were guided by great and righteous sages who were imbued with prophetic inspiration. They sat in the fields as they serenely nibbled, or debated, on the slender blades of dialectic. Some, who were endowed with limited understanding and could not reach the higher fields of study, gnawed on the flat of the meadow or on grass hardly higher than the surface of the earth; while others, whose spirits soared higher, stood on tiptoe in the rough and rugged places of lofty speculation and stretched to pick at the deep roots and sublime fruits of the tree of life, which is the Holy Law;[57] and they meditated, engrossed in its teaching of marvelous secrets.

The udders swelled with milk which the tenderest lambs suckled with relish from their compassionate dams were the fountains of knowledge which even our smallest children imbibed from their loving sages.[58] And those who had filled their souls to satisfaction with higher study prophesied events to come as they drank in the clear brooks and crystalline waters of contemplation in which our Lord and His glory are reflected. Others offered sacrifices by which the people were cleansed and purified. All thus gazed at themselves in these waters of cleanliness, and rejoiced when they saw their reflections in heaven above, alive forever in the bond of the living[59] and in the treasury of the righteous[60]—the farthest point and end of the tempestuous sea of life which we all must traverse.

Others stood by the fountain of heavenly waters and belled yearningly like thirsty deer; they were incensed by the heavy burden of their flesh and sought release from the prison of this life,[61] that they might aspire to the enjoyment of the bliss they contemplated; but they were frustrated in their desire and left in confusion: their souls, which are like incorporeal figures, transparent in life's waters, were held captive to their sorrow and detained by the mite of their bodies' insensitive flesh.

In this way the saintly company was sustained by this heavenly food and water, such as the angel of the Lord gave the prophet Elijah when he fled from Jezebel.[62] With their splendid discussions they fulfilled the divine precept, "Happy are they whose work is in the Law; they bring satisfaction of spirit to their Maker."[63]

Among the worthies who spent their days absorbed in this angelic exercise (which excels all others in the world as a cool and pleasant morning surpasses the impenetrable darkness of the night), there were some who descended to human affairs with a divine intent. They were like the morning dew that drops from heaven to sprinkle and drench the grass, that is, lower and terrestrial matters. Yet they too obediently directed their labors to the service of their Creator. Since they were not pre-eminent, they flew low with the infirm wings of their understanding, and made an example of the less difficult precept of "Happy are they who eat their bread with the sweat of their palms" (Ps. 128.2). And the joys that they received from their achievement were the delightful shades of heavenly bliss they now perceived.

Such was the cool and temperate breeze which refreshed the soul. Such were the shady and cheerful dales where they fed in luxury and passed the days. Such was the thick grove where they took shelter. In it they found the path of their saintly sages and exalted prophets that led them heavenward with glorious steps. Thus they fled the dry, oppressive heat of the world's deceitful sufferings, which, since they are not directed to the true goal of life, are barren and fruitless. Here they took shelter at the foot and shade of the Lord Supreme, who is like a tall cypress or a clear, sweet fountain, for He pours blessings upon all His creatures.

And now—to prove that the day of the death of the righteous is better than that of their birth[64]—the hour arrived for all to taste the reward of their works of divine service, which they carried on their shoulders and on the left sides of their hearts, of varying value, like shepherd's bags of different hides. Each one took the food he had put there and sat down in a place corresponding to his merit.

And as they enjoyed the true honey and the endless fresh white milk of sweetness and delight that is the food of the righteous, and the nutritious fruit of the holy land of Heaven (the children of Israel's real inheritance and the original of its copy here on earth),[65] they felt a fresh, temperate breeze, a divine breath of inconceivable delight. It was the still, small whisper of Elijah's vision,[66] and it breathed immense majesty into the holy and joyous souls of the celestial spirits, who were like tall poplars and huge, luxuriant ashes—as it is written "The righteous are like trees planted" (Jer. 17.8; Ps. 92.13). And softly waving and raising those who had higher branches, that is, more excellent works, to even greater contemplation, its light and stirring melody bespoke an immense felicity and bliss supreme which cannot be described with the low speech of our earthly tongues or grasped by human understanding. This heavenly felicity is like the harmony of the enchanting and melodious nightingales, the gentle blackbirds and the graceful fledgelings of the grove. It is the music of divine proportion by which the celestial edifice and all angelic forms make their heavenly rounds[67] and in supreme obedience affirm God's unity.[68] It is the sweet murmur and purl of the clear, bubbling fountain, to whose sound the shepherds fell asleep after their noontime meal. It is those delightful and glorious afternoons, with their beautiful variety of glowing clouds, some golden with the color of Ophir's pure gold, some crimson like fine scarlet and precious rubies, representing the company of seraphim and cherubim, shining like a glowing fire and furbished sword. It is the fresh breezes, the pleasant, green fields and the charming, gay hills where the sheep and their shepherds reposed after they traversed the tiresome heat of the world's labors. It is the beautiful plain, untrodden by any other people, which led directly to the cottage of the Garden of Delight.[69] This felicity is like the gay, pastoral games, the pleasant recreations of the heavenly field, the joys of flutes and fiddles, and the bands of evergreen laurel, with which the shepherds crowned each other—the perpetual reward with which the victor in the struggle with this world is crowned as an accolade of victory. It is the shepherd's bowers set on the bank of the clear river Jordan, by whose sheen they sat to sup as the final reward of their day. It is the restful, comforting sleep that the shepherds enjoyed, intoxicated with bliss; some outside the cottages, reposing on the grass of their modest merits, and others inside, their spirits carried aloft by profound and glorious contemplation.

ZICAREO: What a glorious existence! What a delightful life! What angelic steps you took in the celestial court while your body was still on earth! What mortal being, while still encased in its earthly husk, has risen to such lofty bliss that it has communicated not with an angel nor with seraphim,[70] but with the Single Essence, and remained alive? Certainly no one but yourself. How perfect are your tents, O Jacob and your dwellings, O Israel.[71] Who is like you O people, hills of such noble pasture, flowers, leaves, grass, shades, soft breezes of the meadows and celestial fields, O sacred waters with which the angels slake their thirst? If merely the sweet recollection of these events exalts my soul in their midst, what joy you should feel, O fortunate Israel, for you not only saw this close at hand through divine contemplation, but touched it with your earthly sight and limbs? But since this blessing soars beyond human comprehension, it is not fitting for my tongue to speak of it further.

YCABO: I have far from completed the thread of my history. I have presented to you only the preliminary, in short compendium and in pastoral garb—as if I were containing the sea in a small vessel. I have not told you of the variety of my continual miracles—the lofty mystery of the Urim and Thummim;[72] the holiness of the heavenly waters;[73] the profound secret of the red heifer;[74] the fire which visibly descended from the heavens to consume the sacrifices;[75] the smoke which returned directly thither and could not be diverted by the winds or storms that blew;[76] the insect Shamir, with which the stones of the Temple were hewed, for the use of an iron tool was forbidden;[77] and the changes and variations of color in the silken thread, placed in the inner sanctum of the Temple, which were a sign of pardon.[78]

And what more can I tell you of my worldly blessings, which the righteous regard as a low and earthly thing, like a flower whose freshness withers and fades.[79] I could tell you of the countless number of golden objects and precious gems of King Solomon in the time of the First Temple, or the Israelite people in the time of the Second, when silver was worth no more than the stones in the street. I could describe my people's physical beauty, or the great worth and handsomeness of their apparel and ornaments. I could dwell on the sturdy architecture of the

Holy City, where the genius of the artist exceeded the beauty of his materials. Compared to any one of these things, the triumphs and achievements of all pagan nations past and present are as brass to gold, as painted glass to precious stone or as cheap tin to English silver. In short, Israel's grandeur contained the finest things of the sea and land in the lower world and embraced heaven, the source of its favor.

But then, compassionate brothers, because I was disobedient,[80] like Adam in the terrestrial paradise, I abandoned the Lord, the fountain of living waters.[81] And as I went up from the desert, the east wind dried my spring and fountain,[82] stripped me of the noble ornaments I treasured, and left me as you see me here, despoiled and bereft of all the blessings I possessed. All my joy has been turned to sorrow. The once flowering and delightful hills are now covered with melancholy and poisonous herbs. The shady groves, with their sweet harmony of birds, have become sandy deserts, the lair of stalking and bellowing beasts. Then why should I not show sorrow in the midst of such misfortunes? O craven Israel, human frailty, open your bosom and tear your guts in pain and affliction, for death is no more than a step between this life and the next. Where is your dauntless spirit? Why do you not put freedom above any kind of torment, as the Israelites did at Masada, the impregnable fortress of Judah? They chose to slay their children, their wives and then themselves and give all their wealth to the fire rather than endure the captivity and cruelty of the Romans, who were almost upon them. But woe to my wretchedness: it would be better for me to raise my weary eyes to heaven, which holds a happy outcome for my hopes. Afflicted and humbled being that I am, if my tongue could somehow wipe out the suffering imprinted on my soul, I would spend the little strength that is left to me narrating the course of my sorrows, as I promised to do for you. But they open like such a vast sea before me that I hardly dare; for on twelve occasions[83] cruel enemies despoiled me of all my glory and tore limb after limb from my crippled body.

TRIBULATIONS OF ISRAEL, ABBREVIATED

(1)[84] First, after I entered the Holy Land, I was enslaved six times—to the kings of Haran, Moab, Canaan (Jabin), the Midianites, the Philistines and the Ammonites[85]—because I imitated their heathen ways. Thus I was given bitter morsels to swallow, since I was removed from God's lovingkindness (for His favor sustains me and without Him I would perish). The prophetic words of Moses and Joshua were fulfilled: "If you will not drive the inhabitants of the land from before you, then those who remain shall be as thorns in your eyes and pricks in your sides, and they shall harass you in the land on which you dwell, and in the manner which I thought to do against them, will I do against you (Num. 33.55-56). Thus God's justice was at work; since I did not obey His command by subjugating them, but rather cleaved to them and imitated their profane works, I was subjected.[86]

(2) I saw the filthy hands of Shishak, king of Egypt, steal the sacred treasures of the House of the Lord, those of the royal palace in Jerusalem, and Solomon's precious gold shields,[87] determined (it seems) to take vengeance for the gems we took with us from his Egyptian countrymen.[88] And my sin led to this. Yet I was warned by Shemaiah's prophecy: "Thus says the Lord. You have abandoned Me and I therefore shall deliver you into the power of Shishak" (II Chron. 12.5).

(3) I saw nine cities and the entire land of Naphtali despoiled of all their riches when Tiglath-pileser, king of the Assyrians, brought all my children to Assyria in pitiful captivity. And when Sennacherib came, he stripped beautiful Samaria of all the children who remained, and brought them to Halah and Habor near the river Gozan, and to the cities of the Medes.[89] Here your threat, O Lord, which you spoke through Micah's lips was fulfilled: "What was the cause of Jacob's prevarication? Surely it was Samaria. Therefore I shall turn it into a heap of the field and a place for the planting of the vine" (Mic. 1.5-6). "Can there fail to be gloom for him who is in pain? This was the first time the land of Zebulun and the land of Naphtali were emptied, but the second was more grievous. It was by the way of the sea, beyond the Jordan, in the district of the nations" (Isa. 8.23). "Samaria is taken away with its king, like foam which is on the face of the waters" (Hos. 10.7).

(4) Then I saw Nebuchadnezzar turn the joy we received from the destruction and drowning of the Egyptians into a sad lament. He invaded Israel's repose as a hungry lion invades a fold of lambs and destroys, tears, beheads, eats, and nonchalantly gluts. Unsatisfied, in his bloody claws he dragged off the rest of my children, along with rich booty, to his lair.[90] Here the Babylonians made us vomit up in blood the clear waters we had drunk from the rock in the desert. They pulled from our entrails, now covered with gall, the sweet manna and tender fowl on which we had fed. The cloud by day and the pillar of fire by night which had guided us became a hostile blaze and later burned the frame of the divine Temple, the marvelous architecture of Jerusalem and countless cities of Judea, and led us astray to unknown lands. Here, Jeremiah, is the lion which you incited against me with these words: "Declare in Judah and publish in Jerusalem. Blow the horn in the land. Cry aloud and say, 'Let us assemble and let us go into the fortified cities.' Set up a standard toward Zion. Put yourselves under covert, stay not, for I am bringing an evil from the north, a great destruction. A lion is gone forth from his thicket and the destroyer of nations has gone forth from his place with warlike sound, to make your land desolate, that your cities be laid waste, and remain without inhabitant" (Jer. 4.5-7). "Behold, I will feed this people with bitterness and give it water of gall to drink" (Jer. 9.14). And Isaiah, here you see me in the flames you kindled for me:[91] "As the tongue of fire devours the stubble, and as the chaff is

consumed in the heat of the flame, so shall their root become rotten, and their blossom shall become vain as the dust" (Isa. 5.24). "The days come when all that is in your house and all that your fathers have laid up in store until this day, shall be carried to Babylon; and they shall take of your sons that shall issue from you and they shall be eunuchs in the palace of the king of Babylon!" (II Kings 20.17-18; Isa. 39.6-7).

(5) After the dross had been purged for seventy years in the burning furnace of Chaldeans and Babylonians,[92] and the Temple had been rebuilt by the order of Cyrus, king of the Persians,[93] I saw Antiochus, the king of Syria, assault the Second Temple and despoil it of its riches.[94] For three and a half years he forbade the continuation of the divine service (the ladder by which God's glory descended to commune with us) and the holy sacrament of the blood of the circumcision, while he sacrificed loathsome swine on the altar in its stead. Woe to me, for after these events I began to fear Jeremiah's words: "Destruction upon destruction calls, it gives a thousand voices" (from Jer. 4.20-21). "Behold, the enemy will come up as a cloud, and his chariots shall be like whirlwinds, and his horses swifter than eagles" (Jer. 4.13). And you, Ezekiel, plainly prophesied this: "They shall strip you of your clothes and take off the ornaments of your beauty and they shall leave you naked, full of shame and abased" (Ezek. 16.39). You, Joel, also foresaw this when you said, "Wail, you ministers of the altar. Be terror stricken and wake all night, dressed in sackcloth, you ministers of God, because the sacrifice is withheld and the drink-offering from the house of the Lord your God" (Joel 1.13).

(6) I saw the cold sword thrust through the entrails of sixty thousand and eight hundred Israelites, by Theodorus, son of Zeno.[95] And I saw the cruel Demetrius kill children while their compassionate mothers watched, then kill the mothers themselves. I saw how he glutted and how he lay publicly with their maidens in order that your word, Ezekiel, might be confirmed: "They shall tear your limbs in pieces with their swords" (Ezek. 16.40); and that Hosea's tongue might not err: "The mother shall be struck on her children" (Hos. 10.14).

(7) I saw Pompey wash his crude hands in the blood of priests, holy shepherds who guided our sheep and who, fearing the death of their flocks, were ceaselessly occupied in the divine service.[96] Other priests, who saw Pompey and his warriors enter the innermost precinct of the Temple, where only the High Priest was allowed, hurled themselves from the high towers into the flames of the fire below.[97] Woe to the father who saw such a thing! The reckoning the Lord took of you was sad indeed; it accorded with these words of Jeremiah: " 'I will go to the great ones in station and knowledge, and with them I shall speak, for they know the way of the Lord, the ordinances of their God.' But these horses had all broken the yoke and burst the bands" (Jer. 5.5). Wherefore Ezekiel, "set your face toward Jerusalem and preach against the sanctuary and prophesy against the land of Israel. Thus says the Lord: 'Behold, I am against you. I will draw forth My sword out of its sheath

and will kill the righteous and wicked among you; and you shall be food for the fire' " (Ezek. 21.7-8).

(8) I saw the marks of Antigonus' teeth on the ears of the High Priest Hyrcanus; he had cruelly torn them off to prevent him from attaining the priesthood.[98] In Antigonus' battle with Herod for the principate, at the cost of his countrymen's blood, I lost so many men that the numbers of the dead prevented the victors from advancing. A shameful victory that was, the act of wild and brutish beasts, and the onset and beginning of the misfortunes that followed! O rebellious children who have turned from my ways, you have confirmed Micah's prophecy: "Hear, princes of Jacob and tyrants of the house of Israel, who cruelly tear the skin from off them and the flesh from off their bones" (Mic. 3.1-2).

(9) I saw the wrath of heaven descend upon thirty thousand Israelite lambs, who were killed by an earthquake in punishment for Herod's ascent to the throne of Judah;[99] for since I asked for a king, I had to suffer for his sin.[100] He put many to the sword and fire who drew sustenance from the full breasts of the Divine Law,[101] because they threw down the Roman eagle, which, in violation of the Law, he had placed on the Temple's main gate. O wicked one, in your wretched story, written with the blood of your brethren, Hosea's words were fulfilled: "I shall give you a king in My anger and take him away in My wrath" (Hos. 13.11). "You shall cry out on that day because of your king whom you shall have chosen for yourselves, but the Lord will not hear you then" (I Sam. 8.18). "O my people, they that lead you cause you to err and distort the way of your paths" (Isa. 3.12). Therefore, "hear, O princes of the house of Jacob and judges of the house of Israel, who hate the just and abhor the right, and pervert all justice, who build up Zion with blood and Jerusalem with iniquity" (Mic. 3.9-10). "Set a horn to your throat," says Hosea; "as an eagle has he placed himself against the law in the house of the Lord, because they have transgressed My covenant and trespassed against My law" (Hos. 8.1).

(10) I saw nine thousand Israelites sacrificed by the butcher, Archelaus, successor of Herod, together with the paschal animals of Passover.[102]

O abominable vessel,[103] these are the thanks you offered to the Lord for the succession to the princedom: you sacrificed human bodies before His altar. You were right, Isaiah, when you threatened me with this villain: "Behold the Lord of hosts takes away from Israel and Judah the excellent man and the perfect man, and the man of rank commanding respect, the elder and the sage. And I will give children to be their princes and babes who shall rule over them" (Isa. 3.1-4). The words are accurate which you, Amos, prophesied against me: "I shall turn your days of feasting into crying, and the end thereof as a bitter day" (Amos 8.10).

(11) I saw the Roman general Sabinus, as if sent by the heavens as the executioner of its sentence, deliver the riches of the Temple

to plunder and the holy dwelling itself to fire, and many sheep to the sword.[104] So, Isaiah, was your prophecy fulfilled: "Therefore is the Lord's anger kindled against His people, and He has stretched forth His hand against it and smitten it" (Isa. 5.25). "And he shall carry off the treasure of all the precious vessels" (Hos. 13.15).

(12) I saw the magnificent buildings near the Jordan burned by Simon the Hebrew, who wished to reign by force and not by right.[105] O enemy, Ezekiel clearly foresaw you when he said: "He learned to catch prey, and turn their cities into wasteland" (Ezek. 19.6-7).

(13) I saw eleven cities in the two Galilees and all their suburbs razed by fire and sword by the powerful armies of Vespasian and Titus, his son. Vespasian did not spare the noble edifices of Chabulon and Joppa, nor did he have compassion on the pitiful groans of women, maidens, young men, old men, or children. He and the other Romans threw them to the flames and sword; some died by their own hands; others who fled in ships were caught in a storm and dashed to pieces against huge cliffs and rocks in the sea.[106] Of those who fled on land, eleven thousand and six hundred were killed by the sword on the mountain of Gerizim in Samaria.[107] Unavailing was the great effort of Netir and Philip, the Galilean brothers who jumped from the walls with such great force that they broke the Roman battle line; many Romans escaped, but those who resisted were killed. No less outstanding was the prowess of Eleazar, son of Abdia, against the battering ram. But since heaven's determination mocked his strength, the land, the fields, the mountains, the sea and the beach were covered with devastation, dead bodies, and the blood of a hundred and twenty thousand lambs. And the enemy carried off many captives and rich spoil in its claws.[108] Here is your foreboding fulfilled, Joel, and what you, Jeremiah, also prophesied: "A mighty people and without number is come upon my land" (Joel 1.6). "Therefore, on the mountains I will take up a weeping and wailing and on the dwellings of the wilderness a shout" (Jer. 9.9), and "I will make your lands desolate and your cities shall be burned with fire" (Isa. 1.7), "and the carcasses of men shall fall as dung upon the open field and as the handful after the harvestman, and there will be none to gather it" (Jer. 9.21). Even the animals were carried off in prey: "I will make the cities of Judah desolate, in such a way that there will be no manner of inhabitant in it" (Jer. 9.10).

(14) I saw the necks of all the sheep (that is, the human inhabitants) of Jerusalem, offered, by their own will, to decapitation, rather than suffer the images of Tiberius and Gaius Caesar in the city, because they were an abomination against the Law of the Lord. Many were cudgeled to death by Pilate, the Roman captain.[109] O divine justice, how you requite measure for measure, a tooth for a tooth, an eye for an eye. Indeed, You threatened me with this through Jeremiah: "Their kings, their princes, their priests, their prophets, all Judah and the citizens of Jerusalem turned their backs to Me, and not their faces. They have will-

fully set their abominations in the house consecrated to My name, to defile it. Wherefore the Lord God of Israel says: 'This city is given into the hand of the enemy by the sword' " (Jer. 32.32-36).

(15) Of the multitude that had come to the Passover sacrifices, I saw thirty thousand lambs crush and kill one another at the gates of the Temple as they rashly went forth, agitated by fear of the Roman general, Cumanus; and the joy of the festival was turned into a sad lament.[110] But you predicted this, Jeremiah, when you told us: "All the tents are spoiled" (Jer. 4.20), and "the hills trembled and moved to and fro" (Jer. 4.24). "And their fallen bodies became as refuse which is thrown into the midst of the streets" (Isa. 5.25). "Songs will flee from the Temple on that day, says the Lord God. I shall turn all your songs into pitiful lamentations and I shall make that wailing to be like the wailing at the death of an only and beloved son" (Amos 8.3, 10).

(16) Like a great earthquake which strikes suddenly and destroys everything in its path, I witnessed the devastation of a flock of twenty thousand sheep at the cruel hands of Caesar's troops.[111] Your words were discharged, Hosea: "They shall be as the morning cloud, or the dew that falls early in the morning and forthwith passes away" (Hos. 13.3). And you, Jeremiah, be satisfied, for the threat which you made to me has been executed: "They shall eat up your daughters and your sons; they shall eat up your flock and your herd" (Jer. 5.17).

(17) I saw all the cities of Syria bathed in Israelite blood, and an infinite number of bodies of men and women of all ages strewn naked along the ground. This calamity befell my people at a time when they were most at ease and prospering in that realm.[112] A prophecy of Isaiah: "When the daughters of Zion are haughty and walk with necks outstretched, the Lord will lay bare their secret parts" (Isa. 3.16-17). "And the enemy shall cast many bodies on the ground" (Amos 8.3).

(18) I saw the traitorous Scythopolitans offer deceitful displays of friendship and then plunge their spears into thirteen thousand defenseless sheep in an ambush. Here I beheld Simon the Hebrew, renowned for his strength and daring. Upon finding himself betrayed by these enemies, with whom he had allied himself against his brothers, he pulled up his old father by his hair and thrust a hard sword up to the hilt through his entrails. He did the same to his mother, wife and his children, who were content to die in this way rather than by the traitors' weapons. Then Simon unsheathed his own sword and resolutely stabbed himself, thereby executing the penalty which his wickedness deserved.[113] O grievous sin, O hapless creature, because you had given the blood of your Israelite limbs to enemy nations to spill, your words, Hosea, were fulfilled: "I am become unto them as a snare. A wild beast shall destroy them" (Hos. 13.7-8). And you Ezekiel [sic], saw this calamity clearly from your heavenly abode. You had prophesied it: "Each one shall swallow the flesh of his own arm" (Isa. 9.19).

(19) I saw five thousand lambs decapitated by the cruel Tiberius

Alexander, who had no pity for the shouts of tender children or the supplications of beautiful maidens, or respect for old age.[114] The words of Jeremiah have been accomplished: "The voice of the daughters of Zion bemoaning great things: spreading their hands, they said, 'Woe is me, for my soul is faint' " (Jer. 4.31). "A voice is heard on the heights, the weeping of the supplicants of the children of Israel" (Jer. 3.21).

(20) In the short space of an hour, on a clear day, I saw twelve thousand sheep swallowed up by the fierce Damascene wolves, who pent them in a narrow place in their own city of Damascus.[115] O luckless hour, how you swallowed in so brief a time what so many years had reared! Indeed, I saw your threat come true, Amos: "I will darken the earth in the clear day" (Amos 8.9). "And they shall be just like chaff which the whirlwind drives and like smoke from the chimney which forthwith goes away" (Hos. 13.3). And you, Jeremiah, also prophesied this destruction and saw these words of yours fulfilled: "The wolf of the deserts will destroy them" (Jer. 5.6).

(21) I saw eighteen thousand lambs pitifully stretched out around Ascalon's walls by the Roman general, Antonius.[116] O gloomy and luck-less day! You had already darkened it, Amos, when you uttered: "I will cause the sun to fall at noon" (Amos 8.9).

(22) When Vespasian entered the city of Tarichaeae and destroyed it, I saw him feeding on the flesh and blood of eight thousand sheep, as the fierce tiger in the fearsome forests of Hyrcania[117] feeds on the blood of other animals. He filled the lake of Gennesaret with blood and dead bodies, which swelled and decayed with a noxious stench. And he carried away thirty-six thousand and four hundred captives.[118] A prophecy of Jeremiah: "Death has come up into our windows; it has entered our houses and killed the children at the gates and the young men in the broad places" (Jer. 9.20). "They will overthrow with the sword your fortified cities in which you trusted" (Jer. 5.17), and "your men shall fall by the sword" (Isa. 3.25). "It will be for musk, rottenness, and corruption" (Isa. 3.24).

(23) On the road from Gischala to Jerusalem I saw foul Roman weapons dyed with the blood of five thousand lambs, most of them women and children. With their swords they cut off the sighs that came forth pitifully from their victims' throats.[119] This is what you, Hosea, had foretold: "Just like the lion will I lie in wait for them by the way. I will meet them and tear them to pieces as a bear bereaved of its whelps" (Hos. 13.7-8).

(24) I saw twenty thousand and five hundred Israelites killed in cruel prisons and with the sword by the Idumeans when they entered Jeru-salem, acting on traitorous intelligence from the tyrants in the city. They were cast naked into the field as food for the birds, the dogs and the wild animals. Many sacred priests were among the victims. Here the just Hananiah, Joshua and Zechariah perished, and the body of the extraor-dinary hero Niger was dragged cruelly through the city.[120] What abomi-

nable wickedness! This was the stamp which sealed the story of the total destruction of Jerusalem, written already by Antigonus and Herod in their first tyrannies. This was the effect of the prophetic words of Ezekiel and Jeremiah, "O city that sheds blood in the midst of itself. You are defiled with the idols which you have made, and you have caused your days to draw near. Behold, the princes of Israel have been in you, each according to his might, to shed blood." "They have wrought evil in your midst" (Ezek. 22.3-6, 9). "They shall be consumed by the sword" (Isa. 1.20). "They shall not be buried, and their bodies shall be food for the birds of the heaven and for the beasts of the earth" (Jer. 34.20).

(25) I saw the traitorous Sicarii kill and rob the possessions of seven hundred sheep in Engaddi. Some of the women were shot through with arrows and killed with their children in their arms; others were torn to pieces by the cold sword, their children still in their wombs.[121] What you said, Jeremiah, was fulfilled here: "Their quiver is an open sepul-chre" (Jer. 5.16). And you also, Hosea, threatened me with this evil: "The children shall be dashed to pieces with their mothers" (Hos. 10.14), "and the pregnant women will be cut to pieces" (Hos. 14.1).

(26) I saw the river Jordan run red with the blood of thirteen thou-sand decapitated Israelite lambs, and their bodies offered to the animals of the field by the cruel Placidus, the Roman general. He took captive two thousand and two hundred others, and carried away rich spoils.[122] Woe to such a sad exchange: all the waters of Egypt were turned to blood out of love for Israel, and now Israel itself changed the waters of the Jordan to blood. And out of this came a calamity unlike any other: the beasts fed on human flesh, on the people of Israel. Your cruel judg-ment was carried out, Jeremiah: "He shall be buried with the burial of an ass, torn to pieces and cast forth" (Jer. 22.19). And the angry words of Moses became a reality: "And I will send upon them the teeth of beasts" (Deut. 32.24).

(27) I saw the flames of the large, rich buildings of the beautiful region of Idumea ascend to the clouds, and the shrieks of the children of Israel open the heavens. And the idolatrous Vespasian and the execrable Hebrew Simon burned magnificent populated cities and high towers, cruelly slaughtering an infinite number of people, and leaving a frightful desert in their wake. And when the fattened spears and ferocious swords could no longer kill because they were so glutted, the people were delivered to the cruelty of the fire. No trace of life remained. And Vespasian took an extremely large number of captives.[123] Thus I tasted here every misfortune that was prophesied concerning the land of Israel. And many prophecies were fulfilled: "I will gather all your lovers, with whom you have been promiscuous and whom you have loved, along with all those that you have hated; I will gather them together against you from every side, and will deliver you into their hands" (Ezek. 23.22, 28). "They will give forth their voice against the cities of Judah" (Jer. 4.16). Thus there is coming "a day of the horn and alarm against the fortified

cities and against the high towers, and on it I will distress men, and they shall be just like blind men, and their blood shall be poured out as dust" (Zeph. 1.16-17). Then, "your fortress, Israel, will fall in such a war" (Hos. 10.14) and "the dead bodies shall be like dung on the face of the land" (Jer. 9.21). And furthermore, "they will burn your houses with fire" (Ezek. 16.41). Thus "I will make your land a desert, and your cities shall be desolate and remain without an inhabitant" (Jer. 4.7). After this will have been fulfilled, "I beheld the earth and lo, it was waste and void" (Jer. 4.23). And about Simon, Ezekiel said, "This one became a lion and learned to catch prey and devour men and make widows" so that "the land is desolate, and the fullness thereof, because of the noise of his roaring" (Ezek. 19.6-7).

(28) And after all Judea was destroyed, as Jeremiah's words had foretold ("All these cities shall be broken down, in the presence of the Lord, and they shall be laid waste before His fierce anger"—Jer. 4.26), the death pangs came to the great city of Jerusalem (which surpasses all others in the world as the head surpasses the human body). Titus had besieged it and he was awaiting a propitious time to muster the terrible fury of his anger like a lion that stops when it sees its enemy near. I saw three tyrants, John, Simon and Eleazar, princes of the Jews, arise from among the people from all parts of Judea who had taken refuge in Jerusalem and fight with one another. Turning their hatred of their enemies against their own people, they incited brother against brother, and son against father. They used the Temple as a fortress, and the battle raged so fiercely that it became an abattoir and a huge lake of blood of the bodies of the Israelites—commoners, nobles and priests—the sacrificial animals, and the Greeks and other pagans who came to worship there. What a shameful blending and abominable confusion, a monstrous affair which banished holiness from God's abode.[124] This is the way, O rash people, that you were uniting to return to the Lord with repentance for past sins and to defend the holy edifice from idolaters! Alas, in my blindness, I did not see all the evil laid before me. My repeated defiance blinded me so that my depravities were apparent to my enemies, and so that all of you who prophesied against me proved correct. Jeremiah: "They proceed from evil to evil" (Jer. 9.2). Hosea: "The throes of one about to give birth shall come upon it" (Hos. 13.13). Ezekiel: "You have brought near the time of your years" (Ezek. 22.4). Jeremiah: "They were against her in siege all about" (Jer. 4.17). "You have despised My holy things; wicked men have been in you to shed blood" (Ezek. 22.8-9; 28.18). I was bereft of understanding, and the words which You spoke through Isaiah's lips, O Lord, found fulfillment here: "Make the heart of this people fat, and make their ears heavy, and their eyes cover with cloud, lest with their eyes they see or with their ears hear or with their heart understand, and repent and be restored to safety" (Isa. 6.10). Therefore "your destruction, O Israel, is at hand, and in Me alone is your help. Where is your king now to protect you?

Where are your judges, against whom you said, 'Give me a king and princes' " (Hos. 13.9-10). Now it is obvious that "O My people is foolish" and "they know Me not; they are sottish children, and without understanding; yet they are wise to do evil but to do good they are totally ignorant" (Jer. 4.22). "Because you have all become dross, I will gather you into the midst of Jerusalem, a heap of silver, of brass, of iron, of lead and tin, into the midst of the furnace, and I will blow fire upon it to melt it" (Ezek. 22.19-20), and "the people will be just like the spark of fire. A brother will not spare his brother; Manasseh, Ephraim, Ephraim, Manasseh, together they shall be against Judah" (Isa. 9.18-20), and then there "I will uncover your nakedness in their sight, and they will see your shame, O Jerusalem" (Ezek. 16.37).

This frightful sin, and the infinite sins already committed, brought a terrible famine into Jerusalem, the first mark of a great calamity. I saw husbands ravenously snatch already chewed food from their wives' mouths and throats, and mothers from their children's; and many choked as their windpipes were pressed. But when all the food had been consumed, men and women raged and searched the sheepfolds and stables, to sustain themselves with animals' dry dung; and they chewed on their belts, their shoes, and the leather straps which they drew off their bucklers. Once beautiful maidens and youths now resembled exhumed bodies. And when all remedies had been exhausted and they could no longer stand on their feet (which had become swollen or numb with cold), they fell and died on the spot. Some, barely alive, threw themselves into open graves so as not to remain unburied. No crying or tears softened these misfortunes, because hunger and thirst, the most painful of the peoples' adversities, had dried their eyes, parched and cankered their mouths, and scorched and swollen their tongues. The terror of the famine went further; it entered even the marrow of Miriam, Eleazar's daughter, and I saw her snatch her only child, suckling at her breasts, quarter and boil it, and eat half of that sad repast. What an abominable deed! What a terrible act, unheard and unseen even among barbarians and uncommon even among wild beasts; how horrible then among our people, known for their compassion! This is what you, Moses, warned me of: "When of everything there is no longer anything else left to her in the siege and affliction with which your enemy will afflict you in all your gates, the tender and delicate woman will eat in secret the children which she engendered" (Deut. 28.56-57). "And the days are coming, says the Lord, when I will send a famine in the land, not a famine of bread nor a thirst for water, but of hearing the word of God. At that time the fair maidens and the young men shall faint for thirst; they shall fall and not rise up again" (Amos 8.11-14). And you, Jeremiah, should be completely satisfied seeing all your judgments completely fulfilled against me, and yet this prophecy was left: "Thus says the Lord, concerning the sons and concerning the daughters born in this place, and concerning the mothers who bore them in this land: 'They shall die with the dead of the sick rooms, and they shall not be lamented, but by famine shall they be consumed' " (Jer. 16.4). "And instead of a girdle, there shall be faintness of limbs" (Isa. 3.24). "We all will growl like bears and will mourn unceasingly like doves" (Isa. 59.11). "I will make them eat the flesh of their sons and their daughters, and each one will eat the flesh of his companions because of the siege and the straitness wherewith their enemies shall straiten them" (Deut. 28.54-58).

(29) Among those who were crazed by unbearable hunger and feared no other death, however pitiless, I saw many surrender to the cruel enemy who besieged them. The Arabs and Syrians who had come to aid Titus opened the captives' bellies and searched their entrails for the gold which some had swallowed to keep it from the tyrants.[125] Thus they escaped from the mouth of the famished wolf, but fell into the claws of the hungry lion, as Ezekiel first foresaw: "They have come forth out of the fire and the fire shall burn them" (Ezek. 15.7). "The lion which lies near their cities will tear to pieces everything that goes out of them" (Jer. 5.6).

(30) And as a fitting conclusion to all my misfortunes, I saw the Roman eagle, in the hands of the ferocious Titus, enter Jerusalem with the savagery of a bull from the deserts of Spain, with the strength of an irate African lion among sheep, and with the rabid claws and mouth of the monstrous tigress of Hyrcania seeking her stolen whelps. Loosing its wings and thirsting for blood, the eagle destroyed throngs of people, swallowed flesh, sucked blood, pulverized bones, and tore to pieces the bodies of thousands of priests, princes, old men, young men, pregnant women, beautiful maidens, and infants. The fire of the holy sacrifices was forbidden. With its hard beak the eagle set fire to the altar and the entire body of the divine Temple and finally penetrated into its innermost and forbidden part.[126] It flew nimbly with the holy fire to the proud height of the city towers, setting aflame its walls and its lavishly designed buildings. Many priests, though they could have saved themselves by defecting to the Romans, threw themselves into the fire and burned with the Temple. Among these were Meirus, son of Belgas, and Josephus, son of Dalaeus. And many others were burnt to ashes, with their treasure chests and boxes. The fire did not spare the great holy library or the building of the Royal Council, which burned with eight thousand Israelites inside. Finally, when the Roman enemies wallowed in the blood of a million bodies; and when the spirits which had informed and sustained these bodies in life had been driven out by the force of the sword, fire, and frightful pestilence; and when the heavy marble slabs and huge stones in the buildings had been burned to their very foundations, [the Temple,] the head of the world, unable to sustain its weight any longer, fell to the ground with such a frightful din and awful tremor that it seemed that the entire structure of the universe had been disjointed, and the end had come for the world's many ages and achievements, the time for everything to return to its primaeval chaos and confusion.[127]

Alas, the fortress where I defended myself from my two enemies[128] is demolished. The nest of the only phoenix is destroyed.[129] The tree which sustained me with its divine fruit is uprooted. Its leaves, which provided a delightful shade for me, are withered. The true soul of my spirit has gone up to the heavens and left my body where it dwelt,[130] stretched out on the ground in the claws of cruel beasts. O wretched me, they have expelled me from my terrestrial paradise. They have trodden under foot the virgins of Israel, who were the delicate daisies and flowers with which it was sown. They have destroyed noble youth and revered old age, its new cedars and ancient cypresses, whose roots were planted above the farthest heaven. They mingled with blood and gall the clear waters of the divine Law which refreshed the people. Near its walls they destroyed worthies and prophets who warded off the indignation of the Lord.[131] My clear sun has clouded and left me wrapped in gloom.

O eyes of mine, which are dried from endless weeping, pour forth floods of gall across my sad cheeks, as you behold all the other members of the body of my people plagued with strange torments—the head, representing the righteous princes and priests; the arms, the angelic beauty of lovely women, the inspiration of young manhood; the weak and tired knees, the honored elders and the aged, and the innocent, hapless infants who had hardly begun to travel on the road of life;—and the soul, life-giver to this entire structure, the Temple, the abode of the celestial king, which is now burned with fire, laid waste, and turned into a desert. Now, indeed, all you prophets should be satisfied, for you have battled me until you destroyed me and the pillar on which I leaned. Ezekiel: "A great eagle with large wings and long pinions, full of feathers of diverse colors, came to Lebanon, and took the top height of the cedar, and breaking off the topmost of its boughs, it gathered them together" (Ezek. 17.3-4). Joel: "His teeth are the teeth of a lion, and he has the jawteeth of a lioness. He has laid my vine waste; he has blasted my fig tree and made it clean bare" (Joel 1.6-7). Jeremiah: "Lo, I will bring a nation upon you from afar, O house of Israel" (Jer. 5.15). "Lament like a virgin girded with sackcloth" (Joel 1.8). Then, "the meal offering was cut off and the drink-offering from the house of the Lord your God; the priests, even the Lord's ministers mourned" (Joel 1.9). Ezekiel: "I will gather you and burn you with the fire of My wrath, and I will melt you in the midst thereof" (Ezek. 22.21). "And when I thus set My face against them, I will make the land desolate (Ezek. 15.7-8). "I will appoint over them four kinds of vengeance, says the Lord: a sword to slay, dogs to tear in pieces, fowls of the heaven and beasts of the earth, to devour and destroy" (Jer. 15.3). "Its [i.e., Jerusalem's] gates will become sad and will cry and it shall be seated desolate on the ground" (Isa. 3.26), so that "Zion shall be ploughed like a field, and Jerusalem shall be as a hill of stones, and the temple mount shall become as a high place of forests" (Mic. 3.12). "And I shall convert Jerusalem into hills of sand and lairs of serpents" (Jer. 9.10). "A third part of you shall die with the pestilence, and with famine shall it be consumed, and another part shall fall by the sword round about you, and another third I will scatter to all the winds and I will command a sword after them" (Ezek. 5.2).

(31) I saw countless refugees from the destruction of Jerusalem, men and women of all ages, slain in Antioch of Syria,[132] in the fortress of Herodium, in the mountains of Jardes,[133] in the fortress of Masada in Judea,[134] and in Alexandria in Egypt. Fire compelled some to break the rest of the seventh day. Some died by their enemies' swords; others used the sword and fire to destroy their children, their wives, their wealth and themselves so as not to fall into the Romans' cruel jaws; while others, who refused to acknowledge Caesar as Lord instead of the God of the heavens, were tortured with all sorts of torments.[135] The words of Isaiah: "What will you do in the day of visitation and ruin which is coming from afar? To whom will you flee for help?" (Isa. 10.3). "A day of fire shall that day be, a day of tribulation and anguish, a day of darkness and thick darkness, and a day of clouds and mists" (Zeph. 1.15).

(32) Of those who remained alive I saw ninety and seven thousand captives led by Titus to Rome; many were consumed along the way in the provinces through which they passed. For the Romans' diversion some died in games of fire, others in duels which they fought in the nude armed with swords and spears like enemies.[136] O afflicted Israel, how different are these sacrifices from those you offered at Jerusalem in the time of your prosperity. They pour you out and sacrifice you among the heathen. They carry the delicate daughters of Zion with tough ropes tied around their necks, instead of the rich necklaces of gold and precious stones they used to wear, dressed in sackcloth instead of the brocade and purple cloth in which they used to wrap themselves.[137] Your eyes turn back and they run with bloody tears as you gaze at the fields and valleys of your holy motherland,[138] lost to you for so long a time. With wearied sighs you behold the crests of the hills decked with clouds and the holy mountains gradually receding in the distance. Here is the result of your words, Jeremiah:[139] "Cast them out of My sight and let them go forth, and when they ask you, 'where are we going forth?' you shall tell them: 'Thus says the Lord: Such as are for death, to death, and such as are for famine to famine, and such as are for captivity to captivity' " (Jer. 15.2). "Wantonly winking and mincing," the daughters of Zion "put ornaments on their feet" (Isa. 3.16). Therefore, "there shall be instead of curled hair baldness, instead of rich clothing sackcloth, and a great burning instead of facial beauty" (Isa. 3.24).

(33) Finally I saw Vespasian and Titus, triumphing over their spoils (the sacred candlesticks, the tables and golden goblets, the holy belts and vestments and a large number of captives), enter the gates of voracious and haughty Rome with a small and wretched residue of my children. Deprived of their good fortune, their faces were drained of color. They were like a gay flower which had once flourished above all others in the field, but having suffered the blade of the plow which cut it apart, it had lowered its head,[140] lost its natural charm, and withered. On passing through these bitter gates the Israelites, my children, lowered their faces

to the ground; their beauty withered and blanched with the pallor of death; their joy turned to melancholy, their prosperity to wretchedness, their exaltation over all to abasement and humiliation by all the nations assembled in that populous city at the hue and cry of this sorrowful and wretched triumph.

A large number of captives were thrown into fights with lions, panthers, and other fierce beasts to vilify and humiliate them. The hapless victims were eaten alive; now a leg was devoured by a cruel lion, now an arm by a voracious bear, and then they were pricked like bulls and put to death. And since the Romans derived much pleasure from the bitter feast of my flesh, Simon, the Jews' prince and captain, was executed. And when he expired, the innumerable Roman populace broke out in a vehement shout of joy,[141] as great as the powerful army of African Moors raises when it attacks in battle; while I, with my miserably faint voice and my streaming eyes fixed on the heavens, asked for a bit of mercy from the King of the heavens, pleading that since He observed and saw everything from His abode most high, He should remember the contentment they were receiving in being the executioners of His first-born, Israel.

This was the rest which awaited me after such a long and bitter journey. The words of Isaiah: "I shall give him a charge, to swallow the spoils and seize the prey, and with a thrashing to turn the people into the likeness of the mire which is in the streets" (Isa. 10.6). "Though your people, O Israel, were like the sand of the sea, they will be converted into a remnant, and I will transport you and your mother who bore you to another land, in which you were not born, and there you shall die; and I will not show you any manner of mercy there" (Isa. 10.22; Jer. 22.26). Thus "the Lord will carry you away and your king whom you appoint over you to a people whom you did not know, nor your fathers, and there they will cite you as an example and a derision" (Deut. 28.36-37).

Behold, brothers, what the history of my sad days has been like thus far. Now, tell me, have you ever seen a lightning bolt fall from heaven with a frightful crack, penetrate a closed and hidden place, set a building on fire, tear out and shatter its heavy marble slabs, and send their pieces flying up to the stars? That is how the anger of heaven fell upon me and upon Jerusalem. It razed the city to its very foundations, scattered its inhabitants to the ends of the earth with the swiftness of flight, and so broke and fragmented the body of my people that its enemies shattered even its smallest unit into a thousand pieces, as you have seen.

NUMEO: On the one hand your story has confused us, but on the other it has moved us to great compassion, since you have been impoverished and despoiled of such great blessings, which the heavens did not share with any other people under the sun. Though you have no visible wounds, your sad appearance, your austere and melancholy face, your laments, sighs and groans, and your feeble voice have cast gloom and a thick pall of sadness over our spirits. That is why we have offered to help you bewail your misfortunes, that we might in some measure alleviate your burden. Now, having heard your abundant reasons for complaint, we would join you willingly. But first we entreat you to restrain your groans and heavy sighs and hold back your tears for a while, so that you may dispel our doubts. Tell us for what reason heaven was cruel to you and harsh to your obedient children, and why God removed His face and favor from those who served Him. Is not God called merciful and benign, favorable to the righteous, and near unto them who strive to follow His ways and delight in maintaining His precepts? For Israel was making the journey of his life with such happy steps, as you told us, in the pastoral garb in which Holy Scripture depicted the righteous patriarchs.

FIRST[142]

YCABO: Now I see that just as you did not understand the metaphor of the first phase of my life, so, too, you have not comprehended the second phase. Therefore, although each step I take with my tongue or with my thought through this sad history is like a step toward death, I want to relate to you fully how my misfortunes began and who threw down the pillar of strength on which I leaned. In short, I will tell you how the storm arose which sank the cedar ship with golden nails laden with all my riches,[143] and impoverished me.

THE FIRST EXPERIENCES OF ISRAEL IN THE HOLY LAND {EXPLANATION OF THE METAPHOR ENTITLED "HUNT OF CONIES AND HARES"} {PART I}

You should know that when I eventually entered the Holy Land, guided there by our Lord through Moses and Joshua His servants, with many marvels and favors, I was governed by the elders and served the Lord well by obeying them.[144] But there came a time when that entire generation passed from this life to the next and was gathered to its fathers, and a new generation arose which did not know the Lord or the deeds He had wrought for Israel.[145] And since they dwelt among the Canaanites, Hittites, Amorites, etc. [sic], they married their daughters and gave their own Israelite daughters to their sons and served their gods besides. In this way I broke my covenant and oath, strayed from the divine precepts, and followed the idols Baal and Ashtoreth.[146] But divine mercy, to rouse me to the fact that I had a God and Lord whom I was to obey out of obligation and promise,[147] immediately chastised me by delivering me into the power of Cushan-Rishathaim, king of Aram and Naharaim.[148] He kept me there as a slave for eight years.

But since God's purpose was to punish me like a merciful father punishes his beloved son, He freed me from that place after this time by the hand of Othniel, son of Kenaz. Inspired by divine spirit, Othniel judged me for forty years, and I did not stray from God's precepts while under his dominion. However, when his days came to an end, I returned anew to my sins, and the Lord again punished me by delivering me into the hand of Eglon, king of the Moabites, as a slave for eighteen years. And when I cried out from there to heaven, He heard me and delivered me by the hand of Ehud, son of Gera, an Israelite. In one battle he killed my enemy Eglon, who held me in subjection, and ten thousand of Moab's finest warriors. And Shamgar, son of Anath, an Israelite, killed six hundred Philistines with no weapon but an ox-goad in his valiant arm.[149]

Despite all these favors which I received from the kindness of our Lord, I persistently returned to my idolatries and sins when Ehud died; and the scourge of heaven did not slacken. I was delivered and sold as a slave to Jabin, king of Canaan, who dealt cruelly with me for twenty years. At this time, Deborah, the prophetess, the wife of Lappidoth, judged me, and through her counsel the Lord delivered me from this Jabin. Under the captaincy of Barak, his great army was destroyed, and Sisera, its first general, was slain by the righteous Jael, a woman worthy to be praised above all others. My repose after this captivity lasted forty years;[150] but when I returned once more to the skein of my wickedness, the Lord delivered me for seven years into the power and whip of the Midianites, and they afflicted me grievously.

With little shame, I again asked help of the heavens, whence it is wont to come in all misfortunes, and God answered me again and had me freed by the hand of the humble Gideon. He immediately destroyed and burned the altar of Baal which his father had and built an altar to the Lord. Here he put a fleece of wool, and uttered these words: "If the dew fall only on this fleece and all the rest of the land remain dry, I will take it for a sign that Israel is to be freed by my hand" (Judg. 6.37). And so it happened, when he arose the next day and pressed the fleece, he wrung out a large bowlful of water (the dew it had absorbed), while the ground was dry. Gideon spoke again: "I beseech you, O Lord, do not be angry with me; if you wish to prove it to me further, make it that there be dryness in the fleece alone, and on all the rest of the ground let there be dew." And the Lord did this, so that there was dryness in the fleece alone and on all the ground there was dew.[151] When Gideon was convinced, the Lord said to him, "The Israelite people are more than the Midianites, and in order that it should not vaunt itself against Me and say, 'My own power has saved me,' tell it that whosoever is fearful should return and not come to battle" (Judg. 7.2-3). And thus twenty-two thousand of the fearful remained behind, while Gideon took with him ten thousand men. Of these he further ordered nine thousand and seven hundred to remain behind because they went down on their knees to drink by a fountain and lapped the water like dogs with their tongues;

and he took with him only the three hundred who quenched their thirst by lifting water to their mouths. With these he conquered a great number of Midianites and Amalekites, as infinite as the sands of the seashore, and released me from their yoke.[152]

After this, impelled by ignorance, I entreated this Gideon to be my king and lord, since I had been delivered from the Midianites by his hand and did not fully comprehend that I had received this victory from heaven. But he answered me like a great sage and worthy, "Neither I nor my sons will rule over you. The Lord will rule over you."[153]

When Gideon had passed from this life and left seventy-one sons, I forgot the many times the Lord had delivered me from the hands of enemies, through whom He had punished me for my sins. I again dallied with the idol Baal,[154] and chose Abimelech, Gideon's son by a slave, to be my king. On taking power, the first thing he did was to kill his seventy brothers on a rock. He did not spare even one member of that family from which I had received such great kindness—except Jotham, who was hidden at the time of this cruel murder.[155] But King Abimelech received his punishment when he was killed by a flimsy stone thrown by a woman.[156]

After him, Tola judged me for twenty-three years and Jair for twenty-two. When Jair died, I turned to the idols again, only much more so, and I abandoned the Lord and His service. But punishment immediately befell me when the Lord sold me to the Philistines and Ammonites as a slave for eighteen years.[157] At the end of these years I called upon the Lord, and acknowledged my rebelliousness by abandoning the idolatrous worship of other gods, and He freed me. He destroyed the Philistines by the hand of Jephthah, who sacrificed his daughter to the Lord for this conquest, since he had made a vow that he would sacrifice the first thing he saw on entering his house.[158] Jephthah judged me for six years, and when he died, Ibzan followed in his place for seven years, and Abdon for eight.[159]

Still not sated with sins and punishments, I returned again to my idolatries and rebelliousness. At this point our Lord doubled my punishment. He again delivered me to the hard yoke of the same Philistines for forty years,[160] since I did not heed past punishments. During this captivity the mighty Nazirite, Samson, was born. With the rotten jawbone of an ass[161] he killed a squadron of a thousand men. But when Delilah, his concubine, at last deceived him and he disclosed to her that his hair was the source of his strength, the Philistines cut off his hair and with it, his power.[162] Samson judged Israel for twenty years.

Afterwards I was given a chance to become thoroughly purged of sin. Strife began between the tribe of Benjamin and the rest of Israel over the wife of a Levite whom the tribe of Benjamin had dishonored and killed.[163] Her husband cut her body to pieces and sent them to all the cities in Israel;[164] they arose against that tribe and twenty-five thousand and one hundred men of Benjamin and forty thousand men of Israel died in the battle. As a result, the tribe of Benjamin was reduced to a shred.[165]

Then Eli, the priest of the Lord, succeeded to the helm of all Israel. When he learned of the death of his wicked sons and the capture of the Ark of God by the Philistines at the cost of thirty thousand Israelites, who died in its defense, he fell from his seat. He exclaimed twice, "The glory of Israel has been carried away, for the Ark of the Lord is taken" (I Sam. 4.17), and died with these words on his lips.[166] But when the immense holiness of the Ark was placed in the filthy hands and abominable temples of the Philistines, it killed an extremely large number of their people. Because of the fearful toll it was exacting from their people and their idols, they transported it from city to city and province to province. Finally, they resolved to remove it from their midst so that they would not all perish.[167] They therefore took it to the fork of a road and placed it on a new cart, drawn by two milch kine that had never been yoked. Showing the kine their tender suckling calves, they began to lead them back home. The animals' natural affection struggled within them and drew them toward the young they were leaving behind, but the cart could not resist the mighty will of God. The kine themselves, guided by heaven, chose the road leading to the land of Israel, and they arrived there with their sacred cargo, after I had repented and removed the abominable idols from my midst under the rule of and in obedience to Samuel, the son of Hannah.[168]

{PART II}

THE LIFE OF THE WICKED,
IN THE GUISE OF CONIES AND HARES

These are the causes and sins which led to my enslavement and removal from the Lord's favor the six times I have related to you, brothers, as the first misfortune.

This was the life of my children, who preferred the hunt, the cruel and heathen custom in which they imitated their brethren, Ishmael and Esau, the hunters,[169] to the pastoral way of life which my Creator favored and which I had chosen. The light of God, the divine Sun, which had guided their fathers descended no more upon them; and they did not see their error. Blind and deprived of this light, their priests rose early to perform the service of the idols Baal and Ashtoreth. They carried on their shoulders the sheep-hooks of false sacrifices, the nets of deceitful miracles and idols' diabolical answers, and with them they ensnared and tripped the now soiled Israelites, who had been changed into conies and hares, animals that are forbidden and ritually unclean in the divine Law. And their loathsome idolatries were the ferreters which drove them from the land and the houses that gave them rest and shelter; and in dread and confusion, they emerged and delivered themselves into the mouths of ravenous dogs—Cushan-Rishathaim, Eglon, king of the Moabites, Jabin, the cruel king of Canaan—and into the teeth of greyhounds—the Midianites, the Philistines and the Ammonites.

{EXPLANATION OF THE METAPHOR ENTITLED "HUNT OF STAGS AND HERONS"}
{PART I}

After this I repudiated the Lord, the King of Kings, and showed myself ungrateful for the blessings and favors which I had received from the Rock of my salvation: I asked for a king of flesh and blood. Through Samuel's lips, I heard of the nature of the king I asked for and how harsh and rough to bear the yoke of the mortal king would be.[171] But my ears were blocked by obstinacy and my understanding blinded by the false representations and deceitful reasons of the Enemy, who was weakening me with temptations from within. Vanquished by the Enemy, I answered that, despite the obstacles, I desired a king in order to be like other nations.[172] O, what a terrible answer—a thing which the Lord always abhorred and forbade! But since this was what I wanted, though He was greatly grieved at the ignorance which had overcome me, He gave me Saul as king. Saul's height was appropriate for a king, for from the shoulders and above he was taller than all Israel.[173] At the first war which he waged with the Philistines, I sinned under his banner by eating the blood and flesh of the animals he captured.[174] Saul committed two acts of disobedience: he did not wait for Samuel at the sacrifice before entering into battle;[175] and he spared Agag, king of Amalek.[176] As a result of these sins, he was vanquished in battle by the Philistines at the cost of my limbs and three of his sons; and Saul died by his own hand, pierced through by his sword on the mountain of Gilboa.[177] Thus I immediately began to pay for the king I had asked for.

When Saul's dominion was cut off, the Lord gave it to David, who had killed the well-armed giant Goliath with a single furious stone from his sling.[178] David administered justice and repeatedly showed his kindness. On an occasion when he desired water from a fountain located in the camp of his Philistine enemies, and three young men learned he was thirsty, they went through the entire enemy camp and obtained it for him. But David refused to drink it. He lifted the cup and said: "May I be delivered from doing such a thing. Is this not the blood of the men who went for it with patent danger to their lives?" And so he offered it as a sacrifice to our Lord.[179] He showed great penitence[180] for his sin against Bathsheba and Uriah,[181] and when he purged himself of it in this life in the pursuit of his son Absalom,[182] his penance was received. But it seems Satan the Distorter then rose against me. He pointed out to the divine Majesty the sin of the kings I had requested, and as a result the Lord incited David to count the people.[183] For this offense He brought a pestilence over me and partially avenged Himself by the death of seventy thousand men of Israel.[184]

David was followed by his son, Solomon, who built the holy Temple to our Lord.[185] But he allowed prosperity to undermine morality, for in exchange for the gifts of wisdom, wealth and glory with which the Lord favored him over all other earthly beings, he followed the gods of the Sidonians and Milcom, the abomination of the Ammonites. Out of his love and lust for heathen women, he built a temple for Chemosh, the idol of Moab, as an expression of his love for them.[186] Because of his sins, Ahijah the prophet tore the new mantle he was wearing into twelve pieces as a symbol of the tribes; he gave ten to Jeroboam, leaving only two, Judah and Benjamin, to Solomon's house.[187]

{PART II}
KINGS OF ISRAEL

But this wicked Jeroboam was ungrateful for the kindness and the spacious kingdom which the Lord had given him. He made two golden calves, set one in Bethel and the other in Dan, with their houses, temples, altars and priests, and forbade the people to go to Jerusalem to worship in the Temple. And he said to them, "Here you see your gods, O Israel, who brought you forth from the land of Egypt" (I Kings 12.28). But when he raised his hand and arm against the man of the Lord who rebuked him, they withered.[188] Thus, in such wicked company, I again plunged into the whirlpool of my idolatries; I made groves, raised pillars and used other signs of heathendom. But woe is me, for Jeroboam's limbs and bones, and mine, and those of his entire lineage paid for it in the land where I idolized and on the altars where I sacrificed, according to the word of Ahijah the prophet; for when Nadab followed his father Jeroboam's wicked footsteps, he and all his family were killed by Baasa, after he had reigned for two years.[189]

But the evil seed of these men continued to grow, for Baasa, who had destroyed it, brought it to life again when he occupied the throne. He put himself in their place, and, during the twenty-four years he reigned, he revived all the sins of Jeroboam.[190] And since the divine scale of justice balances the penalty of the wicked with their crimes, a similar fate befell Baasa and all the others who wrought evil in the kingdom of Israel; for when Elah, his son, had reigned for two years, he became drunk and was killed by his general Zimri. As soon as Zimri had possession of the crown, he murdered all of Elah's relatives and friends. But because Zimri gave such early indications of his evil nature, his rule lasted only seven days. Omri captured his capital, and Zimri set fire to the palace where he had taken refuge and was cremated.[191]

After he took possession of the kingdom, Omri proved worse than all of his predecessors. Not content to equal even the vile deeds committed by Jeroboam, he surpassed them, and committed destructive evils for twelve years. Then he died; but so that his death should not free me from his poison, he left a son, the venomous serpent Ahab. During the twenty-two years I was under his yoke, his evil acts were so enormous that his deeds obliterated the memory of the evil of all the kings in Israel who had preceded him. He took to wife Jezebel, daughter of the king of the Sidonians,[192] in order to drown me in the deepest sea of idolatry and to add sulphur and tar to the great fire of evils already enveloping me. She had Naboth put to death with false evidence because he refused to sell his vineyard to her husband,[193] and she harassed the divine Elijah,[194] who later was carried to the heavens in a fiery chariot.[195] Four hundred and fifty of her false prophets, representing her sinful idols, contended with Elijah, who spoke for the truth of the Lord. They agreed to offer two sacrifices: victory would belong to the side whose sacrifice was touched by heavenly fire. Fire came to Elijah's offering only, and he decapitated the false prophets.[196]

Under the wicked trees of Ahab and Jezebel, I suffered many calamitous periods of long famine. These evil rulers were finally uprooted in a battle which Ahab waged against the king of Syria in Ramoth-Gilead. Ahab was struck dead by an arrow. Dogs lapped his blood and wicked women washed the chariot in which he was riding.[197] And later I saw his seventy sons decapitated all at once in Samaria by Jehu's sword.[198] And in fulfillment of Elijah's prophetic words, I saw Jezebel thrown out of a window in her tower; she was smashed to pieces, and her blood spilled over the walls; and dogs and birds ate her flesh in the field of Naboth, whom she had unjustly killed.

Ahab was succeeded by their son, Ahaziah. Like a sponge, he sucked in and absorbed the lethal poison of his wicked parents' works and helped me persist in my rebelliousness for the two years that he ruled. But he was afflicted with a deadly disease; and when he sent to ask Baal-zebub, the idol of Ekron, whether he would recover, Elijah met the messengers and spoke the following words to them for the Lord, which he later repeated to Ahaziah himself, "You sent to ask of Baal, as if there were no God in Israel whom you could ask. Therefore you shall not go down from the bed of your sickness, but shall die in it" (I Kings 22.52ff.; II Kings 1.16).

So Ahaziah ended his days with that illness and left me subject to Jehoram, who did not depart from his evil ways for the twelve year period I was under his yoke. While I was under him, my sins and his caused the Lord to send the king of Syria against Samaria with a huge army, and such a great famine came over me during the siege that I heard two women agree to divide and eat their children between them.[199] When the king of Syria prepared an ambush, Elisha succeeded in discovering it by his prophetic gift, and sent to advise Jehoram, king of Israel, to keep clear of the place; and Jehoram prepared accordingly and set up a guard there. When the king of Syria discovered this, he was astonished and asked: "Who is it among us that has been revealing this?"; and he was answered, "It is no one save Elisha, prophet in Israel, who reveals to his king everything that you say in the secret chamber where you sleep." Amazed by such a prodigious feat, the king immediately sent to find out where Elisha was. He sent a powerful army against the city of Dothan where the prophet was staying. They besieged the city by night, and when the man of God arose in the morning, he found it was surrounded. His servant was very frightened, and said to him, "O my lord, what shall we do?" Elisha answered him, "Fear not, for they that are with us are greater than they that are with them." And Elisha asked the Lord to open his servant's eyes and he saw a mountain covered with horses and chariots of fire around Elisha. Then Elisha prayed to the Lord to blind the enemy army, and He blinded it. And Elisha approached the enemy and said, "This is not the road nor is this the city. Follow me, I shall guide you to the man whom you are seeking." And all that people followed him and he brought them into Samaria, among my children and their enemies. When they arrived there, Elisha again made supplication, and had the Lord open their eyes. And when that army of Syrians saw themselves in the land of enemies and surrounded by a number much larger than they, they swooned, astonished at the great marvel. And when the king of Israel asked Elisha if he should cut their heads off, he answered no; he could decapitate only those he could have reached with his sword and bow; but rather he should have food placed before them. And after he had made them a sumptuous banquet, he let them go back to their lands, and they never returned against the land of Israel.[200]

After leaving Jehoram's yoke, I entered Jehu's for twenty-eight years. As soon as he took the scepter, he feigned friendship toward the idolatrous cults. In this way he assembled all their priests and prepared a sacrifice. He declared in the presence of all that those who did not serve Baal should leave or court death, and he showed them animosity. And when only those who were priests of the idol remained, he suddenly ordered them decapitated, and all the temples of Baal destroyed. Thus at the beginning of his reign he proved very acceptable in the sight of our Lord. For this the Lord promised him that his sons would sit on the throne of Israel until the fourth generation.[201] Nevertheless, he was finally deceived by the Enemy, and the great force of his wicked predecessors' wheel[202] led him in his latter days to accept the cursed heritage of abominable works that was handed down from one king to another. And when the merciful Lord, who governs all, saw that there was no longer any spot within these princes to which a single strand of justice could cling, He struck me forthwith through Hazael, king of Syria,[203] and He thence forth began to diminish me and shake me from my base.

And in order that the punishment should be meted out to a greater sinner, Jehu was succeeded by Jehoahaz, his son. He did not swerve from Jeroboam's wicked way, but pursued his sinful path for seventeen years. The Lord's anger was kindled against me, and He delivered me into the hands of Hazael and his son, Ben-hadad. They made my yoke so heavy and afflicted me so cruelly that they gave cause to the Lord to remember the merit of my holy fathers.[204] He lifted His anger from me and transferred it to the enemies who abused me so. Thus I was restored to my liberty and lands.[205] But, woe is me, for I was so deeply rooted in sin and subject to its bridle that at each step it led me where it wished and made me forget the punishment I had just received.[206] So Jehoash, who next followed and ruled over me for sixteen years, refused to disengage himself from the company of malefactors. Indeed, one of his first acts was to lead his army against Amaziah, king of Judah. He threw down the wall of Jerusalem, entered with a hostile hand and violently seized all the vessels and treasures of the house of the Lord.[207] And in order that I might see that the light of my salvation was beginning to dim, Elisha the prophet, the lamp that illumined the darkness enveloping me, died at this time. When a dead body, cast into his grave by mistake, touched his bones, it quickened and rose to its feet, revived.[208]

Then Jeroboam II[209] took the royal crown and followed the execrable custom of his predecessors. He did not deviate from any of Jeroboam's sins, but on the contrary, lengthened the skein of my wickedness. I remained in his company for forty-one years. When the kingdom was then given to Zechariah, he gave indication of his evil intentions in so short a time that at the end of six months he was killed by Shallum, who usurped his crown. The Lord's promise made to Jehu, the great-grandfather of this Zechariah,[210] that his children would occupy the throne of Israel until the fourth generation, was thus fulfilled.

After one month of rule, Shallum's wicked deeds were such that he was made to drink from the cup of bitterness which he made others take: He was killed with the sword of Menahem. Menahem held the scepter for ten years,[211] and loyally continued the evil deeds of his predecessors. When he was refused entry to the city of Tipsah, a city of his Israelite brethren, he put to the sword all the pregnant women he found there. He left his son, Pekahiah, as heir to me and to his terrible ways. Pekahiah ruled for two years and feasted well on Jeroboam's pestiferous vices. But he perished because of his sin, which equaled his father's. He was killed by Pekah's sword. Pekah took over his dominion, and continued on the throne in his master Jeroboam's evil deeds for twenty years.[212] And when the Lord most high, who beholds our ways from above, saw how estranged they were from His service, and that we outdid the brute animals in obduracy and stubbornness and we fled from human nature and reason, He began to threaten me with the final destruction that was being prepared against me. I had already woven the greater part of the net into which I would fall on my face and which would entangle my wings.[213] The Lord presently sent the king of the Assyrians against Pekah, and he vexed me with a heavy and hard punishment. He sacked nine cities and the entire land of Naphtali,[214] and carried all the children I had there into wretched captivity in Assyria. And he took out the golden calf which Jeroboam's hand had placed in Dan.[215]

When I had drunk this vial of gall, Pekah, too, tasted of it, since he deserved to. He was suddenly killed by Hoshea's sword; and Hoshea sat on his royal throne for nine years.[216] But he and I were planning grave sins against the Lord. The Lord's compassion and kindness had been communicated to me through the prophets. His superabundant promises for my safety and hopes for my repentance were the admonitions of His paternal love. He had also given me many warnings concerning the harsh punishments to be meted out by His sovereignty and majesty, to the extent that His lovingkindness permitted. But I had been transfixed by a host of sharp arrows of sin and my wounds were so many that my body was like a single sore.

With this the limit of my offenses was reached. Disgusted with Israel, the mighty God on whose favor the blessing of this world and the next depends, now completely stripped me of all His grace which had protected me. I was thus left deserted by divine favor and unprotected. Like a tree in a huge, open wasteland, stripped of all its green foliage after the bloom of summer and attacked by fearsome winter storms until it is shaken and finally uprooted by the increasing fury of their relentless assault, I was attacked by the fierce king Shalmaneser. He covered all my fields in Samaria with enemies, assaulted me with a military storm, felled me[217] and tore my roots, my children, from the center of the earth[218] where they had been planted by the hand of the Lord Supreme. He stripped me of my rich apparel and clothed me with the wretched, poor garb of a distressed captive.[219] Half dragging my children, their cheeks streaming with tears[220] and their delicate virgins' feet dripping with blood because of the sharp thorns on which they tread, he brought me to Halah and Habor near the river Gozan and into the cities of the Medes[221] to feed on bitter and deadly herbs among the human animals of these regions. Here I have until now been plunged into a deep sleep of forgetfulness by God, who alone holds my salvation in His grasp. Then Shalmaneser, and afterwards Esarhaddon, kings of Assyria, brought over many idolatrous peoples from diverse kingdoms to the lands I had possessed. But since these had no knowledge at all of the true Lord, the very land, which in itself was holy, disowned them and reprehended their idolatries. Cruel lions emerged from the woods, entered the inner rooms of their houses, and tore them to pieces. The king of Assyria sought to remedy this. He sent a priest of Israel to teach them the First Cause[222] and to perform works for His pleasure, so that the land might suffer them. But they were so inured to their strange rites that they mixed one service with another. They feared the Lord, but they also honored their idols, [223] and as a result they limped on both feet. And until this day they have remained in this confusion, for now they neither fear the Lord nor do they keep their ancient ceremonies.

{PART III}
THE HUNT OF STAGS TRANSFIGURED
INTO THE LIFE OF THE WICKED

This is the description of the life of those children of mine who applied themselves to the customs of heathendom and the second hunt, the hunt of stags, as I related to you. Once their kings were in the saddle in the heat of the day (when the cool morning had passed in which our

Lord alone was their king and governor), twenty or thirty huntsmen went forth. Their names were Jeroboam, Nadab, Baasa, Elah, Omri, Ahab, Ahaziah, Jehoram, Jehoahaz, Jehoash, Jeroboam II,[224] Zechariah, Shallum, Menahem, Pekahiah, Pekah, Hoshea, kings of Israel. They held their long javelins in their hands (scepters of the kingdom with full power to kill); they wore green fur-caps on their heads (crowns with great hopes); at their sides, they carried full leather bottles and provision bags (bellies stuffed with forbidden foods); and they were riding on their pampered mares (false and shameful opinions). They rode to that vast and beautiful open land, stippled with deer and roebucks, the pleasant, spacious kingdom of Judah, all of it occupied by Israelites. And as they discussed evil thoughts concerning the idolatries so delectable to their palates, they blocked the flight of the beaten game (the poor populace) to cut off its independence (the means to save itself). As they moved away and succeeded one another in the kingship for certain periods of time, they laid a siege of pestiferous abominations. Jeroboam had the captaincy and stood in his station as chief with his two golden calves. Next to him was his son Nadab. There followed the awful Baasa, Elah, Zimri and Omri, who took great pains to surpass their leaders. Ahab set himself apart, trying to appear sovereign in wicked deeds when he had conquered his predecessor. With his wife Jezebel at his right hand, he was haughty and presumptuous amidst his groves and statues and filthy altars. Lying prone at his feet were a large number of bodies of the Lord's prophets, in whose blood he and his wife had bathed their faces and hands. Ahaziah, his son, held fast with both hands to their skirts, and yet he, as well as Jehoram, his brother, had their eyes fixed lovingly on Jeroboam. All the rest of the company stood at the posts where their first captain had stationed them. Thus, armed with their abominable works, they moved from Samaria and struck the holy mountain of Jerusalem, where the divine Temple was established. Their intent was to throw down the lofty and marvelous edifice and drive from Jerusalem the nimble stag, the fickle populace, who were still sheltered and protected by the Temple service they performed there, inadequate though it was.[225]

When the stag left its covert, that is, when the people's favor was removed, its enemies made it drink from waters streaming with idolatries, and it could not make up its mind which to choose.[226] But Jeroboam, a hunter cunning and shrewd in wickedness, strove to set the stag in the midst of his army and the terrible path of the two golden calves which he had contrived. He astutely confronted it wherever it turned until, in that sad condition, it reached the station of his successor, who was to follow him on the throne. The new king was annoyed at having to wait so long for this pleasant moment, so much did the poison of wicked acts seethe in his and his successors' breasts. But when he arose with the kingdom, though still dazed with sleep, he immediately pursued the stag. In this way each one of those who took the crown pursued the persecuted people (who had been turned into a wild animal), just as the malefactors before them had run their course. Thus the last hunter easily killed the tired game and removed it completely from the presence and favor of God, whose grace gave life to my soul and prosperity and rest to my afflicted body. When I had been thus deprived by Hoshea, the last king, to the great joy of the Enemy, our tormentor, all my children were removed from their estates. And Shalmaneser and his army, with festivity and great rejoicing, carried me and the dead cattle, that is, the wretched, overthrown people, afflicted and moribund, to captivity in his lands, and my memory has until now remained dead in this world.

LAMENT OVER THE LOSS OF THE TEN TRIBES

O disconsolate old age, distressed father and afflicted old man, who sees such great affliction before him and whose offenses make him swallow so bitter a morsel! O beloved children, where are they taking you? To whom are you leaving the houses you built, the vineyards and trees you planted, the delightful gardens you arranged, the cities with rich build' ings and strong walls which you erected? To your enemies to enjoy. What has become of your joyous occasions and festivals? They have been swiftly changed into days of lamentation for the dead and the captive. Who has begrudged you the splendid ornaments of your clothes? They have covered you wickedly with sackcloth instead. Where will you drink the clear water of the Holy Law, since they have removed you from the Fountain whence it flowed? Where are they carrying you to be exiled so far from the motherland which bore you?[227] Indeed, your utterance, Ezekiel, found fulfillment here: "I will bring shepherds from the nations to occupy their homes" (Ezek. 7.24).

O holy land, how can you consent to your children being taken from before your eyes? Loosen your hair over your shoulders[228] and pull it out in anger and affliction. Raise a howl and a shout that heaven may take pity on your widowhood and solitude.[229] Open the spring of waters and let loose tears like brooks across your cheeks. Do not give to strangers the fruit which you gave your children. Change your nature, and let your covering be holm-trees, thorns, caltrops and desert herbs, for there is no longer any reason for you to dress in merriment, to wear the beauti' ful flowers and luxuriant verdure of your fields, as you used to for your loved ones. Let those who tread on you feel the frown with which you receive them, and let them understand that you are a stepmother to all peoples, until the Lord, your husband,[230] will gladden you by the restitu' tion of your legitimate children. O my beloved ones, do not cast a back' ward glance, for seeing what you are leaving behind, you will bear away a greater pain. Lift yourselves up to the heavens whom you have offended, for from there your remedy issues. O Lord, what cruelty was this that You practiced with Your first born? If his ignorance diverted him from

Your service, cannot a father's love accomplish more? Would not my wickedness have been overcome with the infinite mercy in which You are clothed, whose bounds cannot be comprehended?

ZICAREO: So far we have clearly understood the causes which impelled your Creator to bring you to your present state. And as we understand from your words, you have only yourself to blame, since you wounded yourself with your own hands; through the vein of idolatry, you let the blood of your entire body and so fortified the wall of your rebellious acts that you left no entry for celestial compassion, which strove greatly to help you at every opportunity. Consider and judge dispassionately how much kindness heaven employed with you. In Egypt you were the most humbled and lowly slave of all the earth; yet the Lord, whose intelligence and will governs all worlds, took you for His people, and made you inherit the possessions of those who ruled over you in payment for the time you served them. He drowned all their men and their king because of the afflictions you received from them. At the crossing of the sea, He opened the heavens for you and favored you with the sight of the whole heavenly court.[231] He gave you water to drink, even from the sterile and arid place where you asked for it, forcing the stone to change its nature. He gave you the food of angels in the sterility of the desert, where wheat could not be sown nor pleasant herb grown. He battled against your enemies without your taking arms; nor was your blood shed; and He delivered them vanquished into your hand. He gave your people possession of the happiest land which He created in His world. You did not erect its beautiful cities and noble buildings; but rather He delivered to you, for you to enjoy without labor, the trees which other hands had planted; the flowers and elegant plants which they had sown; the houses, towers, palaces which others had built with so much sweat and labor; the gold and silver and a great quantity of other riches which they had striven so hard to acquire.

And as a reward for such supreme benefits, such solicitous actions and testimonies of many greater blessings to come, you disobeyed all His precepts and you practiced them in reverse. He commanded you when you entered the land that you should not ally with the heathen: and you took up friendship with them; that you should not intermarry with idolaters: and you married your daughters to their sons, and you gave your sons to their daughters; that you should not worship their gods: and you offered sacrifices to the idols of Baal and Ashtoreth in contempt of Him, and you humbled yourself to them. Though you deserved to be uprooted from the world for such acts of disobedience, He punished you at first with only eight years of captivity in the power of Cushaim [sic], king of Aram, and He immediately returned His mercy to you and restored your liberty. You rebelled again, four times, and from the straits where your offenses delivered you, that you might be purged of them, He again saved you in the hour when you acknowledged your sin and asked Him for mercy and aid with all your soul. And He not only delivered you from the inimical hands which harassed you, but He took vengeance upon them in your presence for the evil they had done to you while you were in their power.

Who ever had such a friend and benign king? Who was ever protected by such a mighty prince? And who was ever defended by such an invincible leader? Why then, in this fortunate position, did you ask for another lord who was subject to human wretchedness; and who would be overcome at every step by his spiritual and corporeal enemies; and further, who would not only be powerless to deliver you even from the hardships and constant tribulations where your rebelliousness put you, but would even be unable to save himself from them without divine help? What did you expect from this king for whom you asked? Indeed, in nothing of what you needed could he assist you; he could only submit you to greater afflictions, as you have seen from experience. For the errors of Solomon, with all his wisdom, made two parts of your body. And as for the part over which Jeroboam reigned in Samaria, consider the tribulations with which he and all his progeny afflicted you:

First, the two golden calves, at which he made you perform idolatry, cost you a large quantity of blood, spilled from your veins and your children's on the land and altars where you practiced your abominations. The perseverance of this sin in Ahab's reign desiccated your land with a frightful sterility. And the persistence in this wickedness by his successors brought you to the point where, under Jehoram, tender-hearted women were driven by hunger to eat their children. Pekah's obstinate continuation of the same offenses and rebelliousness first invented by his master, Jeroboam, laid waste nine cities of yours in the land of Naphtali with great destruction, and all your children there were carried away as captives to Assyria. And Hoshea's abominations, which had taken deep root in the land, planted by so many predecessors, finally dispossessed you from that entire region in the storm which carried off the remainder of the Ten Tribes.

Thus you can consider the wickedness you committed and the benefit you received from the Lord's company when He was your king, and what you have attained from the earthly and mortal prince whom you requested. In his power your sins multiplied, your abominations increased, and the baseness of your works surpassed that of your heathen neighbors. Truly, if you examine well the number of your rebellious acts, you will find there was no longer any room for pardon. Just as a wife who breaks the faith of her beloved husband, so did you break your faith with the Lord, O house of Israel.[232]

YCABO: O brothers, your reproof is so justified that its truth congeals the blood in my veins. And I can tell you that when my memory recalls my faults and my imagination reminds me of the abominable and ugly deeds that my hands committed, the fears which the Enemy of mortals inspires are very great. I fear above all that the Lord, so provoked and offended, has now rejected me as His people. And then I fear lest He has gone over to another people, after seeing how little effect His remedies and punishments have had on me. And if He has left me, I dread still a third evil, namely, that being thus deprived and absent from His favor, my memory may end and be consumed in the paws and teeth of the animals of this world, this frightening desert through which I travel.

CONSOLATION ON THE CAPTIVITY OF THE TEN TRIBES

NUMEO: There is no doubt, Israel, that you have been plunged into a deep sea of sins, and that your hands alone have been your murderer. With your own hands, you set fire to your land; you leveled and reduced its walls; you delivered it to the nations, for them to enjoy it; you chained your own feet with captives' shackles and fetters; and finally, you brought about your perpetual ruin though you expected the merit of your fathers to stave it off. But now at this point where you have arrived, hear the mercy of the Lord, who is roaring against the North. "If the heavens above can be measured, and the foundations of the earth which are beneath searched out, then will I cast off the seed of Israel for all the sin which they have done" (Jer. 31.37). "He who gave the sun for light by day, the moon and the constellations of the stars for light by night, who made the sea roar so that it becomes stirred and makes a tumult with the waves, the Lord of Hosts is His name" (Jer. 31.35). Then "if these laws of the sun, moon, stars, and sea cease so will the seed of Israel cease from being a nation before Me forever" (Jer. 31.36). "For I will make a full end of all the nations where I have thrust you; but I will not make a full end of you" (Jer. 30.11). "Unto all the families of Israel will I be God, and they shall be My people" (Jer. 31.1). Thus, "for I am with you, says the Lord, to protect you" (Jer. 30.11), "who found favor in the wilderness, the people that were left from the sword" (Jer. 31.2). Therefore, "fear not, my servant, Jacob, neither be dismayed, O Israel, for I will save you from afar and your seed in the land where they have you in captivity" (Jer. 30.10).

Your doubts and ailments are cured by these words and divine medicine which were sent down from heaven solely for this purpose. And if you wish an earthly remedy to satisfy you further and to reassure your timorous spirit, I will prove to you that there is no merit in any other people here on earth on whom God's grace and favor might rest, so that He should remove you from His intimacy.

ORIGIN OF IDOLATRY[233]

If you believe that because you were subjected by Him to the Egyptians, it was possible that they were a better people, then you have conceived a very wrong opinion, for they never recognized the Cause of all Causes to be God, as you did. The first god they worshiped was Ham, son of Noah, the worst of his three sons. For when Noah left the ark in Greater Armenia near Persia, next to the river Araxes,[234] after the deluge in which all flesh perished, he divided your world into three parts, and placed a son in each dominion. To Shem he gave the fortunate Asia, stored with gold and precious stones and decked with scented and excellent trees. To Japheth he gave the scepter and lordship of all Europe, whose nobility, knowledge and culture surpasses that of all other parts of the universe. And to Ham, the wicked sorcerer, who uncovered his father's shame[235]—some say that with magic he made him incapable of procreating—he delivered Africa, whose metropolitan city was in Egypt.[236] Thus these peoples took him for a god, and as such they obeyed his laws and judgments and did not attain to any higher knowledge of God than of seeing Him as the first king and monarch whom they were subject to in their region. And changing his name, they called him the god Saturn. They built cities and many temples in his honor, and offered sacrifices to him.[237]

You have mentioned the Assyrians, who tormented you so harshly, and under whom you are captive. Shall I show you the vanity of their foundation? Like the Egyptians, they worshiped mortal men as gods. The first was Asshur, a grandson of Nimrod, who built the proud tower of Babel[238] which led to the variation and change in languages among all nations. This Asshur determined to lay the foundations for a kingdom. He left Babylon with a large host and began to build a strong city, called Nineveh. His name was changed to Ninus, while the entire province of Assyria derived its name from Asshur.[239] All the peoples who came from this region built altars and offered sacrifices to him and considered him their god; but not only him, for they venerated any man who taught them knowledge and did not perceive that there was a Creator of the world. And they performed these barbarous and heathen rites at the time when you were punished for your crimes by them.

And as for the Babylonians, Persians and Chaldeans, what can I tell you save that, blind like all these others, they strayed from true knowledge in pursuit of similar vanities. The first heathen god they worshiped was Saturn, the god of the Egyptians, and after him his son Jupiter Belus, who was also called Osiris. His worship and that of his wife, Juno, granddaughter of Noah, extended among all the heathens because he gave them laws, while she was the first to sow seeds in Egypt, where they changed her name to Isis.

Then they worshiped Sabazius the wizard, another mortal man, who was the first to till the soil in that region, and for him, too, as for the others, they made statues, festivals and sacrifices.[240] Thus Persians and Chaldeans, Egyptians and Babylonians in Asia (where the seat of dominion was at that time) and all the rest of the heathen peoples throughout the world worshiped idols. They regarded Noah and his wife, Tithea,[241] as the chief gods above all others, because they were the ancestors of the people who arose after the flood, and they called by various names.

To some peoples Noah taught astrology.[242] He divided the year for them according to the course of the sun, and made the months according to the rotation of the moon. By astrology he was able to guess at the events that would occur at the end of each epoch. The people thought he had a relationship with heaven and the celestial bodies; and at his death they said he had become one of them, the chief one.[243] Others believed him to be not only the father of the three men, Shem, Ham and Japheth, who were leaders of the world and kings of all the earth, worshiped as gods,[244] but also the father of the entire human race, which had multiplied throughout the universe after the flood. The people called him Celus, and his wife Arithia,[245] which means earth. (She was also known as the goddess Vesta). And these names signified that just as the earth, with the help of heaven, brings forth all things, so they two had engendered all mortals and all were descended from them.[246] Other people, seeing that he was the first planter of the vine,[247] called him Janus, which in Aramaic means "worker of the vine." (The derivation of Janus corresponds somewhat to ין.)[248]

Finally, deeply rooted in their blindness and confusion, these peoples were not satisfied to make gods of human beings, but they humbled themselves even further by bestowing the divine name upon monstrous animals that appeared in the world. This we can see in the time of Daniel—who was thrown by the Chaldeans into the lion's den—[249] when the Chaldeans worshiped a poisonous and monstrous dragon who lived in a grotto in the wilderness. They offered it many sacrifices at night and brought gifts of food; and when they threw their offerings in front of its cave, the wild beast came out and devoured them. It grew so strong and fierce with this continuous nourishment that it greatly dispirited those who beheld it, and those who heard about it were overcome with trembling and dread.

Daniel ridiculed this god and the Chaldeans were offended. Since he had already destroyed their god Bel and all his priests besides, they angrily determined to deliver him to the power of the terrible dragon. But Darius, the king, forbade this punishment because of the great love he had for Daniel. He told Daniel that the dragon was a living, strong and robust god, whom he could not resist as he had resisted Bel. But the great worthy answered him, "Do not deceive yourself, O king, for this beast is subject to the power of men, and the spirit of the Lord is not in it. If you desire to see this, give me permission, and I shall kill it without a sword, spear or any other instrument of battle. For this is only a common reptile, and the Lord most high has instilled in it the same fear of man that all animals have, because man is created in the image of God. I do not desire any aid from you against this animal, save that when I vanquish it, you do not give permission to your princes to take vengeance upon me." When he was assured by the king, the populace and all the grandees—who believed that the dragon would kill him—were very happy. But the merciful Lord, who stood ready to defend His servant, did not permit it; rather he turned their joyous thoughts into sadness. Daniel prepared an iron instrument, like a comb with which flax is dressed. Its prongs and tines were filed smooth, but they came to sharp points. Daniel placed various kinds of victuals on them, such as suet, grease and other fats, and daubed everything with sulphur and pitch, covering the teeth and tines. He then placed this ingenious device before the dragon. The dragon seized it with its enormous mouth, in great haste to devour it. The instrument went down to its maw; the heat melted the suet and fat from the iron teeth; the sharp edges were exposed and rent the dragon's intestines and organs. The dragon immediately was racked with an excruciating pain, and it expired on the next day with a frightful roar.[250]

Just as Bel, the god of the Egyptians, and Nebo,[251] the god of the Assyrians, fell upon their faces (their icons were carried into captivity on beasts of burden, and they were unable to walk on their own feet),[252] so did this dragon come to an end at Daniel's hand, as I have told you.

These are the beings whom the Chaldeans worshiped, those whom the Egyptians regarded as gods, and those who were so venerated with sacrifices and respect by the Persians, the Babylonians and all the other nations of the world. Indeed, men who enter Africa's deepest mines in search of gold, are not as far removed from the terrestrial light as these people were removed from the divine. Well, do you really think, on your honor, O brother Ycabo, that the Lord of the heavens and earth would choose such a people for Himself when he left you, Israel, punished and chastised because you were imitating the sins of such peoples as these? If, indeed, He had desired to exchange you, He could have chosen another, better people than the one He was leaving. And since I have clearly proven to you here that there was no better people at the time, and the force of the ancient error in worshiping mortal men went on to affect modern peoples—and the rest I shall tell you in your ear[253]— do not fear, because the Lord, the God of your righteous fathers, is with you. "Hear, O house of Jacob, and all the remnant of the house of Israel, that have been carried by Me from the womb, and whom I have borne on my shoulders from the birth," says the Lord, "even to old age I am the same, and even to hoar hairs will I carry you on My shoulders" (Isa. 46.4). O Lord, truly there is none like You. You are great, and great and mighty is Your name. Who will not fear You, O King of the nations, for glory resides in You, and neither among all the wise men of the nations nor in their kingdoms is there one comparable to You. [And yet the people do not realize this.] They are confused and have become like brute animals. They worship a piece of wood and an ornament made of silver, taken out by the drawing iron or stretched out by the hammer, or what is made of refined gold, the work of the goldsmith's and artisan's hands,[254] while the Lord is the true God, the living God and eternal King. At His anger the earth trembles and nations cannot endure His wrath.[255] But concerning the idols of the nations you shall say as follows: "The gods who did not build heaven and earth shall perish from the earth and from underneath those heavens. But He who with His power fashions the earth, and orders the globe with His wisdom, stretches out the heavens with His prudence—when He calls forth, He gathers a great force of waters in the sea, and raises clouds from the end of the earth, and changes lightning flashes into rain and draws out the winds from His treasuries. He makes all creatures foolish with respect to their knowledge" (Jer. 10.11-14). "He makes every sculptor ashamed of his sculpture, because his molten idol is a lie; for there is no breath in it; their works are vain; at the time of their visitation they shall perish" (Jer. 10.14-15; 51.17-18). "But Jacob's portion is not like that of these; rather He who formed all things is his portion and Israel is the tribe of His inheritance. The Lord of Hosts is His name" (Jer. 10.16).

YCABO: Blessed be the hour of your coming and blessed be the feet that brought you before me. The expressions of your lips are divine and they stir my soul with celestial delight. Your answer to my question has left me quite satisfied. But now that you have healed one wound and you assure me that the Lord has not passed over and will not ever pass over to another people, what cure will you give me for my other wound? O wretched me, how can I raise my hope for blessings? My wings are clipped and broken and I cannot see works worthy of blessing within me. And even if the Lord will not turn to another people, how can I hope for heaven's favors to descend upon me as they used to when I have no merits to aid me? My soul and body have become increasingly covered with nodes of rebelliousness, and I cut a thousand wounds in my entrails with the sharp blades of my crimes. I have become so inured to my corrupting diet of sin, that its need is now almost rooted in my nature, like the need for poison in those for whom poison is a food.[256] Sometimes, touched by God's spirit, I make an effort to change, yet I hardly succeed, for the continual practice of sin now draws me like a wheel which is moved at first by a great force, and then continues to turn by its own momentum. "Can the Ethiopian change his skin or perchance the leopard his spots?" (Jer. 13.23). And I, inured to so much evil, can I do good? O, woe is me, I fear that I cannot. Then how am I to have hope of ever seeing again my ten sons who are in captivity in Assyria, or of their being planted again on their joyous land whence they were uprooted with wailing and bitterness? How can I imagine that I will see the land with the joys it once had, and my children, who were its fertile sheep, feeding in its once delightful pastures? Indeed, I believe their sin is sufficient to vex them still further wherever they are in the farthest parts of the earth, never to free them from the power of those who hold them in subjection. O my soul, how sad and dry is your leaf. Since your root is planted in sand and sterility, how then will you produce fruits of joy? O my Rachel, let us make a lament together,[257] for our loss was the same: your children whom you bore, and the creatures I engendered, have been away for many years. O Lord, heal the wound which You inflicted on us, for its cure lies in Your hand alone. "You have chastised me and I received the chastisement, like an untrained calf that refuses to learn from its punishment. Take me back again to You and I shall come near, for You are the Lord my God. I am ashamed and confounded and have borne reproach from my youth" (Jer. 31.18-19). Loosen and break the yoke which has become so weighty on my neck. But O, woe is me, for I cry for mercy with my hands enveloped in iniquity, and its power has already so wearied the righteous works in me that I cannot raise my drooping arms. You, O sin and enemy of mine, have covered the eyes of my understanding with so much mist that at mid-day I walk in dark gloom,[258] and I cannot see the true Goodness whose light I so sorely need. You have blocked my ears and the shouts of those who rightly admonish me cannot reach my soul. O, detractor of mine, how you have trodden me. You have clipped off most of the cords to the holy impulse,[259] by which I might help myself against you. You have carried off my ten branches to Assyria, to engulf them in an abyss of forgetfulness. Tell me, in which alien land did you plant them where they must live contrary to their nature? Their fruits have not come to light in all the years they have been gone.

HUMAN CONSOLATION FOR THE CAPTIVITY
OF THE TEN TRIBES

Strengthen yourself, strengthen yourself, Israel.[260] "Strengthen the weak hands and make firm the tottering knees" (Isa. 35.3), for the force of God's mercy toward you has not been diminished, nor does the pardon of your children and the healing of your wounds depend upon your good or evil deeds alone. Many and incomprehensible are the ways by which the Lord performs lofty actions and new marvels. His infinite power is not subject to the frail reasoning of mortals, who think that with their understanding they can determine what is just or unjust. The Lord's ways and His thoughts are so sublime and so distant from those of humans as the highest heavens are from the lowly earth.[261] Loosen not your hold on your merciful God, but fasten your hopes on Him and cast your eyes on the infinite and bountiful marvels which He has performed for you when you did not merit them. Take them as your guide and example, for God's works are the light and true lodestar of mortals, and you will possess the firmest and strongest pillar of hopes that you have yet had to lean on and embrace.

Did you not see the Lord drown millions of Egyptians in the Red Sea for your Israelite children, although your children were engulfed by that people's heathen practices and sins?

Did you not see them worship a golden calf in the desert in reward for this kindness,[262] and the Lord yet despoil all the Canaanites, Hittites and Jebusites, etc. [sic] of the lands and possessions which they owned and deliver them to your children to enjoy?[263]

Did you not see your children then intermarry with their heathen neighbors and worship their idols—a thing so forbidden—and the Lord yet free them four times from the hand of the enemy who punished them for their sins: from Cushan-Rishathaim; Eglon, king of the Moabites; and from the peoples of Midian, Ammon and Philistia, with a cruel slaughter of these heathens?[264]

Did you not see the victory He gave your execrable son, King Ahab, whose wickedness and poison dried the grass where he planted his feet and fouled the air and earth? The Syrians once came down mightily upon him, together with thirty-two kings, saying blasphemously that the God of Israel had no power save in the mountains because they had lost one battle against them. And when Ahab asked heaven for compassion and help, he went down by God's command on a level field with only seven thousand Israelites, and the mighty Lord gave him a marvelous and triumphant victory against that entire innumerable heathen people, with the frightful slaughter of a hundred twenty-seven thousand Syrians. And the kings, dressed in sackcloth and with ashes spilled over their heads, came to kneel humbly before Ahab and ask mercy for their lives.[265]

Did you not see the lofty miracle He performed for your other son, King Jehoram, the grandson of Ahab and the perfect likeness of his evil deeds, when the same Syrians turned against him with an even more powerful and mighty army than before? They besieged the entire prov-ince of Samaria and brought it to such anguish that tender-hearted Israelite mothers were forced to eat their own small children out of hunger. And here, to show you God's power, whose remedy is reserved for a cruel moment like this when men despair of human resources, He suddenly one night cast a fear and dread on the Syrians. He made them hear a frightful din of horses and the tumult of a host of warriors. Alarmed and weakened by fear, the Syrians immediately lifted the siege and fled, leaving all their spoil and riches scattered along the fields and roads where they sought refuge.[266] And thus when it dawned, O Israel, you saw all your children who had been at death's doorstep quickened with life once more, although they deserved to be punished with a thousand kinds of death for their abominable sins. Therefore raise your tired and fallen hopes from the ground and lean on the prop of God's mercy, that it may sustain you. Then open your heart wide, and receive it in the very midst of your soul, for you yet have much greater reason to hope than this natural reason I have given you. I would like to tell you of these hopes, but you must have a better predisposition than you show now in order to receive them.

YCABO: You have raised my afflicted spirit from the earth's mud and dust to heaven, and there the contemplation of your words keeps my spirit buoyed. Their force has wrought such a sublime change in me in so short a time that I perceive you are more than a human being, though un-recognizable in earthly garb. If you have the angelic quality which I suspect and you bring me news from heaven concerning my children in Assyria,[267] I beg you as I would a lord, with all humility, to speak some-what more clearly with this wretched creature, as befits the remedy for my dejection. And if perchance you still imagine that I have persisted in the state of incapacity in which you saw me until now, you are mistaken; rather be assured that I am completely changed, because I now find my hope, which was so weak and drooping, very much strengthened within me. And if you desire a greater state of readiness for me to merit your words, I dare not promise you more until you have influenced me with your holy arguments.

DIVINE CONSOLATION FOR THE CAPTIVITY OF THE TEN TRIBES

NUMEO: Since you assure me that you have resolved the three doubts which you first voiced to me, I am content for the time being to have raised you to this degree of hope, for this is one of the chief gates by which God's compassion comes forth to visit the world. "Those who wait for the Lord renew their strength; they mount up with wings like eagles, they run and shall not be tired; they shall walk and not be faint" (Isa. 40.31). "He that hopes in Me, says the Lord, shall receive the land as a possession and shall possess My holy mountain" (Isa. 57.13). This is the disposition I had desired you to have before hearing my words, and since you now have it, hear the message which I bring you from heaven concerning the children who have been in Assyria in captivity for so long a time:

"Says the Lord of hosts: 'I will break his yoke from off your neck, and will burst your bands, that strangers might not subjugate you any more; but they shall serve the Lord their God and David their king, whom I will raise up unto them'" (Jer. 30.8-9). "There shall come a time in which Jacob shall take root, Israel shall blossom and bud, so that its fruitage will fill the face of the earth" (Isa. 27.6). "And on that day a great horn shall be blown, and they shall come that were lost—or the memory of whom had died—in the land of Assyria, and they shall worship the Lord in the holy mountain at Jerusalem" (Isa. 27.13). "They shall no more say 'As the Lord lives, who brought up the children of Israel from the land of Egypt,' but 'As the Lord lives, who brought up the seed of the children of Israel out of the north country and from all the countries where I had driven them'" (Jer. 23.7-8). "These shall come from afar; some from the North and from the West, and others from the land of Sinim" (Isa. 49.12). And then you, Israel, shall say, and the nations, bewildered and amazed by your so unexpected prosperity: "Rejoice, O heavens, and let the earth be glad; let the mountains break forth in great joy, for the Lord has comforted His people and upon His afflicted will He have compassion" (Isa. 49.13).

And you see the other doubts which you raised in your lament dispelled here, for the Lord says, "Then shall the deaf hear the words of the book and the eyes of the blind shall see, with obscurity and darkness removed; then shall the humble be glad in the Lord and your poor and your afflicted shall rejoice in the Holy One of Israel" (Isa. 29.18-19). And at that time, you, Jacob, along with your beloved Rachel, shall lose the melancholy that has been so deeply seated in your heart. And thus says the Lord: "At that time Jacob shall not be ashamed, nor shall his countenance become red with shame, when he sees his children, the work of My hands, come from the midst of him to sanctify My name, and sanctify the Holy One of Jacob, and stand in awe of the God of Israel" (Isa. 29.22-23). And to you, O Rachel: "Refrain your voice from weeping and your eyes from tears, for there is a reward for your work, says the Lord: your children shall return from the land of the enemy (Assyria)[268] to their own border" (Jer. 31.16-17).

"How is it you do not know how I prize my son Ephraim, and that he is a delightful and darling son to Me? I remember him still as when I used to speak with him in the past, and My heart still yearns for him. I will yet have compassion upon him, says the Lord" (Jer. 31.20). Therefore "set up waymarks and guide-posts and consider with your heart the steps of the way by which you went, and return, O virgin of Israel, return to your cities" (Jer. 31.21). "And Jacob shall return and have rest and shall be full and secure and none shall make him afraid" (Jer. 30.10), "for I am with you, says the Lord, to protect you" (Isa. 41.10). Here, O brother, you see how the Lord is sending you remedies for all the ills and hardships you have bewailed in your lament. They are now on the way. Wait a little while longer and they shall come.

YCABO: O happy and celestial being in human form, great is the consolation which my soul receives from the answers you have given to my doubts, and the message you bring me has been a healing balm to my wounds, for with it you have assuaged a good part of their pain. O King of the Heavens, Your mercy, diffused through all the veins of the world, gives sustenance and life to an infinite multitude of its creatures; without it this great structure which You have created would perish. I, one of the world's smallest beings, am overwhelmed in the abyss of baseness where I have been sunk by my sins. I beg You, high above all exaltation, now to fulfill for me at last this promise of blessing which You have given me, for I am fallen into the extreme of anguish and wretchedness. And you, saintly and sovereign messenger, I entreat you, by the love which you must employ with your fellow creatures and those distressed as I, tell me your name and which of those you are whom we are awaiting.[269] Then shall I become staunch and have the faith I should in your message of great joy.

ZICAREO: We cannot as yet divulge our names to you. We must first learn from you the cause of all the ills you have suffered, and whether you have more wounds to which we may apply our remedy. After we have heard the entire history of your tribulations, we shall satisfy your desire to have your blessing come to pass. As for your other question, we can tell you that we are not the men you await, but others, to whose words you may lend as much credence as you would to any of theirs.

CHAP.[270] OF THE KINGS OF JUDAH
{EXPLANATION OF THE METAPHOR ENTITLED
"HUNT OF STAGS AND HERONS"}
{PART IV}

YCABO: Since this is so, I shall do what you bid me. You must know, brethren, that the Enemy did not stop pursuing me. Therefore prepare a new remedy and another healing balm, for you shall have to cure still more open wounds in my body and my soul. They are so many that if you take my past troubles, which you have heard, and compare them to those you are about to hear, they will seem trifling. It is as if the powerful rock of Gibraltar were uprooted and thrown into the greatest abyss of the ocean deep. The ocean would cover it as it sank, immense as it is, and no trace of it would remain.

And so that my entire body should be converted into a single wound (Isa. 1.6), this happened: On the other side [of the border between Israel and Judah], my children, Judah and Benjamin, who lived under the dominion of Solomon's son, Rehoboam, in Jerusalem, provoked the Lord to great wrath there. They made statues and groves, performed idolatrous ceremonies under leafy trees, and they defiled themselves in all the forbidden abominations of the nations. And for a small part of these sins[271] Shishak, king of Egypt, came as the instrument of my punishment. He emptied all the treasures and riches from the house of the Lord and the palace and carried off the golden shields which Solomon had made.[272] As I have already related to you, this was the first punishment which I received from alien hands after the Temple had been completed.

I was oppressed by Rehoboam for seventeen years. When he died, he left me in the service and under the yoke of his evil son, Abijam, who clothed himself in the terrible garb of his father.[273] But when Abijam died after three years, Asa entered into possession of the kingdom. He ruled for forty-one years and corrected some of the evils committed by his predecessors; he forbade idolatrous practices, though not completely.[274] His successor, Jehoshaphat, followed the same road for the twenty-five years that he wore the crown; yet he failed to do away completely with my abominable places, because I sacrificed in them against his will and burned incense to the shameful idols.[275] And I became even more dissolute in this abominable sin under the yoke of Jehoram, his son, who followed him in his kingdom, but by no means in his virtue; his perversity gave great assistance to my errors, and he conformed to Ahab's terrible doctrine for eight years.[276] At the end of these eight years he left Ahaziah as heir to his wickedness and royal scepter. In a single year Ahaziah showed the depth of his venomous character. And in order that such a poisonous viper should not completely corrupt the land which provided the people's sustenance and the air from which they received the breath of life, he was killed by Jehu, a general of Jehoram, king of Israel.[277] But with his demise, the ravenous hunger for dominion fully revealed how far the force of evil extended, though it went against divine and human law; for Athaliah, Ahaziah's mother, not respecting the great distance in life she had already traveled and the little distance left for her to go according to the course of nature, usurped the kingdom by force from her own grandson. Yet her tyranny lasted only six years. She was slain by the sword and the crown was handed over to Jehoash, to whom it rightly belonged.[278] Jehoiada, the priest, made a covenant with him and with me[279] that we should return to the Lord with penitence. And for this purpose I destroyed all the altars, groves and images of abomination with that first impetus of zeal.[280] But when the divine spark had passed which illumined me for so short a period of time, I was left in my former darkness, weak in goodness, and even more steeped in evil than before, and I began again to sacrifice to idols and restored the forbidden places. In the forty years that Jehoash reigned, he rebuilt those parts of the Lord's Temple that had been destroyed, but he did not restore the vessels which were missing, for Shishak, king of Egypt, had taken them away. And when Hazael, king of Syria, attacked and besieged Jerusalem, Jehoash paid him in tribute all the wealth which had been consecrated to the Temple of our Lord by the previous kings of Judah. Finally, two of his servants killed him.[281] But then his son Amaziah sat on the throne for twenty-two years. He avenged his father's murder by putting the assassins to death, and followed him closely in his righteousness. Yet I broke all restraints of virtue, and under his rule, I pursued idolatries at full speed. Amaziah was killed by a conspiracy, perhaps because he did not employ full severity and punishment against me and was negligent in the execution of my penalty.[282] After him his son Azariah ruled as king for fifty-two years, and he did what is considered right in the Lord's eyes, though he was afflicted with leprosy, which accompanied him to the grave and made him live in a house apart during his lifetime. His perfection was insufficient to divert me from the crooked and erring path I followed. Indeed, I disobediently abandoned his virtuous example for the groves and hills of idolatry, the source of my perdition.[283] And thus I persisted under the dominion of Jotham, who succeeded Azariah to the royal scepter. He held it for sixteen years and imitated the righteous steps of his father, which were acceptable to our Lord. He built the Temple's upper gate.

By now the divine Majesty had seen that I had become as obstinate and intractable as marble and that the power of the virtuous wheel of these four worthies was too weak to budge me from the sins which I had embraced with both hands.[284] He therefore began to send the serpent, in the form of the King of Syria, into the kingdom of Judah.[285] A hundred and fifty cities were attacked and part of the tribes of Judah and Simeon taken captive; they were seized on the road and the Lord transported them to dark hills.[286]

And in order that I should receive the just punishment for my [ever-increasing] transgressions, Ahaz succeeded to the scepter. He put wood on the fire of my abominations for six continuous years. He built altars, set up groves, made his son pass through fire and employed other heathen ceremonies for which the Lord had driven the heathens from that land. So that he might avoid a siege by the Assyrians, who were coming to punish him and me, he gave the treasures of the Temple and the palace in Jerusalem to the Assyrian king as tribute.[287] Thus this king's wickedness blazed so high that it threatened grave misfortunes in his days for his punishment and mine.

But the righteous Hezekiah intervened to make amends. On Ahaz's death he took the crown and held it for twenty-nine years. His ways were like David's. He obliterated the high places, broke the statues and burned the groves. The clear and spacious stream of his righteous acts absorbed the filthy pools of my abominations and led me with its swift current to spread the sails of my hopes on the vast and spacious sea of the God of Israel.[288] And so that I might place my confidence in Him alone, he shattered the metal serpent called Nehushtan, which Moses had made in the wilderness to bring healing to those who had idolized the calf and which was still worshiped with sacrifice and reverence. Hezekiah was a tributary to the Assyrian king. He gave him the silver which was in the Lord's house and on the Temple gates and the royal treasures as well, in order to bring peace to the kingdom. Though a worthy, he did not rely upon his righteousness alone, but sought rather to appease Azazel[289] with that sacrifice. But the wicked Sennacherib was not placated. Eager to devour still more, he besieged Jerusalem with a large army and showed beastly haughtiness to Judah and offended the Lord's name. For this the Lord of vengeance avenged Himself upon him. He sent a cruel massacre against him in his own lands: during a siege upon Jerusalem a hundred and eighty-five thousand of the Assyrians were killed one night by an angel of the Lord. Terror-stricken, the army broke camp in the morning and ran for refuge. But death continued to pursue the king, and it overtook him when his son, Adrammelech, stabbed him inside of his idol's temple in Assyria.[290]

When the last days of the righteous Hezekiah had arrived, and he was ailing in his bed, the prophet Isaiah came to advise him of his death. He turned his face to the wall and cried out to the Lord and entreated Him with tears. And before the prophet had gone down the stairs,[291] he turned and told the king that the Lord had heard him and granted him a gift of fifteen years of life beyond his allotted days. But then, envied by the Enemy, who diverts and distorts our good steps and is constantly on the watch to trip us, Hezekiah showed all his riches to some ambassadors of the king of Babylonia as a gesture of honor. The Lord was offended by this sin and the prophet threatened Hezekiah with captivity in Babylonia, where his children and all their possessions would be enslaved to Shalmaneser.[292] And though I wished to do penance to avert this threat, Manasseh, who followed on the throne, harmed me rather than helped. During the fifty-five years he reigned, his wickedness resuscitated all the idolatries and abominations of the nations that had been expelled from our land and revived everything that had been destroyed by his father Hezekiah: he raised up the vile altars of Baal, prepared groves like Ahab, the wicked king of Israel, worshiped the planets of the sky and erected two altars for them in the very house of the Lord—something all the more prohibited and forbidden in the place where our Lord had said He would place His name. He made his son pass through the fire; he divined; he practiced witchcraft and thereby communicated with demons. In essence, he gave himself over fully to those evils which would provoke our Lord to anger and went so far as to place an abominable image in the holiness of the Temple, something most vile and outrageous for such a divine place.[293] Thus with his hands he removed the mask I wore—if I still wore it—when I committed my sins, and I brazenly abandoned myself to more dissolute evils than even the idolatrous nations had committed in the land.

The web of my destruction was being woven with these threads, and the need for my punishment was becoming increasingly evident to our Lord. And in order that my sins might take deeper root, when I had been freed from Manasseh's yoke, I entered that of Amon, his son. Since Amon had imbibed his father's lethal poison, at the end of the two years he enjoyed the crown, he was slain by his servants in the very palace where he lived.[294]

Josiah followed him on the throne, but not in his wicked deeds. He was a perfect king like David in the sight of our Lord.[295] He began to reign at the age of eight. In order to lift the exile of righteousness, which his father and grandfather had banished, and give it the choicest place in the land, he killed all the priests of Baal; he cut off the execrable soothsayers with the sword; he uprooted the wizards and diviners from the world; he destroyed and burned all places where idolatry had been committed by past kings, and the altars which Manasseh had erected in the palace of the Lord. As soon as he had cleaned the land of so much abomination, he and the rest of the people of Judah[296] who remained agreed upon a covenant to serve the true God, whose might gives being to all things created. And he spread the sails of his will so freely in His service, that a favorable wind blew upon him from the sky and led him to the encomium which Sacred Scripture gives him with these words: "Before him there was no king like unto him that turned to the Lord with all his heart, with all his soul, with all his might, according to all the Law of Moses, nor after him was there born any like him" (II Kings 23.25).

Yet, all this notwithstanding, the dark fog of my offenses was already so thick that, though Josiah's clear sun shone with all its might upon it, it was unable to find a place where the smallest strain of divine mercy might descend upon me. To the contrary, the great fervor of His wrath which He kindled against Judah did not diminish any of its strength, on account of the terrible Manasseh's abominations, from which my soul and body were still blemished and blackened with fresh stains. That the thoughts of the debased might be confused and that exalted spirits might realize that in the true life, the life to come, there is a sure reward for the righteous; and at the same time, to warn me of the penalty and grave punishment which my wicked deeds could expect, since even the perfect and the good were being punished, the worthy Josiah died at the hands of Pharaoh, king of Egypt, after he had reigned thirty-one years.[297]

And when Jehoahaz, who had learned little of his father's virtues, took possession of the royal scepter, he spurred on the total destruction which was advancing toward me furiously to overthrow me. And he projected so many evils in the sight of the Lord, that, like a plant whose roots are but three months old,[298] he was uprooted from the kingdom by the Pharaoh named Necho and carried captive to Egypt. After killing Jehoahaz, this heathen enemy thenceforth made Jerusalem tributary to himself.

When the poisonous tree of Jehoahaz was thus uprooted and withered and when I presumed that a king similar to the righteous Josiah would flourish, Eliakim, with his hands full of wickedness and his heart made of lethal poison, took possession of the kingdom. He dressed himself in the garb of his wicked predecessors and placed his feet in the dirty footprints they had left on my body and in the Holy Land. But the rod of punishment with which the Lord had threatened Manasseh and which had already begun to touch me, first with Josiah's unfortunate death and then with Jehoahaz's captivity in Egypt, now gave me a third punishment: Nebuchadnezzar, king of the Babylonians, carried away Prince Eliakim from me as a slave for three years. During this time the oppression of captivity sapped part of his venom and he thus atoned for his offenses. His freedom was therefore restored and he was returned to the throne in Jerusalem.[299]

Then a great number of Chaldeans, Assyrians, Moabites and Ammonites attacked me. They fiercely brandished their spears against me, and, as the Lord already determined, Eliakim ordered me to prepare myself patiently and make myself ready to drink the bitter vial of the captivity of Babylon. The Lord had warned me of this on many occasions through His prophets, because of my continual rebelliousness and because of the innocent blood Manasseh had spilled in Jerusalem. And, in order to prevent the woeful sentence from being suspended by some worthy act or righteous deeds which would intercept the Lord's anger, the Lord set Jehoiachin, one of the most wicked kings, in Eliakim's place when He took Eliakim's life after he had ruled eleven years. Jehoiachin showed himself to be so iniquitous in the short three months he had control of the kingdom that he deserved Nebuchadnezzar's attack against me. Nebuchadnezzar took him captive along with his mother, his servants, his princes and his eunuchs, and took for booty all the treasures of the Temple of the Lord and the royal palace. He uprooted all the nobility of the house of Judah, as many as ten thousand from Jerusalem (such a happy city, where tall and noble trees sprang forth and grew so luxuriantly), and brought them into the sterile land of Babylonia to be planted, so that their green branches might wither, for these trees could not take root there. Of all the people, none remained in Judah save the lower classes of the population, the poor and mendicant. Over these Nebuchadnezzar appointed a king of his own choosing, and named him Zedekiah, according to his own pleasure.[300]

The burden of my sins had now reached this unhappy state, and my hope hung by so thin and feeble a thread that a frail hand could snap it. Zedekiah (the last king) clutched this thread with all the strength of his wickedness and continually strove to break it during the eleven years he ruled. He succeeded without difficulty. As a result, Nebuchadnezzar again sought Jerusalem out, leveled its walls and set fire to the holy city and to the Lord's divine Temple, where abominations had already put God's Presence[301] to flight. Nebuchadnezzar arrested King Zedekiah, whom he had personally appointed, killed his children in his presence and then gouged out his eyes. He cruelly tied him with two iron chains and he carried him and the rest of my children in wretched captivity to Babylonia, leaving behind only a few, whose extreme poverty and wretchedness made him number them with the dead and buried. And besides these, there was a small and inferior number left who were fit only to cultivate the land, so that it might not go entirely untilled.[302]

I was thus delivered into the power of their hapless captivity. There seventy years of punishment (and some divine compassion) succeeded in lifting only slightly the scale of my sins, whose weight had brought it to the ground. But the King of the heavens—my true Father, I confess—was moved to pity. Like a merciful father who feels his natural love in the midst of his anger and punishment and is touched with remorse at his child's cries of woe, He slackened and relaxed the hand with which He whipped me. To mitigate the severity of my punishment, He touched Nebuchadnezzar's spirit. Nebuchadnezzar ordered Jehoiachin released from prison, restored his regal garb and gave him a seat of honor at his royal table.[303]

{PART V}

HUNT OF HERONS,
ADAPTED TO THE WICKED KINGS OF JUDAH

The punishment inflicted by Nebuchadnezzar's hand was my fifth, and my way of life, which I narrated to you in the metaphor of the hunt of herons, brought this punishment upon me.

This life was led by Judah and Benjamin in a region near Israel.[304] Twelve or fifteen other hunters of similar stock (whose names were Rehoboam, son of Solomon, Abijam, Jehoram, Ahaziah, Athaliah, Ahaz, Manasseh, Amon, Jehoahaz, Eliakim, Jehoiachin, Zedekiah)[305] came out to hunt in a fresh, green clearing, the terrain of Jerusalem, airy with divine favor and covered with the fresh hopes of the greater blessings the Lord had promised its inhabitants in the heavenly Jerusalem. And while they reigned in the pleasant fields of Jerusalem's happy land, they saw the divine Law on high and from afar. It was like a noble and delicate heron which soared on pinions of inventive speculations, cutting the thin airs of subtle and exalted secrets.

Against it they loosed the thoughts of evil they had been concealing and the false views which lay secret in their breasts, and they impetuously attacked it with the falcons of heinous deeds, idolatries, divinations, sorceries and internecine murders. And wherever the heron flew, wherever the Law's holy precepts and purposes wended their way, they took up a contrary position, for it seemed to them that in this way they would eventually control (rather than be controlled by) the graceful bird of the heavenly Law.

Solomon's determined start in this pursuit gave his successors incentive to attack, for under the shadow of such a notable their errors seemed less grievous, and therefore they committed them lightly, as Rehoboam, Solomon's son, and Abijam, his grandson, soon did. And the wheel of sins, which was turned forcefully by three strong arms in succession, continued to turn by its own momentum. Thus, though the gentle heron's truth swelled with pride and brought remorse to their souls, it was trampled by the weight of pernicious deeds with which its enemy had surrounded it. Thus the holy Law, finding itself at the brink of destruction, endeavored to save itself by the good kings Asa and Jehoshaphat, who succeeded these evil ones. But Jehoram, Ahaziah and Athaliah attacked it fiercely from all sides and the noble game, unable to withstand their furious onslaught, tenderly and pitifully lamented before our Lord of the blows, the cruel sins, committed against it.

Moved by compassion, the Lord sent the divine priest Jehoiada, and the righteous Jehoash, Azariah, Jotham, Ahaz, and Hezekiah to aid and succor it. The heron towered aloft trying to free itself and fly to the most exalted and righteous of these kings. But its foe kept rising and subduing it; it harshly wounded the heron and slashed it repeatedly with the long, sharp claws of the execrable Manasseh and Amon, who erected the two idolatrous altars in the house of the Lord and put the abominable image in the sanctity of the Temple. Thus pieces of the limbs and principal organs of the body of the Law and its divine cult and observance were rent and shattered, and it was stripped of its holy ceremonies, which had covered it like plumes. The populace lost its respect for the heron of the Law and the bird's torn fragments floated aimlessly through the clear, fresh atmosphere created by a few worthy men. Now and then its feathers alighted upon a pure, green blanket of grass; this was the life of the righteous few, a life where true hopes could flourish.

When the wounded heron saw itself at the point of death, it again sought help from the heavens with pitiable cries. And since mercy is never lacking for those that sincerely request it, heaven sent the great worthy Josiah to aid it. He was like a large kite, for he destroyed and overcame all the abominations of the malefactors. But the shrewd enemies then retaliated with Jehoahaz, a spirited sparrow-hawk, the energetic saker Eliakim, the beaked gerfalcon Jehoiachin, and the large hobby Zedekiah, and when they all came together a fierce strife and battle were begun before our Lord. The forces of the wicked were greater in number and power. In addition to the cruel attacks with which its previous enemies had staggered the wearied heron, it was assaulted by these new enemies in large numbers and all at once. Though divine mercy spurred her to fight, her resistance weakened at their harsh onslaught; she there-fore submitted and fled to the heavens with her invisible spirit,[306] leaving her body—the people—in the power of her enemies here on earth.

Shishak, the king of Egypt, attacked my people, tore off the clothing it wore in Rehoboam's reign and carried off all its treasures and riches. Then the ferocious Sennacherib, king of Assyria, took parts of the limbs of Judah and Simeon and ran off with them in his mouth,[307] leaving a hundred and fifty cities empty and in ruins. On the way these two tribes were taken from him by the lupine king of Ethiopia, and the Lord has kept them hidden to this day in the dark hills commonly known as the Caspian Mountains.[308] Then, in Jehoiachin's time, Nebuchadnezzar came with great fury and tore off Judah's head: he took in captivity all the ten thousand nobility of Judah and Benjamin. He later returned after Zedekiah, the last king, and completed the dismemberment of my entire body. He burned and destroyed the holy Temple and its priests and worthies, and the rest of my limbs he carried off to Babylonia, where he had previously enslaved the others.

ISRAEL'S LAMENT ON THE LOSS OF THE FIRST TEMPLE

Alas! Alas! O tears, offer yourselves to this lament, for since you were created, you have never streamed across cheeks for a better cause. Come cloaked in such distinctive grief that even the blind may see the light which is no longer mine. Come not forth from my eyes, for such display befits a common ill. Seek a different way that suits my unusual loss and its towering pre-eminence. Let the world through your changed condi-tion feel the greatness it has lost.

O hapless and luckless day, the most gloomy, blind, bitter and infernal of all those that have been or are to come! You ought not to be counted in the number of days which fill the month and year, nor in the web which they weave in mortals' lives.[309] You were the sword of death that severed life; your gloom and darkness smothered it when it banished the divine light which illumined the entire universe.[310] O hapless day and sad, how right is the land of the Israelites to blaspheme and curse you. You have broken the ladder by which its children rose to commune with the angels, by which the supreme and incomprehensible Glory descended to visit them and to favor the undeserving world of earth. You have snapped the thread of the blessings it gained through such a happy communion. You have cut off its prophecy, the angelic wisdom and divine providence that gave us warnings necessary to the inhabitants of this nether world.[311] You have uprooted the great and holy worthies, those fruitful trees that ennobled and honored the land. You have forbidden us to behold its miracles contrary to nature, which implant the fear of God and the desire to serve Him in the soul of man.[312] You have stripped it of all its rich adornments, and when our blessings ceased, you were the means by which it was sown and swelled with perverse and errant spirits, to the prejudice and scandal of all mankind.

Alas, beloved children, what has become of you? You have more to lament and regret than all the misfortune that can be seen with mortal eyes. You have felt the iron in your entrails and I, who am your soul, perceived the delight your enemies felt as they tore you to pieces. You were appalled by the wounds which the wild fire imprinted on your flesh, and I by the fire which burned the sanctuary of your souls. Oh Israel, Israel, how dearly and bitterly you paid for your good fortunes. The animals you sacrificed before the Lord delivered you from the punishment which your offenses merited, but you were not satisfied. Therefore you, yourself, must now be offered in sacrifice for your sins, for the heavens are no longer content with a substitute. Indeed, even now that your limbs are torn and your blood is spilled on the earth, the Lord's ire has not abated, but His hand still remains outstretched over you.[313] Your errors and wickedness have brought you to such a lowly state that brute animals have attained a superiority over you. They were sacrificed [to the Lord] by the holy hands of divine priests, but you must be sacrificed by the profane and earthly hands of cruel heathens.

Yes, ill-fated Israel, you have a right to grieve. You have suffered more at the hands of the wicked butcher Nebuchadnezzar than from your enemies Sennacherib and Shalmaneser. They offended only your perishable and terrestrial body while Nebuchadnezzar bruised your soul and its blessings when he destroyed your sanctuary, the road to your salvation. They avenged themselves only on your external garb; Nebuchadnezzar destroyed your divine ornaments and inner vestments. They ate only the branches of the tree; he consumed its root and fruits. They mutilated only one finger of your left hand while Nebuchadnezzar, a crueler killer, tore out your right hand and gouged out your eyes. They wounded you with an arrow in the least vital place; he, a most vicious enemy, stuck all his arrows into the side of your heart. They fed their wrath on everything in the element of the air and below, while he, more pernicious, put his hands on the quintessence of all the heavens above. O Nebuchadnezzar, if your understanding could grasp what you have offended! You did not wish to obey God's will, which directed you, and because of your wickedness you deserved to become the executioner and rod of His punishment. Do not act haughtily toward me, for you were only the axe that hewed me out, while the Lord was the hand that moved it.[314] Neither the power of all the earth nor the forces of the entire universe are strong enough to resist God's might. How could your weak and puny army block the heavenly host that used to defend me? But woe, wretched me, I am raving. I am drowning amidst the hazards of the sea and I threaten those who watch me from the calm of the land. My hands and feet are tied like a calf in the fold, and the slaughterer's knife is at my throat;[315] I have received the lethal blow, and yet unconsciously chew the food which he offers me in consolation.

O tears, do not cease to run. Let the milk I once suckled fall with you, turned to gall and poison. And if you cannot satisfy my sorrow, then stop, for I do not want you to fall. O limbs of mine, what secret or marvel do you hold, that the turbulence and force of my great misfortunes can fit into your small, weak and fragile frame? O Lord, why do You give the light of life to the afflicted[316] and humble the conquered, by showing them others in happy repose? If You desired me to enter this world, I should have been returned from whence I came when my feet first touched the earth and I uttered my first cry; then I would not have offended You or wronged You, nor would my own faults have tempted me to rush like a fool to the brink of destruction.[317] You have placed me in a frame made of clay and adobe, subject to temptation's unabating winds and storms; how can that which rots and is infirm by its very nature sustain itself when it is buffeted to and fro?[318] O mortal tongue, I own you and yet you offend me. Give expression now to everything I feel within. For my grief and sorrows are struggling to come forth; they cannot be contained in the infinite soul where they settled, for they have surpassed its compass.

O Jerusalem, once holy and happy city, what has befallen you? What has become of your riches human and divine? Which lack shall I now sense anew and lament? One misfortune is as terrible as the next: which shall I say is most important, when they are all equal?

Shall I bewail my divine riches, like the cherubim on the Ark of the firmament of the Lord? Here His glory made its nest and hovered over them. Here sounds like words issued forth from the One who created the worlds[319] with one word alone.[320] Here my sad eyes now see ravens and birds of the night build their nests.

Shall I shed bloody tears on my sad cheeks for the tablets, inscribed by the hand of the Infinite Power and delivered to His servant, Moses, on the mountain of Sinai with many miracles—tremors of the earth, bolts of lightning, sounds of fear and fright and other marvels which an earthly tongue cannot depict? Shall I bewail his rod, into which the Lord infused such a lofty power that it split the Red Sea into twelve parts,[321] and as its waters congealed into mountains,[322] it made a dry road through which I passed; and to slake the thirst I suffered in the desert, it changed the course of nature by making water run from hard rocks?[323]

Shall I cover myself with black, coarse wool for the Urim and

Thummim engraved on the High Priest's breastplate, which could marvelously predict victory or defeat in battles?[324] Shall I bewail with bitterness and dejection the loss of the divine fire which descended miraculously from the heavens and accepted and consumed the sacrifices in the sight of all the living? Shall I raise the cries of my doleful plaint to the stars for the priests and Levites who administered such a lofty service and whose lives were cut off by sword and fire? Shall I flee from human conversation and seek fearful deserts where I may share the wild beasts' victuals in sorrow and grieving for the greatest loss that mortals have seen—the loss of righteous men, the preceptors of the Law who were transfixed on the sword's edge, and their virtuous disciples who were impaled on spears?[325] With what manner of sadness shall I sorrow in my distress for my newly-born children who, undefended, were cast to the ground by the sword and swaddled in dust and blood or dashed against walls, as I heard their plaintive cries and piteous groans, with no mourners to look upon them with compassion and be grieved?[326]

How shall I express my grief as I see my foe waiting for a child to leave its mother's womb so that he may cut off its days before her eyes?[327] O cruel, voracious hands, could you not show to those who had not tasted one moment of the world some of the consideration reserved for those who have already spent many days and years in it?

Israel, Israel, your rupture is incurable and your wound is sore.[328] So, brothers, is there a remedy so complete and sufficient that it can heal this long illness, or a net of consolation so spacious and large that it can contain these grievous and prolonged disasters? Consider it well and you will see that my enemies have overcome all means of comfort and remedy. What medicine shall I apply to the wounds which the fire burned in my entrails, what ointment to the mortal blows which the sword struck and cut within my soul? Their marks are not removable, however much they are purged, and my scars will always leave a trace, no matter how skilled the surgeon.

O enemies of mine, you were swifter than the eagles of the sky when you flew upon the mountains of Jerusalem to injure me; the wind of my offenses favored your wings. O my daughters, whiter than pure milk and more beautiful and delightful than the clear sun, I saw hunger turn your skin the color of the Brazilians, your covering the color of the Ethiopians. I saw your faces slashed by the sword and cloaked in deadly anguish. O infants, tender and delicate, I saw your souls depart on the dry nipples of your mothers' breasts, and I saw the spirits of valiant youths, enfeebled by hunger and thirst, leave their bodies stretched out and abandoned along the city's squares. O honored and venerable elders, how shall I mourn the destruction and eradication of your great authority and knowledge? I saw them uncover your hoary heads with disdain and scorn, and split the tonsured heads of your honored elders with their swift, sharp swords. O death, how in a few hours you have uprooted and swallowed the fruit of so many years!

O frail and earthly blessings, I would miss you but little if, in compensation for your absence, so many spiritual and divine blessings still remained to me. Who will now, like Ezekiel, see the divine Glory atop a chariot of fiery flames, moved by holy animals?[329] Who will now see the lion with eagles' wings, the bear, the ferocious tiger, and the large and more dreadful animal with ten horns and iron teeth, as Daniel did, and have revealed to him through such visions the fall of kingdoms, the rise of others, the humbling of some peoples and the prospering of other nations?[330] To whom shall the admonitions to fear the Lord now be communicated, as they were to Jeremiah and Isaiah and the rest of the great company of prophets? "Prophecy has now abandoned the prophet; the law is perished from the priest and counsel is lacking from the elders" (Ezek. 7.26).

O miserable and persecuted body of mine, all your organs must be altered and sensitized still more, for the exquisiteness of the pain of my misfortunes cannot be felt with usual and customary feelings. My eyes, which have bewailed only lowly and terrestrial losses, are unworthy of participating in a loss so lofty and divine. My thought and heart, which have been afflicted with only common disasters and misfortunes, do not possess the merit to mourn a disaster so pre-eminent and unique.

Yet whither shall I direct my lamentations, O heaven, for my mortal anguish will not let my tongue cease. O, affliction of mine, offer me an argument that I can plead against heaven.[331] Could it be that like a surgeon, you wished to amputate the rotten limbs, the perverts and sinners, from my body? Then you have exceeded moderation with your treatment, for in your wrath your hands and knife have moved beyond the sick limbs and cut the healthy ones as well. Did you not wish to see that you have cut off some righteous and good people who did not deserve to be included in that company?

ZICAREO: Do not proceed with your complaint. Cease lamenting now, O Israel; you are raving from your pain. Let not your tongue touch again what is forbidden, for you have nothing to complain against heaven, as your true history attests. And be reminded that the Lord said to the man clothed in linen: "Go through the midst of the city of Jerusalem and set a mark[332] on the foreheads of the men that sigh and are grieved for all the abominations that are committed in it. And the others smite without pity, but to those who have the mark do not draw near" (Ezek. 9.4-6). Thus your healthy flesh was not cut off, nor was any creature punished with death or exile who had not first, with his own hands, made the sword that cut him and prepared the snare into which he fell. "For the land has become full of the judgment of murderers and the city has filled with violence" (Ezek. 7.23). "Your whole body was sick from the sole of your foot unto your head, O Israel" (Isa. 1.6).

For if Jeroboam, king of Israel, made two golden calves in Samaria for the people to idolize, Rehoboam, king of Judah, set up groves and erected statues to foul idols in Jerusalem to provoke the Lord's wrath. If Nadab, king of Israel, followed in his father's filthy footsteps, Abijam, king of Judah, also dressed himself in his sire's wicked garb. If Baasa revived all Jeroboam's sins in Samaria, Jehoram conformed to the evil Ahaz and practiced his execrable doctrine in Jerusalem. If Elah, king of Israel, imitated all the wickedness of his forebears, Ahaziah, king of Judah, inherited all the abominations and idolatries of his predecessors. If Zimri was converted into a scorpion in Samaria, the woman Athaliah was transfigured into a viper in Jerusalem. If Omri, king of Israel, decided to venture beyond all his predecessors in the performance of deadly evils, Ahaz, king of Judah, put wood and tar on the fire of your abominations by making his son pass through the bonfire and practicing other false ceremonies of heathendom. If Ahab, with his exploits and brazen sinning, killed the memory of all who had reigned in Samaria before him, Manasseh revived everything that had been destroyed by his father, Hezekiah, and erected altars to the idol Baal inside the Lord's house in Jerusalem. If Ahaziah, king of Israel, imbibed and absorbed the noxious liquor of his father, Ahab, Amon, king of Judah, did not depart from the wicked and shameful ways of Manasseh, his progenitor. If Jehoram fed you with abominable idolatry in Samaria, Jehoahaz gave you poison to drink in Jerusalem. If the other Jehoahaz, king of Israel, went full speed ahead along Jeroboam's road of wickedness, Eliakim, king of Judah, marked out footsteps as dirty as his forebears' in the clean land. If Jehoash did not remove himself from the company of the evil doers in Samaria, Jehoiachin entered their number in Jerusalem. If Jeroboam (II), king of Israel, did not swerve from the execrable path of his forebears, Zedekiah, king of Judah, clung with both hands to the wicked deeds of his predecessors.

Thus you were justly punished by the Lord and punishment for your wickedness was meted out by a just scale, for these two tribes of Judah and Benjamin which the seed of David ruled in Jerusalem were as rotten as the Ten Tribes which separated with Jeroboam in Samaria. "The iniquity of the house of Israel and of Judah has become exceedingly great, for they have said: 'The Lord has forsaken the land, and the Lord sees not'" (Ezek. 8.6-12). And in order that you might understand how much more Judah sinned than Israel, hear these words of the Lord: "Israel's backsliding has proved her more righteous than Judah, the forsaker of His Law" (Jer. 3.11). "The sin of Judah was written with a pen of iron and with the point of a diamond was it engraved" (Jer. 17.1).

YCABO: I acknowlege that my wickedness prepared the trap for me and my rebelliousness snared me in it, but I have wanted you to remove from my eyes a veil of other doubts which now covers them. You have told me that my two limbs, Judah and Benjamin (for whom I now mourn and lament as much as I did for the Ten Tribes of Israel) that were carried into captivity by Assyria, were rotten. I have given you indications that Jerusalem's offenses were qualitatively as grave as Samaria's great sins; but in quantity it was not so, for the nineteen kings of Israel who ruled over the Ten Tribes were all poisonous plants whose venom-ous fruits killed my children's freedom and destroyed the blessings they possessed. And even Judah, whose dominion began with the dawn of a light of righteousness, changed its course in the middle of its road, turned backward, blocked it, and finally completely covered it with a thick, dark cloud of sins. Thus on neither Judah nor Israel was there any place for God's compassion to alight. But these two sons, Judah and Benjamin, for whom I am now celebrating such bitter nuptials, had among their twenty kings, eight plants which bore healthful and choice fruit. Their names were Asa, Jehoshaphat, Jehoash, Amaziah, Azariah, Jotham, Hezekiah, and the one resembling an angel of the Lord, Josiah, as you, brothers, well know. Then why did these men not resist and ward off the penalty and punishment which was descending from heaven against the sinners? And how is it that they did not find the mantle of God's mercy to cover and repair the destruction and captivity of their erring and murderous people?

ZICAREO: You have stated your case very well. Now be attentive, for you will see born from your doubt the merciful purpose which you seek. You recall well that the nineteen evil kings of the Ten Tribes of Israel, gathered in Samaria under Jeroboam, only reigned a total of two hun-dred forty-one years, seven months, and seven days. At the end of this time they were overcome by their final captivity, that of the Assyrians, which has lasted so long and has cloaked the Ten Tribes in an enduring oblivion. But the scepter of the twenty kings who ruled over Judah and Benjamin in Jerusalem lasted for three hundred and seventy-six years and six months. Thus the righteousness of the eight worthies whom you have mentioned prolonged the life of the kingdom of Judah over that of Israel by a hundred and thirty-five years. For while the wicked were daily undoing the web of human lives and endeavoring to turn the wheel which would begin the seventy years of captivity in Babylon,[333] these eight worthies moved among them with their righteousness. They rewove part of the web, and at times the power of their holy works even re-strained the wheel of captivity which was about to begin its furious whirl. But against the haste and speed which the wicked devoted to undoing the web and the might which their numbers applied to the wheel, all the righteous men's resistance proved powerless, although God's mercy bestowed upon them as much favor as they were capable of receiving. For the compassion of the heavens is prepared to give infinitely as long as there is room for it in the recipient.

Therefore, here is the mercy you seek, attained by the righteousness of the eight good men, and the benefit which you received from the Lord's hand on their account. This mercy would still be protecting you if you did not choose to go to the extreme with your wicked deeds. And still, now that you have reached the extreme and placed yourself in the hands of the Babylonians, your enemies, you have clearly seen the fatherly mercy with which the Lord visited you even in their land, as He cast aside your rebelliousness and recalled His love for your fathers.[334]

But my talk is long, and so let us leave it for the morning; night is falling and we must walk a good distance to our cottages. Wherefore, brother Ycabo, I entreat you earnestly to return home with us for shelter. A pleasant supper and delightful sleep await you, and you will temporarily dispel the anguish which the memory of your past happiness brings you in your present sad state. In the morning we shall speak further of this, and you shall also favor us with the continuation of your story.

YCABO: Let us go, for it would be folly to reject such company and hospitality, especially when they are so graciously offered.

END OF THE FIRST DIALOGUE.

SECOND

DIALOGUE

DEALING

WITH THE REBUILDING

OF

THE TEMPLE

AND

ALL THAT OCCURRED TO IT

UNTIL

IT WAS DESTROYED

BY TITUS,

AND

THE CONSOLATION

FOR SUCH A LOSS.

SUBTITLES

FOR DIALOGUE II

Consolation for the loss of the first temple
Blessings which were lacking in the second temple
Events of the second temple
(The changes which were made by the translators
of the torah [into greek])
[Antiochus' persecution]
[The martyrdom of eleazar]
[The martyrdom of hannah & her seven sons]
[The maccabees & the hasmonean dynasty]
[The coming of the romans]
(The construction of the second temple)
[The rebellions against rome]
Lament on the loss of the second temple
Consolation for the loss of the second temple

ZICAREO, YCABO, NUMEO—INTERLOCUTORS

ZICAREO: Get up, brother Numeo. Let us awaken to hear Ycabo's sorrowful tale. Let us talk with him as we guide our flocks to some luxuriant pasture, for it is my greatest concern to keep the promise I made to him yesterday. And unless I am mistaken, I shall find cogent arguments to ease the burden of his anxieties.

YCABO: I am not asleep, for constant wakefulness provides the greatest refreshment for my wearied limbs. When mortals rest from all their cares, instead of sleeping in serenity, I review in my mind the wretchedness of my life and find comfort in an endless stream of tears. Thus, although last night was one of summer's shortest, it seemed longer to me than December's longest. I spent it in anticipation of receiving some comfort from your quickening arguments, though my misfortunes are so great that it is difficult to find any relief.

But it seems to me that this place is better for threshing grain than for feeding cattle. Let us therefore move away, and I will help you lead your flocks beyond that ridge; as I came I noticed that the grass there had not been trodden by sturdy oxen or trampled by impetuous hunters, and a clear river passes through its midst. As the sun rises on high and the importunate crickets begin to chirp, your sheep will feed there and quench their thirst.

NUMEO: He is right. Let us move on.

ZICAREO: Lead on, Ycabo, and you, Numeo, keep an eye on that pregnant sheep which is grimacing with pain; do not let her remain behind. And I shall return to the matter we were speaking of.

YCABO: I would like nothing better.

CONSOLATION FOR THE LOSS OF THE FIRST TEMPLE

ZICAREO: Is it possible you do not remember that when Nebuchadnezzar died, more than twenty-two years after the destruction of the Temple,[1] and after him his son Evil-merodach, Belshazzar succeeded to the empire of Babylonia and Chaldea?[2] He made a sumptuous banquet for all his princes to celebrate the victory he had won over the combined armies of Cyrus, King of Persia, and Darius, King of the Medes. Afterwards, when he had become merry with wine, Belshazzar sent for the sacred vessels of the Lord's Temple which Nebuchadnezzar had brought from Jerusalem, and profaned them by inviting his filthy, idolatrous company to drink from them.[3] The exalted King of the heavens was moved to anger out of jealousy for His holy vessels. At that very moment he sent down an invisible angel, who wrote these words on the wall before

111

the king: *He counted, He counted, [He weighed,] He divided the Persians.* The letters were Hebrew, but the language was Syriac.[4] The king saw no part of the writer's body but his fingers, and he blanched and fainted in fright and bedevilment. But not another person present saw this marvelous vision. The Chaldean sages, with all their knowledge, vainly attempted to interpret it. But it was Daniel who finally explained it: "The God of Israel has *counted* the number of his enemies and has cut them off. The Lord used the word counted twice, because He had twice counted the days of Belshazzar's reign: once to fix the time Belshazzar was to hold sway over his kingdom, and now to appoint the time of its destruction. He had *weighed* the enemy in the balance and found him wanting. The God of Israel has therefore *divided* the enemy's kingdom and delivered it to Darius and Cyrus, kings of the Persians and the Medes."[5]

This sentence, Ycabo, gave evidence of the Lord's pity and His desire for your restoration. And in order that His judgment might be executed and the seventy years of your captivity completed, as He had informed you through Jeremiah,[6] you recall, do you not, how on that very night Belshazzar was killed by his most trusted eunuch? Since the writing on the wall said that Belshazzar[7] was to be destroyed and his kingdom was to pass over to Cyrus and Darius, his servant wished to gain their favor by accelerating these events.[8] He brought Belshazzar's head to Cyrus and Darius and told them of the defilement of the Lord's vessels, of the writing, and of Daniel's interpretation. When the kings heard of this prodigy, which had occurred in so short a time, they knelt devoutly on the ground, worshiped the Lord of the heavens, and said, "There is no doubt that the God of Israel is much more powerful and true than all other gods, for His power and will decide who will rule over the kingdoms of earth and who will be removed from the thrones they possess."

The King on high then infused into their hearts a love for His people Israel. Accordingly, Cyrus made a vow to the Lord that he would restore His Temple, return His vessels and liberate all your children from their captivity as soon as he had won the victory promised him by the prophet. Cyrus and Darius both went to battle with their powerful armies, and, with heaven's favor, they swiftly subjugated all the land of the Chaldeans and Babylonians.[9]

And to avenge you, the Lord decided that your Babylonian enemies should be punished in the same manner as they had vented their anger against you. Do you not remember how their children were dashed to pieces before their mothers' eyes and how their sheltered virgins were violated?[10] And how, for your greater happiness, the Lord moved King Cyrus' spirit and reminded him of the promise He had made to liberate you? And therefore in the first year of Cyrus' newly acquired reign,[11] did you not see him proclaim a general amnesty throughout his dominion for all your children who were captives in Babylonia, and send them to rebuild the Lord's Temple as it had been in former days? And to this

end Cyrus gave you a large quantity of his own silver, gold and vestments, and a large supply of provisions and men to help in the construction of the building.

Cyrus restored to you all the service vessels of the Temple which
Nebuchadnezzar had brought to Babylonia and placed in his god's
profane shrine. There were five thousand and forty vessels, all made of
gold and silver.[12]

Free and well-provisioned, many of your children immediately departed, taking many priests and slaves of both sexes. They were under
the leadership of Ezra, Eliakim, Jeshua, Mordecai and other princes of
the houses of Judah and Benjamin.[13] Thus they again entered their
lands, prosperous, free and favored by heaven. The people showed their
great joy, singing psalms, playing tuneful instruments, and offering sacrifices and gifts of thanksgiving for the great blessing they had been
granted.

Did you not see the divine Temple rebuilt? How happy were the cries
and shouts of joy when the foundations of the holy house were laid!
They blended with the tears of priests and Levites and old princes who
had seen the First Temple and recalled the greater blessings of the past,
so that the sound of joy of the one group could not be distinguished
from the sad wail of the other.[14]

Your heathen neighbors, who had been brought to Samaria by the
king of Assyria when he emptied that land of the Ten Tribes, attended
this great and tumultuous rejoicing. But they went to Darius to slander
the project and strove to obstruct it.[15] Yet you remember well that until
the Temple was rebuilt the Lord defended it continually, and you saw
the marvelous edifice finally completed on the third day of the month of
Adar, in the sixth year of the reign of Darius the Second.[16]

And from the time that the divine structure of the Temple was erected,
you clearly saw that its prosperity and greatness constantly increased.
When Artaxerxes later succeeded to the Babylonian empire, his spirit
was touched by the Lord most high, who continued to protect you with
His mercy. Artaxerxes sent Ezra, a prophetic scribe, with lavish gifts of
gold and silver to present to the Lord. Ezra also obtained permission for
the city of Jerusalem to be rebuilt.[17] And although your enemies,
Sanballat, Tobiah, the Arabians, the Ammonites and the Ashdodites,
bitterly opposed and obstructed the rebuilding,[18] the Lord gave you
strength and victory: you completed your task. You built a city of strong
walls, high towers and beautiful buildings. And you ennobled it and
made it flourish; and it covered you with new plumage, replacing the
feathers of which you had been shorn and stripped.[19]

Thus you see how the merciful God put a healing plaster on the
wounds which you had inflicted upon yourself with your own hands and
lifted you out of the lake in which you were drowning. You called
the cruel Nebuchadnezzar to raze Jerusalem's walls to the ground, but He
called merciful Cyrus to raise them up to the heavens. You brought the

enemy Nebuchadnezzar to lay your city waste and disperse you, but the Lord brought this friend to prosper it with sumptuous buildings in which you could take shelter. You stripped the priests and Levites of their garb, but the Lord now clothed them with their holy vestments and adorn' ments. You killed them by depriving them of the works of their service, but the Lord now revived them by occupying them with the holy sacri' fices. You exiled yourself from your lands in captivity, but the Lord restored you to them with liberty. You covered the daughters of Zion with coarse cloth and base apparel, but the Lord now covered them with rich vestments. The blackness and melancholy which had disfigured their white flesh and faces you now saw completely cloaked by joy. The dis' respect and scorn with which venerable elders had been treated you now saw converted into high honor and esteem. If the learning of the Law had ceased, you now saw it making its course anew.[20] If those who taught it had been killed by the sword, you now saw others quickened [sic][21] in their place by God's mercy. If the land had cried in your absence, it now joyfully received your new presence and invited you to partake of its marvelous fruits. If the power and scepter had been humiliatingly removed from your kings, you now saw them possess great dominion, their heads covered with royal crowns. Thus you now saw the people who had been carried captive to Babylonia so wretched and afflicted returned to Jerusalem with great pomp and celebration.

And above all this, the Lord wished to apply a still more perfect medi' cine to the wound you had received. He gave you vengeance against Nebuchadnezzar, the rod of your punishment who had offended you.[22] He broke this rod before your eyes and destroyed his entire kingdom— as I have narrated to you—by the hands of the Medes, those extremely cruel archers, whose arrows have no pity even for infants in the womb.[23] Nebuchadnezzar's wicked deeds and many more grievous ills than those which he committed against you fell upon his head to avenge you for his joy and vainglory at your suffering. The Lord overthrew that Babylon which was an ornament of all kingdoms, the Chaldeans' beauty and pride,[24] as He had overthrown Sodom and Gomorrah. In fine, He de' stroyed that entire land on your account in such a way that "the Arab shall no longer pitch his tent there, nor shall the shepherds make their cattle lie down there." "Rather it is a place of lying down for poisonous animals. He has turned it into a dwelling of ostriches and a desert where satyrs (animals in human form)[25] dance about and owls are heard hoot' ing in the place where magnificent houses stood, and dragons roar on the sites of stately and costly palaces" (Isa. 13.19-22). Therefore in this way "the Lord made Lucifer, son of the morning, descend from heaven into the depth of the abyss" (Isa. 14.12) and He avenged you, O Israel, and raised your low estate to the stars.

Let your lament cease, and be consoled, for the Lord beat into wind the haughty thoughts in the heart of the one who presumed to mount to the height of the clouds and be equal to the Most High,[26] and He satisfied your longings for your land and your desires to have your freedom. Cover your face with joy, for "Fallen, fallen is Babylon and all the images of her gods has the Lord shattered to the ground" (Isa. 21.9); and He restored your holy Temple that you might serve the Most High there. Change your sad attire. Since the Lord made the land of Babylonia the sepulcher of all its offspring and gave your barren spouse an infinite number of children from your body,[27] clothe your heart with contentment. Since you have seen the sun and stars darken for the Babylonians and shine more brilliantly for the children of Israel, banish sadness from your soul. This is the origin of the proverb, foretold by the prophet Isaiah, which arose among your children in Jerusalem concerning the king of Babylon: "How has the collector of rents ceased; how has the tributary of gold ceased!" (Isa. 14.4). And you again collected tribute from all kingdoms. Therefore consider yourself among the consoled and the joyous. For this is always the portion of those that spoil you and the lot of those that destroy you, O Israel.[28] Tell me now, what further remedies could you wish for your suffering and what greater relief for the pain of which you complain? It seems to me you should be satisfied, if you have no new ill to complain of.

BLESSINGS WHICH WERE LACKING IN THE SECOND TEMPLE

YCABO: The consolation you have applied to my tribulation regarding Babylonia would have been sufficient if the felicity which I previously possessed had been fully restored to me. Yet the garment with which the Lord now replaced the long and substantial garb of my former blessings (which had been taken away) was too short and most inadequate for me, for in the Second Temple I lacked the most important spiritual and material gems of my previous riches. The gift of prophecy, by which the secret of everything our Lord was planning for the weal or woe of all mortals was disclosed, now left me and visited me no more. The celestial fire which descended from heaven onto the sacrifices and consumed them, ceased. The Ark of the covenant with the Tablets of the Law which Moses fashioned, and the curtains which had been made for it in the desert disappeared, because Jeremiah cached them in the hollow of a cave on Mount Nebo. The urn of manna which sustained Israel in the desert, the Urim and Thummim, the cherubim, and the silken skein were lacking.[29] In the First Temple no woman ever miscarried at the smell of the sacrificial meat, nor was there as much as a fly in the house where the sacrifices were slaughtered. No pollution came upon the High Priest on the Day of Atonement. The rains did not quench the fire of the logs from the woodpile. The wind never succeeded in changing the course of the straight pillar of smoke which ascended to the sky. No flaw was ever found in the first ears of corn or in the two breads or the shewbread.

Though people were crowded in the holy Temple because of the large multitude in attendance, when they prostrated themselves they had plenty of room, even though when they stretched out their bodies, they occupied more space. No snake, scorpion or any other poisonous creature harmed any person in Jerusalem; nor did any man say to another when they went to Jerusalem, "This place is too narrow for me."[30]

All this I enjoyed in the First Temple, but in the Second it was not so; instead just the opposite of all these things happened. Then how can my pain be assuaged, since I have so many open wounds left that need to be closed?

ZICAREO: I confess to you that the medicine of the Second Temple was insufficient to cure all the ills you had received, but it was a visitation by our Lord and a fulfillment of His prophecy to you to show you that this lack was not due to Him, and He told you so through Jeremiah's lips: "After the seventy years are accomplished in Babylon, I will visit you and I will fulfill My good word to bring you back to this place" (Jer. 29.10). But since you still feel your sorrow, I should still very much like to know what you did with this blessing that you possessed, whatever it was.

YCABO: Yet it would be better, brother, for you not to know it, for it will give you pain to hear it and me great sadness to recall it. Still I shall obey you since you wish it so.

EVENTS OF THE SECOND TEMPLE

After the Second Temple had been built, I found myself perplexed when the first sacrifice was offered, since I could not bring any terrestrial fire to it[31] and celestial fire failed to come from heaven as it formerly did. Finally, an old man who had lived at the time of the First Temple discovered a deep well and drew out of it a handful of thick liquid resembling honey; and when he spilled it on the logs of the altar, it suddenly ignited into a terrible fire, so high that it sent forth an immense flame which roamed all over. And it moved and lapped with such agility that all the bystanders were compelled to flee and station themselves far off to observe it, as it went about purifying the Temple. You should know, brethren, that this was part of the celestial fire which used to descend for the sacrifices during the First Temple, and which Jeremiah hid in the well at the time of its destruction.[32] The Second Temple used this, and not the direct fire from heaven which the First Temple had used.

Later, when Jaddua became High Priest, I committed a grievous sin. Manasseh, Jaddua's brother, married a daughter of Sanballat, an inhabitant of Mount Gerizim; and since Manasseh refused to remove her from her father's house and bring her to Jerusalem, as his brethren who married foreign wives used to do, he was compelled to forfeit the priesthood. For this reason his father-in-law, Sanballat, asked Alexander the Macedonian for permission to build a temple on Mount Gerizim, so that his son-in-law might be priest there, since he could not be a priest in Jerusalem. His request was granted. The temple on Mount Gerizim did great harm to the one in the Holy City, for many wicked people of the rabble, who had concealed their wickedness because they had had nowhere to display it, began to go to that sinful temple to offer the required sacrifices; and they abandoned the true Temple of the Lord.[33] With this sin I began to provoke heaven again. This condition lasted until the time of King Hyrcanus, the son of Simon the Maccabean, who destroyed it.

When Alexander the Macedonian died, four princes followed him as rulers of the Empire. One of these, Seleucus [was king in Syria], and another, Ptolemy, was king in Egypt.[34] Ptolemy asked Jerusalem to send him men who could teach him the Law. Seventy priests were sent, and with them, a distinguished man named Eleazar. These teachers expounded the Law to Ptolemy, and they translated the twenty-four books of the Holy Scriptures from Hebrew into the Greek tongue. The king separated them when they began to translate, and they altered several passages so as not to confuse his understanding; yet when each one's work was later examined, it was discovered that they were in agreement in everything they had changed, by a miracle of the Lord.[35] The changes were as follows:

THE PASSAGES WHICH WERE CHANGED BY THOSE WHO TRANSLATED THE LAW[36]

Where it says, "In the beginning God created the heavens and the earth" (Gen. 1.1), they translated "God created in the beginning," so that it should not be presumed that there was anything first except the Lord.

"Let us make man" (Gen. 1.26), they changed to "I will make man."

[And the passage telling of the building of the tower of Babel], "Let us go down and let us there confound their language" (Gen. 11.7), they changed to: "I will go down and I will confound," so that this statement should not lead to the inference that there were many gods.

"Sarah laughed within herself" (Gen. 18.12), they translated "Sarah laughed speaking with those near her," so that the king should not say, "Who told you what went on inside her?"

They translated: "In their anger they slew the ox, and in their self-will they broke the crib" (Gen. 49.6), so that the king should not object, "What relationship is there between a man and an ox?"

They translated: "And Moses took his wife and his sons and set them upon a beast of burden," (Ex. 4.20), so that the king should not mock Moses, master and giver of the Law, for riding "on an ass."

They translated: "Now the period of time that the children of Israel were in Egypt *and in all other lands* was four hundred and thirty years"

(Ex. 12.40). The children of Israel were in Egypt only two hundred and ten years, from the time Jacob said, "I went down there";[37] and the Hebrew letters of these words, "I went down," add up to two hundred and ten years. But their reckoning of four hundred and thirty was from the year of the birth of Isaac, who was Abraham's holy seed.

They translated: "And on the young of the children of Israel He did not lay His hand" (Ex. 24.11); for if they had said "on the big ones," as Scripture says, the king might claim that the adults escaped while the young did not.

They translated: "Nothing that was desirable did I take from them" (Num. 16.15); for if they had followed the Scripture which said, "I did not take an ass," the king would claim: "But he took another gift or present of greater value."

They translated: "For the Lord your God divided them [i.e., the planets of the sky] that they might give light to all peoples" (Deut. 4.19). For if they had followed what Scripture says, "The holy and blessed Lord divided them for all peoples," he would think that the Lord gave the people permission to worship the stars.

"He has gone and honored other gods whom I did not command him to honor" (Deut. 17.3): they added "to honor" so that the king should not say "you have already called them to the cult of strange gods."

For "the hare," they used the metaphor "small of foot" (Lev. 11.6; Deut. 14.7); for Seleucus' mother was also named "Hare," and he might think, "The Jews are mocking me."[38]

In short, they changed all these passages since they understood from the wicked Ptolemy that his intention was to carp on something to divert them from the service of God. But after he saw how all their translations were miraculously in accord, his attitude improved somewhat. He sent them back to Jerusalem with lavish gifts, and he freed a hundred and fifty thousand Jews who had gone to live in Egypt,[39] that they might accompany the others back home. In addition he sent a table of pure, solid gold, weighing a thousand talents, to the Temple of the Lord. On it was etched a lifelike picture of the entire land of Egypt and the Nile River, which runs through it and supplies it with water. Ptolemy also sent various precious stones whose appearance and design were so unusual and marvelous that their like has never again been seen in the world.[40]

[ANTIOCHUS' PERSECUTION]

But after these wonders and mercies had been sent to me from heaven, the Enemy envied me and infused a large draft of bitterness into my sweetness. Malignant thorns began cropping up among my children. They brought into the world a king named Antiochus[41] (who later reigned a short time in Macedonia and Egypt), that I might be punished. From this group of my wicked children came forth also Menelaus, Simon, Alcimus and many other similar men who left Jerusalem to bear slanderous reports to Antiochus, and to my great harm, rigorously followed his evil example.[42] Then a prodigious sign appeared over the Holy City; it could be seen nightly in the sky between heaven and earth. It was a likeness of fiery horses, and their riders held golden weapons in their hands and fought with one another. This sign appeared for forty continuous days. When the wicked Israelites beheld it, they took it for a portent, for it appeared to be an indictment of the vile Antiochus. These wicked men reported it to Antiochus, saying also that the people of Jerusalem thought it was a sign portending his death and that they rejoiced at it. This incensed Antiochus. He attacked me with a powerful army, and inflicted cruel destruction upon Jerusalem. He took captive and put to death by sword a considerable number of people, and dispersed a large group of worthies. They fled in fear to nearby forests, where in their hunger they ate grass like animals and foraged for food like savage beasts.[43]

But this enemy was still unsatisfied, and he left his generals and governors in the land of Judah and charged them to afflict the Jewish people. Antiochus built a large city by the sea, and named it Antioch. Within the city he erected a golden idol in his likeness, and ordered all his subjects to worship it and to bring the children of Israel there to do the same; and any Israelite that refused was to be killed. He further ordered that the Israelites were to be compelled to eat pork and forbidden to keep the Sabbath or to perform circumcision; the death penalty was decreed for anyone who transgressed these commands.[44]

These unfortunate orders were enforced so strongly that Philip, the governor Antiochus left in the land, prohibited the people from observing almost every law. He favored the wicked and killed many good people. But since the holy Law cannot be subdued (regardless of how many threats of death are placed in the way of its observers), two women were found who had secretly circumcised their sons. These Philip punished with barbarous cruelty: he had them hurled down from a tower with their children at their breasts, and they were dashed to pieces.[45]

[THE MARTYRDOM OF ELEAZAR]

After this, Eleazar, chief of the priests, was arrested and brought before Philip. Philip told him craftily, "Eleazar, prudent and wise priest, you will carry your hoary head to the grave wet with blood if you will not eat the meat of my sacrifices." The worthy replied, "I will not take lightly the precept of my God, who is the Lord of all the earth." Philip spoke more kindly to him in an attempt to persuade him, saying, "You know that I love you and that I wish to pardon your old age. Let a little of the meat of the sacrifices that your people are accustomed to eat be brought here secretly, and eat it in front of the people so that they may see it and say that you ate of my sacrifices. And thus you will escape death." To this the saintly Eleazar, in whose goodness there was no taint and whose virtue was unfeigned, replied resolutely, "You have arrested me very late in life. I am already ninety years old. It does not befit my age and authority to feign fear of the Lord my God, and to be the cause for my brethren to err, since those of lesser age would take this deed as an example. They would say, 'Eleazar at ninety years of age has broken the Lord's covenant,' and they would perish[46] in this errant way. Therefore never will I do such a thing; never will I defile my holiness and the purity of my old age, and uproot my people by giving them an occasion to distort the Law of my God. And though I free my soul from your hand, I cannot free it from the presence of the Lord, for no one, living or dead, can flee from His sight or escape from His hand, for He has dominion over the living and the dead. Thus it is better for me to die bravely and leave my people an example of constancy, so that when they see my honorable death they may long to perish in the same way. . . ."

Philip the enemy cut short his words, had Eleazar removed from his presence, and commanded that he be put to death. His order was carried out, but not before Eleazar had suffered a thousand tortures. In the midst of his suffering, he raised his eyes to heaven and groaned, "O Lord, now I recognize that You love me since You have led me to fulfill the precept 'You shall love the Lord with all your soul.' You know indeed that I could free my soul from this death, but that out of love for You I have not done so; and the tortures I suffer here, though they are harsher than the weakness of my old body can bear, are yet nothing in my eyes because of my fear of You." And even as he dauntlessly spoke these words, his martyrdom ended and the candle of his life was extinguished. But the memorable example of his constancy left a light as bright as that which he gave to his people when he was alive.[47]

Still, the death of this worthy did not end the punishment for my iniquities, which increased daily and formed a mountain so high that the righteousness of the few worthies among so many wicked men could not scale it or overcome it.

[THE MARTYRDOM OF HANNAH
AND HER SEVEN SONS]

To afflict me further, a mother and her seven sons were arrested, brought before Antiochus and commanded to eat abominable swine flesh in his presence. And to convince them to do so, he had them brought before him one by one. But the first one said to him, "Antiochus, why are you detaining me with words, teaching me what I am to do? I have already been indoctrinated by my parents and am prepared to bear the yoke of our Lord and His Law." Antiochus became very angry at these words. He sent for a large brass frying pan, and placed it above a fire.

The boy's tongue, hands and feet were cut off and thrown, along with the rest of his body, into the frying pan. The pan was lifted above the fire to make the boy suffer more and to frighten his mother and brothers. But they encouraged and comforted one another and trusted firmly in the goodness of our Lord. And when they saw their brother dying so bravely out of fear of God, they said to one another, "This is what the saintly Moses said in his song: 'For He will repent Himself for His servants and in them will He break the anger He has against the wicked" (Deut. 32.36-41).

When the first child had died, the second was brought, and he answered Antiochus' threats fearlessly: "I shall not do less in the devotion and fear of God than my brother did." For this the enemy ordered his limbs broken so that they too could be thrown into the frying pan awaiting them on the fire. The righteous Israelite then said, "Why do you afflict our souls which you did not give us, or our bodies which you did not rear?[48] They shall return to the Lord, who gave them to us, and when He revives the dead and the slain of His people He will quicken us."

When he had expired they brought the third boy. He raised his right hand toward the enemy Antiochus and said, "What is wrong with you? What advantage do you derive from intimidating us so? All of these afflictions come to us from heaven. This we understand; and therefore we patiently bear them. You are but a puff of air in our eyes, for we await glory from heaven, where the reward of our works will be given to us."

Antiochus and all his nobles marveled greatly at these words and at the admirable courage with which the lad spoke them; but he did not desist from having him killed like the others.

The fourth boy was brought, and when he came, he said with no less valor than his brothers: "Why must I get involved in talk with you, you accursed man? We shall die for our God, who will revive us, but you will never be resurrected."

When he had died, the fifth was brought, and he said with great courage: "You are an ignorant and vile man who does not understand the works of the Lord. You may say in your heart that our Lord has abandoned us and that He loves you since He has brought you to your glory and power, but you are mistaken. He abhors you because you are a wicked blasphemer and a raging dog. He has incited you against us, and you will finish feeding and sate your cruelty on us; but soon He will take full vengeance upon you, without regard or pity for your seed."

When he had been killed like the others, they brought the sixth boy. Undaunted and brave as the rest, he said: "We acknowledge the wickedness with which we have sinned against the Lord and we have therefore been delivered to this death, and we suffer it for all our people. But since you have made your heart haughty by not acknowledging the God of heaven and earth, He will take vengeance on you and will uproot you from the earth."

Finally, as he expired, the seventh, who was a small lad, was brought forward, and with him his saintly mother, Hannah, who had already seen six of her children dismembered. Yet she was overcome by neither fear nor dread. She approached the dead bodies of her children with a stout and invincible heart, raised her pained voice, and cried out to heaven: "O children of mine, I am your mother who bore you and the Lord is your creator, who gave you spirit and soul. He is the one who formed you and made you grow. He built your bones and wove your sinews and covered them with skin, and He breathed the breath of life into your nostrils. We are the work of His hands, and all this which He has made us endure is for His service. He is merciful and just. With much greater glory will he repay us in the true life, the life to come. Happy are you, my children, for your constancy."

The enemy, bewildered by the futility of his attempts to persuade the mother, decided to admonish her small son, so that the boy should not be able to boast of having overcome him.[49] He spoke softly and sweetly to him, and promised him on oath to give him many gifts and to make him a great lord, even to give him the second place in all his kingdom, if he would break God's precepts and obey him. But the blessed lad scorned all his promises and even refused to listen to them.

When Antiochus thus saw himself scorned, he called the boy's mother and said to her: "Good woman, have pity now on this lad, and do not be so cruel to the fruit of your womb. Admonish him to do my will and you will save him." The saintly Hannah answered him: "Hand him over to me, perhaps I can advise him." Whereupon she took the boy aside and kissed him, laughed and mocked the king, and said: "O my son, relinquish every advantage the deceitful world promises you. I bore you nine months within my womb and then I suckled you for three years. And I have reared you and to this day taught you to fear the Creator. Remember this and look to heaven. Consider the earth, sea, fire and water, that all of them were created with a mere word by Him whom we serve, and in His presence man is as if he were nothing. And since you understand this, do not fear this tyrant, O my son, but die for the Lord your God. O would that you were already with your brothers in the inconceivable bliss where they are, so that I might find you all there and be present at your glorious and happy betrothal with heaven."

When she had finished, the child, inspired with lofty zeal and reverence for God, approached King Antiochus and said, "Why are you detaining me and why do you not let me go directly to my saintly brothers? Do not think you will overcome me with your deceits and make me honor your vanities and offend the Lord most high and His holy Law, which He gave the Israelite people by the hand of His servant Moses. You accursed and execrable inventor of evils, enemy and abhorrer of the truth, which you blaspheme and offend so greatly, tell me, whither will you go and where will you flee from the eye of the incomprehensible Lord who owns all the earth and the fullness thereof? He will quicken us all and exalt us above every nation, but you, O wicked one, shall be unable to escape the lash of His wrath. It will be better for you not to have been born, for we shall go to life everlasting after we have suffered your tortures, while you will go down to hell, punished by a strange death and cruel afflictions, and you will remain confounded forever in its darkness."

As he spoke these words he was made to suffer terrible torments never before devised in this world; and thus this blessed creature expired.

And when the mother approached her dead children, she raised her hands to heaven and prayed, "O God most high, infinite and compas-sionate, let this servant of Yours immediately follow her children to see them in that glorious place which You have prepared for them up above." She had not quite finished offering this short prayer when her request was fulfilled. As she lay on the bodies of the children she had borne in her womb, her soul gently departed from her—she did not feel the rigorous crossing of death—and passed on to the place where her chil-dren's spirits had soared.[50]

Brothers, I have narrated these three misfortunes[51] to you in such detail because they are so exemplary and of such great importance that they grieved me to the extreme. And I confess to you that they put me in some confusion as I saw such great worthies come to such cruel ends.

NUMEO: I do not wish to allow further doubts to spring up in your soul, so before they sink their roots deeper, it would be prudent to remove them. The word of Moses uttered in his song, "That the Lord will take consolation in His servants" (Deut. 32.36 and Ps. 135.14) is to be understood as follows: Sometimes the entire people sins and a general punishment from heaven is necessary. If there be any righteous person or persons whose merit outweighs the combined offenses of the sinning Israelites, our merciful Lord accepts your ewe or your pure unblemished lamb as a sacrifice for all the people,[52] and the entire populace is spared exile from the land.

This was the role of these worthies—the holy priest Eleazar, the remarkable woman Hannah and her seven sons. The Lord showed them mercy by taking them in the state of their perfection and removing them from the danger of falling from that state if they continued in this life on earth.

Thus you can change your idea and be consoled. Now proceed with your story, for though it is pitiful, we must see the nature of your wounds in order to determine a remedy.

[THE MACCABEES AND THE HASMONEAN DYNASTY]

YCABO: This constancy which vanquished Antiochus intensified his virulence, and he commanded that no one be allowed to live unless he idolized the statue of himself which he had erected. As a result of this many of my children fled in terror to Jericho and to a mountain called Modin. And they chose as their leader the High Priest Mattathiah, whom our Lord had given five sons of great merit. The name of the first-born was Judah; the second, Jonathan; the third, Johanan; the fourth, Simon; the fifth, Eleazar.[53] These were the Maccabees, renowned for the extraordinary valor which they displayed in battle. When Antiochus' general, Philip, and his huge army arrayed themselves for battle against them, Mattathiah took a thousand Hebrew souls, including women and children and old people, into a cave on a Sabbath day. Philip admonished them to come out and break the rest of the seventh day; but when they refused, he set fire to the mouth of the cave and the dense smoke suffocated them all.[54] And then he prepared to attack the men under the rule of Mattathiah the Maccabee. First he affably asked Mattathiah to worship the image of Antiochus. But the priest answered the idolater scornfully, and assaulted a wicked Hebrew who accompanied him. This Hebrew had attempted to ingratiate himself with Philip by offering a pig on the altar erected for the sacrifices of the Lord. But he did not escape punishment, for Mattathiah, jealous for the service of God, attacked him and cut off his head while Philip looked on.[55]

Mattathiah raised a banner against Macedonia and he encouraged his people to fight on the Sabbath in order to rid themselves of the yoke of those who forbade them to keep their Law. And after a large group of the good people of Israel had assembled, a cruel slaughter was inflicted upon the Macedonians.[56]

Then Mattathiah's son, Judah, left the camp accompanied by all the good men of Israel and headed for Jerusalem. They entered Jerusalem and destroyed all the altars which the uncircumcised idolaters had erected, and cleansed all the vileness and filth in the holy city.[57]

Under the leadership of this Judah our Lord gave me many victories. But afterwards in his time, Timothy, the general of the Macedonians, attacked me with a hundred and twenty thousand armed men and killed a large number of my children in the land of Manasseh and Gilead.[58]

By this time the fame of the Romans had begun to spread. Rome was the fourth beast Daniel saw,[59] which crushed and ate things, and trampled the remainder with its feet. The Romans made a pact with my Israelite children when Judah was general, and when the Greeks dwelling in Joppa and Jamnia learned of this agreement they began to harbor evil thoughts about the Israelites dwelling in their midst. They invited them for a pleasure trip on their ships, and the Israelites, with their wives and children, accepted the offer in good faith. The Greeks took them festively across the sea, but when they reached the deepest part, they threw more than two hundred overboard.[60] After this I saw Judah attack Gorgias, the general of Edom's cavalry, and I saw the Edomites kill some of the valiant men of Judah's army. But when inquiry was made as to why these Israelites had been killed, it was discovered that they had heathen images of gold and silver concealed under their clothes.[61]

In a battle against Eupator, Antiochus' son, I saw one of the Maccabees, Eleazar, pass alone through the enemy lines, killing and wounding as he went. I saw him attack an elephant, which, as it was most conspicuous, appeared to be carrying the king. He thrust his sword into its navel and it fell dead upon him. Thus this noble hero died, leaving to the world the great example of his valor.[62]

Then I saw Bacchides and his army of thirty thousand Greeks attack a city of Judah where there were three thousand Israelites. All of them fled and deserted their general, Judah. With only eighty Israelite horsemen from his guard, Judah attacked one of the enemies' armies of fifteen thousand men and killed two thousand of them in the first encounter. And when Judah saw Bacchides before him, he approached him with a drawn sword and the mien of a frightful lion, but his enemy fled to a nearby city and saved his life. But when another army of fifteen thousand men that stood poised at Judah's flank saw that he was tiring, they attacked him in full strength and vanquished him. Thus that illustrious hero and prince of my children perished. After his death, Jerusalem's enemies increased.[63]

Jonathan, his brother, succeeded him in the principate and enjoyed the priesthood for seven years. Under him I lived in peace. When he died and was gathered to his people, his place went to his brother, Simon.[64] After many battles, Simon was finally killed by his father-in-law, Ptolemy, king of Egypt, who had Simon's two sons tied in chains.[65] Hyrcanus, son of the slain Simon, rose against Ptolemy, and set siege to one of his cities. Ptolemy, seeing his predicament, brought Hyrcanus' mother and brothers to the top of the wall, tied them, and cruelly whipped them. When Hyrcanus saw this, his heart was moved to pity. Tears streamed down his cheeks and he ceased his attack. But his mother stretched forth her hands and entreated him not to have pity for her, but to recall his father's death, and to storm the city again even more fiercely in an endeavor to capture his enemy.

When Hyrcanus heard his mother's entreaties, he blazed with anger. He set up his equipment anew, and beat the walls more forcefully with the battering ram. He was so successful that the city was threatened with complete destruction.

Ptolemy then returned to his first strategem: he again brought the mother and her sons to the wall. He whipped them even more cruelly than before on the tower beneath which the ram battered and threatened to hurl them down if Hyrcanus did not cease his attack. When this noble youth saw the pain inflicted upon his mother and brothers, he could not restrain his tears, and they came forth in profusion. Still his mother encouraged him from the top of the wall, admonishing him not to desist but to avenge his father's death and to ignore his pity for her. Her behest again made a profound impression upon him, and he ordered a powerful attack against the city. Yet, in the midst of his sally, he turned his eyes toward his mother and brothers who suffered as he assaulted the city, and he called off his attack. Confused and bewildered, he was finally overcome by pity for the pain he saw his flesh suffer, thinking, "I am the cause of the tortures and pain they are receiving." He ended the siege and returned, sorry and sad, to Jerusalem, believing that in this way his mother's and brothers' affliction would cease. But the wicked Ptolemy only became more furious, and after Hyrcanus left he killed them, and fled to Philadelphia.[66]

When many days had passed after their deaths, Hyrcanus made a great banquet for all the lords of the house of Judah. And when he sat down at the table with the wise men of Israel, with whom he studied the Law of the Lord, he asked them to tell him if they thought he was deserving to serve as High Priest of the Lord. The wise men responded that he was a righteous and upright man. But one of them had an answer which was not so peaceable as the others': "If you wish to be righteous," he said, "you should leave the priesthood and be satisfied with the kingship alone." Hyrcanus asked why, and he answered: "Because your mother was a captive and was defiled; and for this reason it is not meet for you to enter the Holy of Holies."

The king was provoked to great anger. The joy of the banquet turned to strife, for many evil meddlers told him that all of the sages held this same opinion. Therefore he began to abhor the sages and forthwith commanded that no one should study the Law with them under penalty of death. And he changed his beliefs to those of the Sadducees, and in his wrath he killed many good people.[67]

From this time on, infinite discords and rivalries began because of the favor Hyrcanus showed to the Sadducees and his consequent aversion to the Pharisees, whom he had once preferred.[68]

These Sadducees held the view that the observance of the Law was to be understood literally, while the Pharisees taught the Law in the manner in which our fathers handed it down to us, declaring it as it had been declared to them.[69] At the same time another sect arose, that of the Essenes, and they took part of both laws.[70] Because of the differences and contentions of these sects, much blood of the people, who held the true law of the Pharisees, was shed, for their side was the weakest, while that of the Sadducees, who were aided by the king, was the most powerful.[71]

When Hyrcanus had been gathered to his people, after ruling for thirtyone years, he left three sons—Antigonus, Aristobulus and Alexander—and Aristobulus succeeded him on the throne. He was called a great king because he greatly expanded the Jewish kingdom. He vanquished the Tyrians and Sidonians, he killed an infinite number of Israel's enemies, and he compelled the conquered to be circumcised, and submitted them all to the Israelite yoke. He did not desire the priesthood, but was content with the throne alone.[72] But in order to enjoy his rule as he wished, he arrested his mother and had her put in chains, expelled his brothers from Jerusalem, and showed affection only to Antigonus, the youngest.

When Antigonus was returning with great honor from a war to which Aristobulus had sent him, he learned that his brother was very ill, and he hastened to Jerusalem to see him. When he arrived, he went first to the Temple of the Lord and entreated Him to spare his brother's life. But wicked people were not lacking who envied Antigonus, and they falsely informed Aristobulus that his brother returned intending to kill him, for he was in the Temple in military uniform preparing to attack the king with his men.

The king became alarmed, set up a strong guard, and ordered that anyone that tried to enter armed to see him should be killed. And when the queen, Aristobulus' wife, who hated her brother-in-law, learned of these events, she deceitfully sent a message to Antigonus telling him to come fully armed, for this was the way the king wished to see him. The youth trusted the queen, and did as he was bid in order to please his brother; but as he approached the palace, he was killed by the king's guards because he was armed.

When Aristobulus heard of his brother's disastrous death, he was so grieved and became so ill that he began to vomit blood. When he sent a page to his physician to show him the blood, the page, by a miracle, fell with the chamber-pot on the very spot where Aristobulus' brother's blood still lay spilt, and the blood of one brother spilled over the blood of the other.

When the king heard of this he grieved much more over his brother's death, and acknowledged his own sin. And his grief killed him after he had enjoyed the royal scepter for only two years.[73]

He was succeeded by Alexander, the son of Hyrcanus, whom he had hated during his lifetime. In the first war Alexander waged he captured all the land of Zoilus, king of the Sidonians, and returned to Jerusalem with a great victory. Afterwards Alexander secretly sent an embassy to Cleopatra, the mother of Lathyrus, proposing they attack Lathyrus, for the mother desired very much to destroy her son. When Lathyrus learned of this, he burned with fierce anger, and attacked Galilee with a powerful army. He took the city of Assochis and twenty-two thousand Israelites on a Sabbath day and carried them off as captives.[74]

And on top of this misfortune, another one overtook me:

Alexander, wishing to avenge this loss, attacked Lathyrus with fifty thousand Israelites. Since he had a large number of men, he relied so much on his own strength that he did not remember the Lord. He gave Lathyrus battle at the bank of the River Jordan, and thirty thousand Jews were killed by the sword because of the little confidence they placed in the Source of all their past victories, and the great confidence they placed in their own might.

These enemies continued to pursue the Israelites, taking another town of Judah. Lathyrus killed all the women and children he found there and cooked some in pots to instill a fear in the Jewish people that he ate human flesh.[75]

On a Succoth festival, when the people were rejoicing with the palm-branch and citrons, I saw one of the sages throw a citron at the king in jest. The monarch, however, took it as a sign of contempt. Shouting "To arms! To arms!" he massacred more than six thousand scholars of the Law, filling the holy Temple with their blood. But this cruel slaughter still did not quell his anger. He commanded that thenceforth the people should be governed by the orders of the Sadducees.[76] During his reign the true sages[77] suffered grave tribulations, and since they saw that the king hated and persecuted them so, many went over to Demetrius, king of the Greeks, with their adherents, and asked him for favor and help. He received them gladly and put into the field forty thousand cavalry and a large number of infantry to battle against Jerusalem.

When Alexander heard of this powerful army of Demetrius advancing toward him, he fled from the city by night and went to hide in the hills. And when the Israelites throughout Judea saw that the holy city was in danger, they attacked Demetrius with only ten thousand cavalry. They fought him, routed him, and forced him to return to Greece[78] in dishonor and shame, while Alexander came back to Jerusalem. Here he assembled an army and attacked a territory which was under the control of the Pharisees. Arresting eighty of their most noble men, he brought them in irons to the Holy City and hanged them all at a banquet while he laughed and drank.[79]

When Alexander fell gravely ill—his illness lasted three years—and when his wife saw that most of the populace was on the side of the Pharisees and that with her husband's death all his family would fare badly, she took counsel with him. He told her, "When I die, embalm me secretly and let not my death be discovered in any way, but tell those who ask for me that because of my illness I abhor seeing people. In the meantime, assemble all the Pharisees and deal with them in a friendly manner, with words full of love, and tell them to take vengeance on me while I lie sick in bed. And if you do this, I am sure that they are so merciful that they will pardon my past and they themselves will bury me."

This is what happened, for when the Pharisees learned through the queen that he had died and how he had repented, they answered that he was the anointed of the Lord, and though he had sinned so gravely, his long illness had served as an expiation for his offenses. And they bewailed him and carried him on their shoulders to his grave. Alexander ruled over Israel for twenty-seven years.[80]

His crown was taken by his wife, Alexandra. She had two sons by the king, one Hyrcanus, a righteous man, and the other Aristobulus, a mighty warrior. This Hyrcanus loved the Pharisees, the true sages. As soon as Alexandra began her reign, she freed the scholars and righteous men her husband had arrested, and commanded the people to obey their ordinances and their exposition of the Law. She appointed Hyrcanus High Priest and Aristobulus head of the army, and she gave the true sages power to punish the opposing sect of the Sadducees, whom they considered heretics. Thus during the reign of this queen the adherents of the wicked sect found themselves in great tribulation, so much so that they decided to leave Jerusalem. They went to live in various cities, and chose Aristobulus as their leader.

When Alexandra died, after reigning nine years,[81] the Pharisees elevated her son Hyrcanus to the throne in Jerusalem, and he continued to serve as High Priest. When Aristobulus learned of this, he became envious of his brother. He attacked Jerusalem with a host of heretical Sadducees and besieged the city so forcefully that the priests and elders begged him not to destroy the Lord's people. They made a covenant with him, in which they named him king and agreed that Hyrcanus should be left with only the dignity of the high priesthood.

As these tyrannies and iniquities blazed, they spurred the Enemy, who is always pursuing us, to seek an occasion by which the kingdom might be removed from the seed of the Maccabees; and further, by which the Maccabees should be destroyed for the sins which their descendants had committed, since they had shed so much righteous and innocent blood and led Israel away from obedience to the holy sages and prophets to the heretical Sadducees. The Enemy found an opportunity. The Sadducees were King Aristobulus' closest confidants and friends, and they advised him to kill Hyrcanus; for as long as Hyrcanus was alive, they urged, Aristobulus could not enjoy his kingdom in safety. And Aristobulus determined to do this.[82]

At this time this secret was discovered by one of the hectors in Israel, a man named Antipater, a great sage both in the Law and in Greek learning. His lineage was of the Romans who had been captured by Israel.[83] Antipater had four sons—Joseph, Phasael, Herod, and Pheroras, and a daughter named Salome.

Since Antipater was very fond of Hyrcanus because of his great ability, he disclosed to him what his brother Aristobulus was plotting with the advice of the Sadducees. He advised him to flee to Arabia to King Aretas, and offered to accompany him and help him in every way. Hyrcanus followed his counsel, and was received very amiably by King Aretas. He told the king that his brother Aristobulus was plotting to kill him without cause, and asked for assistance, that he might regain the throne which had been usurped from him. King Aretas promised to help him, and they made an agreement that if Hyrcanus were victorious, he would restore to Aretas all the cities which had belonged to Arabia. Hyrcanus then gathered a large army and attacked Jerusalem; and when the city was besieged, most of the people of Judah came forth and defected to him.[84]

The festival of Passover fell at this time, and the Temple services could not be completed on account of the war. A righteous man, a priest named Onias, inspired with noble zeal, secretly went out of the city to Hyrcanus and asked him not to fight until the Passover service had been completed. Hyrcanus answered him that since the priest was a holy man, he should entreat the Lord to give him victory against his brother Aristobulus, so that war might cease in Israel. The worthy replied that he was not capable of attaining such a favor, for the wars had been brought about by the commission of great sins and wicked deeds. His answer enraged Hyrcanus' servants, and as the priest left, they attacked him. With their naked swords they tried to compel him to pray to our Lord for what Hyrcanus had requested of him. And when Onias refused, they killed him.

In anger at this sin, which had been committed without cause, our Lord cast a great pestilence on His people, and a large number of Israelites perished.[85]

[THE COMING OF THE ROMANS]

And to our further distress at this time, Pompey, a Roman general, left Rome on his way to conquer Armenia. Aristobulus bribed Pompey to send a letter to Aretas, the king of Arabia, ordering him to make Hyrcanus lift the siege of Jerusalem, and threatening to break the treaty the Romans had made with him in the event that he refused.

At this time, the greater part of the world was subservient to the Romans. Aretas therefore obeyed Pompey's embassy, and Hyrcanus and his friend Antipater were compelled to lift their siege of Jerusalem and to turn away to their disadvantage, as their sins merited. Aristobulus and his men pursued Hyrcanus and killed many of his troops.

When Pompey arrived in Damascus, Aristobulus, in gratitude for his assistance, sent him an ingeniously sculptured golden vine. Its roots, branches, leaves and grapes were of the purest gold, and it weighed five hundred pounds. Pompey was delighted with this gift, and sent it on to Rome as a remarkable and unusual treasure, and there it was placed in the abominable temple of Rome's great idol, Jupiter.[86]

But the Roman quickly forgot the bribe he had received. He attacked Jerusalem and demanded the Temple vessels from Aristobulus. When Aristobulus refused, Pompey broke the wall of Jerusalem and tried to enter the Temple to take them. The Israelites fought bravely against the Romans and killed ten thousand in the first battle.

But when the Romans regrouped to attack the city, conflicting opinions arose among the people. Some said they should open the gates for Pompey, while others believed that they should defend themselves against him. In the end, those who were of the opinion that they should open the gates prevailed, and the enemy entered Jerusalem to avenge the sins that had been committed until that time. Pompey immediately attacked the holy Temple and killed a large number of priests and commoners. He made Hyrcanus king and Antipater his adviser. He sent Aristobulus as a prisoner to Rome, made the Jews tributaries to the Romans, and left Scaurus in Judea to receive the tribute.[87]

In Rome [some thirty-five years before], a senator's wife had been delivered of a male child, who was named Julius. His mother had died at his birth; the birth was a difficult one and had to be hastened (in Latin they say *caesa*), and they therefore called the child Caesar.[88] Caesar eventually ousted the Greeks from their position of world supremacy, subjecting province after province. He had attempted to force the Roman Senate to make him king, and caused much discord and many deaths in the city.

When this news reached Pompey in Arabia, and it was further heard that Julius Caesar was killing senators in an attempt to gain control of the Empire, he assembled all the men he could and marched against Caesar. And when Caesar learned what had transpired, he removed Aristobulus from his prison, made him general of an army, and sent him against Pompey.

Aristobulus' arrival in Judea frightened Pompey so much that he sought a way to secretly assassinate him: he persuaded some men in Jerusalem who had fought with Aristobulus during his wars with his brother Hyrcanus to send him a poisonous present. They did so; Aristobulus tasted of it and died a few days later, after ruling over the Israelites for only three and a half years.[89]

Hyrcanus gave the government of Jerusalem to Phasael, the son of his counselor Antipater, and appointed Herod [his other son], over all Galilee. In this way Antipater and his sons eventually ruled over the kingdom together, and Antipater controlled almost all of Judea. But when Hyrcanus realized that his kingdom was gradually being usurped, he poisoned Antipater.[90]

Amidst all this, Antigonus, a son of Aristobulus (Hyrcanus' brother whom Pompey had killed with poison) made a secret pact with Pacorus, king of the Persians. Pacorus promised to assist Antigonus against Hyrcanus, and Antigonus, if he won, was to give Pacorus five hundred pounds of gold and a hundred virgins of Israel in tribute. Pacorus approached Jerusalem with a powerful army, and Antigonus and a large throng of Israelites left the city to join him. Both armies fought against the Holy City, entered it, seized King Hyrcanus and stabbed Antipater's son, Phasael, to death.[91]

There Antigonus bit the ears of his uncle Hyrcanus, the High Priest and king, and tore them off so that, thus blemished, he could no longer enjoy the priesthood.[92] Antipater's other son, Herod, escaped and fled to Augustus Caesar, the Roman emperor.[93]

Thus Pacorus was victorious. He made Antigonus king and took Hyrcanus captive to Persia.

In Rome, Augustus Caesar proclaimed Herod king of all the land of Judah and put a large Roman army at his disposal. As Herod advanced he met Alexandra, daughter of Hyrcanus, and Mariamne, her daughter by Alexander, son of Aristobulus. He brought them back to the land of Israel and took Mariamne for his wife.

Thus Herod marched forward with his army, and with the help of the Syrians he engaged Antigonus in a battle in which many children of Israel and their enemies died. Ultimately the persecuted Israelite people fared the worst: their enemies broke down the wall of Jerusalem, entered the city, and went as far as the sanctuary, creating havoc as they went. They would have entered the Holy of Holies, had Herod not prevented it, sword in hand.

In Jerusalem Herod arrested Antigonus and delivered him to the Roman Sosius, who took him along with him. But after they had left, Herod feared that Antigonus would yet return to the throne. He there-fore sent a substantial gift to Sosius, and bribed him to kill Antigonus.[94] Thus was the iron net being woven which would imprison my liberty until this very day.[95]

When matters were in this state, Pacorus, king of the Persians, released Hyrcanus from prison and made him king over all the rebels and fugi-tives of Israel who were in the land of Shinar[96] and in the land of the Persians. Herod feared Hyrcanus, and sent him letters feigning friend-ship, asking him to meet with him in Jerusalem, for he eagerly desired to see him. Hyrcanus came confidently and Herod showed him great affection and called him father; but he secretly contrived to kill him. Hyrcanus discovered his design and resolved to flee to Malichus, the king of Arabia. But the letters which he wrote Malichus reached Herod's hand through a faithless messenger. Herod accused him of treason against the Jewish Senate, and had him executed in the sight of all the people. In this way he secured his kingdom against the seed of the Maccabees, according to his earthly judgment; he did not consider that the Lord was observing and contemplating his deeds from His abode on high.

Thus Hyrcanus died after ruling intermittently and with great anguish for forty-six and a half years.[97]

Herod's wife, Mariamne, had a brother, Aristobulus, who had the handsomest face and physique of all the children of Israel. Though he was often asked by his wife to promote Aristobulus to the high priest-hood, Herod refused, for he feared him, since he was of the seed of the Maccabees from whom he had usurped the kingdom. At last, after he had slain Hyrancus, he was compelled to do so.

Despite this appointment, however, Herod could not placate his mother-in-law Alexandra for Hyrcanus' death; indeed, she spoke so angrily to Herod that he imprisoned her. From prison Alexandra wrote to Cleopatra, the queen of Egypt and the wife of the Roman satrap, Mark Anthony, asking for her help and complaining of the evil Herod had inflicted upon the seed of the Maccabees, to whom the throne rightfully belonged.

Cleopatra replied that she would do as asked if Alexandra came to meet her. After Alexandra read the letter she sent it to her son Aristob-ulus, the High Priest, and told him she wished to flee to the coast at Joppa and thence to Egypt by ship. She advised him to flee with her, and suggested that they make two large coffins for the flight and pay a handsome bribe for someone to take them.[98]

The messengers revealed these plans to Herod, and he advised them to keep the secret and to bring mother and son to him when they were in the coffins. Thus when Alexandra and Aristobulus entered their coffins to flee to Egypt, the coffins were brought before Herod and opened, to the great chagrin of those present. This did not prevent Alexandra from railing at Herod, while he pretended to ignore her and dissembled his sentiments.[99]

One year later, as Aristobulus, dressed as High Priest in his pontifical vestments, was offering the sacrifices near the altar of the Temple, the Israelites contemplated his charm and prudence, and rejoiced greatly in seeing him, and some said, "Praised be the Lord of the heavens, for He has left someone who can still avenge the destruction of the Maccabees' seed." King Herod heard these words and marked them well. He was fearful, and they irked him, for he thought, "Surely the Israelites want to restore his forebears' kingdom to him." When he saw the hearts of all the people inclined toward Aristobulus, he took counsel, and a bitter sentence emerged for the hapless youth.

When Herod and his entire retinue went to Jericho for the Feast of Booths, he prepared a sumptuous banquet for all his princes and servants. Each one sat down by rank, and he placed Aristobulus, the High Priest, at his right hand. When they had finished eating, several men requested the king for permission to take a swim in the Jordan. Herod had secretly instructed them to entreat the High Priest to join them, and to overcome him and drown him in the river. As they were bathing, they entreated Aristobulus to join them. He agreed, if the king would permit him. Herod told him to do as his heart pleased. The youth entered the Jordan, and as he swam with his companions, the king suddenly saddled his horse and returned with his retinue to Jericho. The swimmers stayed late, and after sunset they approached Aristobulus and drowned him. Feigning sorrow, they went to inform the king that Aristobulus had drowned. Herod appeared to be greatly shaken at the news of his death, but the populace, who loved Aristobulus dearly, understood what had really happened. The iniquity could not long be concealed: it was soon discovered that the king was responsible for the crime. His wife, Aristobulus' sister, and her mother, Alexandra, flared with greater wrath against Herod and his offspring.[100]

Within the Roman Empire Octavian Augustus had conquered Mark Anthony, king of Egypt, of whom Herod had been an ally. Fearing Octavian, Herod planned to visit him with a substantial gift; but before leaving he told Joseph, his sister Salome's husband, to poison his wife Mariamne if he should be killed by Octavian. Joseph revealed this secret to Mariamne, and from then on she bore an ever increasing hatred toward her husband.

When the king returned safely from his visit to Octavian Augustus, he sensed, from many indications, that his wife now abhorred him, and he discovered that Joseph had revealed their secret to her. Certain that Mariamne had therefore committed adultery with Joseph, Herod informed the people that Mariamne had wanted to poison him, and had her decapitated in the public square.[101]

In this way, Herod became drunk with innocent blood, and wove the web of my destruction and total ruin. But now the Lord did not delay His punishment. He immediately sent a grievous plague over all Herod's house, and his maid-servants and his closest favorites died. And besides, a terrible pestilence spread over the land, so deadly that Herod clearly recognized that he had killed Mariamne undeservedly, and he repented. And Herod was afflicted by a severe illness. His mother in-law, Alexandra [seeing an opportunity for revenge], attempted to poison his medicine; but her plot was discovered, and she was put to death by Herod. Thus the family of the Maccabees came to an end.[102]

The king had two sons by Mariamne, Alexander and Aristobulus, who had been sent to Rome to study Latin. When they learned of their mother's death, their hearts hardened in hatred for their father.[103]

In the midst of this wickedness, Herod decided to raze the Holy Temple, which had been constructed according to the plan of Cyrus, and to rebuild it in accordance with the specifications of Solomon. The people objected because they feared that after it had been torn down Herod would not rebuild it; but it was razed, and Herod erected it anew with its original marvelous structure.

THE STRUCTURE OF THE SECOND TEMPLE[104]

The length of the Second Temple was a hundred cubits, as were its breadth and height. It was built all of one stone, white marble. The height of the stones was a hundred and twenty cubits: twenty in the foundation and a hundred above ground. The length of each stone was twelve cubits, and its width eight cubits, and the stones all were of the same size and thickness. Herod covered the doors of the house with the purest gold, and had the posts and sockets made of silver; he had many precious stones set in the windows; he had a golden vine of daedal artistry made, all solid gold and so large that it weighed a thousand pounds. Its ingenious workmanship was so marvelous and exquisite that the world has never seen another composition like it. And at the entrance to the Temple, he had two silver walls built, wrought with the same daedal artistry as the rest of the building.

The Temple had a courtyard, with a floor of clear, milk-white marble. On its western side, the length of the courtyard was a hundred and fifty cubits and its width one hundred. On the southern and on the northern sides, the courtyard was also a hundred and fifty cubits long and a hundred wide. Around it Herod had a hundred and fifty columns of fine white marble set in four rows. Each row was forty cubits long; each column was forty cubits high and three cubits thick, and all were identical. The courtyard and its columns on the southern side thus exactly resembled their counterpart on the nothern side.

On the eastern side of the Temple, however, the courtyard was seven hundred and twenty cubits [long].

At the end of the courtyard Herod had built a number of cloisters, so high that anyone walking in them could easily see the waters of the brook Kidron.

Herod also built a silver wall half a palm thick, with a door of solid gold between the threshold and the house itself. On it he placed a sword of gold weighing twelve pounds, which was engraved: "Let the stranger that comes near be put to death."

In short, the objects with which Herod adorned this Temple were so amazing and distinctive that the most superb and skilled artisan could not effectively imitate the beauty of any one of them, nor could any other king in the world succeed in erecting such a building.

For the first sacrifice King Herod sent to Sharon's fields for a large number of cattle. The building of the Temple was completed on the day that the monarch usually made a banquet for all his court, and this provided even greater contentment for both the king and the entire populace.

At this time Herod's sons, Aristobulus and Alexander, returned home from Rome and came to Jerusalem; they were greatly angered against their father. Herod quickly found them brides—Alexander, who was the older, was married to the daughter of the king of Cappadocia, and Aristobulus, the younger, wedded the daughter of his aunt, Salome, Herod's sister.

When his sons entered Jerusalem, they did not go immediately to pay homage to their father; and as a result he was offended, and conceived a dislike for them. Herod had still another son, named Antipater, born of a poor woman whom he had brought into the palace after he had killed Mariamne. [In his anger at his sons], he decided to make Antipater heir to the kingdom in his will; as a start, he invested him with much authority and gave him a substantial gift of money. Leaving Antipater in this position, Herod went to Rome to visit Emperor Augustus, taking his eldest son Alexander with him. The emperor effected a reconciliation of sorts between father and son.

When Herod returned to Jerusalem, he divided the kingdom into three parts and gave one to each of his sons. Antipater, the son of the common woman, feared his two half-brothers because they were of noble blood, and determined to persecute them by malicious reports in order to remove them completely from their father's favor.[105] He went so far as to bruit that Alexander wanted to kill the king, and as a result Alexander was arrested and sentenced to death.

In these straits Alexander wrote to his father-in-law, Archelaus, king of Cappadocia, who was a man of shrewd judgment and great wisdom. Archelaus immediately traveled to Jerusalem to aid his son-in-law. He astutely and cleverly told Herod that he had come because he understood that Alexander was plotting to kill him, and that his daughter could also not fail to know about this; he vowed that because she had also committed treason, he would kill her if Herod killed his son.

Herod was very happy to see the great friendship which his son's father-in-law showed him. But Archelaus' stratagem enabled him to attain his desire; he persuaded Herod to order a new inquiry into the matter, and the charge against Alexander was found to be false. Herod therefore freed him.[106]

But the sin would not be content without venting its wrath, for when Archelaus returned to his land, Antipater again accused the youths. He induced a barber to testify before the king that they had bribed him to kill Herod when he shaved him. There was no opposition to this accusation; Herod immediately had his two sons hanged and decapitated the barber who had incriminated them.[107] Thus he continued his cruelties, shedding innocent blood because he trusted in malicious reports.

After he had murdered Alexander and Aristobulus, Antipater was confident that the kingdom was within his grasp, and he was untroubled by the fact that the Lord of the heavens was weighing all his thoughts.[108]

Herod's sons left five sons of their own. Alexander left two: Tigranes and Aristobulus, and Aristobulus left three: Herod, Agrippa and Alexander.[109] Herod betrothed Tigranes to a daughter of his brother Pheroras, and Alexander to a daughter of Antipater, who had brought about his parent's death.[110] But Antipater was against the engagement and he managed to break it. He made an alliance with his uncle Pheroras, and the friendship between the two men was so great that Herod came to suspect them of treason, and it was not long before Antipater was accused of plotting to kill his father with a certain poison he was alleged to have sent in a phial to Pheroras from Egypt. As a result of this accusation, Antipater was imprisoned in a narrow cell.[111]

Later Herod became seriously ill. He wept aloud in his bed, crying, "O wretched me, I have no heir left who loves me." Recalling how he had wrongly killed his beloved wife Mariamne and his two children, he lamented piteously day and night.

One day while peeling an apple with a sharp knife, he was so troubled by his sad thoughts and forlorn over the evil he had committed against his own blood, that he lifted himself from the bed, supported himself with his hand and tried to thrust the knife into his stomach. But his servants who stood nearby rushed to him and swiftly took the knife away. Thwarted, Herod cried aloud, and those with him joined with such a wail that their sad voices were heard beyond the palace and the people said, "the king is dead."

Antipater, too, heard this inside his prison, and rejoicing, he begged the jailer, "Let me free for my father is dead, and I will favor you." But the jailer refused, and when told that his father was alive, Antipater lamented and was very dejected.

The jailer thus learned how Antipater truly felt, and since all Israel hated him because of the deaths he had caused through his devilry, the jailer reported to the king everything that had transpired. Herod burned with even greater anger against his son. He swore that Antipater would never see his desire fulfilled, and ordered him to be removed from prison immediately and executed. And so it was done. Five days later Herod died and left another son, Archelaus, heir to the throne. Herod had ordered that his body should be buried in the city of Herodium, two and a half days distant from Jerusalem.[112]

As king, Archelaus gravely forsook the service of heaven. He married his brother Alexander's wife, who already had children,[113] and committed many greater evils besides. After reigning for nine years, he dreamed that he saw nine ears of corn sprouting full and perfect on a single stalk, and being devoured by a huge ox in a single gulp. When he awoke, he sent for the sages in Israel to interpret his dream. The sages said that the nine ears represented the nine years of his reign, and that the ox which was devouring them was the great king Octavian Augustus of Rome, who would take his kingdom away in that year because he had sinned by marrying his brother's wife. Archelaus did not reply. Five days later Octavian Augustus came, arrested him, and put his brother, Antipas, in his place as king over Israel.[114] After performing this deed, which seemed to have been commanded by heaven, he returned to Rome.

Octavian Augustus died, and Tiberius Caesar reigned in his stead. When he took the crown, Antipas committed even more wicked deeds than his predecessors. While his brother Philip was alive, he married his wife, who had already borne children.[115] Rabbi Johanan, the High Priest, reproved him for such a great sin, and for this rebuke Antipas had him put to death.[116] But neither of these sins was left unpunished, because the Lord forthwith sent Tiberius, the Roman emperor, against Antipas. He took Antipas captive and sent him in irons to Spain, where he died. In his stead, Tiberius placed Agrippa on the throne. Agrippa was the son of Aristobulus, one of the two sons whom Herod had executed. During Agrippa's reign Tiberius died, and Gaius Caesar [Caligula] replaced him and proclaimed himself a god.[117] He was succeeded by the cruel emperor Nero.[118]

[THE REBELLIONS AGAINST ROME]

Agrippa reigned for twenty-three years over Israel, and in his days he was forced to submit to the Romans' grievous yoke. For Florus, the Roman general, shed an infinite amount of Israelite blood and dishonored many virgins. Moreover, Florus impoverished the rich through false accusations, not leaving them even the bare necessities of life.[119] While he was in Jerusalem he desired to live in the Temple, and he hanged many Israelites on the beams of the holy house.[120] Since the harried people could not endure such vexation and hardship, the youth of Israel rebelled. They selected Eleazar (the son of Hananiah), whose father had been High Priest, as their leader. They attacked the Romans by surprise and killed a large number of them, and Florus was compelled to flee on horseback to Egypt.[121]

After this successful foray, King Agrippa, in great fear of the Romans' might, admonished the common people and the nobles to obey them.[122] This counsel pleased the elders, and they were disinclined to start a war against Rome. But Eleazar and his band refused to resubmit to them; instead, they killed two ambassadors of Rome and their entire retinue. When the elders of Israel saw this, they left Jerusalem and fled to Mount Zion,[123] fearful of what was going to happen.

Eleazar was angry at their flight; he pursued them, fought with them and killed a large number of the elders. When Agrippa heard of this massacre, he sent six thousand men to aid them. Both groups attacked Eleazar's army and inflicted heavy casualties. Thus began the internecine war among the Israelite people. This war and the sins I had previously committed brought on the desolation[124] which has continued to this day.

Later, the revolutionaries on Eleazar's side prevailed. They expelled King Agrippa from Jerusalem and killed many great princes and lords in Israel. Many others took refuge with the king outside the city.

The revolutionaries now had the field to themselves. They set the royal palace on fire, emptied it of all its treasures and took all the finest things in Jerusalem as spoil.[125]

When the Romans saw that Israel had rebelled against them, they took counsel, and voted to kill all the Jews in their lands. The cruel slaughter began in Damascus, where ten thousand Jews were put to the sword in the first onslaught. They repeated this massacre in Caesarea.

As this great evil spread throughout the Roman Empire, Eleazar and his army attacked Damascus, the city where the massacre had been inflicted on his brethren. He captured the city and cruelly executed all the Romans and their confederates. He did the same in all the cities of Syria to which he came, killing and destroying, and he returned to Jerusalem victorious over his enemies. As he approached Scythopolis, a Syrian city a day's journey from Jerusalem [a Hebrew named] Simon came forth from the city to fight them as an ally of the Scythopolitans. When the Scythopolitans saw that Simon had left, they took counsel, and expelled all the rich Israelites from the city. They shut the gates upon them, and put to the sword some thirteen thousand poor people who remained.

When this was done, the Scythopolitans attacked Simon, who had done so much for them against his Israelite brethren. Simon realized his cause was lost, but before his enemies could kill him, he grabbed his old father by his hair and cut off his head; then he stabbed his wife and children and finally threw himself on his sword. Thus they all died a more honorable death than they would have at the hands of the uncircumcised.[126]

When King Agrippa saw the insurgents of Eleazar's band committing destruction and robbery in Jerusalem and burning his palace, he went to Rome to remedy the situation by seeking aid from Nero. Nero sent back with him his general Cestius [Gallus] and an army as numerous as the grains of sand on the seashore. They arrived in Judea, battled, and captured many of the Israelites' cities. Cestius found greatest resistance in the area of Chabulon, where he put eight thousand and four hundred Israelites to the sword. He carried out similar massacres in Caesaria and Sepphoris.[127]

Then Cestius and his army turned toward Jerusalem. Agrippa first entreated him to propose peace to the defenders of the city. Ambassadors were sent, but Eleazar did not allow them to answer, for as soon as they entered the city, he executed them. In anger, the Roman general Cestius set siege to the city. Yet fear did not grip the people within, even when the attacking enemies increased in number. On the contrary, on the third day Eleazar opened the gates, attacked the Roman army and killed five thousand of its infantry and a thousand of its cavalry, while Israel suffered almost no casualties.

The foe, amazed at such extreme valor and bravery, began to fear the Israelites, and Cestius moved his army away from the city. He set fire to all the surrounding villages and commanded trumpets to be blown.[128] Fearing a reprisal, he and Agrippa fled and covered in one night a distance that normally took three days to reach; and when dawn broke, the rest of the army that had remained likewise fled.

When Eleazar saw the Romans fleeing for refuge, he followed hot upon their heels. He killed a great number of them and took as booty all the spoils which they had left in their haste.[129]

When Nero learned of the Israelites' victory, he fumed with anger. He had sent a great army with Cestius, but now he sent Vespasian (and his son Titus) as general of another army to avenge this affront. He charged them not to pardon or spare any human being, but to put all cities to the sword and fire.[130]

O my brothers, it was not Nero who was bringing this cruel sentence upon me; the multitude of my crimes and the high mountain of my rebellious acts required it of God's justice, and it was entrusted to Vespasian and his son Titus. The news of their coming encouraged many of Israel's enemies to move against her; and when Vespasian arrived, all of these and others who were tributary to my children went over to his side, and the Roman army grew more powerful day by day.

When the Israelites saw their enemies' preparations, they divided their land into three parts and placed a general in charge of each. Hananiah, the High Priest, was over Jerusalem. Eleazar, his son, general of the insurgents, was in charge of the rest of Judea to the Red Sea; and Josephus, the son of Gorion, was over Galilee and all the land of

Naphtali.[131] When Josephus assumed command, he assembled an army and marched against Syria, then called Halah,[132] where King Agrippa's treasures were stored. He captured them[133] and then he went down to Tiberias, which had rebelled against Israel. He entered by force of arms, and when he captured a Roman general, he tied his hands behind his back and sent him thus as an affront to Vespasian. Then he attacked Sepphoris, which had rebelled, and killed a large number of my children. Capturing the city, he avenged the blood of his brethren when he put all the people within to the sword and set the city's buildings on fire.[134]

Vespasian turned his army against Galilee. He besieged the city where Josephus was and attacked it for many months. Destruction and casualties were heavy on both sides, but in the end the city was breached by the Romans, and Josephus and the other nobles took refuge in a fortress, where they negotiated a pact with Vespasian. Josephus' companions, however, refused to accept the pact and decided to kill one another by lot rather than deliver themselves into their enemies' power. When only Josephus and one soldier who was afraid to kill him remained, both surrendered to the Romans.[135]

When the city was conquered, Vespasian left, took Josephus with him and went on to Joppa.[136] From there he sent his son Titus against Judea, commanding him to kill anyone refusing to surrender, and to tell all his captives to be grateful that he spared their lives. Titus complied with his father's command and went through all Judea perpetrating unparalleled cruelties.[137]

Vespasian then marched on the city of Gamala, which was located on the summit of a hill. At the request of King Agrippa, who accompanied him, he offered peace to the city and advised it to surrender without resistance. The Israelites drew near the wall and called lovingly to Agrippa, who went to speak with them. But they revealed their treachery and threw a huge rock down at him, which broke his shoulder and arm, and he fell senseless to the ground.

Vespasian was greatly angered. He fiercely attacked the city, captured it and massacred many people. And when he left Gamala, he laid waste all the other cities of Galilee with the sword and fire.[138]

In this province of Galilee there had arisen an Israelite named Johanan (John), a very factious and bloodthirsty man. The wicked and perverse men of Israel were attracted to him, and he became their leader.[139] When Galilee was lost, he fled with his men to Jerusalem.

In the meantime, Vespasian left for Mount Tabor. He captured all the towns and cities on the way, killing and destroying as he went. Finally, he and his son turned their armies toward Jerusalem to inflict a mortal blow upon the capital city.

Many perverse people from all over the land of Judea had taken refuge in Jerusalem. A large number, unstable by nature, defected to Johanan's command, betraying the High Priest, who was then the supreme master in Jerusalem.[140] With their aid Johanan became powerful in the Holy

City and began to persecute its righteous and noble citizens. In order to confiscate their estates, he accused them of wanting to defect to the Romans. His wickedness knew no bounds; he even despoiled the priests of their vestments and prevented them from performing their divine offices.[141] In short this wretch grew so powerful that he deprived Hananiah of the priesthood and ordered that High Priests be chosen by lot. And the lot fell to a rustic, whose name was Faruth, the son of Faniel.[142]

The righteous and worthy men among the people witnessed this great catastrophe and the degradation of the holy faith. Though they were powerless to prevent it, they were aroused to anger by this great offense, and they exhorted one another to risk their lives to remove it. A number of them assembled and attacked the malefactors with such fury that they and their leader Johanan were compelled to flee to the Temple. When the pursuers arrived there, Hananiah commanded that they shed no blood in the sanctuary. But he put about six hundred armed men around the Temple to watch them and to prevent them from leaving.

When Hananiah again took counsel on the matter, it seemed better to call the foe to come outside the Temple peacefully, and they did so. Their enemies, however, refused to trust them. Instead, they contacted the children of Esau,[143] who lived in Seleucia,[144] to ask them for aid. The Idumeans marshaled twenty thousand armed men and immediately came to Jerusalem. When Hananiah saw the army that was coming against him, he attempted a peaceful approach. Speaking to them calmly from the wall, he told them he was amazed at their coming to the aid of such wicked men, and suggested that they had been misled. To this the Idumean traitors deceitfully responded that they were coming only to aid Jerusalem.[145]

In the meantime Vespasian's army also arrived, and with it a great storm with thunder, lightning, fire, flashes, and an earth tremor so powerful that the people were forced to flee the wall. They said that the Lord was fighting for the Romans,[146] but they did not know that the hapless hour of their final ruin and destruction had come.

This storm forced the six hundred men who guarded the Temple against the insurgents to take refuge, for they were unable to withstand the great earthquake and the wind, rain and thunderbolts. Johanan's following, seeing themselves thus released, left the Temple to open the gates of the city to the Idumeans; when the treacherous Idumeans entered, they killed eight thousand Israelites, took possession of Jerusalem, and daily helped Johanan inflict great suffering upon the populace. Among their other evil deeds they arrested a wise and wealthy man named Zachariah, and charged him with sending Vespasian a letter promising to open the gates of Jerusalem for him. Johanan had him hurled down from the wall to the bottom of the valley of Jehoshaphat; he was dashed to pieces. All of his possessions were confiscated, and his children were left destitute.[147]

Johanan enjoyed this tyranny and sought to extend it. He told the righteous judges of Jerusalem that unless they invented similar accusations against other men of wealth, he would judge them as he had judged Zachariah. They therefore had to placate him. He soon arrested another worthy, Gorion, and sentenced him to death because of his wealth. When the innocent man pleaded that his body be buried after the execution of his sentence, Johanan refused, and had him torn apart by dogs instead.[148] And he inflicted similar cruelties upon many other innocent people in Israel.

Finally, when the righteous people saw themselves thus harassed and persecuted by the wicked, they had no recourse but to surrender to the Romans. They told Vespasian to come and free them from the hold of these wretched insurgents and said that they wanted to be his subjects.[149]

At the time of this embassy Vespasian had gone to another city, called Gadara, to help its good people, who were also harassed by Johanan's partisans. Vespasian[150] entered the city and massacred the insurgents. As he turned away and crossed the Jordan, he came upon a great number of Israelites in flight. Vespasian's army attacked them and killed thirteen thousand men in the first encounter, for the Israelites were disorganized and unarmed. The remainder of the people rashly jumped into the Jordan, believing that they could save themselves in this way. But what the enemy Vespasian failed to do was accomplished by the river, for though the Israelites thought they could easily turn back, the waters swelled over them. Ninety-two thousand Israelite men and women, old and young, were drowned, and the Jordan carried their bodies into the Dead Sea.[151]

When my Enemy had executed this frightful vengeance on my limbs, news reached Vespasian that fire from heaven had fallen upon Nero in Rome and killed him, and that Galba was ruling as emperor in his stead. The Romans then killed Galba, made Vespasian emperor and immediately sent ambassadors for him.[152]

Vespasian departed for Rome, taking Josephus ben Gorion with him as a prisoner; but as soon as he was crowned emperor, he freed him, and sent him back with great honors to his son Titus in Judea. He charged Josephus to accompany Titus in his wars, and he killed Agrippa, the king of Israel.[153]

Titus attacked the city of Gaza and captured it and all its environs in Judea. Afterwards he took Ascalon, Joppa and Caesaria, inflicting massacres and setting fires in each.[154]

Despite these misfortunes, the discords and iniquities within Jerusalem did not abate. Three divisions or parties had now been formed among the people. One faction followed Hananiah, the High Priest, who had been deprived of the priesthood. Another followed the wicked Johanan, and the third the equally wicked Simon. Thus brothers and kinsmen fought against each other. The more their discords and struggles multiplied and reduced their numbers, the more the camp of the Romans swelled with men and arms from all sides.

When Hananiah saw matters in this state, he gave the leadership of his faction to his son Eleazar. Eleazar was a major cause of the troubles which ensued. Though only Nero had manifestly hated Israel, Eleazar determined to harm the Roman army, and he provoked it to anger against me.[155]

These three factions fought continually and shed so much Israelite blood in the city that it ran like water through Jerusalem's squares and reached the gate of God's Temple. Nor was this the extent of their abominable activity and crime. Johanan and his perverse company moved to the highest terrain in the area, and from there they attacked the city by hurling arrows and large rocks from above, demolishing homes and killing the people who were walking in the squares.

Then he entered the Temple and killed many worthy priests who stood, sacrifices in hand, making offerings to the Lord. The blood of the animals was mingled with the blood of the holy and righteous people in Israel. This misfortune was so great that people could no longer bring their sacrifices to the Temple.

Johanan also set fire to most of the sumptuous houses and palaces in Jerusalem and to the stores of oil, wheat and other foods which the people had gathered in anticipation of the siege. Hunger and pestilence increased until the city lay desolate, while those who fled from the city's misfortune fell into Titus' captivity.[156] O my brethren, I cannot tell you even one of a thousand misfortunes which were suffered, for the Israelite tyrants who fought inside the city were much crueler to my children than the enemies who assailed us from without.

Having conquered Caesaria and other cities, Titus moved on and pitched his entire camp in Ellon, two days' journey from Jerusalem. There he chose six hundred of the most valiant Roman cavalry and took them to survey the Holy City to determine its vulnerable flank, and to see whether it might surrender peacefully.

When Johanan learned of Titus' arrival, he prepared an ambush. He attacked the Romans and killed all their men, except Titus, who alone escaped and fled the way he had come. It appears that the Lord was determined to preserve him that he might serve as the instrument of my punishment. In his anger, Titus immediately turned his entire army against Jerusalem, and exhorted his troops, saying, "You are now going to fight with a people which has no equal in the world in valor! They are stronger than lions, tougher than panthers and fleeter than deer."[157]

When the Israelites saw that their enemy had encircled them, they agreed to make peace among themselves and enthusiastically went forth to attack the Romans. They killed such a multitude in that attack that the Romans' lines were broken in many places and Titus was left with only a fraction of his troops. Though disgraced, he rallied his men and re-grouped his dispersed army. He went down from the Mount of Olives, where the battle had been waged on the first day, and re-engaged Israel near the gates of Jerusalem.

The Israelites, however, had cunningly stationed some of their horsemen in an ambush at the enemy's rear. Then they opened the gates of the city and prepared to battle Titus. The fighting began and the trap was sprung. The Romans, realizing there were enemies both behind and in front of them, cried out to Titus, "Save your life, sire. Do not die at the hands of the children of Israel; but if you do not leave, we will all die here with you." Titus preferred death to saving his life by flight.

Both sides battled valiantly; though the Romans appeared to be getting the worst of it, the damage to their ranks was actually small. After a few days of such skirmishing, the Israelites finally made a truce with the Romans. Yet no sooner had the war ceased outside, than it flared up more fiercely within the city than ever before. Titus was delighted to see that the Israelites' actions were helping him to win the war.

When the truce came to an end, the Romans and Israelites again drew their swords and brandished their spears against one another. Titus approached the walls of Jerusalem to consider how best to attack the city. When he saw a place suitable for his purpose beside the tomb of Johanan the priest, he told one of his men, "Speak to the men who are on top of the wall and find out if they are interested in making a pact with me. Then I will speak to them." The Israelites did not answer, and when the Roman repeated his statement, they shot an arrow at him. It sought out that part of the body which holds the chief source of life, and the Roman fell dead upon the ground.

This incident so incensed Titus that he ordered the battering rams to be brought against the wall. The impact of the machine was so powerful that it demolished the entire area around the first wall, penetrated it, and began to destroy the second.[158]

At this time a valiant Israelite horseman, Castor, who relied upon stratagem when his strength did not avail him, came to Titus and said, "O liege and king, pardon the stupidity and futility of the defense against you and have pity on this city and on the house of the sanctuary which is in it." "Come over to my side," Titus responded, "and I will let you live." Said Castor, "Let me first consult my companions, for I would like to go over to your side."

Titus trusted in this answer and approached the wall; but at this Castor and his men hurled down a massive door, aimed to kill Titus. It did not hit him, but it did not fall in vain, for it struck many Romans broadside, killing them, and its edges wounded many others. The rest of the Romans ran for refuge when they saw how badly their comrades had fared.

A large number of arrows and spears were directed at Titus, but he refused to display weakness and preferred to remain exposed to danger. Though he received several injuries, his wounds were not mortal. God's will defended him; and the fine shirt of mail and the excellent helmet he wore protected him. When he had no strength left to withstand such a multitude, he was finally forced to flee.[159]

On the following day Titus returned to battle. Before fighting he spoke kindly to his foes, and urged that matters should not be allowed to progress to the point where the city and the holy Temple might be destroyed. Upon hearing these arguments, many good and peace loving men who could foresee the dangers ahead wished to surrender to him. But Johanan and Simon and their perverse gang prevented them, sword in hand, and forthwith killed most of them. They closed the city's gates until the end of the war, and the people suffered the most severe and dire pangs of hunger, and were forced to eat dogs and dead rats.[160] And when even such food as this was lacking, mothers and fathers attacked and killed their children, and satisfied with their own flesh the faintness and craving of their bodies.[161]

The enemy continued to bring battering rams to the wall and to beat with great fury until valiant Israelite youths set fire to the rams. The resistance by the people inside the city lasted so long that Titus, to insure his victory, decided to starve the city by a long siege, for he recognized that it was impossible to hasten his victory by active battle.

My sins brought him the results he expected. Because of the famine, my people's corpses soon became so numerous that there were not enough graves to bury them, and they were thrown over the walls into the brook Kidron.

When the foe Titus saw the multitude of corpses, he raised his hands and eyes to heaven and said, "O Lord, I am innocent of the blood of these slain, for I sought peace."[162]

Despite famine's unbearable and frightful visitation, my iniquity continued its course. The wicked accused the priest Mattathiah before Simon, one of the Sicarii,[163] of wanting to defect to the Romans. Without respect for his venerable age or his holy calling, Simon executed him and four of his sons with the sword; only one of his sons escaped.[164] Then he executed the priest Hananiah of the family of High Priests and threw his body with the others. He continued his execrable deeds, executing the excellent scribe Aristeus, fifteen worthies, and eleven of the greatest and most renowned sages in Israel, because when they were stunned by Simon Sicareus' wickedness they had said to one another: "Blessed be He who is so patient in avenging Himself on the prevaricators against His will. How long will He delay in executing His wrath on this wretch?"[165]

Simon's cruel deeds were so frightful that all the other sages of the Law, fearing that they would soon fall into his hands, met in assembly, and decided to surrender to the enemy Titus and to look to him for kindness; they therefore secretly defected to him. He received them cheerfully and provided them with food to allay their hunger. But the hunger had so affected their systems that even as they ate their souls left them; the remedy came too late.[166]

Many others had swallowed their riches to prevent the wretched Israelite tyrants from taking them. Once in the Roman camp, they dropped gold and precious stones when they relieved themselves. When some Arabs and Syrians heard about this, they lay in wait for Israelites outside the camp, beheaded them, ripped them open and removed the remaining gems and gold from their insides. This misfortune affected as many as a thousand Israelites.[167] When news of these events reached Titus, he expelled from the camp the Arabs and Syrians who had committed this outrage, though he punished them no further.

The fire of my punishment burned so brightly and the enemy's sword was so bathed in blood that outside one gate in Jerusalem a hundred and fifteen thousand and eight hundred bodies, felled by the might of the sword and the plague, had been cast out for burial. And those who walked through the other gates were killed and thrown upon the corpses around the city; their number was six hundred thousand. And there were many others, of whom no count could be taken. Some were thrown into the valley of Kidron; others received no burial because of the Sicarii's cruelty.

Because of the might of the Sicarii, Jerusalem was not able to surrender to the Romans. As a result my children suffered the cruelest and most frightful famine mortals have ever experienced; for their once delicate and tender stomachs could not refuse even filthy and fetid animals which had never before served as human food. They gnawed at the leather of their shields, and bolted any herb they could find, without examining whether it was poisonous or noxious. There were thus many who ate death enveloped in the remedy they believed they had found to sustain their lives. Yet even this did not last; soon Jerusalem, which had been surrounded by luxuriant orchards and delightful trees, like a terrestrial paradise, was turned by the insurgents into a desert, a wilderness where grass or green herb could not be found.[168]

The Romans attacked the wall again with their battering rams, and their attack was so furious that they threw it to the ground. Titus rejoiced, but his joy was short-lived, for when this wall fell, behind it was a newer and much stronger wall which the Sicarii had erected. The Romans scaled the demolished wall, the Sicarii climbed the new wall, and a bloody battle was begun. The Israelites displayed such prowess that the Romans were about to abandon the wall and the hope of capturing Jerusalem, had not my sin called Titus at that moment.[169] He exhorted his men that the name of the Romans would suffer dishonor and infamy throughout the world if they lifted the siege of a city reeling from famine, pestilence and the countless other ills brought on by the internecine discords and struggles. One of Titus' knights, overcome by shame, drew his sword and shouted, "If any of you takes pride in being a valiant knight, let him join me and let us fight against those sickly weaklings."[170] A squadron formed around him and they rushed furiously up the wall. But the Sicarii, who waited for them with equal bravery, attacked them so valiantly that they left very few Romans alive; the survivors turned and fled with greater haste than they had come.[171]

Finally Titus, seeing the great resistance to his attacks, introduced new tactics. After taking counsel on what strategy to employ, he resolved to mine the city, and therefore immediately planted mines from the camp all the way inside Jerusalem; and when this was completed, the Romans again scaled the fallen wall.

The hour had now arrived in which my repose and freedom were to come to an end. Because of my constant rebelliousness, hunger had so weakened the guards who watched the wall and the fatigue from battle had cast such a deep sleep upon them that they did not perceive the enemies mounting until their swords were at their throats, about to snap off their lives. The enemy Titus suddenly entered the Holy City with all his soldiers, some jumping over the mines they had sown and others hurdling over the broken wall. Thus they captured Jerusalem, which used to be the defense and impregnable fortress against all my tribu- lations.

When the Sicarii saw themselves attacked, they regrouped into one band, and took refuge in a courtyard of the holy Temple, determined to resist valiantly. Titus attacked with his army and the Sicarii dauntlessly came forward to receive him at the entrance to the courtyard. Like men thrown to the lions, who have no choice but to try to muster all their strength and save their lives at the expense of their enemies, so the Israelites now engaged the Romans. The battle raged so furiously that one could hear from afar the clash of arms, the clang of swords, and the groans of the mortally fallen, hurled on their compassionate brothers, whose souls were forced to depart before their appointed hour. Within the city and without the number of corpses was so great that the way of those who wanted to pass was often blocked.

The Sicarii, seeing the extent of the battle, realized that they were at the brink of their destruction. Inflamed with anger, like a fire pent in a dusty container breaking out in search of air, they rushed out intrepidly against the Romans. They broke through their ranks like raging lions, and savagely killed and destroyed so many of them that the Romans were compelled to yield to their anger, and to flee in near defeat from the sanctuary and the city. Those who achieved this victory were Johanan (John), captain of the Sicarii and Alexas Gyphthaeus, captain of his cavalry; Simon, their chieftain and Jacob (James) the Idumean, his co- captain; and Malachiah, Arisimon and Judah. On the fifth day of the month of Sivan, in the afternoon preceding the festival of Shavuot, a countless number of Romans fell lifeless between the Temple walls in that encounter.[172]

And so as to leave the city defenseless, Titus had the walls thrown down. On the following day he again approached the sanctuary where the Sicarii were assembled, and once more, through Josephus, son of Gorion, spoke gently to them and admonished them to surrender. He consoled them and reproved them because they had defiled the sanctuary by shedding so much blood, and continued to profane it. Were they waiting for him to come with all his might, to set fire to the holy Temple and to put all the people in Jerusalem to the sword and thus bring the divine cult and service to an end?[173]

To this they answered, "As long as we fight the wars of our God and die free men in His house we need no other sacrifice than our lives, our flesh and our blood, and these we offer here near His altar. And we suffer this more cheerfully than the prospect of subjection to your heavy yoke and the shameful prison of your captivity."[174]

Many of the worthies, who saw how desperate their situation was and how the Lord had patently unsheathed His irate sword against them, defected to the Romans and delivered themselves into Titus' hands. He received them kindly and sent them to live in the land of Goshen, charging the Roman generals in the land of Egypt not to mistreat them.[175]

Then, seeing that the Sicarii refused to surrender under any conditions, Titus assembled an army of thirty thousand men, appointed the Roman Arustius their general and surrounded the entire Temple.[176] The Sicarii fought there for seven continuous days. At night they secretly infiltrated the Romans' camp in search of food, satisfied their famished bodies, and then returned. They did this so regularly that it came to be discovered, and guards were stationed to prevent it. When the Israelites could no longer endure their exquisite hunger, they began going out through the eastern gate to the Mount of Olives to seize horses, mules and asses. They slew the men guarding them, brought the animals into the city with great joy, and there ate them and shared them with their companions.[177]

But this hapless remedy diminished by the hour, and despairing of their lives, they performed amazing feats to harm the enemy, so that they might not die in vain. Thus, when they saw the city's walls demolished and those of the Temple sanctuary almost broken, the Israelites covered their sticks with sulphur, grease and fresh pitch, and gave the appearance of fighting with the Romans. They feigned to be fleeing from them, and when the Romans pursued them, they led them behind the Temple. From the time of the Temple of King Solomon of Israel, a large building stood here which the kings during the Second Temple had covered with logs of cedar. The Israelites used these to climb to the roof of the Temple, and the Roman knights followed them. No sooner had they reached the top when a soldier, who was hidden below, set fire to the building. The fire spread so quickly that the Romans had no chance to escape. Titus watched them being devoured by the flames and wept at his helplessness. A large number of his knights perished there.

But the fire in that mighty edifice was so great that it spread to nearby buildings. It burned countless houses and noble palaces of the princes and lords of Jerusalem, and finally reached the palace of King Hezekiah of Judah.[178]

At this time the famine had become so fierce that a sweet and warm-hearted young woman was found who had killed and eaten her young son.[179]

Titus now let loose the reins of his anger. Losing respect for the sanctity of the Temple, he brought the battering ram, beat the wall and felled it with two thrusts. The Romans rushed through the debris and reached the Temple gate. When they found it fastened, they set fire to the hinges, which were covered with silver. The fire melted them, set the wood ablaze and the holy portals fell to the ground.

On the next day their idolatrous and filthy hands set a far crueler fire in the divine Temple, burning the terrestrial home of the King of the universe. Many priests and worthies jumped into its flames and were destroyed with it. But before the Temple was completely consumed, Titus profaned it further by entering the place where only the High Priest was permitted. He cast his eyes in wonder in every direction and said, "Now I know that this house truly belonged to the heavenly King. With good reason did the nations come to it from the end of the earth to offer silver and gold to the Lord of the heavens."[180]

The Romans marveled at the building, and wanted to honor their gods with it. Accordingly, they spared some places from the fire. There they placed the abominable idols they worshiped and made their customary sacrifices to them, mocking my children and ridiculing my holy Law and its sacred ceremonies before their vile images.[181] Later, all of Israel's royal family humbly prostrated itself before the heathen Titus. Johanan and Simon had still not cooled the great ardor of their hatred. They set fire to all the noble houses and stores of wealth in Jerusalem to prevent the Romans from enjoying this glory along with all their others. Yet the vengeance I could now take on my enemies was of little consequence. Titus immediately ordered that all Israelites found in the squares of Jerusalem should be put to the sword; and a large part of the populace perished by this decree.[182]

At this time every man abandoned his leader to seek the Romans' mercy. Simon's horsemen, who had come from Idumea, offered to surrender to Titus if he would promise to spare them.[183] But when their general Simon learned of this, he executed many of them; the rest escaped to the Romans.

Titus stripped the Temple of all its valuables—the tables, the golden lamps, the pontifical vestments and the treasures of the Lord's house, and also the purple vestments consecrated by the kings in the period of the Second Temple.[184]

When Johanan, the chief of the Sicarii, saw his life dangling by its last threads, he threw himself at Titus' feet and now meekly begged for mercy. But his enemy was so hostile and angry toward him and Simon that he ignored his humble and pitiable petition and fettered him in heavy irons. Tied in this way, he was led through the Romans' camps, where he was mocked and vituperated. Seven days later he was dismembered, and he thus came to a hapless end.[185]

Simon, who did not know what had happened to Johanan, emerged shortly thereafter from his covert, attired in a rich purple garment and full royal regalia. He let himself be found by the Romans and was brought before Titus, who had him put in iron chains as he had done to Johanan, and made him run through the entire camp with great affront and disgrace. He did not permit him to die there, but brought him tied in this way to Rome, where he was slain in the triumph.

The number of dead in Jerusalem totaled a million people, not counting those who died from pestilence and hunger,[186] and the number of those captured was ninety and seven thousand. These numbers do not include the people who died with Eleazar, the son of Hananiah the priest.

This Eleazar fled Jerusalem before it was subjugated by Titus and took with him a large number of the finest people of Israel; and they went to take refuge in a fortress called Masada. Titus advanced against them after the battle in Jerusalem and fought them with mounds of earth, battlements and battering rams. He put them in such straits that they were about to surrender to him. But Eleazar their leader said to them, "What advantage or benefit can there be in our lives, now that we see our land destroyed and the building of our sanctuary laid waste? Why, will we not be considered vile and low, a shame and derision for all nations? Will we not be helpless to prevent the uncircumcised from sleeping with our daughters and wives before our very eyes? And furthermore will they not place the grievous yoke of their captivity on our sons before our very eyes? Therefore would it not be better for us to kill all our women and children as a sacrifice and set fire to all our possessions to prevent these heathen foes from enjoying them? And furthermore, would it not be preferable for each of us to receive death patiently at the hand of his companion rather than from the Romans who are before us? Certainly it will be nobler for our souls and more honorable for our bodies than to fall into the hands of these filthy and barbarous pagans."

When all the men had heard this speech, they assembled their wives and children in the city square and put all to the edge of the sword. Then they set fire to all their wealth and their houses just as they were. Finally they killed one another by lot and the last one thrust his cruel sword into himself.[187]

And forty-eight and a half years after the destruction of the holy Temple, there arose in the city of Bethar in Judea a Jew by the name Bar Cozba. His knowledge surpassed that of most people in his day, and he announced that he was the true Messiah whom we await, and offered amazing proofs of his identity. In short, his ways and manner were so effective that he incited the people of this city[188] to rebel against the Roman Empire. Hadrian Caesar, who was then emperor, learned of the rebellion and attacked the city with a mighty army. After a siege that lasted three and a half years, he captured it and inflicted such a cruel and frightful massacre upon its people that our enemies' horses wallowed up to their mouths in Israelite blood, and the current of the blood was so great and powerful that it swept large and heavy stones along as it coursed to the sea, four thousand paces from the city. Finally, a third part of the two rivers which flowed in the area of Jericho ran red with the blood of forty-five thousand men who were slain, and for seven years the heathens round about fertilized their vines with the putrid blood of Jews. Among those slain was Bar Cozba; his head had been cut off by a Roman soldier.[189]

LAMENT ON THE LOSS OF THE SECOND TEMPLE

O Lord, why did you restore me from the shattered state in which I was left after the destruction of the First Temple? Was it to have people who could bear great torments, such as those I see before me in the Second? Why did you again clothe me in joyous garb if I was destined to be covered with such exquisite pain and sadness? This second glory seemed a shadow, and this second prosperity a lightning flash. It made me recollect and thus bewail anew the loss of the First Temple, for this Second Temple did not equal in excellence the one I formerly possessed. Like a man inured to pauperism, I was already reconciled to captivity in Babylonia, and rejoiced in it. But my misfortune envied me even this estate. It stationed itself in my way like an enemy, sword unsheathed, to block the forward moves I made with my strokes of good fortune, after I had taken only a few steps of the journey.

O hapless Israel, how fleeting are your pleasures and satisfactions here on earth! How briefly joys tarry with you! They pass through your gate with the swiftness of a courser. Blessings appear like a dream to you; they come to visit you only to increase your torment, for they momentarily slip from your hands. Like a survivor at sea, tossed by the tempest onto a deserted beach and stripped of all his earthly riches, so was I, O Lord, after the torment of the cruel Assyrians and Babylonians. Would that you had left me in this condition if the remedy of the Second Temple was to be so curtailed. You consoled me with only one son[190] in this second house for the many thousands of my children whom death swallowed in the first. I know not why you granted it so little life. Instead of a merciful consolation and help, it was a way by which I regressed and bewailed anew all those lost ones whom I had lamented before.

If I had enjoyed no further blessing than the First Temple, which I lost, time would have assuaged my grief and pain. But since I was again allowed to taste part of the blessing, and its sweetness immediately turned to gall, I could not bear such suffering. O hapless me, water was raised to my parched lips, but before I could taste it, it was taken away from me. I found myself destitute in the cold deserts of Norway, and I was helped by a will-o'-the-wisp, which vanished with the wind. Blessings quick to come and go leave greater wounds than pain felt from their continued privation.

Among the Babylonians, O Lord, I thirsted so for liberty, dominion and wealth! Since for some reason it was Your wish to visit me at the end of seventy years, why did You immediately despoil me and impoverish me through the Romans? And if I had to fall if You raised me up, would that You had let me lie fallen and not lifted me. For if I had to bear the captive's yoke under heathen peoples, I already bore such a yoke among the Babylonians. And if I was to be deprived by idolaters of the Holy Land which You gave me in part, I was already far away from the Holy Land and longed for it in pain in Babylonia. And if because of my lack of merit You did not wish to seek a way by which I might avoid the misfortunes which You prepared to punish me, would that You had done so, O merciful Lord, for the honor of Your sanctuary. For since Nebuchadnezzar's filthy hands had already profaned it, why did You deliver it anew into the power of the heathen Titus?

Here, in a short compendium, brethren, you see the history of the Second Temple and the sins which I committed there. This was the axis or hinge on which all my prosperity and rest turned and were transformed, giving all my blessings this disastrous end. Does it seem to you that these misfortunes are designed merely to sting[191] and these losses merely to bring regret?

Then, later, in the time of Emperor Trajan, I saw the multitude of Jews who dwelt in the province of Cyrene (in Africa, to the east of the great Syrtis)[192] conspire and rise up against the Romans and Greeks who lived in that province and kill most of them. And the Jews who lived in Egypt did the same. When the Jews living on the island of Cyprus learned of this, they too rebelled and inflicted such a great slaughter on their enemies that two hundred thousand persons were killed. This resulted in the promulgation of an imperial law that no Jew could enter the island of Cyprus, and anyone coming there would be put to death, regardless of the circumstances of his arrival. This statute was so rigorously enforced that even if any Israelite stopped there during a storm or by error, he was immediately put to death. But since my sin deserved even greater punishment, the Emperor Trajan dispatched a large army against the Jews in the territory of Cyrene, and carried out a general massacre among them. Such a savage slaughter had never before been witnessed in the world; four hundred thousand Jewish souls left their bodies by the force of the sword.

And when, after this terrible misfortune, Emperor Hadrian succeeded to the throne, he ordered the rebuilding of the holy city of Jerusalem, which had been leveled by Titus not long before. The city soon rose again, due to the amazing speed of the Jewish builders, who were chiefly responsible for this achievement. Hadrian named the city Aelia Hadria Capitolina (derived from the name of Hadrian), and forbade it to be called Jerusalem. Despite this, my children greatly rejoiced at its rebuilding. But when they saw it being populated by many heathens, who worshiped their idols there and erected abominable temples to their gods, they could not bear to see the holy city so profaned.[193] Their jealousy and anger reached such a peak (they were also greatly harassed and subjected by the heathen and could not freely practice their holy Law), that they rebelled. They routed all the auxiliary troops and the Roman garrisons from the provinces of Judea and Galilee and all the rest, and killed as many as they could.

When Hadrian learned of this, he dispatched against the Jews a large and powerful army under the command of Julius Severus. Severus slew a large number of my children. And after they were conquered, the Romans desolated their entire province. They razed fifty noble castles and many key fortresses, and burned nine hundred and eighty-five towns and inhabited villages. Fifty thousand Jewish warriors died in skirmishes and battles, and many others perished from the famine, disease and hardships which accompanied the war. And when this extremely cruel vengeance had been executed, Severus expelled and permanently exiled all my children who remained in Jerusalem.

CONSOLATION FOR THE LOSS OF THE SECOND TEMPLE

ZICAREO: How rough and heavy was this wheel, for it trampled your earthly limbs and bruised your divine soul. I realize that flesh cannot help but feel its suffering. But this does not mean that the heavenly spirit infused in it should in such circumstances reject reason, which offers it consolation. Thus if your flesh has suffered, its pain should not have blinded your understanding. Omitting for now the discussion as to whether you deserved the punishment you received in the time of this Second Temple (since the truth of it can be understood by your history), let us come to the reasons you have presented in your lament.

You say that it was not necessary to raise up one who was to fall again, and that one who was to become a slave once more to the Romans could have done without dominion, since he was already a slave to the Babylonians. You speak with passion and not with reason. Now listen to me; you will see how mistaken you are.

When the Lord decided that the Second Temple should be built, it was not with the intention that it should necessarily be destroyed. On the contrary, if your works deserved it, the promise made to your fathers would have been fulfilled through it; and it would have lasted forever. Do you wish to see proofs of this truth?

(1)[194] Do you not recall how God's mercy came to aid you one night, when Alexander the Macedonian, emperor of Greece, attacked Cyrus, the king of the Persians, and led his army against Jerusalem with the intention of harming you because of your alliance with Darius? (The truth was that your sins now called for punishment.) While Alexander was serenely sleeping on his couch, during his journey to Jerusalem, the Lord made a man clothed in a white linen tunic appear near the head of his bed. In his hand he held an unsheathed sword, flashing like a lightning bolt, and he lifted it to strike Alexander. The king of Macedonia was frightened, and said, "Sire, why would you strike your servant?" The man answered, "The Lord of the heavens has sent me to subject great kings and many nations to you, and I am therefore accompanying you to favor you in your wars. Yet you must die now if you intend to attack Jerusalem and harm the Lord's people and priests."

"I beseech you," said Alexander, "to pardon this evil which your servant until this moment has committed with his thought alone."

Alexander's coming had made you swallow a bitter draft, and the Lord wanted to put him in your hands that you might receive consolation from the foe himself. Therefore, when He saw Alexander's repentance and humility, the man answered him: "Go on to Jerusalem, and before the gate you will find a man dressed in white linen, as I am, and similar to me in his appearance. Kneel down before him and worship him, and do exactly as he tells you; do not deviate one jot, for if you do not do this, know that you will die on that very day."

The king arose, terrified, and continued his journey. As soon as he arrived in Jerusalem, he saw Jaddua, the High Priest, who calmly awaited him in front of the terrorized populace. Alexander jumped quickly from his chariot, knelt on the ground, and worshiped and obeyed him. Because of his humility, the High Priest made entreaty for him to the Most High. The Lord gave Alexander victory against Darius, king of the Persians, against whom he had come to wage war, and you were freed from the great misfortune which threatened you.

(2)[195] Do you not remember the great marvel the Lord performed before your eyes a short time later when slanderous Israelites went to Seleucus, one of Alexander's four successors, and exaggerated to him the riches of gold, silver and precious stones which you possessed in your Second Temple? Seleucus sent his general Heliodorus to bring him all the treasure he could find there. When Heliodorus came to Jerusalem and entered the Temple to strip it of its riches, there within the Sanctum Sanctorum, the Lord made him and all his cohort hear the sound of a terrifying and frightful earthquake, which rent the mountains asunder and shattered the rocks.[196] In fear, they took to flight and left Heliodorus alone. When he raised his eyes, a man of frightening mien appeared before him, wearing a golden vestment spangled with precious stones and girt below with golden weapons ready for battle. He rode a mighty steed, and he attacked Heliodorus so furiously that the horse hoofed and wounded him, and threw him to the ground. Moreover, the horseman ordered his two servants, clad in white tunics and holding whips in their hands, to scourge Heliodorus; they did so with such cruelty that they left him tottering between death and life. In this condition, he was lifted up and thrown out of the Sanctum Sanctorum. From there his men carried him to a bed, and he lay paralyzed, unable to open his mouth either to speak or to eat. And when they saw him in this condition, all the elders and nobles of Macedonia humbly asked the High Priest Onias to pray to the Lord on his behalf, saying: "We recognize that all the gods of the nations are vain and only your God is the supreme truth. He made the world and in His hand are the souls of all the living." When the holy priest heard this, he prayed to the Lord for Heliodorus. In that instant, Heliodorus saw the two youths who had whipped him in the sanctuary. They said to him, "Arise and go to the priest Onias and throw yourself at his feet, because for his sake the Lord, whom you offended, will have compassion upon you." Heliodorus immediately received strength, arose and went to Onias. He fell to the ground before him, blessed the Lord, the God of Israel, and the priest, and offered silver and gold to the Temple's treasury; then with all speed, he left the city to take refuge in Macedonia. From that time forth King Seleucus never again dared to harm Jerusalem; rather, as long as he lived, he continued to send presents to the Temple of the Lord.

(3)[197] Do you not remember the first victory which the Lord gave to Mattathiah the Maccabee against Antiochus' general, Philip? With only a small group of the good people of Israel, Mattathiah and his sons attacked the enemy's powerful army, which had come against them near the mountain where they had withdrawn because of the foe's cruel deeds. And they inflicted such a massacre among the heathens that from then on no trace of them was left in the land of Judah. And they circumcised all the Israelite men who had not been circumcised for three and a half years because the enemy Antiochus had forbidden it under penalty of death.

(4)[198] And when Antiochus' son, Nicanor,[199] later returned with a large army and, confident of his victory, brought many merchants to buy the children of Israel that he would capture, do you not recall how the Lord thwarted his intentions, and how his entire army was routed and destroyed by only seven thousand Israelites, led by Judah? Nine thousand Macedonians[200] were slain in the battle, countless others were wounded, and the rest took to flight as swiftly as their horses could carry them. And Judah took much booty of silver and gold, both Nicanor's as well as his merchants', which they had brought to purchase the captives. And God's mercy did not stop here; it inspired your children to increase their victory. After the Macedonians had regrouped, the Israelites destroyed twenty thousand more, including their general, Philip, who had slain the saintly Eleazar. And Nicanor himself would have joined his soldiers, stretched out lifeless in the field, had he not taken refuge alone in Macedonia, disguised in common garb.

(5)[201] And when his father, Antiochus, angered at this defeat, uttered many blasphemies against the Lord and vowed and threatened to destroy Jerusalem, do you not remember how the Lord afflicted him with a serious illness? Even with this punishment, his haughtiness did not lessen, and he attacked you with a countless host. But the chariot in which he was riding overturned on the road and crushed his limbs, and the Lord heaped wound after wound upon him. He cast such a stench on

Antiochus that when his men tried to lift him from the ground, they could not bear the noxious odor which issued from his body, and they dropped him. Everyone fled from him; his flesh and bones began to rot and you saw him come to a wretched end in a foreign land as a punishment for the great ills which, according to your story, he had inflicted on your children.

(6)²⁰² Do you not recall that when you attacked the Idumeans under the captaincy of this same Judah, the Lord gave you victory against them and twenty thousand enemies were slaughtered in the battle?

(7)²⁰³ And to avenge the evil which you say Timothy the Macedonian general committed against you in the lands of Manasseh and Gilead, do you not remember that the Lord delivered to you eleven thousand Macedonian foot soldiers and a thousand and three hundred horsemen? You decapitated them with your own hands, while Lysias, Antiochus' successor, and all the rest of the army fled and cried with reproach: "The Lord is fighting for Israel."

(8)²⁰⁴ Do you not remember how the Lord delivered to you the Greek cities of Joppa and Jamnia, where you say by means of a ruse, your women and children were drowned in the sea, that you might take vengeance on them? When the Israelites had been removed from the two cities, you put all the inhabitants, young and old, to the sword's sharp edge and set fire to both.

(9)²⁰⁵ Then, when a large number of Greeks came to their aid under Timothy's command, cursing Israel and your leader, Judah, do you not remember how the Lord showed you the kindness of delivering thirty thousand of them to you? You avenged yourself by impaling them on your spears. And moreover, do you not recall how you seized their leader, Timothy, who knelt on the ground and begged Judah to spare his life? And how the King of the heavens favored you even further and enabled you to increase your victory; for as you turned toward the Arabian desert, you met the army of the king of Macedonia coming to attack you, and on that day, before nightfall, you felled twenty-five thousand of your enemies? And in order that you might return to Jerusalem from that journey with greater triumph, the Lord then delivered the entire province of Idumea to you. You overthrew most of its cities and subjected the rest to your tribute.

(10)²⁰⁶ Do you not remember that when Nicanor angrily blasphemed these victories and threatened to destroy your Second Temple, the Lord, by your hand and under Judah's leadership, killed thirty thousand of his fighting men; and Judah himself cut Nicanor's head in two; and the Lord delivered the rest of Nicanor's army into the hands of the peoples in the surrounding Israelite cities? Encouraged by His favor, they attacked the fleeing Macedonians, and did not leave a single man alive, so that there was no one remaining in their entire army to bear tidings of the event. And after they were cast along your fields, you stripped them of the gold and silver and precious stones which were sewn all over their rich garments; and you cut off Nicanor's right hand, which he had once menacingly stretched forth against the Temple. In remembrance of this lofty marvel and the mercy received from the Lord, you placed this arm over a gate in Jerusalem thenceforth called Nicanor's Gate.

(11)[207] Do you not remember the many enemy cities, including the Idumean cities of Dora and Merissa, which the Lord delivered to Hyrcanus, the son of Simon the Maccabee, and which he submitted to Jerusalem's tribute? Under compulsion, they performed circumcision and kept Israel's Law until the time of the Captivity. And all the other peoples over whom the Lord gave Hyrcanus victory did likewise. Heaven's favor toward you was so generous, that although the Romans were already very powerful in the world, they sought your friendship in a peace treaty, and were greatly pleased when you granted it.

(12)[208] Do you not remember when this same Hyrcanus sent his sons Antigonus and Aristobulus to war against Samaria? Hyrcanus remained in Jerusalem, greatly worried about their safety. On a day when he was offering a prayer for the people inside the Temple, he suddenly thought of his sons and the danger to which they were exposed, and then he heard a voice saying, "O priest Hyrcanus, do not fear any danger to your sons. Finish your service, for you have entered in peace and you shall leave in peace." And when he left the Temple he informed the people of this, but they did not believe him. Do you not remember that he immediately sent to his army in Samaria for news and learned that his sons had vanquished Cleopatra, Queen of Egypt, and Epicrates, Prince of Macedonia, who came to the aid of the Samaritans?

(13)[209] And to avenge the actions of the Gazites and Lathyrus against you, do you not remember that the Lord—in addition to the countless victories He granted you against the heathens, the Syrians and others—by the hand of Alexander, the son of this priest Hyrcanus, delivered Gaza to you, the city from which you had received so many misfortunes? You put to the edge of the sword all the people in it, except Lysimachus and his family, whom you spared because they had opened the gates for you.

(14)[210] And after you had executed a cruel vengeance on the city, you should remember that you set fire to the temple of Apollo, whom these same heathen worshiped, and burned the golden idol itself and all its priests in a huge bonfire.

Because of all these mercies, and an infinite number of others which you have received from the Lord, and which I have omitted in order not to burden you,[211] it is appropriate that when you recall the misfortunes you suffered in this Second Temple, you bear in mind your blessings as well.

Thus He who defended your Temple and city against Alexander the Macedonian clearly did not intend to rebuild it merely in order to destroy it.

And He who dealt so ill with Heliodorus, Seleucus' general, because he had come to attack the holy house, did not wish to strip it of its wealth and treasure.

And He who so cruelly killed Antiochus to avenge your righteous children and to ward off the threat which Antiochus had made and the determination with which he was marching against Jerusalem, clearly did not plan to injure your limbs or to lay waste the holy city in which you dwelt.

Even blind and base people may understand that He who destroyed Nicanor and his entire army, and caused the arm which he had stretched forth menacingly against the Temple to be cut off and placed upon its gate, did not have any intention of destroying the Temple, because He was defending it.

He who made it possible for you to burn the temple of Apollo, and the idol itself and all its foul priests, doubtless did not desire to have noxious fire touch His most holy Temple, or His divine priests to burn in it.

And He who killed so many Macedonians, Idumeans, Samaritans, Egyptians and countless other heathens to save you cannot be said to have desired that your blood be shed.

And He who subjected so many nations to Israel's yoke and service in this Second Temple did not desire to put you into the captivity of the Romans. Rather He wished to preserve the Temple's structure, to prosper the city of Jerusalem, and to defend your children's lives from their enemies. But you with your evil deeds brought the Assyrians and the Babylonians to destroy your first Temple and now the Romans to level this second one.

You refused to fear the comet, resembling a tongue of fire, which appeared over the city of Jerusalem as a warning a full year before its destruction. Nor did you take heed of the huge and splenderous shaft of light which in the first hour of the night illumined the area of the altar and the entire Temple like broad daylight, and threatened to set it all afire as it consumed the superfluities of your hatreds.[212]

And when a sacrificial cow so unnaturally bore a lamb in the Temple itself, you did not heed this as a warning that your works were contrary to nature and opposed to the will of God.

You saw another portent when the east gate of the inner Temple, which even twenty men could not close since it was made of heavy metal, opened by itself at the sixth hour of the night, though it had been bolted with iron and latched on top. This omen signified that the gates were calling to the enemies to enter. Yet you still could not close the gates of your soul to envy and hatred, but kept them always wide open so that they might easily lodge within.

On the day of Pentecost when the priests heard a noise and great tumult in the Sanctum Sanctorum at night and a voice which said painfully, "Let us go away from here," you did not have a voice to ask the Lord for mercy, to beg Him not to depart and abandon you.

When your people were at peace before war came, a rustic went about in the streets for four years saying, "A voice is heard from the east and a voice is heard from the west and a voice from the four winds and a voice against Jerusalem, against the Temple, against the bridegrooms and the brides and a voice against this entire people: 'Woe to Jerusalem.' " But he did not frighten you, nor did he make you turn to the Most High with true repentance, to deter the great punishment which was coming down upon you.[213]

None of these warnings broke your hardness.

Do you wish to know further how you alone have hurt yourself, and how much the Lord did not want you to receive these misfortunes, and His holy Temple these profane destructions? Hear His words: "Your ways and your thoughts have procured this unto you, O Israel. This is your wickedness which enters your heart, bitter though it be" (Jer. 4.18). "My bowels, my bowels, I writhe in pain! The chambers of my heart! My heart moans within me! I cannot be still! I cannot rest! Because, hear, O my soul, the sound of the horn, the war alarm" (Jer. 4.19). "Give your glory unto the Lord your God, before it grows dark and before your feet stumble on the mountains of twilight; and, while you look for light, He convert it into deadly shadows and it be made into darkness. But if you will not hear it, my soul shall weep in secret for your pride and I shall wail wretchedly and my eye shall shed a tear, because the Lord's flock is being carried away captive" (Jer. 13.16-17).

Does it seem to you that that infinite Majesty could have spoken sweeter words in this life to a mortal creature than He spoke to you, or given clearer indications that He grieved over your misfortunes? Certainly with only these proofs you can regard yourself as the happiest of all creatures, for you will find that He has not employed any of these means with any other people that was or is yet to be punished.[214] All nations and princes who offended you and who set their hand on your sacred objects were destroyed for your sake, in order that you might see more clearly how deeply He feels the pain you suffer for your punishment.

What befell the empire of the Egyptians, who plagued you in their lands? How did the monarchy of the Babylonians end who soaked you in blood? What has become of the memory of the Persians, whose subjection you suffered? And what happened to the great power of the Greeks who offended you? You have seen the end which all of them suffered, even while your sins were calling them to punish you. Their fate is notorious. A great number of Egyptians were drowned in the Red Sea and the rest were then nearly destroyed by the Babylonians; the Babylonians were subjugated by the Persians and Medes and then the memory of their rule toppled [like their tower] to the ground; the Persians' name was consumed by the Macedonians, and the Macedonians were laid low by the prepotent Romans.

And the Romans, of whom you now complain, had a cruel and fearsome punishment, that you might be avenged, for they killed one another and destroyed themselves with their own hands.[215]

The wretch Pompey, who so haughtily entered the Temple with his cavalry, was destroyed in a fierce battle [45 B.C.E.][216] by his own father-in-law, Julius Caesar,[217] and the traitor Ptolemy presented Caesar with Pompey's head. And so that Pompey alone should not bear the punishment for what so many others helped him commit, God's will decided that in this war all the Roman forces should assemble in the Pharsalian Fields. Here all those who had injured you perished from the direst hunger and the most fearsome cruelties, greater than the cruelties they had inflicted upon you. The sword of one brother did not pardon the heart of the other. And the barbarity went so far that whosoever showed his general his father's head impaled upon a spear was considered to have accomplished a signal exploit in his service.

Even the Roman consuls and the other great leaders reached hapless ends. Marcus Cato slew himself [49 B.C.E.], and Caesar, who had won so many famous victories and attained the title of emperor of nearly the entire earth, was cruelly daggered and killed in one of the abominable temples of the Romans, by his own kith and kin [44 B.C.E.]. Octavian Caesar, who succeeded him in the emperorship in King Herod's time, took the lives of three hundred senators and many other noble Romans. And Brutus, an illustrious prince, killed himself so as not to fall into the hands of Octavian [42 B.C.E.]. Then Cassius, a satrap of greatness and power, ordered a servant to kill him after countless Romans had perished on land and at sea in the wars he waged against Sextus Pompey and many others in his fatherland [42 B.C.E.].

The emperor Gaius Caligula was stabbed thirty-three times by his subjects [41 C.E.]. And after him, do you not recall the wretched end of Nero [68 C.E.], who dispatched Vespasian and Titus against Jerusalem, and the hapless death of Servius Galba, his successor, who was decapitated in the center of Rome [69 C.E.]? Galba's body was left without burial, and his head was presented to Otho, who accepted it and assumed control of the Empire. And afterwards, this Otho expired in his chamber when his own hands pierced his chest with a dagger [69 C.E.].

Emperor Vitellius was carried through the streets of Rome like a malefactor, with his hands tied and a rope around his neck, and he was mortally beaten and wounded by the populace [69 C.E.].

Titus, who also wore the serrate crown of the powerful Roman Empire, and whose hands had shed so much Israelite blood, suffered a wretched illness and was cut off in the prime of his glory after only a brief reign [81 C.E.].

Emperor Domitian, who saw in a prophecy that a king would arise from David's family to destroy Rome, and, out of fear, executed many members of David's line, also had his life taken by the sword in a conspiracy [96 C.E.].

As for Emperor Hadrian, who was responsible for the extermination of the remnants of your people in the regions of Syria and Jerusalem, he was plagued by the Lord with a painful illness for your vengeance. In desperation, he killed himself by depriving himself of food and drink [138 C.E.].

Not satisfied with this punishment, the Lord of vengeance, in the time of Marcus Aurelius [161-180 C.E.], sent against the Roman people the most terrible pestilence ever witnessed in the world, and millions suffered a hapless death.

And who does not know of the disastrous end of Commodus, who followed Marcus Aurelius on the imperial throne? He was poisoned by his concubine, Marcia [192 C.E.]. And the death suffered by Pertinax was also disastrous; his own soldiers put an end to his life with their spear thrusts. They seized control of nearly all of Rome, and put the Empire up for sale at auction, announcing that it would become the property of the person who bid highest and promised them the most favors [193 C.E.]. Do you think that the Romans, for all their greatness, had attained a healthy state of affairs? It is true that their emperor ruled over nearly the entire world. He held peaceful sway over everything that the Christian kings possess in Europe today; over everything that the inhabitants of Africa control; over everything that the Great Turk rules in Asia, Greece and Egypt; and over much that other lords and princes possess elsewhere throughout the world. Yet, that you might be avenged, as few as three hundred soldiers were able to take Commodus' life and usurp his dominion from him while he was in Rome, the source of his strength and the capital of the entire Empire. No buyers were found for Rome, nor was there much demand for it.

Thus you can see how the Romans took vengeance upon one another for your sake, and that God's will consented to these events, for no other force would have been sufficient to conquer them.

There is also the story of Didius Julianus, who finally bought the Empire for gold. After he had ruled for only seven months, two other emperors, Pescennius Niger in the East and Septimus Severus in Germany, rose against him. Septimus Severus prevailed over Julianus and executed him in his royal palace. Pescennius lost his head in a very bloody battle in which a large number of Romans perished. His head was presented to Septimus Severus mounted on the point of a spear; Severus later disdainfully trampled on his body with his horse [193 C.E.].

Emperor Bassianus Macrinus Caracalla was killed by the dagger of Opilius Macrinus and this same Opilius was later despoiled of the rule and killed with dishonor and shame by Elagabalus [217-218 C.E.].

And who does not know of Elagabalus' luckless end, the most miserable fate of all the emperors? When he fearfully hid himself from his soldiers in a shameful place, they removed and killed him, and then threw him into an even dirtier and more fetid place. Because this place was too small they moved him again. They dragged him through all Rome like the body of a dog, and then tied weights to him and threw him into the Tiber River, so that he was forever lost and without a place of burial [222 C.E.].

Alexander Severus, to whom the scepter then fell, had his life taken with violence and hatred by his own Roman subjects near the city of Mayence, in Germany [235 C.E.]. And fierce wars, dissensions, robberies, acts of violence and many other evils grew among Roman citizens and lords after his death and that of his successor, Maximinus [238 C.E.]. In addition to the large number of deaths which occurred there, the city of Rome was set on fire, and a large part of it was burned. In short, in the three full years that Maximinus held the scepter, all kinds of tribulations and calamities continued unceasingly throughout his Empire. Nor did he escape the evil end of his predecessors. As he was quietly sleeping in his tent, his soldiers killed both him and his son, who was heir presumptive to the Empire.

Pupienus and Balbinus, who ruled together after him, were stripped of their imperial robes and borne ignominiously through the center of Rome, like two thieves. Outside Rome's gates they were stabbed by the Praetorian Guard and their bodies left stretched out on the road, so that their place of burial was the bellies of dogs and wild beasts [238 C.E.].

Gordianus, who succeeded them, had his life and dominion taken from him by Philip. And so that Gordianus' executioner should not boast of his feat, in Verona Philip's own soldiers decapitated him at the upper row of his teeth, and killed Philip's son in Rome, so that his family should not rule as emperors [244-249 C.E.].

Gallus' strange and hapless death after he took possession of the Empire is well known. Despairing of his life, he rode his horse headlong into a large lake, in which he drowned [254 C.E.].

In brief, all the rest of the gang that followed came to an evil end through violent deaths. They killed one another or brought on their unhappy end in other ways, the details of which I must omit, for they will make my story too burdensome.[218] I shall only remind you of the low estate to which the Goths reduced the grandeur of Rome, and how they avenged those nations throughout the world whom Rome had harmed. They killed Rome's children; they sacked her wealth; they set fire to her proud buildings and sumptuous palaces; they broke the memorable statues of her emperors and illustrious generals; and they pickaxed the marble slabs, the noteworthy antiquities which gave life to Rome's fame, on which the Romans had sculptured the account of their victories and exploits. The Goths were not content to avenge themselves on the living Romans; they determined to destroy the memory of their past, which they had preserved in sculptured stone. And for an entire year Rome was not inhabited by rational creatures, but by wild and poisonous beasts. Thus you see that the Roman Empire suffered a grievous punishment; it was not only left impoverished, without territory or subjects, but its memory and fame (like that of other peoples who committed so much evil) were nearly expunged.

And so that you may be assured that all were punished on your account, hear the words of the Lord which testify to it! "O My people, be not afraid of the Assyrian, that he will smite you, and lift up his staff against you on the road to Egypt. For in yet a very little while, the fury of My indignation shall be accomplished, in their dishonor. The Lord of hosts shall stir up a scourge against him, as He did in the slaughter of the Midianites at the rock of Horeb" (Isa. 10.24-26).

And about the Babylonians, of whom you said when you found your-self among them, "The violence done to me and to my flesh is in Babylon and my blood is among the Chaldean inhabitants," the Lord therefore says, "I will plead your cause and take vengeance for you. I will dry up her sea, where the wealth of all kingdoms flowed, and make her fountain dry. Babylon shall be converted to heaps of stones" (Jer. 51.35-37). "Israel is a scattered sheep. Lions have driven him away. First the king of Assyria devoured him, and after him Nebuchadnezzar, the king of Babylonia, pulled his bones apart. Therefore, thus says the Lord of hosts, the God of Israel, 'I will punish the king of Babylonia and his land, as I have punished the king of Assyria' " (Jer. 50.17-18).

Then as for the Romans, the Lord threatened them with no less a punishment, and they indeed received it in full. The Lord said: "I have taken out of your hand the cup of staggering and the beaker of My fury, and you shall no longer drink it, Israel. And I will put it into the hand of them that afflict you and who say to your soul 'Bow down, that we may go over, and lay your body flat upon the ground so that it might serve as a street for those that pass by' " (Isa. 51.22-23).

Thus you see how the Lord repaid those who were the instruments of punishment for your iniquities, though your sins no longer permitted any other blessing and it was necessary for Him to employ the full justice of His office. Thus you should receive great consolation on seeing God's power mix such abundant mercy with the punishment which your sin perforce required of Him, and ordain such bitter ends for the enemies who punished you.

YCABO: According to your arguments I now recognize that the Lord again clothed me with new feathers in this second structure, so as to keep multiplying my blessings daily and to fulfill His spiritual and temporal promises if my merits permitted. And because I did not ac-knowledge Him but remained obstinate by flouting His precepts and living in this Second Temple with discords, jealousies and bloodshed, I received His cruel punishment through the Romans; but it was less than my iniquities required of His justice. Nevertheless, since this was so, and the Lord deigned to give me that punishment in compensation for my wicked deeds, why is it that He did not return to me with His mercy once I had received the punishment for my sin? Instead, from that time to the present, I have received cruel punishments and pitiful wounds on my afflicted body—some from new nations who arose amongst these same Romans in the West after their heavy wheel had passed over my bones, and others at the hand of modern peoples in the East.

ZICAREO: You have observed well, and I shall answer you. But first I desire that you recount these misfortunes to me as you have been doing, so that I may apply the proper remedies. Let us leave this task for the morning, for the shadows descending the mountains are now longer than is usual for us, and our neighbor Yronio's reapers, their toil ended, and their scythes on their backs, have begun to return to their cabins singing joyous songs. Let us also retire to ours; where, tonight, like last night, we shall not lack ripe apples and a fresh cheese made in the morning from the milk of my speckled ewe.

NUMEO: You have spoken very well; let us go, Ycabo.

YCABO: Let us go.

END OF THE SECOND DIALOGUE

THIRD

DIALOGUE

WHICH DEALS WITH

ALL THE TRIBULATIONS ISRAEL HAS SUFFERED

SINCE THE LOSS OF THE SECOND TEMPLE,

DESTROYED BY THE ROMANS,

UNTIL THIS DAY,

AND,

AT THE END,

ALL THE PROPHECIES

WHICH THESE TRIBULATIONS HAVE FULFILLED

AND FINALLY,

THE CONSOLATIONS,

BOTH HUMAN AND DIVINE.

SUBTITLES

FOR DIALOGUE III

INTERLOCUTORS
YCABO, ZICAREO, NUMEO

━━━━━

YCABO: I rested more than usual last night. Zicareo's words were certainly good medicine for my old wound. People are right when they say that there is no better doctor for a troubled spirit than a persuasive talker. I trust that he will help me find relief for the troubles I am about to narrate to him. But I see that Numeo and his companion are up. I shall go to greet them. Good morning, brothers.

NUMEO, ZICAREO: Good morning, Ycabo.

NUMEO: We got up earlier than you think this morning. Our mastiffs smelled wolves and began to pursue them, and we had to move quickly. But fortunately, the wolves did not harm our sheep. It even seems that one of them was badly bitten, for our long-eared hound is covered with blood, though he has not been injured.

Now, shall we lead our cattle to a luxuriant plain that lies beneath this slope? There we can rest beneath a green poplar and continue our talk and watch our sheep as they graze.

YCABO: I should like nothing better.

NUMEO: Lead on, Zicareo.

ZICAREO: Let us go. It is only a short walk. . . . Here we are! Now sit down, Ycabo, and continue your story.

YCABO: I shall continue. Listen carefully.

After I had passed through the Romans' stormy rule, the fury of which scattered me throughout the universe, I suffered countless and varied misfortunes.

FIRST MISFORTUNE. SPAIN. YEAR OF THE WORLD 4077[1]

First I saw Sisebut, king of the Goths,[2] who sat on the throne of Spain for eight and a half years, force the Jews in his lands to change their religion. If they refused he warned that he would permit the populace to put them to the edge of the sword. This proclamation was so frightful and cruel that many craven Jews, unable to support the thought of punishment, surrendered to the Christian faith just as the vanquished submit to conquering enemies.

The king sent a courier to the Pope with this news to inform him of the new converts, and there was great rejoicing in both realms, for it was but a short time since the Christian faith had been established in Spain.[3]

Many other Jews, who had valiantly resisted the Enemy's threats, were aided by God's mercy. The many conversions made the king feel that he had done enough, and he went no further with his violence. Thus at last the Jews were freed from the death penalty; instead, they were exiled with reproach from the king's dominions.

At this time Mohammed, who is now venerated by so many peoples, was driven from Spain[4] because he preached his doctrine throughout the world.

After their misfortune, the King of the heavens sent a quick consolation to the afflicted Israelites when he took Sisebut's life and placed Witiza[5] on the throne. As soon as Witiza assumed power, he sent for all my children whom Sisebut had exiled from Spain, and welcomed them back. As a result of this favor, the Jews who had been forced into Christianity gradually returned to the faith of their fathers.

The error which they had committed in fearing bodily death more than the life of the soul was foreseen clearly by Micah, when he spoke these words: "Part of My people exchanged its Law" (Mic. 2.4).[6] And what the prophet Moses had told me so long before was fulfilled in every way in those who were put to this test and trial, and emerged alive, cleaving to the Lord: "I call the heavens and the earth to witness against you this day. I have set before you life and death, a blessing and a curse. Choose life that you and your seed may live, loving the Lord your God and hearkening to His voice and cleaving unto Him, for He is your life and the length of your days" (Deut. 30.19-20).

2. FRANCE. YEAR 4077[7]

During the time that Henry VII ruled as Holy Roman Emperor, I found myself wallowing in riches. My children in the kingdom of France were thriving materially and were secure spiritually. And, as every happy estate in this mortal life is naturally envied, their serenity and wealth were envied by many Christians, and they devised a false accusation against the Jews in order to destroy them.

They sent a woman to a Jewish broker on the pretext of pawning a garment. On Easter eve, she returned to the broker and asked to have it back, entreating him to lend it to her so that she might celebrate her holiday. She promised him, as a good Christian, to return it the day after the festival.

It was claimed that the Jew had answered her, "If you bring me the host after it is consecrated and as a communicant receives it during Lent, I shall not only give you your garment for nothing, but I shall also pay you its worth."

The woman, the Christian conspirators said, was overcome by the promise of reward, and brought the Jew the host she had received at communion. As soon as he had it inside his house, the broker secretly kindled a blazing fire in his fireplace and set over it a kettle filled with oil and water. When the water began to boil, he threw the host inside and said to it, "You are the god of the Christians. If my forefathers nailed you to the cross, I shall boil you in this kettle." No sooner had he spoken these words than the host turned into a little boy who walked about atop the water inside of the kettle. The Jew tried to strike him with a spit, but could not hit him; miraculously, the boy dodged from one corner to another and strove to get out.

In order to further this malicious lie, a wretched gang of ten or twelve suddenly entered the Jew's house one day, then turned about and ran into the street, making a great tumult and inciting the populace with their tale.[8] They told how they had seen the woman give the Jew the host and had witnessed the great wonder that followed.

When word of this reached the magistrate, the hapless Jewish broker and his entire family were arrested. Though he was subjected to cruel tortures, he did not confess to the truth of the charge against him. But his wife, weak as a woman often is, could not bear the torture and confirmed everything they claimed. They demanded that she become a Christian and promised to spare her life. She accepted the terms for herself and her small children, but her husband was burned alive, embracing the Talmud, according to the account I have read.[9]

On learning of this incident, the entire populace of France rose up and killed many Jews in towns far from the capital, and the enraged monarch ordered all Jews found in his kingdom to be banished. The Jews departed in wretchedness, leaving their property in the hands of strangers. Constantly harassed and robbed, they dispersed to many lands of Christendom.

O Moses, before this calamity came you had already warned me of it, and told me that my rest would be disturbed and others would enjoy my possessions: "The Lord will send upon you a discomfiture and punishment in everything you decide and do until He destroys you" (Deut. 28.20). "You shall build a house but shall not dwell in it" (Deut. 28.30).

3. SPAIN. TOLEDO[10]

I saw further misfortunes after the calamitous death of King Roderick, the last of the dynasty of the Goths. The Goths were constantly warring with the Moors, who then occupied most of Spain. When the Goths took Toledo, killing and capturing many enemies, the Africans resolved to recover it, and tried everything possible to achieve their aim. Though they tried often, they did not succeed in their intent until a holiday, which the Christians call Palm Sunday, when most of the people left the city to go to a distant church. Informed of this in advance, the Moors had prepared an ambush, and they attacked and entered the city by force, killing or capturing everyone in it. Included were a large number of its Jewish inhabitants.

After they had taken possession of the city, the Moors left a large number of men there [to maintain their victory] and with the rest they attacked the unarmed populace outside. They captured all the commoners and killed many of them, although most of the nobles escaped. Among these were the chief lords, into whose care the king had entrusted the city.

Realizing how bad their account of the city's capture would appear to the king, the nobles sought an adequate reason or excuse for such a loss, and decided to lay the blame on the afflicted Israelites, on whom all misfortunes are unloaded. When the king angrily demanded an account of the city, they informed him that the Jews had sold it out to the Moors and advised them to capture it. They had not been on their guard against the Jews, since it could not be imagined that they would betray the city. The king accepted the excuse. My children in Toledo suffered a calamity, and in addition the king was angry with all the other Jews who lived in his lands.

When the masses sensed the king's frame of mind, they rose up against me. But my sin had already brought me to such exquisite anguish and grief that when my children were threatened with murder and destruction, the most merciful King of the heavens took pity and touched the king's heart with compassion for all these souls. With great difficulty, the king managed to restrain the populace, though they roared like angry lions, claws and teeth bared in readiness to tear apart their prey. The king explained that if the Jews of Toledo had committed the offense, they alone deserved the punishment, and those who had not been involved did not have to pay, since according to divine and human justice, only the soul which sins must die (Ezek. 18.20).

O Lord, behold how innocent we are of such charges and how unjustly we are persecuted, for all their faults[11] are imputed to us, and besides, we participate in the misfortune they suffer. This is what the prophet Isaiah foretold concerning the nations and us: "Our diseases does he (Israel) suffer and our pains he also bears, and we esteemed that he had been smitten by the Lord because of his own wickedness and crushed (by his own friends), while the truth was that he was wounded to cover our errors and afflicted because of our iniquities. We chastise him for our welfare and with his stripe we heal our infamy" (Isa. 53.4-5).

4. TOLEDO. YEAR 4923 [1163]

After the city of Toledo was retaken by the Moors, I saw a gang of Arabian thieves descend from the Arabian desert and enter the city of the prophet,[11a] or Mecca, by night. Aided by spies they had planted in the city, they succeeded in robbing the ornaments of the casket in which the Moors reverently kept (and still keep) the embalmed body of Mohammed; and they stripped the casket of many diamonds and rich gems which were enchased all over it.

The casket guards, realizing the disgrace which would befall them if they failed to name a suspect who could bear the blame, struck a blow at the weakest and feeblest part of the entire body of humanity: they declared that the Jews had committed the robbery.

In order that the Enemy (who constantly pursues me because of my offenses) might bring this evil plan to fruition, he convinced the Moors of Toledo, who bore a hatred toward my children, that a certain Abraham With The Cloak[12]—being extremely poor, he owned nothing else and thus he had acquired this name—and other Jews who left Toledo to live elsewhere, had been sent by their fellow-Jews to rob the casket.

This report spread through all Islam and the reaction was violent; merely on the basis of this rumor and supposition, the Moors killed many Jews and destroyed forty of their synagogues, the first being the one in Toledo.

And as a result of this report the Jews' distress increased in the entire land of Barbary and elsewhere in the East.[13] Eventually the Moorish kings, in their anger and fury, desired to force all their Israelite subjects to convert to the sect of Mohammed in payment for their alleged offense. But since God in His mercy rushes to aid His people Israel when it is in dire straits, He at last made the Moors cease and be content that they had made many suffer in the initial onslaught. And the Lord punished my iniquity, which cried out to Him to destroy me, with the noxious draft I had swallowed in my great fright.

You prophesied this to me, Jeremiah, when you said, "I will deliver them to be harried by all the kingdoms of the earth" (Jer. 24.9), "and I will afflict them with the sword before their enemies and by the hand of those who seek their life" (Jer. 19.7). Yet at last, when the Lord saw in what anguish we submitted to His mercy, He fulfilled the holy word which He had spoken: "If they submit, I will not cast them away" (Deut. 30.2-3; cf. Isa. 41.17).

At this time Rabbi Moses bar Maimon fled from Castile to Egypt and spent the rest of his life there in great honor as physician to the sultan. There he wrote the letter which is entitled "Concerning Yemen,"[14] in which he consoles its people, encourages them to remain steadfast in the Law of Moses, and gives them great hopes of deliverance.

5. FRANCE[15]

Because the Christians in France hated the Jewish usurers, the poor Israelite people living in Paris were charged with having killed a Christian youth in order to celebrate the Passover with his blood. This news reached the king while he was on a hunt, and since he was accompanied by counselors who were unfavorably disposed toward me, they colored the slander in such a way as to make the king believe it. He did not wait for time, or the customary inquiry, to reveal the truth. He turned, falcon in hand, and galloped back to the city; when he arrived there, he angrily condemned to the stake eighty-four Jews who were alleged accomplices in the crime. But the oppressed lambs were innocent, and what they were charged with was something prohibited by their Holy Law and contrary to its precepts.

"You shall be fuel for the fire," you, Ezekiel, said against me (Ezek. 21.37). Here you see your threat executed.

6. FRANCE

Throughout the province of Normandy my children were hated and envied because of the wretched profit they made from loans, and in one town I saw some wicked men decide to plunder and destroy them. After many unsuccessful attempts, the gang of rascals, with the aid of a sorcerer, finally agreed on a diabolical scheme.

The sorcerer told them that he would bury a pig's heart. This, he hoped, would attract all the pigs in the neighborhood, and when they assembled near the heart, he would make them fight and bite one another to death on this spot. In order for the Jews to be convicted of a criminal deed, they bribed an executioner, who promised to accuse a number of Jews publicly and to testify against them secretly before the governor. He was to aver that the Jews had asked him for as many hearts of Christians as he could get when he carried out sentences, and that he had agreed in return for a consideration. He was to say, however, that since he had pity for his Christian brethren, he had given the Jews pigs' hearts instead. Then, when he had gone to observe what the Jews were doing, he had seen them burying the hearts in that very place.

After the wicked band had agreed to this plan, the sorcerer dug a grave outside the city. As he buried the pig's heart, he conjured the devil with oaths and magic spells. He covered the grave, and then, with his amazing witchery, produced a circle, conjuring and summoning the devils at length.

Within a few short days, a multitude of wild and domestic pigs were seen waging such a horrible fight on this spot that they tore one another to pieces with their teeth. The people ran toward this loud noise and were greatly astonished at what they saw. Then, in the presence of all, the executioner revealed the false accusation he had carried against the Jews. Some of the other participants in the conspiracy abetted him, saying that they had indeed seen the Jews burying something there, but they knew not what.

At this point the people exclaimed, "Certainly these Jews intended to kill all of us Christians as they killed the pigs, since they requested Christian hearts. Is it not therefore right for us to kill someone who wanted to kill us?" With this outcry, they rose up and set the city against my innocent children killing many by the sword and robbing others who were somehow able to save their lives.

O, woe is me! How far it was from my thoughts that I could fall into such a strange misfortune. This is one of those misfortunes contained in the prophecy that you, Moses, uttered against me: "If you do not keep all the words of this Law which are written in this book and you do not fear the glorious name of the awesome Lord your God, then new plagues will come upon you which were never thought of nor are they written in this book" (Deut. 28.58-59).

7. SPAIN[16]

In Tabara, a town in Spain, I saw my people so despised and perse-cuted by the populace that every day at sunset they hid in their houses in fear; for many Jews who had been met by Christians at dusk had been killed.

To my misfortune, it happened that the son of a Jewish smith com-mitted a certain crime. It was not a capital offense, but since he fell into the hands of our despisers, he was sentenced to death. When his hapless old father saw his one and only child taken by so miserable and disastrous a death, he grieved and brooded so much that he went mad.

My enemies' hatred toward me had constantly increased, and they could no longer refrain from carrying out the evil thoughts they con-ceived. One day a large group of Christian youths assembled, pretending to be jousting, which is a customary diversion at festivals in Spain. But with their spears at their shoulders and their swords at their sides, they attacked my Hebrew sheep with such fury that only a few survived.

When news of this tragic event reached the king, the populace, by common consent, sought an alibi so as not to implicate their sons and brothers in the city, who were the real murderers. They declared before the king that the Jewish smith had pretended to be mad in order to avenge his son's death; that for two straight months he had knocked on peoples' doors day and night so that they thought him mad and paid him no more heed; but that during all this time he had been secretly making many locks and crow's-feet, such as are usually strewn on the battlefield to prick the feet of men and horses. They claimed that one midnight he had locked all the houses in the city, spread the crow's-feet through the streets, and set fire to the city; and that if one door had not remained open, permitting a Christian to get out and unbolt all the others, they would all have been burned alive. This, they concluded, was the reason they had carried out the swift massacre against the Jews.

The king and the members of his council saw that all the people testi-fied alike, and that if any of them were to be punished, they would all have to be punished. They decided that the law did not permit them to take vengeance on a whole people, and they therefore set them free. But, woe is me, for the minds of those that reached this decision also partici-pated in the conspiracy, and there was no heart under the heavens that did not turn against me. Moses' prophetic words were fulfilled: "You shall be mad because of what you will be forced to see with your eyes"

(Deut. 28.34). And Jeremiah's prophecy also came to pass, to my misfortune: "Let their men be killed with slaughter and their young men be wounded with the sword, and let a cry be heard in their houses" (Jer. 18.21-22).

8. PERSIA. YEAR 4924 [1164]

At this same time, I saw a very great misfortune befall me in Persia. In the city of Hamaria there was a Jewish community of a thousand families. It was the foremost[17] of the communities that are nestled on the bank of the river Chaphton, at the gateway of the kingdom of Media, whose language is Syriac.[18] These communities are spread throughout the province of Samamaria as far as the province of Ghilan, fifty days' journey away from the dominions of Persia.[19] Here all Jews over fifteen years of age paid an annual ducat of tribute to the king.

In Hamaria there lived an Israelite named David Alroy. He had studied under Chisdai, the most learned Jew in all the Diaspora, and later under the head of the academy in the city of Bagdad. He thus became an expert in Talmud and in all other disciplines, including witchcraft and magic.

Made conceited by his knowledge, he assembled a large group of Jews living on Mount Chaphton and informed them that he was the Messiah. They joined him in a rebellion against the king, and killed many of the king's troops.

The ruler finally realized that the best way to handle David was through a stratagem. He feigned friendship toward him, inviting him to visit the palace, and gave his word that he would be well received. David believed him, and fearlessly came to the palace. The king questioned him, asking if he had really proclaimed that he was the Messiah whom the Jews were awaiting, and who would perform many miracles. David answered that he was, and that the king should treat him accordingly.

Furious at David's arrogant reply, and at the lie he was trying to sustain, the king retracted his word and his courtesy, and had him thrown into a dark prison.

David, deceived and imprisoned, availed himself of his wisdom. He used his magic so effectively that he broke his fetters, freed himself, and left the prison grounds after demolishing a strong wall with a mere word.

The king, on hearing of this, sent a host of men on horse and on foot to search for him and recapture him.

When David Alroy heard that so many men had been dispatched to seize him, he again used his skills. He came before all of them, invisible, and spoke to them. They only heard his voice, but were unable to see him, and they were dumbfounded and confused. David then returned to the palace, where he spoke to the king in the same way. He said to him, "You are not powerful enough to catch me. Instead, you will now see me go my way before your eyes, and you will not harm me in any way."

As soon as David had spoken these words and descended the palace steps, he became visible. He removed his turban, spread it over the river Gozan, and crossed to the other side.

When the king and all his men saw this, they were astonished and amazed. The king could not bear such an affront; he ordered his men to take boats and pursue and capture David. Yet all their work was in vain, for on that day David traveled the equivalent of a ten-days' journey by skillfully harnessing the power that resides in God's ineffable name.[20]

The king saw how little his might availed against David and how his forces were mocked. He therefore sought revenge in another way. He proclaimed throughout all Persia that the Jews had to deliver David dead or alive or face death by the sword.

In tribulation and anguish, the innocent Israelites were compelled to draft a letter to Emir el-Mumenin in Bagdad, asking him to discuss with the princes of the Diaspora whether they should kill David or deliver him alive, so that only one individual might be sacrificed and the rest escape death. And they wrote to David himself, who was in that city, entreating him to desist from his folly and not to involve them in any more difficulties than those they already suffered in their captivity;[21] if he did not listen, they warned, they were in danger of losing their lives, and they would be forced to excommunicate him.

To deliver these letters they sent Zakkai, the Prince of the Captivity, whom they summoned from Syria, and Rabbi Joseph Borhan. However, these letters had no effect, and David paid no attention to what they wrote him.

The people realized their predicament. They continually offered prayers and fasts to the Lord for their deliverance until He answered them by raising up a Turkish king named Sin-el-Din, a tributary of the king of Persia. Sin-el-Din sent for David's father-in-law, who lived in his domain, and promised him ten thousand ducats if he would deliver David dead or alive. David's father-in-law, moved by the affliction of his brethren in Persia (not by the reward), chose to kill him rather than deliver him to the enemy's cruel tortures. While David was asleep on his bed, his father-in-law killed him with a single blow on the side of his heart, and my children were at last freed from their anguish.

Then Sin-el-Din, the Turkish king, informed the king of Persia of David's death. The king was delighted with the news and granted an amnesty to the rebels. They were a very large and rich group, and agreed to pay a hundred quintals of gold to be restored to the king's favor.

Our Rabbi Moses [Maimonides] writes about this event in a letter.[22] He tells us that when the sultan asked David whether he was the Messiah, and he answered that he was, the king said to him, "What proof will you give?" David answered that they should cut off his head, and he would revive. The king said, "If this be true, I will compel my people to become Jewish," and he ordered David's head to be cut off. However, David has not yet come back to life, since this was really a shrewd trick;

he preferred to die in this way rather than by the many tortures he feared the enemy would inflict upon him.

When this occurred, your warning to prevent it, Jeremiah, had already been born, and the penalty which he was to receive had been decreed: "Hearken not to the words of the (false) prophets who prophesy unto you and delude you and speak what occurs to them in their heart and not from the mouth of the Lord" (Jer. 27.9; 14.14). "Behold, I shall rise up against the prophets who dream lies, says the Lord, and who cause My people to err with their falsehoods" (Jer. 23.32). Thus it shall be said concerning him, "The Lord did not send you, and you have given this people false hopes to imbibe" (Ezek. 13.6). "Therefore, the Lord says: 'I shall remove you from the face of the earth, and you shall die this year'" (Jer. 28.16).

9. GERMANY [1420][23]

I saw another misfortune in Vienna, a city in Germany, at the time when Frederick was emperor.[24] A large pool had frozen as a result of the terrible frosts in this region. As was their custom, three small boys went to play there; but the ice broke while they were on it, and they were drowned.

These children were sought everywhere in the district and beyond, but they were not found, and there was no news of them. The populace raised false charges that the Jews had killed them to make a sacrifice of their blood, and testimony was offered that the youngsters had been seen entering certain Jewish houses. To support the false testimony, the people asserted that any wicked act could be believed of the Jews, for the year before they had learned that a Christian maid, induced by money, had brought a Jew a host, and he had mistreated it.

When the report of this accusation, on the heels of the first charge [concerning the desecration of the host] reached the emperor—whose counselors were ill-disposed toward me—he had all Jews throughout his kingdom imprisoned. He was about to carry out a frightful massacre among them, when God's mercy made him spend his fury on only three hundred Israelite souls, whom he ordered to be burned at the stake.

After I had suffered this cruelty, the pool thawed, and the bodies of the children rose to the surface. The people realized how falsely they had charged me with that crime, and there were many who declared publicly that the three hundred who had been burned were innocent of the charges. But, woe is me, not in this way did they or could they any longer correct the mistake.[25]

Indeed an angry word of yours, Jeremiah, prophesied this misfortune: "I will make you pass with your enemy into a land which you knew not, and there a burning fire of My wrath will be kindled in you" (Jer. 15.14).

10. FRANCE. YEAR 4943 [1183]

In the time of Philip Augustus, king of the French,[26] I saw the Jews in his kingdom prosper to such an extent that they had bought half the city [of Paris] where they lived. But since envy follows wealth, and the more so when its possessor was once poor and lowly, the populace resented my children and hated Israel intemperately. Their hatred was such that if the fear of punishment had not restrained them, they would have committed some great brutality against me.

Finally, desiring greatly to see their evil design carried out with impunity, they thought it best to persecute me with false charges. Thus any wicked attack they made might have an excuse.

Some people stated that I made sacrifices of Christian boys, killing them in underground vaults, and that I taught Judaism to the servants who came to work for me. Others claimed that I accepted church vessels such as chalices, cruets, crosses and the like in the brokerages as collateral from thieves, and that I used them for unclean purposes and drank from them—despite the fact that my religion strictly forbids me to utilize any vessel or furniture used in the worship of other gods—and finally, that I had thrown a book of Christian evangels and a cross into a dirty place.

Thus I was beleaguered with many accusations, so that one of them might cause me harm. Their hatred made it impossible for my truth and innocence to prevail.

King Philip, moved to anger against me, sentenced many bankers and other Jews to death at the stake. Many who were in the synagogues on the Sabbath were taken off to prison and stripped of all their possessions, even the clothes they were wearing; countless others, threatened by the sword, permitted the waters of baptism to be poured on their heads in order to save their lives. These were given back their estates.

By such acts my enemies clearly revealed that their intention was to divert the Jews from their Law, and that the accusation with which the Jews had been charged was false.

The truth of the matter was that since the Lord had given me large wings of prosperity[27] and a people whose number was twice that which left Egypt,[28] I flew to terrestrial things and attributed those blessings to my own industry. I was daily becoming more remiss in God's service and distorting many precepts of His will. Because of these sins—since the punishment inflicted on our bodies and estates was no longer sufficient—the king further ordered all synagogues where we assembled for prayer to be confiscated and converted into churches. And with the wealth of which he despoiled them, he erected many noble structures in France. Among these were the palaces and walls of the Wood of Vincennes, a delightful place near Paris, and Champeaux, which they now call Les Halles, where the market of that city[29] is now held.

Just consider, princes, the reason or cause which moves you to harm me. Why can you not see that it is clearly a case of false testimony and that I am punished unjustly, for it is not possible for any harm to be committed against the holy vessels without their defending themselves against it. Do you not recall when the Ark of the Lord was captured by the Philistines and placed with great reverence near their idols in their lands? Its holiness was offended at seeing itself in filthy and profane places and killed an infinite number of those heathens in the cities where they kept shifting it, out of fear of its wrath. It threw their abominable idols to the ground and it caused great devastation among them; it did not cease its destruction and killing until it was returned to the land of the Israelites where it belonged.

As for the hosts, chalice, crosses and the gospels which you hold so holy and consecrated, how can you give credence to the charge that they allowed themselves to be mistreated and harmed? And why do your monks note this and write it in their books, with the intent of provoking the masses against me, since there is no reason for you to believe it? On the contrary, there is more reason to punish the fools who raise such a charge out of hatred, not considering how much they thereby prejudice themselves.

But in truth these misfortunes come to me from a much higher source, for it seems that little fear of God's punishment had settled in the heart of some of my children,[30] so that Amos' prophetic words might find fulfillment: "By the sword shall all the sinners of my people fall that say 'Evil shall not reach us nor overtake us'" (Amos 9.10). Jeremiah's threat has also been realized in this misfortune: "Because you have forsaken Me and served strange gods in your land (willingly), so shall you serve strangers in a land that is not yours (against your will)" (Jer. 5.19). And furthermore, "I shall offer all your treasures and wealth as a spoil" (Jer. 15.13).

11. NAPLES, IN ITALY. YEAR OF THE WORLD 5000 [1240][31]

I saw my children, who had been thriving in population and wealth in Naples and Trani and other cities in the Kingdom [of Sicily], suffer a misfortune far worse than violent death.

The king[32] who was involved in a very important and dangerous war, was near defeat, for it was lasting longer than he could afford. He had depleted not only all his own funds, but those of all the lords and noble-men who followed him, and he had overtaxed his people time and again.

While he was in this dilemma, perplexed and pondering on how to solve his problem, the Jews who lived in his kingdom decided to aid him by offering their possessions; they went immediately to lay before him their fortunes and persons. Their wealth enabled the king to emerge from the war with victory and great honor.

Since he was thus aided by my children, the king did them countless favors and esteemed them as highly as he did the highest nobles in the realm. And things went so well for the Jews that they placed all their reliance upon the favor of the terrestrial and mortal king. Trusting in him, they imagined that they could never again fall in that kingdom, since the prince and the people were indebted to them. Thus they did not found their hopes on heaven. As a result, the Lord was provoked to great anger against them, and their offense was so great that it attacked and overthrew them, and turned all their thoughts to smoke.

As this king was approaching the end of his life, he left the kingdom to his son and praised the Jews who lived in it, telling his son that for the satisfaction of his conscience, he should pay them for the help which he had received from them.

Determined to fulfill his father's behest, the new king took counsel regarding what type of payment would be proper to give the Jews. Concerning this there were many and varied opinions. But all came to the conclusion that the favor had been so great that no temporal payment was sufficient to satisfy it, and that his highness ought to pay the Jews spiritually by saving their souls and making them all Christians.

The advice seemed very good to the king and he approved it. He therefore immediately sent for the leaders of the Jewish community and apprised them of the kindness he had resolved to do for them.

When they heard this they became very sad and disturbed, and replied that this was not the kind of favor they desired to receive; rather, if his highness no longer talked about the matter, it would be the greatest favor he could do for them.

The king answered that he had already determined to pay them with this gift for the obligation his father owed them, and that he considered this reward to be the greatest of all; after they had received it, they would recognize it as such.

The distressed Jews, seeing the king's determination, said that since his highness so willed, they desired time to think so that they might answer more deliberately. The king replied that they should think only of receiving the favor with gladness, and that he was prepared to give them whatever else they requested.

The Jews discussed what they could ask the king so as to divert him from his resolve. Since he was going to make them Christians, it seemed plausible to all that if he were asked to unite them in marriage with all the landed gentry in his kingdom, the request would be so excessive that he would not accept it.

But things happened differently than they anticipated. The king granted their petition, since he and all his nobles believed that in this way they would be saved [from their financial difficulties].[33]

When the Jews realized that their aims had been thus thwarted, they changed their plan and revealed that conversion had not been their intention. The king, however, made a proclamation throughout his kingdom, stating that from the moment of its publication until the time it took a taper to burn out, all Jews were to become Christians or face death.

When my children found themselves threatened by such a swift misfortune, many weak-hearted ones, fearing the punishment, rashly turned their backs on their faith and allowed themselves to be baptized. No sooner was this done than they became excessively prosperous, for the king united them in marriage with the nobles and leading citizens of his realm. And he converted the great synagogue of Naples into a church, naming it Saint Catherine.

The Jews who steadfastly resisted the great temptation and did not convert were deprived of this life by the sword, but they passed on to life everlasting.

This was one of the most illustrious examples in history of how every Jew must reflect on his situation and realize that his hope must be separated from all earthly hopes. It cannot rest on mortal men; it must depend on the infinite might and favor of the King of the universe, who holds both souls and bodies in His hand.

As a result of the conversion of the Jews, the stock of the grandees of Naples was mixed with Jewish blood.

What will you say, O brethren, to this new devilry? For in return for the blessing and benefit received from me, they requited my love with evil and hatred. O how true did I find these threats of yours, Jeremiah: "Cursed is the man that trusts in man and puts his fortress (and hope) in human flesh and removes his heart from the Lord. He shall be like a lonely tree in the desert, which does not see the good when it comes, but will always be in sterile places, in a salt land and one uninhabited" (Jer. 17.5-6). Thus "we looked for peace, but no good came, and at the time of healing we expected, terror and fear overcame us" (Jer. 8.15). And concerning their change of religion, the judgment of Amos also was carried out: "I will slay the residue of them with the sword" (Amos 9.1).

12. ENGLAND. YEAR 5002 [1242][34]

On the isle of England, I saw the Israelites increase their numbers; and in London alone, the capital city of the kingdom, there were two thousand very rich families tranquilly spending their time in exile[35] as the Jews did elsewhere in this kingdom.

Yet my security is not natural, but alien and deceptive, and mis- fortunes in this life are the garb which my soul always wears. My trou- bles refused to leave me. They made a predicant friar fall in love with a beautiful Jewish girl, contrary to the tenets of both their faiths. Though the friar secretly wooed the girl for a long time, he found no way to win her; she spurned him and mocked his notes and promises. This only further inflamed his illicit love. He could no longer resist his rash desire, so he doffed the garb of his Christian faith, and donned the garments of Judaism.[36] He secretly became a Jew. And when he had made this change, he was more successful in getting the beautiful Jewess to pay attention to his courting.

The Jewess was poor and fatherless, and under the influence of her mother, who was a woman of weak character, easily swayed by a chance for gain. When the mother saw the wealth of the erstwhile monk, she gave him her daughter in marriage on the condition that they leave the kingdom of England because of the great danger of their situation.

But their actions were discovered, and the monks were greatly offended by what the friar had done; and the people taunted them. To repair the honor of their order, the monks endeavored to incite the king against the Jews by working through the queen, whose relative and private confessor was a predicant friar. Further, whenever the monks ascended the pulpit to preach, they directed their messages against the Jews. Under their influence the populace developed a mortal hatred toward me, and sought ways to discharge it.

Many false charges and accusations they leveled against me came to naught because they were patently mendacious. But the slander that I was clipping coins[37] was easier for them to maintain. Many of the people arranged to assemble with coins they had secretly clipped in their houses and complained against the poor Jews, claiming that they had received the coins from them. Many other people made similar accusations to lend credibility to the charge. As a result, when the complaint was received by the court, which did not need much persuasion to turn against me, it decreed, with the king's consent, that all my children be expelled from the kingdom. They were also to forfeit their estates in lieu of suffering the death penalty, the punishment prescribed for this crime by the laws of the land.

When the monks saw that the fortunes of the harassed Jews were waning, and that little effort was now needed to destroy them completely, they devised a new accusation. They charged that the Jews had converted a monk to Judaism in a Christian land, and that in return they had to be converted or die for the crime.

Since by this time everyone—the king, the princes, and all the people—was bent on my destruction, and any insignificant occasion was sufficient to throw gunpowder and sulphur into the fire of their wrath (let alone this one which they considered so weighty), the demand of the monks and my enemies was granted.

To implement this punishment, all young Jewish children were taken from their parents and sent to the end of that island, a place called "The North."[38] There they were taught the Christian doctrine and faith, so that, separated from their elders, they should not recall their ancient Law, and should completely lose the nourishment of the Jewish milk they had imbibed. Many of their parents perished from the unbearable grief which stifled them.

Further, to fulfill the first sentence, the Jews were banished from the kingdom. Seeing their children[39] remaining behind, they left with such lamentation as would have moved hard rocks to pity. Thus, contrary to divine and human law, these people were given two deaths or two punishments for their crimes, though according to all laws, no one should suffer more than one penalty.

The converts spread over the entire kingdom, and buildings of former synagogues that were converted into churches are still found, and a large number of the people have Jewish names.

Here, O Lord, I saw Your word fulfilled, as prophesied by Moses: "Your sons and your daughters shall be delivered to another people and your eyes will constantly stream with tears as you behold this, and you shall not have sufficient strength to endure it" (Deut. 28.32).

13. ENGLAND[40]

In this same country, England, I witnessed another fierce and terrible calamity. After that king had left this life he was succeeded by another,[41] who disregarded the past expulsion and recalled all the Jews who had left the kingdom, offering to take them back and let them live in peace.

The Jews took counsel among themselves in France, Flanders, Spain and other lands where they had dispersed. They decided that for no reason, including ease or material gain, would they re-enter a place where they had suffered so great a calamity except to see the children they had left behind, to talk with them and convince them to return to the faith of their fathers and to leave England. This reason seemed sufficient for their return: they desired to win back their lost children.

When they arrived, the populace received them kindly because of the good will the king showed them.

After a few years, the plague broke out all over that island; it was so severe that a large number of people died every day. A terrible famine also hit the land at this time, and not long thereafter these misfortunes were increased by a bitter war against the English by many peoples, including Scotland, a kingdom close by. Clearly this was a punishment for the sin which that people had committed against Israel, so manifest that even fools came to recognize it. But the English, blind and ignorant of God's secrets, did not perceive it. The king, astonished at these many simultaneous tribulations, began to look for counsel concerning a way to check their causes.

After many possible causes had been considered, including events in their kingdom and in the history of other peoples, the king and his advisers resolved to strike a blow in the weakest spot, where it would hurt them least: all agreed that the sins of the Jews were responsible for the calamities the kingdom was suffering. For this they found no better remedy to assuage the wrath of the heavens than to make all the Jews Christians by force, since they could not convert them through love.

The king forthwith proclaimed that any Jew attempting to leave the kingdom would be put to death. Then he assembled all the Jews. He admonished them to change their religion and promised them many favors and benefits, but they refused to convert. He finally baptized them by force, against their will, hoping that the famine, pestilence and wars would then abate.

But after the Jews were forcibly converted to Christianity, these calamities multiplied to such an extent that the land was almost desolate. The people's understanding was confused, and they marveled at the opposite effect which their action had accomplished. The king again took counsel, and there were many who voiced the opinion that the calamities had doubled because of the force which had been used to bring the Jews to the Christian faith; spiritual matters, they asserted, should be freely decided, since our Lord had granted freedom to the human will. For this reason, they advised the king to restore the Jews to their former estate. If any Jew should wish to come to the Christian faith through love, he alone was worth more than all the forced converts.

The council would have unanimously favored this way of thinking, had not the Adversary intervened, dressed in human clothing, to condemn it. Another point of view arose: "It is obvious that if the Jews are given their liberty, not one of them will choose the Christian faith over the Jewish Law. Their Law is deeply rooted in them; the resistance which they showed to becoming Christians is proof of this. Thus, if they become Jews again, the sin which is the cause of the misfortunes our kingdom is suffering will again be present.[42] Our troubles have now doubled because of the force used against the Jews. No other remedy remains for us to consider except to uproot the cause from the world; then the sin and its punishment will cease."

This argument pleased the king, and his counselors approved it. But the Jewish people were numerous and, if killed, their bodies might contaminate the air. The king therefore ordered two pavilions to be set up by the seashore, one distant from the other. In one he placed the Law of Moses received from the Lord on Mount Sinai, and in the other the cross of Christianity. In the middle an elaborate scaffold was erected. Here the king sat down. He ordered brought before him all the Jews whom he had made Christians by force. With a cheerful countenance and feigned joy he spoke these words to them:

"It is true that I believed that if I made you Christians, it would remedy the adversities my kingdom has suffered. Now I see that not only did they not abate, but they are increasing daily, and I realize that the force I used against you has been responsible for their having doubled. Since this is so, I would now restore to you your freedom of religion that you may freely choose which of these two religions you desire. There in that pavilion near the sea is the Law of Moses, and in this one the Christians' faith. Let each one run to the one he likes, and I shall let him live in that faith without any hurt whatsoever."

The Hebrew people greatly rejoiced at the liberty which the king was granting them, not realizing the deceit which lay beneath his cogent arguments. With their wives, and their children in their arms, they ran to the pavilion where the Law of Moses had been placed. There they fell into the snare which the Enemy had set for them. They were able to enter only one at a time because the entrance was very narrow, specially prepared for this purpose; and when an Israelite lamb entered, he was decapitated by a hidden English butcher and cast into the sea. Each one knew not what happened to his brother; their lives were taken by the sword, and their bodies fed to the fish.

O cruel Englishmen, were you so righteous and holy a people that you could not presume that your misfortunes were a punishment for your own deeds? What do you say, brothers, to these secrets—no matter how far away from me the blow is struck, I am the one who gets hurt in the end. O people so quick to hurt me and so blind to the reason for which you harmed me! How is it that you have not become inured to crime from of old? Are not the ways of your princesses adulterous? Is not the garb of your masses woven of robberies, hatreds and killings? I do not need to cite ancient histories to tell this, for modern and contemporary records proclaim and testify to it.

Consider in the few years that King Henry reigned, how many acts of adultery were committed by his own queens; how many treacheries were attempted by the king's noblest and closest associates; how many heads were placed on London Bridge because of these and other ghastly crimes; and how many queens were killed by the sword, and others deprived of dominion. The churches where you prayed were demolished by your own hands or converted to stables. Your priests were shamefully expelled. The gold and silver images to which you bowed were broken apart. The wooden ones were burned in the fire. Others were strewn on dunghills and filthy places. And your pope, cardinals and bishops became a laughingstock and byword among you.[43]

According to your religion, all these acts, singly and collectively, are regarded as sins. They manifest extreme wickedness, and you deserved punishment for them. Misfortunes did not come to your land because of the Jews' sins alone, as you say. When your sins made supplication,[44] you received an answer from heaven. Why, you even refused to acknowledge that you had been like the passengers in the ship that carried the prophet Jonah. Heaven thought little of them, except for the righteous Israelite; and when he was cast into the sea, the storm abated. Yet the others considered themselves righteous and innocent.[45] You tried hard to make your case bear a resemblance to this one.

But what shall I say, O wretched me? Who blinded me to return again to this England, where I had fared so ill in former times? How many devices sin employs to bring me punishment. It made my children remain on that island so that they might be the means by which these prophetic words were fulfilled against me:

"I will lay stumbling blocks before this people, that the fathers and their sons may fall in them" (Jer. 6.21). Thus "calamity shall come upon calamity" (Ezek. 7.26). "You feared a sword: I will draw out a sword upon you, says the Lord, and none will escape by flight, though he strive to escape" (from Amos 9.1-4).

These judgments, O Lord, were cruel. And, moreover, "with treacherous talk have they led me (to slaughter)" (from Ps. 109.2-3). "And
(My children) did not recognize the Enemy's thoughts, nor did they
understand the Lord's counsel" (from Mic. 4.12),[46] in order for this
prophecy of yours to be carried out, Isaiah: "The wisdom of their wise
men shall perish and the understanding of their prudent men shall be hid
at that time" (Isa. 29.14).

14. FLANDERS[47]

In Flanders I saw myself beset by a most terrible hardship. Since my
children in that earldom had been living in peace, tranquility and wealth
for some time, the Enemy, who watches my prosperity constantly in
order to find an opportunity to demolish and destroy it, came forth to
confront them.

He chose, as his means, to move some of the populace, those who were
most hostile toward me, to raise up a false charge against me that might
lead to my destruction.

A band of people, ill-disposed toward the Jews, assembled and alleged
that the Jews had stolen their host; then, to abuse it, they had broken
it and immediately, as it broke, the host had shed blood as if grieving at
the affront it had received. And, they said, the blood also meant that
revenge had to be taken.

So much credence was given to this false accusation that they stabbed
or burned the innocent flesh of a large number of my children. And—a
torment equal to death—they enticed many with a promise to spare
their lives if they became Christians, and many were converted out of
fear of a death penalty.

That generation of converts has spread over nearly the whole realm;
and though a long time has elapsed, these converts still give an indication
of their non-Catholic origin by the new Lutheran beliefs which are
presently found among them; for they are not comfortable in the religion
which they received so unwillingly.

Here your judgments were fulfilled, Ezekiel, when you said, "A third
part I shall scatter to all the winds and I will send a sword after them"
(Ezek. 5.12), and "fears will enter My people's hearts from this sword"
(from Ezek. 32.10; cf. Ezek. 32.23). Thus this fear that enveloped me
was quite strong; as a result of it, I turned my back to the Lord, exchang-
ing His Law for fear of the sword.

15. GERMANY. YEAR 5022 [1262]

In the town of Foreheim,[48] in Germany, I saw all the Jews who lived
there at death's doorstep.

There was an inveterate feud between two powerful men of the region over an inheritance which each claimed. In the struggle, the son and legitimate heir of the party that was expected to win was secretly slain.

The two sides had kept their enmity concealed for a long time, but finally the hour arrived when the dead man's relatives could take vengeance. With the help of an old woman, they kidnapped a seven-year-old girl from their enemies, killed her and buried her in an unfrequented place outside the town.

When the girl disappeared, extensive searches were made to find her. But when she did not turn up, the populace suspected that she was kidnapped by the Jews to be used as a sacrifice on Passover, for they were of the opinion that we needed Christian blood to celebrate the Passover, though such a cruelty is strongly forbidden by our Law.

In short, stirred up by this mere supposition, these people already had weapons in hand, ready to carry out a massacre among my innocent children.

You can imagine, brethren, with what anguish my soul was afflicted. Finally God's mercy came to my rescue and infused reason and justice into the prince's heart. He informed his people that they were greatly burdening their consciences by perpetrating such a cruelty on the basis of mere suspicion. He gave them other reasons, and finally he placated them.

After several days, the truth about the kidnapping by the old woman was discovered. But, despite this, the ignorant populace did not cease to believe that I was accustomed to make sacrifices with Christian blood.

This misfortune was not unforeseen by Ezekiel when he said, "I have set the fear of the sword in them" (Ezek. 21.20).

16. MISFORTUNES IN MANY PLACES. YEAR 5080 [1320][49]

In France and Spain, two great calamities befell me at the same time.

[In Spain], a young boy, seventeen years of age, said that a dove had appeared to him one afternoon and had alternately alighted on his shoulder and on his head; that then the Holy Ghost, as they call it, had begun to visit him. When he tried to take the dove in his hand, an exceedingly beautiful maiden appeared to him and said, "I now make you a shepherd on the earth. You shall go forth to fight with the Moors. And here is the sign of what you have seen with your eyes." When the lad took a look at himself, they say he found the account of this event written on his arm. At the same time, another man came forward who announced that the lad had discovered the sign of the cross inscribed on his shoulder. People said, however, that he had only dreamt all this while sleeping near a fountain.

But, however it may have happened, the meek dove turned into a venomous scorpion for me, and the dream became a true and disastrous reality; for when the nobles of the land heard the news, they all became excited, treated the boy like a saint, and conferred solemn honors upon him. When the masses saw this, a large rabble attached itself to the lad and followed his call to conquer the Kingdom of Granada.[50] But woe is me: although the people were only against the Moors, Heaven had secretly decreed that a cruel blow be struck against the Jews. And when the Devil, our Enemy, gave an Israelite a chance to scoff at this miracle, the people were filled with bitter hatred against me. They abandoned the project against Granada and began to carry out the bitter sentence against me which my iniquities demanded of God's justice. These shepherds had been so innocent of such iniquities that they were made the executioners of my limbs.

The enormous crowd, whose number had swelled to thirty thousand men, attacked all the Israelite lambs that had gathered in Tudela and put them to the edge of the sword. A group moved on to the town called Cordel with murder on their wicked minds, but the prince, Meltsar Tolosa (or rather, some merit of my fathers, the Patriarchs, who stationed themselves before our Lord to speak in our defense against our transgressions),[51] sent many well-armed men to arrest them. They fought so valiantly that they brought back ten wagons full of prisoners.

When the monks learned of this, they rose at midnight and stole out to the road. They mingled with the people, released the shepherds from prison, and spread a rumor that they had been miraculously set free. All the people in the district cried, "Behold, behold, the miracle of the shepherds." Inflamed by this false rumor, they furiously attacked the Jews, acting in such accord that in the first onslaught two hundred people were killed by the sword. And the lord of the city himself was in great danger because he defended the Jews.

A large number of my children had taken refuge in a fortress in Narbonne. When the news reached them that ten wagon-loads of enemies had been captured and bound, they returned to the city.[52] In order to give them greater security, Meltsar Tolosa sent a relative of his to accompany them, charging him to lead them to safety in the fortified city of Carcassone. But the traitor revealed the hatred he secretly bore toward me; he sold me to the peasants in the villages and advised them to kill me on the road. And they fell upon that flock of sheep and ravaged them like famished wolves who see meat set before them. They had no pity on little children, on young or weak old women; they put people of all ages to the sword, forming a huge pool of Israelite blood. The bodies and bones of some were strewn along the roads, while others were left where they fell as a meal for the birds and dogs.

This stroke of misfortune spread swiftly to many distant places— Bordeaux, England [sic], Castelsarrasin and Agen; and in all these regions it was constantly proclaimed that any Jew who was found was to be killed.

In the province of Toulouse-Bigorre,[53] in the cities of Marsan and

Condom, and in many others, a total of a hundred and twenty congrega-
tions were destroyed by the sword as a result of this unfortunate rumor
and the arrest of the shepherds in the wagons. The Lord's punishment
moved over me so frightfully that some Jews chose to take their own
lives rather than await the enemies' wrath, as the lesser of the two evils.
Among these were the Israelites who were hiding in Castelsarrasin. They
cast lots to decide who would kill his fellow; they all died in this way.
The last two that remained, whose hands had spilled their brothers'
blood, hurled themselves from the high tower and were dashed to pieces.

In Toulouse all the Israelites either died by the sword or converted to
save their lives—except one, who escaped because of his close friendship
with the lord of the city. And of the large number of Jews in Gascony,
only twenty were left alive; a cruel massacre was carried out against
the others.

In the town of Lourdes, where I thought that my shrewdness would
help me avoid the Enemy (who in one hand carried the sentence from
heaven, and in the other the sword to execute it), seventy people gave all
their possessions to the lord of the city in return for his promise of safe-
conduct to the Kingdom of Aragon; but when they left the city, the
nobleman revealed his deceit and brutally massacred them all.

The Jews in the Kingdom of Aragon would have been at death's door
had God's mercy not temporarily stayed the Enemy's hand by giving
them favor in the eyes of a bishop, the son of a king. But when the shepherds saw that the Accuser was not succeeding with his evil plan, they
split into four groups, and proceeded to Valencia, Barcelona, Jaca and
Monserrat.

When the man with the cross imprinted on his shoulders arrived in
Jaca, all the people prostrated themselves before him. The Jews had gone
up on the wall, but four hundred were killed on the morning of the
seventeenth day of the month of Tammuz.[54] Only ten escaped into the
castle.

When a thousand and five hundred shepherds (devils for my people)
then went on to the city of Barbastro, all the Jews in the city and its
environs felt anxiety and trepidation, like condemned criminals who look
in vain for pardon.

In this predicament, the heavenly King had pity on His people. He
touched the princes' hearts with compassion and moved them to try everything within their power to save the harried Jews who had escaped from
such great misfortune.

The king of Aragon forthwith sent his son to destroy and wipe out all
the shepherds and their company who were to be found in his kingdom.
By his command, more than two thousand were hanged or impaled by
spears, and many others fled. The whole region was thus cleansed of
their venom.

The king of France exiled the shepherds from his entire kingdom, and
allowed the people to kill any who still remained. And the Pope commis-

sioned all bishops and prelates to destroy all of the shepherds under their jurisdiction.

When they were thus pursued, through the kindness of the One who governs the world, He at last rid all these kingdoms of those serpents; but my Enemy brought them over to the Kingdom of Navarre. The Jews of the congregation of Pamplona, terror-stricken at the news of their enemies' unwelcome arrival, set out for the nearby town of Monreal, three leagues away. But the men whom they paid to accompany them betrayed them and delivered them into the mouths of the famished wolves, the hostile shepherds, and several Jews were killed. The rest fled and took refuge in Monreal, pursued all the way by the opprobrious shepherds.

But when the hunted Israelites arrived in the city, our Lord gave them strength. They turned against the enemies and fought very valiantly, killing a hundred and seventy. Among these was their leader, who carried the cross. He was killed by an arrow shot by the servant of the nobleman who was protecting us. When the others saw their leader lying dead on the ground, they lost courage and swiftly turned their backs in flight.

Then the shepherds began to weaken. When three hundred moved to the city of Tudela, and saw that the Jews were strong there, they left, unsatisfied, like a vixen which sees a tender chicken safely perched on a high roost.

The rich among my children who were spared considered the great kindness which the Lord had shown in letting them escape, and they provided their poorer brethren with sustenance for three years, so that they might recover from the extreme poverty and destitution in which they were left. And in a short while the gang of hostile shepherds was heard from no more, and their noxious memory was dissipated.

All of the prophets were avenged and satisfied in everything they had prophesied against me. The dove announced that the time of Ezekiel's prophecy had arrived: "They (the children of Israel) shall be like doves on the mountains, all of them moaning, each one in his wickedness; and all hands shall be slack at that time, and all strength shall soften like waters" (Ezek. 7.16-17). "They provoked Me to anger with their vanities; and I will provoke them with a no-people; with a foolish nation will I harm them" (Deut. 32.21) for these shepherds who hurt me were very ignorant rustics. "I will appoint over them four kinds of deaths, says the Lord: a sword to slay, dogs to drag, birds of the heaven and beasts of the earth to devour and destroy" (Jer. 15.3). And "though they dig and penetrate into the nether-world, My hand shall take them from there; and even if they were hidden on the top of Mount Carmel, I will search and take them out thence" (Amos 9.2-3). And this was clearly fulfilled, for it availed me not to hide in towns or castles. "I called my friends and they deceived me. They spoke to me with a lying tongue" (from Lam. 1.2; Jer. 38.22). "Their silver and their gold will not be able to deliver you on the day of the Lord's wrath" (Ezek. 7.19). "And they shall seek peace but shall not have it" (Ezek. 7.25); rather, "rumor shall be upon rumor" (Ezek. 7.26). "If they go out into the field, there shall they be slain by the sword" (Jer. 14.18). "But I will leave some, so that there be of you some that escape the sword among the nations, when you shall be spread throughout the countries" (Ezek. 6.8).

And in addition to all these misfortunes, O Lord, I saw Your merciful words fulfilled in me, and Your vengeances executed on my enemies. You said: "I will sift the house of Israel among the nations and I will vex them as corn is sifted in a sieve, yet shall not the least grain fall upon the earth" (Amos 9.9). "Many shepherds have spoiled My vineyard; they have trodden under foot My prized portion" (Jer. 12.10). Since besides all their vexations, "they have defiled My hereditary possession, which is My people Israel, I will also pluck them up from their land (which is this life)" (from Jer. 12.14). "When you have ceased to spoil, then you also shall be spoiled" (Isa. 33.1). "Then shall those of My people remember Me" (from Isa. 33.2 ff.).

"O throne of glory, exalted eternally, place of our sanctuary, in fine, You, O Lord, are the true hope of Israel" (Jer. 17.12-13) and "You are my refuge in the day of affliction" (Jer. 16.19).

17. ITALY. YEAR 5081 [1321]

After this terrible affliction which made destitute so many people, I was soon threatened by a new disaster. The following year there arose a sister of the Pope, named Sancha.[55] She was as hostile toward the Jews as Haman, who determined to destroy Israel in Esther's time.

She often tried to provoke a massacre against the Jews, but her wicked plan did not succeed. Finally she alleged a thousand crimes against me, and begged the Pope, her brother, to banish me from all his domains. In this she succeeded. But when the general exile was proclaimed, bringing me great anxiety and vexation, our Lord elected to show me kindness and favor through the virtuous King Robert of Naples and Jerusalem.[56] He came to my defense, petitioning the Pope and reprimanding all who persecuted me. In this way, he delayed the Pontiff until I had cast a sacrifice of twenty thousand ducats into Azazel's mouth.[57] This was given to the Pope's sister, and thereupon she had the sorrowful verdict revoked.

Here I was overcome by the curse which you, Moses, cast upon me as you departed this life: "The Lord will smite you with sudden discomfiture" (Deut. 28.20).

18. FRANCE. YEAR 5081 [1321][58]

In the same year I suffered such an affliction that my flesh shrivels and trembles when I recall it.

Throughout France a strange disease broke out which caused many deaths. There were diverse opinions as to the nature of this illness. Some doctors said that it was a mysterious plague which showed no symptoms in any part of the body. Others suspected that it was a poison. Most people came to believe the latter explanation. As they were considering the place of its possible origin, the enemies of Israel declared that the Jews, in league with the lepers, had in all likelihood poisoned the waters.

No sooner had this accusation been uttered, than it was given as much credence as if it had been witnessed. The tale began to spread, and it achieved notoriety throughout the kingdom. It was maintained as certain that the Jews and the lepers had poisoned the rivers and wells in an attempt to destroy the kingdom. And since my misfortunes, even when they begin in jest, end as serious realities, all the Jews in France were arrested on this charge.

In their predicament my children sought to demonstrate my innocence and the falsity of the charge. At a great cost to themselves, they sent for the most renowned and eminent physicians from abroad to examine the sick. After extensive examinations and experiments, in which they gave this water to dogs, they proved to the local physicians that it was not poison [which was killing the populace] but a strange illness (as a punishment for their sins).

These discussions and experiments continued for nine months, and during that time the Jews were kept imprisoned, with the threat of death hanging over them continually as they awaited the gloomy hour when the enemy would tear out their souls.

Finally, despite patent proofs given by the doctors and despite the fact that the French had no reason or evidence sufficient to condemn me, the great offenses[59] which I had committed throughout that kingdom saw to it that they sentenced five thousand souls to death as a sacrifice,[60] while the rest were freed. The French offered to spare the lives of these five thousand after they had been condemned if they became Christians. The Jews refused to accept such terms; with the divine name of the Lord upon their lips, they were cast together into a fire whose flame was so high that it seemed to touch the stars. But their pitiful shouts and cries and those of all their brethren who saw them soared still higher.

The large number that perished here under such great torment, as you can well imagine, brothers, left many widows and orphans shrouded in anguish, hunger and destitution.

This is the water which you meant, Jeremiah, when you prophesied: "I will feed this people with bitterness and give it waters of gall to drink" (Jer. 9.14). And this is the incurable leprosy mentioned by Moses: "The Lord will smite you with the boil and the scab, whereof you cannot be healed" (Deut. 28.27). This is the fire and the enticement—to see whether they would exchange the Law of the Lord—with which I was threatened by you, Jeremiah: "I will smelt them and try them" (Jer. 9.6). "Their men shall be killed with slaughter and they shall deliver their children to famine, and their children shall be orphans and their wives widows; a cry shall be heard in their houses" (Jer. 18.21-22).

And into all this misfortune You mixed salvation, in order that Your holy word might be fulfilled in the remnant which escaped: "I will not utterly destroy the house of Jacob, says the Lord" (Amos 9.8).

19. GERMANY. YEAR 5006[61]

In Torti,[62] a province of Germany, where my children were thriving in number and riches, I saw envy breed such a hatred in the populace that they sought any means to plunder and destroy them. When a dread disease came to the land, they found the best opportunity to put their evil inclination into effect, for not many years had passed since the plague had occurred in France. They asserted that the Jews had poisoned the water in the wells and rivers, and cited the events in France for evidence. My offenses[63] gave such force to this false charge that the populace did not wait for further proof but acted on this rumor, which was circulating throughout Germany. They armed themselves and rose up against the Jews, and with sword and fire killed as many Israelite lambs as they could find.

Nor was my misfortune satisfied with these deaths in Germany. When the noxious rumor reached Catalonia and Provence, where the devastation of the contagious illness had spread, similar killings and burnings were executed on my limbs. Out of fear of this punishment, some Jews changed their religion to save their lives; they escaped death by becoming Christians.

If these misfortunes had increased, brothers, I think that there would not have been a single Israelite left to relate these events in any European tongue. But God's mercy saw fit to take the sword from the Enemy's hand and not to destroy me completely.

This tribulation, stemming from water, had to pass over me that these other prophecies of yours, Jeremiah, might be fulfilled: "He will give us waters of gall to drink because we have sinned" (Jer. 8.14). "I will deliver them into vexation and misfortune in all the kingdoms of the earth" (Jer. 24.9).

20. FRANCE. YEAR OF THE WORLD 5106 [1346][64]

In this same year, in France, I was bruised by another kind of blow. I had returned to that kingdom to begin a new life,[65] and acquire new possessions with which to spend my wretched exile amidst enemies.

Another Philip[66] came to the throne, a son of Louis and grandson of Philip Augustus, who had treated me so cruelly. The new king, without offering any explanation for his action but a hatred whose flame was stoked by wicked counselors, proclaimed that all Jews found in his kingdom must convert to Christianity; if they refused, all their possessions were to be confiscated and they were to be banished from the kingdom.

Of the large Jewish population, very few were moved by this demand to barter their faith. They chose to endure patiently the dire poverty and misery to which they were reduced (they were left nearly naked) rather than to annul the covenant which the souls of Israel had made with the Lord on the mountain of Sinai. Thus, my children left France in the month of Ab, on the Christian holiday known as St. Magdalene's Day, mourning for all their stolen possessions as well [as for the destruction of the Temple].[67]

Some were unable to endure their wretched state. Finding themselves naked, they could not resist their enemies' offer of twice the amount of possessions which had been confiscated, and further great benefits if they converted, and they consented to baptism. Foremost among these were the Jews of the community of Toulouse—except for a few, who remained loyal to Judaism. In this way that province was sown with Jewish seed,[68] and many of the descendants of these Jews are probably still uncomfortable in the faith which their ancestors accepted so reluctantly.[69] It would not be implausible to assume that from these people stem the Lutherans, who have sprung up everywhere in Christendom.[70] For since throughout Christendom Christians have forced Jews to change their religion, it seems to be divine retribution that the Jews should strike back with the weapons that were put into their hands; to punish those who compelled them to change their faith, and as a judgment upon the new faith, the Jews break out of the circle of Christian unity, and by such actions seek to re-enter the road to their faith, which they abandoned so long ago.

Wherefore, O princes, you should consider how much harm you bring upon yourselves by compelling the Jews to accept your faith; for the ways by which mortals believe they can strengthen their purposes through injustice in the end become the means that undermine them and destroy them.

This king did not go unpunished for his tyrannical deed. Nine years later, while chasing a stag on a hunt, he was led astray through rough terrain, and fell down a mountain into a deep gorge. He and his horse were dashed into a thousand pieces. The French people clearly recognized this as a punishment for his misdeeds.

When his son, the virtuous Catholic King Louis, succeeded him, he sought to correct the wrong his father had inflicted upon me. He recalled me to his kingdom and permitted me, through my industry, to replace my possessions. Yet this blessing lasted no longer than a will-o'-the-wisp. Seven years later, on the people's petition, I was again exiled from France, though I was not deprived of my worldly goods.

Afterwards King John took the crown, and then his son Charles, who welcomed me once more to the kingdom. I lived tranquilly there as long as these two ruled. But when they had departed from this life and another Charles[71] had taken their place, the populace rose up against me, mercilessly killed me and robbed me,[72] and expelled me from the kingdom even against the king's will.

You foresaw this misfortune, Micah: "We are utterly ruined. Part of My people changed (their religion)" (Mic. 2.4).[73] "You cast out from their pleasant houses the women (and their companions)" (Mic. 2.9). "They shall gird themselves with sackcloth and horror shall cover them" (Ezek. 7.18). "For everything I have given them will pass over from them into the power of another" (from Jer. 8.10; Jer. 6.12). "But in the end he who afflicts you will not endure forever; rather he shall speedily disappear and when he has been thrown into the pit, the memory of him shall end" (from Isa. 51.1 ff., 12-14; cf. Ps. 9.6 f., 55.24; Job 18.5 ff.).

21. SPAIN. YEAR OF THE WORLD 5850[74]

At the time of the discord in the Roman See regarding the election of the pope, I saw a pope named Benedict chosen in Spain. His former name was don Alvaro de Luna.[75] In Rome, the opposing factions selected a different pope, Innocent.[76]

At this time there was a monk in the Dominican order named Brother Vincent,[77] the greatest persecutor and enemy of Israel in a long time. He was highly favored by the king, Ferdinand of Aragon; when Ferdinand was a prince, Vincent was one of the twelve who had voted to elect him king of Spain.[78] With the king's protection, Brother Vincent determined to implement an accursed design against me. He led an aroused mob through the cities of Spain, carrying a crucifix in his hands and a scroll of the Law in his arms. In loud and fearsome tones he called upon the Jews to gather under the cross of Christianity and convert. His gang, armed with spears and swords, would attack and kill those who refused, and he made Christians out of the others, who surrendered out of fear of death.

In this way he traveled over nearly all of Spain, and made more than fifteen thousand Jewish souls abandon their faith. Because of his violent persecution, many of my children took refuge in Barbary, abandoning all their possessions in order to save their lives.

Those who turned their backs to our God out of fear for their bodies were principally the Jews of Aragon (Valencia, Mallorca, Barcelona), Lerida, Seville, and many other cities.

Since all this food did not satisfy Brother Vincent's hunger, this enemy tried to extend his power over foreign kingdoms. He undertook to cross over to Portugal, where a large number of my children were living, and he requested the king's permission to enter. The reigning monarch, Edward, answered that he could enter if he consented to having a crown of glowing iron fagots placed upon his head. When my enemy recognized that his reception in Portugal frustrated the fulfillment of his wretched desire, he abandoned his efforts.

Since the calamity involving Brother Vincent lasted for a long time, some who had converted under threat of death [left Spain, and as they] journeyed from land to land, they returned to the religion of their fathers. A great many migrated to lands belonging to the Moors. Some went into Portugal, and many to other Christian lands where Jews were to be found.

To distinguish them from other Christians, the epithet *confesos*[79] came to be applied in Spain to the converts who remained Christians. The other Jews, who could not be overcome by force or threats of death, and continued to live in Spanish lands, were subjected to many disabilities by the king. They were compelled to wear a red badge, by which they could be recognized and thus abused, and they were forbidden to lend money on interest, or even to own land.[80]

You threatened me with this misfortune involving Brother Vincent, Jeremiah: "I will bring over them an evil from which they shall not be able to escape" (Jer. 11.11). "And the fury of this anger of the Lord shall not return until it is executed" (Jer. 30.24). "Because I will cast you into a land where (by force) you shall serve other gods day and night, and there I will show you no mercy" (Jer. 16.13). "And the residue (who do not wish to serve them) I will dash to pieces with the sword before their enemies" (Jer. 15.9), since your sins demand it.

22. SPAIN. YEAR OF THE WORLD 1215[81]

In Spain, I was again made to suffer great anguish.

In the territory belonging to Louis of Salamanca,[82] the young son of a rich merchant appeared on a holiday dressed in finery, wearing gold in his chains and studded belt. Two thieves contrived to rob him. They lured him outside the city, and stripped him of his costume. When the weeping boy turned to return to the city, the thieves (also natives of the city), fearful that their actions would be disclosed, pursued him, cut off his head and gave him a hasty burial in an unfrequented place.

When the lad was missed, a diligent search was begun. The public was asked to help, and rewards were promised for information leading to the boy's discovery.

A few days later some shepherds happened to guide their flock near the murder scene. And since dogs generally scent everything, the sheep dogs chanced on the boy's body. They unearthed one of his arms with their paws, and prepared to eat it in front of the shepherds. The shepherds recovered the arm and brought it to the city for identification.

When the boy's father learned of these events, he, his relatives and friends and most of the townspeople went with the shepherds to the field to see the place where the dogs had disinterred the arm, and they finally discovered the rest of the body.

After the father had identified his son, and he and the other relatives had bitterly bewailed him, they gave their opinion as to who could have committed the cruel deed. All maintained that it could not have been a

Christian, since the child was too small and innocent to have offended anyone, and that it must have been some captive Moor or Jew.

And when Jews were mentioned, many in the group who violently hated the Jews accused them of this evil act. They related how in many parts of Christendom, and principally in Germany, the Jews had stolen children to offer a sacrifice with their blood.

Convinced of this false view, they returned to the city in great anger. And as the rumor spread from one person to another, it grew so exaggerated that it was said that the Jews had taken out the boy's heart, roasted it, and eaten it publicly in that place.

As this barbarous rumor spread, the lad's relatives and others began to sharpen their swords and brandish their spears; and they would have offered a sacrifice of my flesh had not the Lord of the heavens come to aid me in my distress. The king ordered a thorough inquiry into the matter, and the truth was learned through a goldsmith to whom the thieves had sold the gold pieces they had stolen from the boy. And thus ended the storm which was rushing furiously to drown me after I had nearly swallowed and bolted death.

See, brothers, how my iniquities blind the world when the time for my punishment comes; for though the very people who accuse me know that there is no such cruel precept in my Law, they claim that I want to offer sacrifices of human limbs. They should consider that in order for us to slaughter even a hen, we must do it mercifully according to the precept. How much more unnatural would it be to kill human beings to hold divine services with their blood, which is such an abominable and forbidden thing. But I can say nothing, since my sins must roll on until Moses' prophecies are somehow fulfilled: "The Lord will send a discomfiture against you because of the evil of your thoughts" (Deut. 28.20).

23. SPAIN. YEAR 5216 [1456][83]

I witnessed another misfortune in the city of Segovia, during the reign of John, while he was a young boy and his mother, Catherine, was Queen-Regent of Castile.

A number of Jews had grown very powerful in the Court, and as a result all of the Jews were hated by the people of the city, who sought every possible means to harm them. They did not hesitate to put their evil plan into effect: they succeeded in getting a priest to testify that a Jew had stolen a host from him. He had brought it home, he said, and cast it into a kettle of boiling water. When he later went to look for it, informed of the theft by a person who had seen the Jew leave the church, he found the Jew's house, entered, and saw that the water had turned to blood.

The populace gave sufficient credence to this false testimony for many Jews in the city to be arrested. Among them was Mayer, King Henry's physician.[84] The court sentenced him and two other of the finest Jewish citizens to death, and had them drawn and quartered. The Jews' houses of study[85] were converted to churches, and still greater evils would have befallen them if heaven had not intervened. After the cruel punishment was meted out to my innocent limbs, the charge was found to be false.

In the same city, a nobleman who had long feuded with the bishop decided to kill him. In order that he might take his vengeance with impunity, he callously bribed a cook to poison the bishop.

Persuaded by the reward, the cook resolved to do this, and indeed, had the poison ready. But despite the secrecy of the plot, the poison was discovered. The cook was immediately arrested and put under torture to identify his employer; his life was to be spared if he revealed his name. However, though tortured repeatedly, the cook disclosed nothing. Finally, the nobleman who had planned the murder advised him to blame the Jews and confess that they had given him a sum of money to commit the crime because they hated the bishop, since he was a priest of Christ.

Thus did this wicked man testify. For divulging the information his life was spared, while a large number of innocent Israelites lost theirs by the sword. The rest of them fled the city, abandoning their homes and most of their possessions in order to escape.

The prominence [in the Court of Segovia] which I had achieved at this time corrupted my heart, and Jeremiah's prophetic words found fulfillment: "I will punish you according to the fruit of your thoughts" (Jer. 21.14). And Amos': "Though they go into captivity before their enemies, there shall I command the sword to slay them, and I will set My eye upon them to do them harm and not good" (Amos 9.4). "A strange people shall consume all your work" (Deut. 28.33).

24. SPAIN. YEAR 5248 [1488]

I saw the following in Granada, where a thousand five hundred Jewish families lived prosperously and comfortably in the city and its environs:

The Christians conceived the idea that the Jews ought to exchange the Law of Moses for their Christian faith or perish. Although the penalty the Christians threatened was awesome, the Jews nevertheless chose to sacrifice their bodies rather than offend their souls. When their enemies saw the Jews' determination, they put all fifteen hundred families to the sword on the ninth day of the month of Tebet. They did not spare a single person. They had no pity for the children who clutched their pious mothers' arms, or for the cries of tender virgins, old men, young men, or people of all ages who entreated the Lord on high to avenge this brutality. Among the victims was the renowned and distinguished sage, Rabbi Joseph Levi.[86]

On this same day, the ninth of Tebet, a fast had been ordained long before, and the people observed it without knowing the reason why. It seems that this great tribulation had been foreseen by God's spirit. But the force of this prophecy of Jeremiah prevailed: "Though they fast, I will not hear their cry, and though they offer sacrifice, it will not please Me; but I will consume them with the sword" (Jer. 14.12).

25. THE INQUISITION IN SPAIN. YEAR 5251 [1491][87]

Those whom Brother Vincent left as confesos[88] in Spain thrived so that they joined the ranks of Spain's grandees and noblest lords; they were therefore soon united in marriage with its leading families. They occupied posts of distinction and importance in the court: they held the titles of count, marquis, bishop, and obtained other high dignities which the material world bestows upon those who court it. Those who remained Jews enjoyed their secret favor and also flourished and prospered.

This happiness lasted until the time of King Ferdinand and his wife, Queen Isabel. And like an uprooted flower, which speedily dries and withers,[89] so did this prosperity perish, like all my others. For the enemies of my good fortune found the king, and much more so the queen, Isabel, inclined to persecute me; and they began to encourage them to destroy the confesos. Little effort was required to win the sovereigns' minds, for their stock, it seems, has produced the greatest enemies of my people in the history of the world.

They turned their power against the Jews who were already within the Christian fold. As confesos, they were no longer recognized as Jews, and their minds were at ease and their hearts secure, since they were Christians. The king and queen sent to Rome for a wild monster,[90] of such strange form and horrible mien that all Europe trembles at the mere mention of its name.

Its body, an amalgam of hard iron and deadly poison, has an adamantine shell made of steel and covered with enormous scales. It rises in the air on a thousand wings with black and poisonous pinions, and it moves on the ground with a thousand pernicious and destructive feet.

Its form is like both the awesome lion's and the frightful serpent's in the deserts of Africa. Its enormous teeth equal those of the most powerful elephants. Its whistle or voice kills even more quickly than the venomous basilisk. Its eyes and mouth spew continual flames and blazes of consuming fire, and the food it eats is the fire in which human bodies burn.

Its flight is swifter than the eagle's, but wherever it passes its shadow spreads a pall of gloom over the brightest sun. Finally, in its wake it leaves a darkness like the darkness visited upon the Egyptians in one of the plagues.

And when it arrives at its destination, the green grass which it treads or the luxuriant tree on which it alights dries, decays and withers, and then is uprooted by the monster's devastating beak. It desolates the entire countryside with its poison until it is like the Syrian deserts and sands, where no plant takes root and no grass grows.

Such an animal was brought against the entire *confeso* community (who were supposedly unrecognizable in Christian garb). The monster burned a great many of these children of mine with the fire from its eyes and strewed the land with countless orphans and widows. With its mouth and powerful teeth it wrecked and swallowed all of their worldly riches and gold. With its massive, poison-laden feet, it trampled their renown and their greatness, and with its awesome and misshapen countenance it disfigured and marred comely faces [which were forced to gaze upon it], and darkened hearts and souls with its blight. And it still continues its vile deeds in Spain, against the limbs which were severed from my body. And though my children are parading their Christianity, it does not save their lives.

I do not want to be remiss in telling you that in addition to the enemies, there were at that time some *confesos* who delivered their own brothers into this cruel monster's power. Poverty was the spur and the reason for most of their evil acts. Many poor *confesos* went to the houses of their richer brothers to ask for a loan of fifty or a hundred crusados[91] for their needs. If any refused them, they accused him of Judaizing with them.

These misfortunes lasted for four years. Then the sovereigns determined to uproot the *confesos* completely from Judaism, and remove them from contact with the Jews. They exiled from their domains all the Jews whom the wrath of Brother Vincent had not reached, and those whose constancy had kept them within the Law of Moses. Both groups wandered in great tribulation and hardship through many lands. Some passed over to the Kingdom of Portugal, others to the lands of the Moors, while some dispersed to the Kingdom of Naples and other parts of Europe.

Here many of Your judgments, O Lord, were fulfilled, which You pronounced against me through the lips of Your prophets. Concerning this wild beast and a similar one in Portugal it was said by Jeremiah: "I shall send among you serpents, basilisks, which cannot be charmed, and they shall bite you with an incurable bite" (Jer. 8.17). For with these I shall bring it about that "what comes into your mind shall not be at all, in that you say: 'Let us be like the nations and like the families of the countries to worship wood and stone.' As I live, says the Lord, surely with a mighty hand and outstretched arm and poured out fury will I be king over you" (Ezek. 20.32-33). "And then the great and notable treasure of yours in which you place all your hope will be converted into tow, and the one who acquired it into a spark, and they shall both burn together, and none shall quench them" (Isa. 1.31). Because "they who depart from Me shall be written in the earth, for they have forsaken the well of living waters, who is the Lord" (Jer. 17.13). "At the time of their afflictions they will say to me, 'Rise up, save us,' and

I shall answer them, 'Where then are your gods now whom you worshiped? Let them arise and save you in the time of your affliction'" (Jer. 2.27-28).

26. YEAR 5252 [1492]
WHEN THE JEWS FROM CASTILE ENTERED PORTUGAL

And of those who were ejected from the Spanish kingdom and who remained faithful to Judaism, the majority went on to Portugal. Six hundred families[92] came to an agreement with King John, the second of that name, to pay two cruzados for each one who entered the kingdom. And the king promised to allow them to live in their religion and to provide ships for those who wished to leave.

As soon as these harried Jews entered Portugal, an epidemic broke out, a harbinger of the catastrophe which awaited them ultimately. Many Jews as well as Christians died from this illness.

Shortly after their arrival, a number decided to cross over to Africa and Turkey, for they feared the eventual cruelty of the Christians more than the present vexations of the Moors. They therefore asked the king to keep his promise and provide them with safe passage. The king, however, had conceived an evil plan. He procrastinated and equivocated until he was so importuned by them that he granted their request. My punishment was as my iniquities deserved, and as had been prophesied to me. The hapless Jews embarked, thinking they were in the custody of trusted friends. But they were deceived. They were taken to the high seas, where their cries and shouts could move no one to pity, and there they were tied hand and foot, and their women were dishonored before their eyes and they were despoiled even to their last garment.

O Lord, since these enemies of mine fled from the shame of the nations to commit such a cruel and treacherous deed, I was at least consoled that You were a witness to it. From You they could not flee or hide, and You are the source to which we look for the remedy to all our misfortunes.

After they had so cruelly treated the Jews, they atoned by taking them to the shores of Africa—to its most deserted spot. There they cast them, like victims of contagion, upon a barren beach, far from human help. Babies begged for bread and mothers raised their eyes to heaven for help, while others, reduced to despair by hunger and abandonment, dug their own graves.

But when they were at the end of the thread of life, they raised their eyes and saw a horde of Moors approaching to take them captive. They had entered the land without safe conduct or permission, and they were seized and arrested with great harassment. But they regarded the captivity as a divine visitation and a release from their terrible and awesome plight.

After they had entered the land, their brethren there redeemed them and set them free, and helped them in their need and misery.

Though many of my children in Portugal preferred to spend their captivity in the power of the Moors, and not in Christendom, when this sad news reached them they became so terrified that they did not dare ask for passage.

O, wretched me, for these misfortunes with which you, Moses and Jeremiah, threatened me were now fulfilled: "I will heap evils upon them; My arrows will I spend upon them; they shall be burned with hunger and consumed" (Deut. 32.23-24). "Deliver their children to the famine" (Jer. 18.21). "There shall not be prosperity in your ways, but you shall suffer violence and injury" (Deut. 28.29). And then "you shall be carried off, and there shall be none to save you. You will betroth a wife, but another man will sleep with her" (Deut. 28.29-30). "You will beget children, but shall not keep them, because they shall go into captivity" (Deut. 28.41).

27. PORTUGAL. YEAR 5253 [1493]
WHEN MY CHILDREN WERE SENT TO THE LIZARDS

This dreadful tempest was soon followed by the lash of an even rougher storm. The Portuguese king, eager to find some logical excuse to vex me, called for an investigation to see if the number of my people who had entered his kingdom exceeded the stipulated six hundred families. Since the haste with which my children had left Castile did not allow time for a census, or for anyone to wait and see if there was sufficient number, they found that they had exceeded the number. The king claimed the excess as his captives and slaves; he could thus vex the Jews at will and carry out his evil designs against them. Their willingness to redeem themselves for the price at which the rest had entered, or a higher price, proved of no avail.

To my misfortune, the island of São Thomé had recently been discovered. It was inhabited by lizards, snakes and other venomous reptiles, and was devoid of rational beings.[93] Here the king exiled condemned criminals, and he decided to include among them the innocent children of these Jews. Their parents had seemingly been condemned by God's sentence.

When the luckless hour arrived for this barbarity to be inflicted, mothers scratched their faces in grief as their babies, less than three years old, were taken from their arms. Honored elders tore their beards when the fruit of their bodies[94] was snatched before their eyes. The fated children raised their piercing cries to heaven as they were mercilessly torn from their beloved parents at such a tender age.

Several women threw themselves at the king's feet, begging for permission to accompany their children; but not even this moved the king's pity. One mother, distraught by this horrible unexampled cruelty, lifted her baby in her arms, and paying no heed to its cries, threw herself from the ship into the heaving sea, and drowned embracing her only child.

Thus those innocent souls were removed from their parents' sweet tenderness by such inhumanities and delivered into the power of merciless enemies. O brothers, who could describe to you the hidden and visible anguish which cloaked all my children—the sighs, the tears, the bloody and febrile groans which were heard in all their houses; for there are no words of consolation to relieve a pain so great, though each one had good reason to hope for consolation.

This monstrous cruelty would have induced many people to take their own lives before the time allotted them by God's will, if others would not have suffered by their absence. But husbands feared their beloved wives would be widowed and alone among enemies, while wives were restrained by the hope of seeing their children again.

Finally, when those innocent children arrived at the wilderness of São Thomé, which was to be their grave, they were thrown ashore and mercilessly left there. Almost all were swallowed up by the huge lizards on the island, and the remainder, who escaped these reptiles, wasted away from hunger and abandonment. Only a few were miraculously spared that dreadful misfortune.

O Lord, whose power encompasses the dominion of the entire universe, how shall I fortify my heart and soul with patience so that the great force and onslaught of such tribulations does not shatter it? Consider that "You have oppressed us and broken us in a land of dragons, and have covered us with a shadow of death," as my son David had once foreseen and lamented (Ps. 44.20).[95] In addition to the misfortunes in England, your threats against me were again executed here: "Your children shall be delivered to other peoples, and when your eyes see this they shall continually shed tears, and you shall have no strength to be able to bear it" (Deut. 28.32). "Because I shall set the teeth of beasts against them and the fury of serpents against the people" (Deut. 32.24). "And at this time I shall not hear when you call Me and are afflicted" (Jer. 11.11). Therefore "gird yourself with sackcloth, O daughter of My people, and wallow in ashes. Make you mourning, as for an only son, and a most bitter lamentation" (Jer. 6.26). Now since I have suffered such harsh punishments from Your anger, help me now, O Lord, and delay not.

28. PORTUGAL. YEAR 5257 [1497]
WHEN THEY WERE MADE CHRISTIANS BY FORCE

When death had finally carried off King John, who had persecuted me so cruelly in this world, another enemy then took the scepter in his place.[96] Once he obtained the crown he did not wait long to torment me. He soon proclaimed that all Jews in his kingdom must become Christians or leave Portugal within a stipulated period. If they did not leave, and were still found practicing Judaism, they would be allowed to remain, but their estates would be confiscated.[97]

This proclamation greatly saddened all my children, for their hearts told them that my enemy wished to perpetrate an evil greater than exile, and they determined to leave. Since they had lost their lands, they gathered the rest of their belongings as best they could in this short time, and prepared to leave. But when the king realized the Jews' resolve, and how little they seemed to mind exile in preference to changing their religion, he revealed his evil intent. He commanded all Jews in the kingdom to assemble in Lisbon, bruiting that he would there provide them with ships. But as soon as he had gathered them, he had them herded into large buildings called *Os Estãos*.[98] And when he had corralled them, like sheep prepared for the slaughter, he at last exposed his venomous character, and announced that all were to become Christians; and that they should do out of love what they would otherwise have to do by compulsion.

These threats were not sufficient to make my children turn their backs to their God; instead they answered resolutely that they would not comply with his request.

The king, seeing that greater force was required to jog them, consulted his advisers. They decreed that all the Jewish youth up to the age of twentyfive should be separated from their elders. This separation reminded the Jews of the still fresh cruelty when their children were thrown to the lizards, and they became terrified. What sad words can I find to describe to you the grief expressed by young and old alike, and the fathers' and mothers' screams and groans, which could have cleaved rocks and moved tigers to pity?

After the young people were removed from their families, the advisors spoke to them persuasively, covering their venomous thoughts with treacle and promising them many favors if they converted wholeheartedly. But even this was insufficient to budge them from their constancy.

Finding the children as resolute as their parents, the agents of my temptation attacked them furiously. Dragging some by their legs and arms and others by their hair and beards, they carried them forcibly into the churches, where they threw their baptismal water upon them; it touched some of them but barely reached others. Further, they imposed Christian names on them and placed them in the custody of Old Christians, who were to submit them to their new religion and keep them from their own faith.

No sooner had they completed this violence than they turned to the parents, who clung in anguish to the life they abhorred, and dealt them another mortal blow. They told them that their children had now converted to Christianity and urged them to do the same if they wished to live in their company. But this did not move them. Finally the king commanded that food and drink be withheld from them for three days

to try them with the anguish of hunger, but this they likewise coura-
geously endured.

The king realized that even this was insufficient to change them, and
that if he starved them any longer they would perish. He therefore
determined to use the violence he had employed with their children.
Dragging some by their legs and others by their hair and beards, punching
and mauling them, his men brought them to the churches, where the
waters of baptism were thrown upon them. Many resisted valiantly: one
father covered his six sons with their prayer-shawls,[99] exhorted them
sagely to die for their faith, and killed them one by one, taking his own
life last. One couple hanged themselves, and those who tried to take their
bodies away for burial were slain by the enemies' spears. There were
many who threw themselves into wells and others hurled themselves out
of windows and were dashed to pieces. My children's torturers took the
bodies of these Israelites and burned them in the sight of their brethren,
that they might be gripped with increased terror and fear of their cruelty.
As a result of this violence, contrary to divine and human laws, the
bodies of many Jews were made Christian, but no stain ever touched
their souls. Instead they kept forever impressed upon them the seal of
their ancient Law.

Who can escape from Your anger, O Lord, when it is moved with so
much cause as my iniquities provided? For even here it has overtaken
me, in these farthest parts of the earth, fulfilling these cruel judgments
which You pronounced against me through the lips of Your prophets:
"The Lord will scatter you among all peoples from one end of the earth
even to the other; there you shall serve other gods, whom you have not
known, you nor your fathers, and you will serve your enemy and lan-
guish" (Deut. 28.64-65). "He will place an iron yoke and hunger upon
your neck" (Deut. 28.48). "And all those who remain of this wicked
generation shall choose death rather than life" (Jer. 8.3). "And on the
day of their calamity (in a strange land) I shall turn My back to them
and not My face" (Jer. 18.17), just as they turned their backs to Me and
not their faces and worshiped foreign gods in their own lands." Yet the
truth is that "if we forget the name of our God and stretch forth the
palms of our hands to a strange god, the Lord does not fail to search this
out. (This must needs be so), for He knows the secrets of the heart"
(Ps. 44.21-22).

29. THE SLAUGHTER IN PORTUGAL. YEAR 5266 [1506]

It was not enough for the Portuguese to have brought my children so
forcibly and unjustly to their own religion, and to have removed them
from the faith in which they were born. They did not permit them even
to live peacefully in this way, but insulted and injured them, humbled
them, and treated them with disdain and scorn. My children would no
doubt have borne this patiently, if calumnies and false reports had not

been raised to destroy and uproot them from the world. The preachers in the pulpits, the nobles in the public places, and the city-folk and rustics in the squares began saying that any famine, pestilence or earthquake that came to the land came because these converts were not good Christians and practiced Judaism in secret. As a result, when some inveterate enemies of my children realized how the will of the people was bent on their hurt, they found a way to put their evil designs into effect.

Among these were two Dominican friars, who went through the city of Lisbon with crucifixes on their shoulders, inciting the people and calling for all to join them to avenge the death of their god. Many shiftless and base people attached themselves to them, and they attacked the weak and defenseless group of ill-baptized New Christians with spears and unsheathed swords. They killed four thousand of them, robbed them, and carried out all those cruelties which are perpetrated when a city is sacked: they maimed men, dashed children against walls and dismembered them, defiled women and girls and then killed them. They threw many pregnant women out of windows onto spearpoints awaiting them below, and thus blocked the road of innocent children before they could arrive in the world, where the mercy of heaven was sending them. One woman, driven by her fierce anger and honor, killed a monk who tried to attack her with his own weapons, knives that he was armed with.

If this catastrophe had continued, all the New Christians living in the city of Lisbon would have perished. But God's mercy arranged for the judges of the city to rescue them, and then the king, who returned speedily from his quarters in the town of Abrantes, aided them. Thus that fearful massacre ended.

O merciful Lord, witness our suffering from Your habitation on high and help us. And to prove that in the arcanum of our hearts we never wavered in our Jewish faith, "See that out of love for You we are killed each day, and are accounted as sheep ready to be slaughtered" (Ps. 44.23).

By Your command, Ezekiel pronounced this angry judgment which has been fulfilled against me: "O sword, O sword, keen-edged, furbished for the slaughter. It has been sharpened and furbished. It shall be upon My people. It shall be unsheathed against the leaders of Israel. It is the sword of great slaughter, which will enter into them to make their hearts melt and for many to fall before their gates" (Ezek. 21.14-17, 19-20).

Now when we suffer Your anger, "Awake, why do You sleep, O Lord? Arouse Yourself, do not remove Yourself from us forever. Wherefore do You hide Your face? Wherefore do You forget our affliction and oppression, since our soul now wallows in the dust and our belly cleaves to the face of the earth? Arise, help us and redeem us for Your name's sake" (Ps. 44.24-27). "Bring now upon them the evil day, and with destruction double (that which we have suffered), break them" (Jer. 17.18), O Lord of vengeance.

CONCERNING THE INQUISITION IN PORTUGAL

Fifteen years after this tribulation, King John, the third of this name, succeeded to the throne. At his accession great fears and anxieties sprang up in my soul, since he had shown malice toward my afflicted people while he was prince.

Before he took the reins of the kingdom, the New Christians had become immersed in power and its deceits. They had nearly forgotten their ancient faith, and lost the fear of that Fountain whence our life flows because of the vast riches and the status and rank they were acquiring in the kingdom. They now felt secure in their imitation of the Christians—though they never exchanged the secret of their souls.[100]

While my children were in this state, my faults determined to undo and persecute me. They chose as agent and executor King John, whose will was disposed for the task.

Because no misfortune could be more rigorous than the one my children suffered in Castile, the king decided to inflict this same punishment for my offenses in Portugal.[101] He sent to Rome for a monster, similar to the one in Spain. And though but few years have passed since its arrival there, it has already cruelly and frightfully ravaged that ill-baptized people. Its coming has paled their faces, troubled the repose of their spirits and covered their souls with pain and sadness. It has cast them from the comfort of their homes and made them dwell in dark prisons, where they live in anxiety and continual sighing. For there it prepares a trap for them so that they will fall into the fire and be burned.[102] They are martyred so much that in the poverty and abandon to which they are driven by this monster, they kill their own children, burn their husbands, deprive their brothers of life, increase the number of orphans and widows, impoverish the rich, destroy the powerful, make thieves of the nobly born, and sow base and infamous places with modest and chaste women. It has already consumed many by fire; not one by one, but by thirties and fifties at a time does it administer its punishment to them. And when it burns and destroys them, it attracts a large Christian populace, which exults and rejoices at seeing my limbs burn in the bonfire, lit and stoked with the wood my children themselves have carried on their shoulders from afar.

These ill-baptized people are filled with such fear of this beast that they glance furtively in all directions in the streets to see if it is nearby, and walk and stop in fear, their hearts tremulous and fluttering like the leaves of a tree, afraid that it will attack them. Whenever this animal strikes a blow, no matter how far away it is, all feel it as a blow in the pit of their stomachs, for in this calamity they are all members of one body in their suffering. Even at their tables they eat their morsels in fright, and the beast disquiets and terrorizes them even in the hour when restful sleep is granted to all other creatures. It turns the joys and festivities of marriages and births into grief and disquietude for them. In short, the monster makes them swallow a thousand lethal gulps at every moment, for it avails them not to show by external signs that they are Christians; it must examine their hearts with fire.

O brothers of mine, I could not fully describe even one in a thousand of the ills which this animal causes them, for its ways of inflicting torture are infinite. In fear of its cruelties, many of these ill-baptized people tried to leave Portugal, fleeing the land where this venomous reptile trod; but before they could enter their ships, some families were seized and delivered to the bitter prisons and thence to the fire. Others were drowned by the swell of the sea before they could reach their waiting ships. Many were taken even from their covert within the ships and burned in the monster's devouring flames.

Thus was I caught in the snares which all the prophets had set for me so long ago. They spoke, and it was thus fulfilled. "The Lord will scatter you among all peoples from one end of the earth even unto the other end of the earth. There you shall serve other gods which you have not known, nor your fathers. And among these nations you shall find no repose, nor shall there be a place where you may set the sole of your foot in safety. And the Lord will make your heart beat constantly and give you hollow eyes and sadness in your soul. And your life shall hang before you on a thin thread. You shall fear night and day, and you shall have no assurance of your life. Rather you shall say in the morning, 'Would that evening were given me'; and in the evening you shall say, 'Would that morning were given me,' because of the great fear of your heart and because of what you shall see with your eyes" (Deut. 28.64-67). And even if you, Israel, are compelled, "if you worship other gods and serve them, I declare unto you this day that you shall surely perish" (Deut. 30.17-18).

But in my ignorance, while hidden in the garb of a Christian, I thought that I could thus save my life, although it was just the reverse. "Israel grew fat and kicked back; it abandoned the Lord its maker and proved ungrateful to the Rock of its salvation" (Deut. 32.15).

"You forgot the Rock which bore you" (Deut. 32.18), and then the Lord said, "(Since this is so), I will hide My face from them" (Deut. 32.20), "and since they provoked Me to indignation with what is no god" (Deut. 32.21), fear and terror will be within their houses, for "a third part will I bring to the fire and smelt them as silver is smelted and will test them as gold is tested" (Zech. 13.9). And "their gold shall be held in scorn; their silver and their gold shall not be able to deliver them in the day of the Lord's wrath" (Ezek. 7.19). For "I will do unto them after their ways, and according to their deserts will I judge them until they recognize that I am the Lord" (Ezek. 7.27). For "since you went backwards, therefore I stretched forth My hand and destroyed you" (Jer. 15.6). "And when you raise your hands in prayer, I shall hide My eyes from you, and though you increase prayers, in no wise shall I hear you, for your hands are full of murders" (Isa. 1.15). "And if by chance some one of these whom I would want to punish could manage to hide in secret caves or hiding places that I see him not—(certainly this is impossible since) I fill the sky and the earth, says the Lord, and I am a God close by and not far away" (Jer. 23.23-24). . . .[103]

31. CONCERNING THOSE WHO HAVE LEFT AND WHO ARE LEAVING PORTUGAL SINCE THE YEAR 5291 [1531]

Some of those who escaped with anguish and danger from this animal's fierce claws and ultimately left the kingdom of Portugal, fared ill in strange lands. They were captured in Spain, arrested in Flanders, and despised and abused in England and France. Because of such difficulties, many depleted their fortunes and lost their lives. When their misfortunes brought them to Germany, a large number died from hardship and travail in the Alps because of their utter helplessness and exposure. Many of their wives were widowed when they were about to give birth. And when they gave birth on those cold and intemperate roads, still a new kind of misfortune was suffered.

And as if these troubles were not enough, there arose against me the cruelest persecutor of Israel since the loss of the Temple: Jean de la Foix.[104] He awaited my wandering children in the State of Milan; there he arrested them by the wagon-load. Since he did not have authority to kill them, he despoiled them even of their last garment. He subjected weak women and wearied old men to a thousand tortures to force them to reveal what possessions they had brought with them, and how many others were to follow, so that he could await and arrest them. Thus this man impoverished many and brought them to the brink of despair.

As soon as I had escaped that venomous reptile, I fell into the hands of other strange and ferocious peoples. The sea also devoured a number of the refugees, while others perished in both inhabited and deserted lands.

But of those who escaped with their lives, the great majority soon recognized the kindness which they had received from the Lord; and they went to lands where freedom permits them to return to the ancient and true Law of their fathers, which they had abandoned and forgotten for so many years. Others, on leaving the tempestuous sea, anchored again in many ports of Christianity, and there they are now dying in sadness and desiccation, without arriving at the Fountain, or being able to shatter the illusions of great ease and wealth with which the world entices them.

Many prophecies were clearly fulfilled here: "I shall make them roam all the kingdoms of the earth in fright and they shall be a curse, a horror, a derision and a dishonor among all these peoples among whom they wander wearied and harried" (Jer. 29.18).

"A third part shall call on My name, and I will answer them. I will say: 'You are My people' and they will say, 'The Lord is my God' " (Zech.

13.9). "And they that escape of you shall remember Me among the nations where they are captives and they shall know that I am the Lord and that I did not speak in vain when I prophesied their tribulation unto them" (Ezek. 6.9-10).

And the others, who still refuse to return to My Law and plead excuses, "they do not speak truth in all that they say and there is not one of them who repents him of his wickedness enough to say in his heart, 'What have I done, O wretched me? How is it that I have been mad for so long and still continue?' Rather each one pursues his wicked course as a horse in battle when disturbed and maddened" (Jer. 8.6). Yes, "the stork in the air knows her appointed times, and the turtle and the crane and the swallow each observes the time of its coming. But My people did not realize this concerning the Lord" (Jer. 8.7), that this is the time for them to go forth to serve Him. And you say, as an excuse, "We are wise: we have the Law of the Lord with us" (Jer. 8.8). Therefore, "I the Lord, who search the heart and try the reins to reward everyone according to his way and according to the fruit of his thoughts" . . . "And he who gets riches unjustly and not by right (amassing them without serving Me) shall leave them in the midst of his days and he shall remain a fool at the end and poor in counsel" (Jer. 17.10-11). "They shall not fill their souls, nor satisfy their appetites, because their wealth has been the stumbling block of their iniquity" (Ezek. 7.19). Thus "I will purge out from among you the rebels, and them that transgress against Me; I will bring them forth out of the land where they sojourn, but not one shall come to the land of Israel" (Ezek. 20.38). And it will happen to them like to those who were left in the desert for their sin and this prophecy will be confirmed: "All those who offend Me shall not see the land promised to their fathers" (Num. 14.23).

About twenty thousand souls left the boundaries of Europe to receive the yoke of Judaism, despising the admonitions of their spiritual Enemy, who spoke of the extreme poverty of Turkey which awaited them with open arms, and the grievous captivity [they would be subject to] under the Turks and Moors. May the merciful King and universal Lord of all worlds accept this as an atonement for their shortcomings.

32. NAPLES[105]

Nearly thirty years after King Ferdinand, the king who had thrown me out of Spain, exiled twenty thousand families from the Kingdom of Naples, one noble family[106] of my children still remained in the city, and through its diligent work and means, some of the exiles were allowed to return to the kingdom.

Although the Jews were constantly attacked and threatened with persecution and exile, their situation improved, until Emperor Charles determined to carry out an oft-made proposal.

Among the notable Jews in Naples was a man of esteem, a dignified elder of the Spanish nation [Samuel Abravanel],[107] the foremost and most distinguished man among the Spanish Jews. He had earned the accolade of "Trismegistus," three times great, as the Greeks say. He was a great sage in the Law, eminent in noble society and philanthropic with his wealth, which he generously used to alleviate the tribulations of his brethren. He provided for the marriage of countless orphan girls, maintained many needy people, and distinguished himself pre-eminently in the freeing of captives. He gave his help so extensively that all the qualities needed to receive prophecy were present in him.

In addition, heaven had granted him a companion who was his peer in all virtues [Benvenida Abravanel].[108] Seeing the plight to which her brethren were subjected, she and several Neapolitan princesses petitioned the emperor to revoke the order of banishment against the Jews. Aided by God's favor, she so wisely presented her request that the emperor graciously granted it, and the Israelite people received a great consolation.

Nevertheless, when the emperor left Naples, some wicked counselors, roused by my sins,[109] incited him against me. Five years later, he ordered that every Jew must wear a badge of identification; if any Jew was found without it, he was to forfeit his life and his property—an unbearable punishment.

The Jews were given six months to comply with this order or leave the land, and heavy penalties were fixed for those failing to do so. My children realized that our calamities always begin with trifling matters, and that this limited oppression, if continued, could lead to dire consequences. The prince's act was a patent indication of his hostility toward them. They feared that he would change his mind once more for the worse, and proclaim more rigorous laws against them. Since if they submitted they would incur greater harm than they would face if they departed from the kingdom, all my children decided to leave rather than chance the outcome of the king's inauspicious decree.[110]

With them went the noble family of the Abravanels, who wished to share the troubles of their brethren, though they had been excluded from the decree.

Some wandered to spacious Turkey, many entered the Papal States, while others submitted to the authority of Italian potentates.

Here your prophetic judgment, Jeremiah, was fulfilled: "I shall make them wander in terror through all the kingdoms of the earth" (Jer. 29.18).

33. CONSTANTINOPLE. YEAR 5302 [1542]

And so that this exile and disquietude should not transpire without additional anguish for me [another misfortune occurred].

In Turkey, a Turk was courting a chaste Turkish matron. After she had been greatly importuned and wooed, she decided to reveal the affair to her husband. He told his wife not to disillusion the lover, and to arrange to meet him at night at an appointed place and time.

The lover was thrilled with this great favor, totally unaware of the fate that awaited him. For the husband had hidden himself near the place of the tryst, armed, and when the would-be adulterer arrived, he killed him.

When he saw the lover sprawled lifeless on the ground before him, he bethought himself where he might take the body, so as to lay the blame and punishment for his crime on someone else. Since all misfortunes are directed against the Jews, and since calamities hasten to them because they are the weakest and frailest spot [in the body of humanity],[111] he decided to throw the corpse into a courtyard where Jews lived.

In the morning, when the Jews found a Turk stabbed to death before their doors, they trembled with anxiety and anguish, like the limbs of a single body.

The Turks came in an endless stream to see the corpse, muttering against the afflicted Jews; and they became so incensed that they spoke of a massacre. To my further undoing, many enemies went to the pashas to slander the Jews, and the pashas raged with anger. On the basis of this false testimony, they would have punished many Jews who had already been arrested, had not God's mercy aided the Jews in the person of a distinguished Israelite, the physician of the Great Sultan.[112] As he had done on many previous occasions, this physician [Moses Hamon] went to the aid of his brethren with abounding compassion and love. He requested a careful investigation of the death, and Supreme Mercy saw to it that the truth was revealed in all its details.

It is likely, Ezekiel, that your prophecy was fulfilled here: "I will do unto them according to their ways and according to their deserts will I judge them, so that they may thus recognize that I am the Lord" (Ezek. 7.3-4).

34. SALONIKA. 5305 [1545]

Then another calamity, harsher and of greater import, followed this one.

There is a city in the Turkish kingdom which formerly belonged to the Greeks, and in our days is a true mother-city[113] in Judaism. For it is established on the very deep foundations of the Law. And it is filled with the choicest plants and most fruitful trees[114] presently known anywhere on the face of our globe. These fruits are divine, because they are watered by an abundant stream of charities. The city's walls are made of holy deeds of the greatest worth.

The majority of my children who have been persecuted and exiled from Europe and many other parts of the world have taken refuge in this city, and she embraces them and receives them with as much love and good will as if she were Jerusalem, that old and ever pious mother of ours.

Though this fine, large community of Israel lived under such favora- ble circumstances here, heavenly wrath in the form of a fire descended on several occasions and inflicted severe damage upon it.[115] The last fire burned a hundred Israelite souls to death and consumed a substantial amount of property. It leveled tall houses, wrecked and demolished almost all the holy synagogue buildings and burned to ashes many old and valuable sacred tomes.

This visitation was so frightful that it brought the city's inhabitants and all who depend upon the city to the brink of ruin; many rich people were impoverished, and the poor were reduced to the direst misery.

Incomprehensible are Your judgments, O Lord, since You so harshly scourged these people who were outwardly striving so earnestly to imitate Your ways and obey Your holy precepts. But when we consider Your infinite kindness, and how just You are in all Your ways, we shall believe that You punished them for some iniquity. Perhaps it was the sin of some wicked individuals, whose punishment embraced the entire community because the good people neglected to chastise it. [This would at least be a plausible explanation for what happened in Salonika.] This city being the head of Judaism—all other lands are its limbs—it is understandable why it received the pain and hurt resulting from the actions of Jews in all other lands. Thus was this judgment of Isaiah fulfilled: "The Lord of hosts will send a leanness among the fattest and most powerful, and instead of their glory He will kindle a burning fire" (Isa. 10.16).

35. BOHEMIA. YEAR 1306[116]

I saw a period of great hardship and stress begin for the Jews who had been spending their exile so peacefully in the kingdom of Bohemia and in other Germanic areas.

Some Jewish and Christian boys were playing ball in the city of Prague, and the ball fell into an unfrequented place. One of the Chris- tian boys later went down alone to look for the lost ball at nightfall, but he misguided his steps, fell, and was killed.

When this youth failed to appear, a search was made, and his body was finally discovered. Since the place where he had fallen was located near a Jew's house, the Jews were accused of having murdered the boy. The old people in the city claimed that the Jews had killed the boy to celebrate the Passover with his blood, and that Jews had often been accused of this crime in Germany in olden times, especially in Prague.

This charge anguished and distressed the Jews as much as if Death itself had appeared before them. They feared the populace would attack them and savagely massacre them, as so often had happened in the past on the evidence of similar falsehoods.

O bestial thought, O terrible plague and curse, which blinds people with sound judgments like the Christians to my hurt! O nations, why do you not consider how forbidden and abominable it is for a Jew to eat blood? Can you not see that among the first commandments of His Law, our Lord forbade the Jews to eat blood? He told them to shun blood: not to eat a strangled bird because its blood remained within it, and to decapitate every animal and let its blood. How, then, can you charge the Jews with killing a child to take his blood? It can only be an affliction which the Lord permits the Jews; misfortunes which the Lord wishes to give them; persecutions which their sins bring on; a scourge with which the Lord chastises them; payment in kind for the commandment of blood which they and their fathers willfully broke.[117] God's justice wishes them to be punished through a lie.

Finally, when my children in Bohemia and in other parts of Germany had almost drunk the full cup of doom waiting for the sentence against them to be determined, the lords of the regions came to the agreement that the Jews should be expelled from the kingdom, since their guilt was only suspected.

Some of these exiles traveled to the nearby kingdom of Poland, while others took refuge in Turkey. O merciful God, how You hold back the punishment which my iniquities stir up against me. Your prophecy has been carried out: "For My name's sake I will defer My anger, and for My praise I will refrain in your case, and I will not destroy you completely" (Isa. 48.9).

36. ITALY. YEAR 5311 [1551]

In Italy's safest port [Ferrara],[118] where God's mercy had ordained that I might rest from the distressing journeys I have made from Portugal and Spain, I was again harassed by my spiritual Enemy, who was aided by my iniquities.

It happened that a plague broke out somewhere in the territory of the Grisons[119] and in Germany. Travelers who came from those areas spread the highly contagious disease to Ferrara, and a number of people, including Portuguese Hebrews, died.

The people fancied that the Hebrews had spread the disease, since on leaving Spain and Portugal they had traveled through the Grisons and Germany on their way to this safe port. Their suspicion increased to such an extent that the lord of the region, though favorably disposed toward us and inclined to ease the desolation of the captivity we have endured throughout the world since the destruction of our Second Temple, was forced to take action against me because of the insistence of the people. Reluctantly, he tried to placate them by expelling all the Portuguese Jews[120] in the city. They left under conditions of great hardship and wretchedness, for the populace considered them contaminated and no one could be found to help them with their departure, even for a price.

Further, the time set for their departure expired at night, and they were under penalty of losing their possessions. Here in the darkness, brothers, you could see weary old men, with their boxes on their backs, falling in the middle of the street, too weak to bear their heavy burdens. Their frail old wives cried beside them and bemoaned their fate. Other people dragged the burdens they could not carry in anguish.

When they finally reached the port in such distress, they were attacked by the guards who had been stationed there by the court to protect them. With their bared swords and spears held at their victims' chests, they forced them to surrender the little money they were carrying for the journey. But these guards were later condignly punished by the just prince.

When the Jews boarded the vessels, where they paid for their passage with their weight in gold, they were taken to sea. They disembarked on another beach of Italy, and there they suffered great anguish because of the adverse treatment they received.

Still God's mercy did not permit any of these Jews to die, nor was there a single person among them who even became ill. This was evidence that they were not infected, and that the disease had not been carried by them.

But the plague continued to spread in the city, and the natives insisted that the Portuguese [Jews] abandon their beach and leave. They therefore embarked again. Some set out for Turkey; they were attacked at sea by corsairs and pirates and had to satisfy them with all the gold they desired to obtain their freedom. Others wandered across the Adriatic, not knowing where to turn, for all people at the nearby ports had readied their spears for the Jews' arrival.

Heaven's pity came to the aid of the Israelites through a son of mine, [Manuel Bichacho],[121] one of the exiles from Portugal who lived in a town called Pesaro, in the state of Urbino. He was moved to compassion and pity for his afflicted brethren, and entreated the prince of the city to take them in. There they found rest as the storm subsided.

Others died unsheltered on Italian roads, for they were recognized as belonging to the Portuguese nation; everyone fled from them because they were rumored to be infected with the plague.

With great reason did Jeremiah say: "I will pursue them with the sword, famine and pestilence. I will make them roam in terror unto all the kingdoms of the earth and let them be a curse, an astonishment, a mockery and a reproach among all the nations whither they shall go tired and harried" (Jer. 29.18). In this exile and the exile from Portugal, this prophecy has been effected against me.

37. PESARO. YEAR 5313 [1553]

Only a short time later I was afflicted with a new and deeper wound. It penetrated to my inmost soul, and touched and offended God's honor as much as the wicked Antiochus' profanation of the sanctity of the Second Temple.

At night in the city of Pesaro, enemies stole into the house where my children of the Diaspora of Portugal gathered to voice their prayers to our Lord. With little fear and less respect for the Most High, they removed the scrolls[122] from the Ark, the books of their Law, the support and firm pillar which upholds the world and all its creatures. They dashed one scroll scornfully against the ground and left it there. They carried another outside and threw it into a garden, on whose trees they hung the scholars' phylacteries.

When dawn came and revealed this terrible desecration, boundless shock and sadness struck the hearts of the Jews.

To make this wound still more deadly, the same perverse hands pushed their wickedness to the extreme: with even greater cruelty they profaned everything in the city's other holy synagogue, which belonged to the Italian Israelites. Four nights later they broke the iron grating of this synagogue, and like shrewd criminals, entered and removed thirteen scrolls of the Law from the Ark. They rolled and wrapped a loathsome swine in the scrolls' sacred bands and mantles and then put this filthy animal into the Ark, from which they had removed the Holy Law. Then they closed the doors of the Ark and contemptuously left the Holy Scriptures lying upon the floor.

O Lord of vengeance, help Your sanctuary which is abused. Come to repair Your honor as You used to, for our iniquities have sapped and drained our strength. The time is at hand for You to fulfill Your most holy word: "For My own sake, for My own sake will I do this, that My Law be profaned no more, nor My glory given to another " (Isa. 48.11).

FINAL LAMENT OVER ALL ISRAEL'S MISFORTUNES PAST AND PRESENT

My compassionate brothers, I have related to you the kind of life I have led in my wretched exile since the Romans scattered me throughout the world.

I have told you how the shrewd and malevolent Spaniards wounded my lambs' terrestrial bodies and divine souls, and nearly wiped us out completely; how my sheep suffered the wrath of the first attack by the audacious[123] Frenchmen, who made them retch in bitterness the lush grass they had pastured; how the malicious Englishmen deceitfully beheaded them with their swords and how the arrogant Germans watered them with poison; how they were pitilessly injured by the shrewd Flemish and abused by the harsh and hostile Italians. I have told you how the strong, almost barbaric Portuguese dismembered them and took the tender calves from their dam's udders to throw some into fire and water, and others into the mouths of hungry beasts.

To this day, none of these storms have abated. Like a ship tossed by shifting tempests on the high sea, unable to steer its prow toward any of the four corners of the world, so do I, afflicted Israel, still roll in the troughs of my perils.

Truly, if all my misfortunes were heaped on one side of heaven, its axis would tilt with grief under the heavy load.

O mangled body of mine, where has anyone seen as harsh and unprecedented tortures as you have suffered? In Babylonia you bolted a morsel of venom which nearly destroyed your life on earth. You revived, only to be brutally martyred again by the Romans. Both of these peoples who cruelly dismembered you have perished, yet you continue to live, still nailed to your tribulations, repeatedly suffering new tortures.

Nature makes all creation change; but not Israel, for its misery is never altered or varied. I have acquired the adamantine hardness of a rock in the sea that is continually whipped by relentless waves.

After the earth has been lashed by the rough of winter, which strips the herbs of their charm and the trees of their leaves, You again gladden it with summer, O Lord. You cast on its shoulders a mantle of flowers and countless species of delightful fruits.

In winter some animals molt their colored skins, others their speckled wool, and some their motley feathers. You change the seasons and cover each one anew, and all are content. But in me, poor Israel, summer brings no change. I live continuously in the gloom of winter, stripped of gay apparel, covered with a mourner's garb.

Oxen, wearied from the plow on a sultry day, are loosed from their yoke when their task is done; they preen in the afternoon shade and ramble to their folds to rest. Then the wearied husbandman takes shelter and heartily eats his rustic viands, free from care. He soon forgets the work he has done and spends the night in sound and uninterrupted sleep.[124] But for me there is no time of repose. I live with the yoke of thraldom ever around my neck, and sad memories freight every morsel I consume. My mind and my sleep are always restless and troubled, for my tribulations and torment permit them no repose, but plague me at the beginning, middle and end of every tranquil moment.

Luckless captives, enthralled from the beardless years of youth to the hoary hairs of age, will leave their harsh durance in the twilight of their lives and revive with the sweet taste of liberty. Long forgotten in their dungeons and given up for dead, they see their misfortunes cease and they are free. But for you, afflicted Jacob, the oldest captive of all, in whose long imprisonment your irons and fetters have eroded only to be soon rebuilt, for you the hour of liberty and freedom still has not arrived.

Time heals the yearning of those who have willingly journeyed many years from home and returns them to their lands in joy;[125] and, O Lord, You console bereaved parents with the birth of new offspring. But for me, wandering Israel, the time of consolation never comes—the time when my exile might be lifted, the time when I might tread the joyous meadows and gay slopes of my true and holy motherland, the time when I might be consoled with new children to replace those whose loss I now suffer and lament.

Venturesome mariners, imperiled in the troughs of the heaving sea, are soon visited by calm and propitious weather, and, their lives and cargoes secure, they joyfully reach the shelter of their desired port. But my tempest never ceases, and I never see the port of my hopes.

In the course of time all mortals, however lowly and luckless their lot, find a remedy for their misfortunes and revive from their long entombment—but not Israel, which never finds new life, and buckles under the burden of its perennial grief.

Therefore, O Lord, how long must the winter storm of my misfortunes last, the yoke so heavy upon my neck, the fetters so harsh on my feet, the disquiet and fright in my spirit, the gnawing anxieties in my soul? How long must my motherland bemoan the absence of her children and suffer the shame of barrenness? When will she again be decked with the handsome and gallant attire she once wore, with flowers more beautiful and exquisite than any other land's, with marvelous fruits which surpass the world's best in size and savor, with sweet and clear waters whose continuous flow kept her so lush and gay? Has the time not come for me to have surcease from my misfortunes and a calm port to rest from my storms—or at least for You to restore her once happy nature to my motherland, since being insensitive earth, she could not offend You? Only her children offended You; they strayed from the path of obedience to their Father.

What prevents her restoration and mine? O Lord, since You are also waiting, along with Israel, Your first born, for the day of her restoration, the mountain of my offenses must be formidable and its valley enormous for You to be thus restrained.[126] Yet it seems to my earthly judgment that I have already suffered all the punishments that were prophesied against me and that can be imagined; and others, as well, of so unusual and strange a nature that their like has never been conceived by the human mind.

What remedy can I now seek in my affliction, if all of my alternatives are equally extreme? The earthly sphere and all of its peoples have conspired and plotted against me. Europe, which swallowed me with its noxious mouth, now retches me. Asia, which sorely wounded me with its hands and trampled me with its heavy feet, unremittingly hurts and harms me. Africa, which vexed and persecuted me, even now keeps me in the extremes of wretchedness.

O world, why did you create in your midst one whom you would so abhor and reject? When you wrapped my frame in the first mass of dust and soil, you should have left it to be trodden on by all the creatures, since they later trod upon me in my present form. Yet, woe is me, my senses were infused in my earthly frame so that the pain and the torment inflicted upon me might be doubled.

But what am I saying? Although all that I have uttered is true, I would suffer my afflictions with some forbearance if, O Lord of all creation,[127] You did not disfigure me and increase my suffering and sorrow.

Mortals measure their lives by days of light and not by nights of sleep, but for me all waking and brightness is death and all my good fortunes are in dreams. O eyes of mine, what troubles you, for when you are closed you see the shades and mirages of my blessings, and when you are open you behold the reality of my misfortunes?

Tired animals rest their spirits in refreshing sleep; some repose on thin, white hemp, others on hard rocks, some on green herbs, and others on tall plants and graceful trees. And the sea rests by stilling its continuous swells. Yet at the hour of repose, I, restless Israel, gnawed by cares and tossed by countless calamities, begin my sleepless night. I ruminate on my anxieties and the ills I dread. I open the gates of memory to the misfortunes that have swept over me and bathe myself in tears for the tribulations yet to come. And thus I cannot help but greatly loathe the world.

Further, I defy the nature of every element on earth; for as the aeons pass, the bodies of many peoples and nations that have come to earth and perished are reduced to the four original elements;[128] yet I am not dissolved or destroyed by time. Thus the earth is blameless if it consumes its rightful parts which I withhold; the fire may justly continue to claim its natural heat that forms part of me, the water, the humidity which I have wrested from it, and the air, the vital spirit of which I rob it. The earth reclaimed its share when my children died in France and Germany. The fire received its part when my children were cruelly burned in Spain and Portugal. The waters of England and the Ocean Sea[129] received their share when my children were drowned. And the air has taken the greatest share in the diseases, plagues and continuous illnesses which I have suffered throughout the universe during this prolonged Diaspora.

But what am I saying, O wretched me? If you, O elements dispossessed me once and for all and destroyed me, it would be better than this torture which gradually dismembers my body with a thousand agonies.

O heaven, O earth, O waters, O human beings, have mercy and relax the knot that you press against my neck. Let the long-choked words come forth from the breast of your slave, whose cause has not been heard. Let him dispute your justification of the evils you have committed against him. What dissimilarity is there between my natural reason and understanding and that which was infused in all other creatures of my species? Why do you celestial constellations pursue me? How was the dust of which I was kneaded different from that of all other earthly bodies, that you, O earth, do not want or permit me upon you? What deformity is there in my face, what disproportion in my limbs compared to that of other rational beings, that you, O nations, reject and repudiate me in all? Surely, if you stopped to judge this wrong dispassionately, you would permit me to spend the days of my mortal life in peace, bothered by only the usual vicissitudes of those who live on earth.

What a profound and extraordinary marvel I see in myself! The earth rejects itself in my form. Heaven abhors its spirit in my breast. Humans shun their own image in my appearance. Can you not see that you subvert all nature by not loving what is similar to you in me, for all things love their like? But oh, woe to you, Israel, for in dealing with you, all creation breaks the laws to which it was bound and perverts its natural inclinations to injure you. What can I say, O Lord? From the strange suffering meted out to me, it seems that You desired not only to punish my sins, but to exhibit me as proof to the world that in Your hand lies the power to change the primal nature of the waters, the earth, the heavens and everything You have created in them; and to exemplify in my martyrdom how divine power may be exerted against a body of people. If this be so, why did this sad lot befall me, rather than any of the other peoples on earth?

Perhaps You have punished me for the first sin I committed, when I sold my brother Joseph,[130] who went down into Egypt, the place of my first wandering and captivity. Yet it would have been more natural, I think, for You to have punished the necromancy of the Egyptians into whose power You delivered me, since they were so distant from knowledge of You and Your service.

Perhaps You have punished me for the golden calf in the desert and my idolatries in the Holy Land at the time of the holy First Temple; for this sin You chastised me with Sennacherib, Shalmaneser and Nebuchadnezzar. Yet the Assyrians worshiped Asshur, Nimrod's grandson, a mortal man, who was deceitfully killed and deprived of his empire by his wife, Semiramis,[131] and the Babylonians offered loathsome sacrifices and honors to a poisonous dragon.[132] It therefore seems that these peoples were withdrawn from Your favor.

Perhaps You have punished me for the discords and jealousies I showed in the Second Temple, when I shed my brethren's blood; for this offense I was destroyed by Vespasian and Titus. Yet who does not know of the Romans' vice, and the obscenity of their religion? Consider only Remus and Romulus, Rome's founding fathers. Like Cain, Romulus killed his brother Remus. To build his kingdom, he assembled many criminals who had committed capital offenses and roamed the world as fugitives from justice, and with such accomplices he laid the foundations for the sway and grandeur of the Romans. The Romans proved that they walked in their forebears' footsteps by imitating them in the countless internecine tyrannies, robberies, perfidies and inhumanities which they committed throughout the duration of their imperial rule.

Whoever saw such an abominable iniquity as the Roman emperor Gaius Caesar[133] committed against heaven when he proclaimed himself god and, under severe penalties, forbade the worship of any other deity? [The Roman emperor] Nero's atrocities are notorious. Not only did he burn Rome for his own diversion, but his pity was untouched by the shouts of the children perishing in the flames. He even betrayed his own mother, commanding that she be killed so that he might open her belly and see the place where he was confined for nine months.[134] Domitian, Caligula, Elagabalus, Gallienus [260-268 C.E.] and others of that ilk fell from humanity in their vices and lusts and joined the ranks of the beasts. And yet, O Lord, You kept nearly the entire world subject to their power. Only the heavens have the key to this enigma!

And for as long as their great empire and dominion lasted, these Romans, like brutes, had no knowledge of the First Cause. Their gods were Jupiter, Juno, Venus, Vulcan, Saturn, Neptune, Pallas, and countless other mortals who had been subject to human misery, who had been born among them and were their familiars on earth. In their transgressions the Romans sank deeper than Israel; thus I believe that they should have been the ones to be disciplined by the agents of Your punishment.

But perhaps You have punished me on account of the offenses and new sins which I have been committing daily against Your most holy Law and which I now confess before You. Or perhaps it is because I have persisted in my iniquity until this day, and have not checked its course or repented for all my past transgressions. This I acknowledge and with all humility I beg Your forgiveness for my obstinacy, O Lord. But, O God of vengeance, cast Your eyes upon the works of the contemporary peoples into whose power You have delivered Your world and observe whether they have left the errant path which their forebears followed.

The heathens who occupy Asia and enjoy its delights and lavish wealth murder men in vicious ways and shed the blood of their own kith and kin. Who does not know of the brigands who inhabit all Arabia Deserta?[135] Their number is fifty or seventy thousand. They come together for attacks and rob the caravans of merchants and wayfarers. They have no other means of livelihood, but spend their days on earth in this evil pursuit.[136]

And among the people of Arabia Felix, many are inhuman brutes. In Sana, the royal city, there lived a son of Sultan Sechamir who bit people to death (like a rabid dog) and satiated himself on their flesh.

The people of Persia are also exceedingly cruel. In the metropolis of Hormuz it is known that the son of the sultan gouged out the eyes of his father, mother and nine brothers and sisters, assembled their bodies in one chamber, and set fire to them, burning the entire building.

The people of India also follow customs that contradict human and divine reason. The Sultan of Cambay, the chief and most noble city in the province, daily consumes a quantity of poison. He has three or four thousand wives, and whenever one spends the night with him, she is found dead in the morning. No one dares touch any garment he has worn for fear of the lethal poison it has absorbed. Yet the sultan is unaffected by the poison, because he has been fed this food since childhood.

Such are the customs and practices of their princes. Imagine what those of their subjects must be like!

And, O Lord, You are well acquainted with their infernal religion.

In Calicut, the capital and principal city of all India, the entire populace worships the devil. A metal devil, hideous and repulsive to behold, is seated on a huge throne in the center of their loathsome temple. This idol has four large horns upon his head and four enormous teeth in his gaping mouth; his nose is ugly and forbidding; and even more frightening are his terrible eyes, fixed in a cruel gaze. His hands are hooked, and his feet are like cocks' feet. Merely to look at this bizarre image inspires dread and terror. In each corner of his gloomy shrine is a demon seated upon a throne above a blazing fire, in which a large number of bodies are burning. The devil picks one up in his right hand and eats it, then takes another with his left. The Brahmans, who are his priests, come every morning to bathe him with scented waters. They perfume him, and when they are finished, they worship him and offer sacrifices in cock's blood, over coals aglow in a silver vase. They burn musk, benzoin, incense and other blended perfumes before him.

And what shall I say about the abominable rites and bestial customs of the other heathens in the continent of Asia? On the island of Java, where there are several kingdoms, some people worship the devil of Calicut; some worship the sun when they rise in the morning; others the moon at night. Many worship the ox; and the majority adore the first object they see upon awakening in the morning. And their infernal practices are no better than those of wild beasts, for there are many on that island who eat human flesh and suck their own kin's blood. When a father is too old to work, his children sell him at the market, and the buyers kill him, and cook and eat him. If a youth becomes incurably ill, his father and brothers put an end to him before he can die a natural death, and sell him as food to others. What an infernal people! What demons in human form! Therefore, O Lord on high, why do these people enjoy dominion and repose? Why do they possess a fertile and abundant land of their own, which yields them stores of silk, brass, gold, the finest emeralds and choicest fruits, and other types of nutriment, while I, Your first-born, Israel, despoiled of my lands and possessions, wander through the world in the depths of degradation and misery?

In Africa, the people commit turpitudes beyond all human comprehension. What can be said of the peoples who live in the deserts in Lybia, Zanhaga, Zuenziga, Targa, Lemta and Berdoa, who are called Numidians by the Romans, save that they are hell incarnate, for they spend all their days in malefaction, pursuing, robbing and killing? And above all, they are not Mohammedans, or Jews, or Christians, nor do they have any religion or offer prayer to any thing; rather they live like the beasts of the field. Yet, despite this, they have a kingdom, they possess territory and dominion of their own, and they do not wander in alien lands.[137]

The Africans in the province of Hea have the same evil character, O Lord on high. They live on the continual robberies they commit against peaceful wayfarers. And their deeds are so wicked that they often despoil innocent passers-by of their lives.

But why O Lord must I dwell on what You can know so intimately of the religions and practices contrary to Your pleasure, not only of these people in Africa, but also in other kingdoms in the world? Therefore, O Spirit divine (You who embrace all things with perfect peace and, diffused through the veins of this earthly sphere, are its salvation and sacred love), would that You took one of these peoples as an example of Your might, as a proverb among the nations in my stead, for they live far removed from Your service. Would that the hapless lot did not fall upon Your people Israel, whose understanding attains Your truth and who strives to be obedient, if not in all, at least in part of Your holy precepts, though the flesh, misery, captivity and deceits of the world lead it astray.

And if You could not will this, then where is the source of justice and right? Put an end now to my misfortunes. Calm the tempest of my evil destiny. Rest my anxious spirit. Peace, peace, O Lord, to so much war, for our times already have enough bitter examples of Your wrath, and have suffered the fulfillment of all the judgments which You pronounced against us:

Amos' [sic] judgment: "Samaria is cut off with her king as foam which is upon the face of the water" (Hos. 10.7).

And Ezekiel's: "I delivered Oholah—Samaria—into the hand of her lovers, into the power of the Assyrians, upon whom she doted" (Ezek. 23.9).

These were fulfilled through Sennacherib and Shalmaneser.

And Ezekiel's judgment concerning Jerusalem: "O Oholibah, thus says the Lord: 'You shall drink of your sister Samaria's cup, deep and large'" (Ezek. 23.22, 32). This has been fulfilled by Nebuchadnezzar's rod.

The judgments of Jeremiah and Ezekiel: "Lo, I will bring a nation upon you from afar, O house of Israel, says the Lord" (Jer. 5.15). "It shall cut off with the sword your fortified cities, in which you trust" (Jer. 5.17). "A third part shall die with the pestilence and with famine shall it be consumed, and another third part shall fall with the sword round about you, and the other shall I scatter unto all the winds" (Ezek. 5.12). This prophecy was fulfilled through the cruel Romans.

Ezekiel's other judgment: "A barley cake shall you eat which you shall bake before them in dung of human filthiness. So shall the children of Israel eat their bread unclean among the nations whither I will drive them" (Ezek. 4.12-13). My forebears suffered this plight, and now I continue in it among the peoples where I am fulfilling my exile.

Now since I have suffered all Your indignations, is it not time, O Lord, for me to find a port where my battered body may rest from so many storms? And if You desire to refine me more, consider, O merciful one, that I am too fragile for the mighty fire of Your wrath.

But oh, woe is me, for the One I call is very far from me, for He answers me not. Where is He now who led us across the sea with the shepherds of His flock? Where is He who put His holy spirit upon them, who led Moses with His outstretched arm and cleaved the waters for His people with His right hand so that they might attain everlasting renown?

Where is He who guided us through the depths? They were led by the Lord's spirit as a horse is led without hindrance or obstruction, or as a beast is led through an open field. Therefore, O Lord, since You so generously came to my forebears' aid when they suffered in the Egyptian inferno and exalted them to the heavens with Your bounteous hand, let this hand not be withheld during the long misfortunes of their children. Let my cries reach You, and from Your lofty and supreme abode, lower Your eyes to the abyss of my tribulations, and send Your mercy to help. Where, O Lord, have You hidden the zeal which You used to assume, the fortitude which You donned for the defense of Your people, the continuous compassion which You had for me? Why do You not employ any of these blessings with me at present? For You are the truest of our fathers, for Abraham does not know us in this era, nor does Israel take notice of us (Isa. 63.16).[138]

We see clearly that the multitude of our sins have delivered us into the power of Your wrath, and that we have persisted in these same iniquities, for were it not so our affairs would have a happier and more favorable end. But since it is so, do not permit us on this account to rot in the power of our wickedness; proceed no further with Your fury. Have pity, have pity, O merciful one, for we submit to You. Dispel the dark cloud of my demerits with the strong light of Your mercy: let them be consumed, let them be drowned in the depths, never again to appear before You. Consider instead that "we are all the work of Your hands, for we are the clay and You are our Maker, and that besides this we are Your people" (Isa. 64.7-8) "and part of the tribes of Your inheritance" (Isa. 63.17). "Put before You the cities of Your holiness, which are converted into desert; Zion a waste; Jerusalem desolate; our holy house, the honor and glory of all of us, where our fathers praised You, which is burned with fire, and the fact that all our most esteemed and precious possessions have been turned to desolation. Then will You restrain Yourself, O Lord, for things such as these and will You dissemble for such a long time?" (Isa. 64.9-11). I do not believe it; rather as they and I groan, we remain awaiting Your incomprehensible and bountiful mercy.

ZICAREO: For such complaints a display of emotion and tears is proper, and we shall join you, since much of your loss affects us as well. It is a human trait to show the soul's sorrow by external signs, and our Lord considered it proper for these tokens of sadness to be found in rational creatures; in all great misfortunes He admonishes wailing and lamentation as a precept for the afflicted. All Israel wailed thirty days in the desert when our Lord gathered the brothers Aaron and Moses to Himself, because these pillars on which the entire populace had leaned were now removed. And they displayed no less emotion when Joshua departed from this life. Eli the priest was so grieved when he heard that the Philistines had captured the Ark of the Lord and slain his two sons, that he fell from his chair and died. Jeremiah displayed his sorrow for the loss of your First Temple in heartrending ways.[139]

Thus you are permitted to show dejection and sorrow for your children whom you saw compelled to change their faith in Spain; for those who were burned and despoiled in France; for those who were converted so violently and then killed by the sword in England; and for the un-exampled cruelties committed against them in the past in Germany, Italy and throughout the world, continuing to our own day in Portugal. How many were struck down in the tender years of childhood! Their innocence evokes our pity. How many were stunned with a cruel and violent death in the joyous days of their espousal! Our grief for them surpasses every other. Those uprooted at a riper age had nobler and more precious qualities which we missed. They were already perfect fruits; they had reached mature life and fulfilled their parents' dreams. And what human emotion can do justice to our grievous loss of the sedate elders, the guides of all life's stages? Yet most poignant is the grief which we feel for those who abandoned their most holy Law to save their lives, and have to this day persevered in their error; like rebellious limbs, they refuse to attach themselves to the body of Israel, continuing to wander among the deceitful pleasures of the nations. This grief exceeds all the others com-bined as much as the divine soul surpasses the earthly body.

Therefore, let them be mourned by the father who gave them their terrestrial flesh, and the One on high who infused in them a celestial spirit and enabled them to stand upright.

You may display as great a sorrow now as was shown at the time of your captivity in Babylon, and when you descended into Egypt against your will, for the virgin daughter of your people is struck with great devastation and wounded with a grievous hurt. Let the sound of your laments be so pitiful that it softens even the hardest hearts. Lament the bodies, begotten of you, as it were, which are daily racked with pain before your eyes, and let the Lord, their spiritual father, lament the tarnished souls which have already passed from this life, and those which are soiled in our own days.

HUMAN CONSOLATION FOR THE TRIBULATIONS OF ISRAEL

NUMEO: Now that we have bewailed your wounds, which are as bloody as a surgeon could wish for before he operates,[140] it is time for us to seek the remedy and consolation for all of them, for we have come to the end of them, as we hope, through God's mercy, to explain to you in many ways.

The first is this: You must realize that all human beings are subject to punishment the moment they commit a sin. Our Lord established this law when He told Adam in the terrestrial paradise: "Eat not from the tree of knowledge of good and evil, for on the day you eat therefrom you shall die" (Gen. 2.17). When Adam transgressed the commandment he sinned, and suffered the punishment.

On the other hand, every divine precept which is observed receives its reward. Our Lord appeared to Abraham and said to him: "This is My covenant which you shall keep, you and your generations after you: every male shall be circumcised. And Sarah your wife shall bear you a son and he shall be called Isaac" (Gen. 17.19). Abraham fulfilled the commandment and received the promised reward.

O Israel, on the mountain of Sinai our Lord showed His glory to you alone, and there He gave you precepts to observe. You disobeyed and flouted them. You have sinned like Adam, and have persisted impenitent to this very day.[141] You therefore had to receive punishment, as was decreed in the ancient statute concerning the first man. Thus when the Lord invokes against you the law which is identical and common for all creatures, no injustice is done to you to aggravate your travail. Indeed, it would be proper for you to dwell less on your own grief, and instead to compare it to the grief of others who are also subject to human ills.

The second manner of your consolation is that the ultimate excellence of all things is extremely difficult to attain. Gold is wrought in the fire and purified to bring it to its highest luster. And the diamond has excellence only after the dullness of its natural state is worn off with great effort. But after it is ground on a heavy wheel, it reveals its splendor, and serves the purpose for which it was created.

Our father Abraham was gold, yet before he could receive the epithet "perfect,"[142] he was cast into the Chaldeans' fire and tried with the sacrifice of his son, Isaac. Only then did he reveal the great splendor he had within. The other two patriarchs were precious stones, and they were polished on the wheel of many travails. Thus, O Israel, for you to attain a blessing as great as you expect, and the disposition which merits it, you too must be prepared to be refined from your dross more than any other people, as all other things in nature are before they attain perfection. Indeed, the hardships experienced by the three patriarchs have foreshadowed your sufferings from their time to the present, and through their suffering they were the first to teach you how to endure your misfortunes with patience. Therefore, since incomprehensible happiness awaits you, until the time when you attain it you must brace yourself and resist the importunate harassments of the Enemy with the marvelous constancy which your forebears showed.

The third manner of your consolation is this: Our Lord chooses the lesser of two evils for you. Since you have had to suffer for one of the above two reasons, He preferred that your body suffer in this world; for as for your soul, "You are a holy people unto the Lord and you shall not die, but He has chosen you for His treasure up above" (Deut. 7.6 and 14.2). Every Israelite has a share in the world to come.[143] Do you wish to see the proof of this truth? "Thus says the Lord, the God of Israel: 'You are My witnesses, that I am God and that I am forever the same'" (Isa. 44.6, 8.). You now can understand how your soul will live eternally in glory. The soul must forever be a witness to the Eternal, while the body cannot, since it perishes. And in greater confirmation of this blessing, Hosea says, "Israel is not My people, but a child of the living God, Israel, My first-born son" (Hos. 2.1; cf. Ex. 4.22). For just as the father gives his choicest possessions to his son, so the Lord gave you, as a son among the slaves of His household, the best of the earth below. And because you were also to have a second portion in heaven, He called you by the additional name, "first-born," thereby informing you of the purely spiritual gift which is heavenly bliss. This is the best of all His possessions, the kind the first born among the children inherits from his father.

Elsewhere Scripture says: "Israel is safe in the Lord with a perpetual salvation. They shall not be put to shame, nor shall they be marked with hurt for ever and ever" (Isa. 45.17). This proof is the seal of all the others which I have given you, as is the following: "The idolaters are vanity. On the day of the visitation of their idols they shall perish. The portion of Jacob is not like these, but He who created all things is his portion and the rod of his inheritance: His name is the Lord of hosts" (Jer. 10.15-16; 51.19).

Thus since you shall inherit the Lord, who is the perpetual, glorious and highest blessing, your soul is saved, as His own words attest. How this blessing will help you as you struggle with your memories of past misfortunes or try to resist the furious onslaught of your present ones! This has truly been a miraculous remedy, one attained from the Lord through His sublime favor. Avail yourself of it and let not your flesh feel the cruel fire where it is cast, or the sword with which your enemies punish you; hope for a blessing as great as the one you are destined to enjoy when you leave this life.

YCABO: It would follow from your argument that all Israel, evil or good, is to be saved; and this seems contrary to God's justice.

NUMEO: It must be understood that the name Israel has great pre-eminence and dignity. It was bestowed upon our father Jacob when he attained the final degree of his perfection, and whosoever attains this end by any means is saved.[144]

YCABO: Then another, greater obstacle comes in my way; almost all my children will lose this blessing, since none can attain such a lofty degree of goodness.

NUMEO: You are mistaken, for this state can be reached in many ways; it is being attained even through the punishment which you receive, and it is happening in this way:

When the Lord communicated to you directly, it was easier for you to attain perfection, for you were aided by His manifest favor, and by the temporal blessings He bestowed upon you, which served as a ladder to the spiritual ones.[145] But in our days, when your sin has obstructed God's intimacy, His mercy has provided another remedy by which you may attain this state and save your soul. It has purified you in the fire of this world, and given you the punishment for your iniquities on earth in the countless hardships and misfortunes which you have suffered. You are thus prepared for salvation, as these words of Isaiah confirm: "In this shall the iniquity of Jacob be expiated" (Isa. 27.9). Thus those who suffer for their faults in this life in the garb of Judaism by cleaving to the Lord and His Law, have a share in the world to come. This is what the Most High assured you through the lips of Moses His prophet when he said, "All of you who have cleaved to the Lord (in your travails and temptations) till the present day are alive" (Deut. 4.4). But this is not so for those who drop off from this body of Israel, changing to the laws of other nations.

YCABO: Since this is so, the souls are damned of those who exchanged the Law of the Lord by force, and ended their lives in their new garb out of fear of death. There has been such a multitude of these people in the past, and even in the present.

NUMEO: With these God's majesty employs another great mercy. He makes those souls pass from one body to another until they are refined, and until they are purged of their perfidy, or are finally ruined by the adamantine obstinacy of their sin. I prefer not to speak of this, since it is not food fit for all stomachs.[146] Much remains to be said, and you will delight in it when you are sufficiently versed in the contemplation of God for His lofty secrets to lodge in your soul.

Let me return. Even when God inflicted corporeal punishment, which troubles you so greatly, His compassion made it possible in many ways for you to endure it patiently, and for many benefits to accrue to you because of it.

Firstly, He meted out your punishment gradually, so that your full punishment might not consume you and destroy you. Thus He said through the prophet's lips, "I shall punish you little by little, but consume you I shall not" (Jer. 30.11; 46.28).

Secondly, He punished you immediately after each sin, so that your unrequited iniquities should not accumulate, and so that you should take measures to remedy your works after every lash. The Lord told you this in these words: "Your affliction shall teach you and your travails shall reprove you" (Jer. 2.19).

Thirdly, by scattering you among all peoples, He made it impossible for the world to destroy you, for if one kingdom rises against you in Europe to inflict death upon you, another in Asia allows you to live. And if the Spaniards burn you in Spain and banish you, the Lord wills for you to find someone in Italy who welcomes you and lets you live in freedom. And if the Lord had not dispersed you but instead, as your iniquities merit, had isolated you in one corner of the earth, like your brethren, the Ten Tribes, your life would be in jeopardy and the die for your destruction cast. You would long ago have perished from the wrath of only one of the peoples who had subjected you.

Therefore, what you regard as an injustice from the Lord is a supreme mercy and a special favor which He has employed with you alone. He employed no favor with the other nations of the world. Consider the

Babylonians, whom He left long unpunished for their wickedness, and waited long for them to turn in penitence; when He saw that they did not turn and that their wickedness had reached an extreme, He destroyed them once and for all. He did the same to the Romans and other nations that once flourished in the world. And you may infer that He will do the same to the peoples who rule at the present time, whom you mentioned in your lament. They will pay dearly for what they now enjoy. So did our Lord say to Abraham: "In the fourth generation they shall return hither, for the iniquity of the Amorites is not yet full" (Gen. 15.16). And David in his psalm said, "The wicked flourish like grass and all the workers of iniquity blossom: it is that they may be destroyed forever" (Ps. 92.8), "for the eyes of the Lord are against every sinning kingdom to uproot it from the earth, but the house of Jacob I shall not completely uproot, says the Lord" (Amos 9.8).

Now do you see how potent a love the Most High has bestowed upon your fathers? He turned the threat of His anger in a way that might lead to your benefit, the threat he made to Moses in the wilderness be-cause of your sin: "Let Me alone and I will destroy them" (Ex. 32.10). And in the threat He later made when you persisted in your iniquity—"He was deciding to gather them into the corners of the earth and uproot their memory from among men, save that He dreaded their enemies' ferocity lest they perchance boast of this and say, 'Our valiant hand and might have wrought all this, and not the Lord'" (Deut. 32.26-27)—the Merciful One changed this form of punishment in the manner I have already explained to you. He dispersed you among the peoples and did not herd you together. Therefore acknowledge that heaven has sent you this secret and sublime boon, and not the contrary, as you have thought. Anoint your tender wound with this healing balm, and you will see how effectively it assuages the pain that racks you.

The fourth way for you to receive consolation also derives from this mercy. The Lord not only prepared these grades for the great mountain of punishment which you were required to climb,[147] but in order for you to scale it with less hardship, He from time to time consoles you by redemptive acts and taking vengeance on your oppressors for the malice with which they have inflicted the penalty for your iniquities. Jeremiah's words testify to this: "I will visit upon you nations the wickedness of your thoughts" (Jer. 23.2). You have already witnessed this in the fates of the early nations—the Egyptians, Babylonians, Assyrians, Greeks and Romans, and in the more modern nations of whom you recently complain:

Sisebut, the king of Spain, who was the first to harm you after the Romans, was poisoned in the prime of his life and rule shortly after he vexed you, and the Lord immediately replaced him with a king who favored you.

Consider King Philip of France, who despoiled you of all your wealth and banished you from his realms in misery and poverty. Nine years

later, while hunting, he was lured by a stag through rough and unfrequented terrain; he fell over a mountain, and he and his frenzied horse
were dashed to a thousand pieces.

Recall the fate of King John the Second of Portugal, who sent your
infants to the lizards. His son Don Alphonse later married the daughter
of King Ferdinand of Castile. At the height of the festivities, while
the bridegroom was participating in a race, the devil stepped into his
path and threw him from his horse;[148] he died the following day. When
the king refused to accept this punishment for his crime, he was poisoned
and his own glory dissolved. And since by his sin he had already killed
his heirs, his kingdom passed into the hand of his greatest enemy.[149]

So as not to weary you with more such details, let me tell you
generally that among all your abusers, though they were brethren of one
and the same religion and faith, such an accursed strife has arisen and
continued to this day that great torrents of Latin[150] blood have run
throughout their lands and abroad. We can thus say of Spain that Italy
is its grave; of France, that Spain is the means of its consumption; of
Germany, that all of its neighbors, including the Turk, are its executioners, who make it the wall where their artillery strikes; and of
England, that continual pestilence and hostile Scotland are its scourge.

You have daily observed with your own eyes these specific judgments
of God, and others which I have omitted in order not to be prolix. Thus
Jeremiah's words have been fulfilled: "They that eat you shall be devoured, and they that carry you off shall be carried off and they that
spoil you shall I make a spoil" (Jer. 30.16). Therefore unburden yourself, and lighten the load of your suffering. Your hungry spirit will rest
as soon as it imagines its vengeance.

The fifth road to consolation is the great benefit which has come of
your misfortunes in Spain and Portugal, of which you so bitterly complain; for when a person's limbs are being devoured by herpes, it is best
to cut them off with the knife or the fire, so as to prevent the spread of
the disease and save the rest of the body. At such a time the cruel
surgeon is the instrument of recovery. Therefore, since you had forgotten
your ancient Law, and feigned Christianity with all your might solely
to save your life and property, without realizing that you were jeopardizing your soul, it was proper that in such a perilous and mortal illness
the Lord should not be apprehensive about applying the cautery to cure
you. Truly, if you consider matters carefully, His mercy was great in
being cruel to you, for the noxious wound penetrated your body so
rapidly that in a few years it would have killed the memory of Judaism
in your children. And no more merciful remedy would have sufficed to
save your limbs,[151] which are now out of danger. Therefore cut away
your flesh which is wasting, if you desire life. Let the great benefit you
are receiving soften the unyielding pain of your rigorous cure. And
throw these waters of consolation upon the flames of the Inquisition,
that the heat you suffer may be lessened.

The sixth way to consolation is the help you received in the hardships which you say you had to suffer in order to save your life after leaving Portugal:

Has God's mercy ever appeared to anyone in human garb? It has appeared to you, to help you with your troubles. Has anyone ever seen a woman risk her life to save her brethren, as if she inherited Miriam's innate compassion;[152] or govern her people with Deborah's remarkable prudence; or aid the persecuted with Esther's boundless virtue and surpassing piety; or free the besieged from anguish, like the chaste and generous widow Judith,[153] a woman of true-hearted courage? The Lord has sent you such a woman in our own days from the supreme choir of His hosts. He has treasured all these virtues in a single soul. To your happy fortune, He chose to infuse them in the delicate and chaste person of the blessed Jewess [Gracia] Nasi.

Her inspiration greatly encouraged your needy children in Portugal, who were too poor and weak to leave the fire,[154] and to undertake a lengthy journey. She generously provided money and other needs and comforts to the refugees who arrived destitute, sea-sick and stuporous in Flanders and elsewhere. She helped them overcome the rigors of the craggy Alps in Germany and other lands, and she hastened to alleviate the miseries caused by the hardships and hazards of their long journey. She offered you her compassion and divine largesse in the sudden dire distresses you faced when you were exiled from Ferrara.[155] She provisioned the rich at a time when they could not use their wealth. She helped the masses of destitute people. She denied no favor even to her enemies. She sent boats loaded with bread and provisions and revived the starving people from the grave which famine had prepared for them on the Italian shores. Thus with her golden hand[156] and angelic purpose, she lifted the majority of our people in Europe from the abyss of this hardship and countless others, where poverty and sin had hurled them. She continued to guide them until they were in safe lands, and until she had returned them to the obedience and precepts of their ancient God. Thus she has been a stay in your weakness, a prop for the weary, a clear fountain for the thirsty, a shady tree, full of fruit, which has fed the hungry and sheltered the forsaken. To more aptly describe the great blessing she represents, she has always been a beautiful summer, a refuge during all the misfortunes of our Portuguese people, and a pillar of strength on which its affluent could depend to preserve them and their fortunes. A large number of your children, who have fled from the brutality of the Portuguese, have reached safety on this eagle's outstretched wings.[157] She has imitated the Lord in the Exodus from Egypt, as related by Moses' prophetic words: "As an eagle that stirs up her nest and hovers over her young, and spreading abroad her wings, bears and carries them upon her, so did the Lord alone lead this people and there was no strange god with Him" (Deut. 32.11-12).

The seventh road which leads you to great consolation is the safe and placid port which God's boundless mercy has prepared for you, so that your wearied limbs, your exiled children, might find shelter from the storms of sea and land. It lies in the blessed spirit of a noble prince of Italian blood, sublime and generous, whose abode is nestled on the beauti' ful river Po.[158] Since the day your trouble and trek had their beginning, who can recall any stranger to your Law lifting your lowly, welcoming your dispersed, and embracing the rejected and tormented among your people? Who can remember anyone who came to restore the vital breath sapped by the tedium of a long journey with such generosity, such benevolence and such a measure of love as he did? Indeed in no other hu' man being has heaven infused a more blessed spirit or a nobler soul than in this prince, who is not human, but divine. To this day he has stood with his wings outstretched, waiting to gather you lovingly beneath them. You traversed the lands of Spain terrorized and depressed, but you entered his lands exhilarated and secure. In his quiet and blessed port you calmed your spirit which became apprehensive and anxious when you crossed the perilous passes in the kingdoms of Flanders and France. You were arrested and mistreated in Germany and Milan, but here you were permitted to enjoy the liberty for which you yearn. All of the hardships you faced in your exile from Portugal were mitigated here. Here you were able to doff the heavy cloak you wore, and deck your soul in your true and natural garb.[159] Therefore if you suffered such bitter tribulations up until this time, the remedies now beginning are so sweet that they should arouse your expectation for greater blessings yet to come. So apply this healing plaster to your wounds, for it will certainly bring you great consolation and benefit.

The eighth and most signal way by which you will rise to a higher degree of consolation is in the great nation of Turkey. This country is like a broad and expansive sea which our Lord has opened with the rod of His mercy, as Moses did for you in the Exodus from Egypt, so that the swells of your present misfortunes, which relentlessly pursue you in all kingdoms of Europe like the infinite multitude of Egyptians, might cease and be consumed in it.[160] Here the gates of liberty are always wide open for you that you may fully practice your Judaism; they are never closed. Here you may restore your true character,[161] transform your nature, change your ways, and banish false and erring opinions. Here you have begun to embrace your true ancient faith and to abandon the practices opposed to God's will, which you have adopted under the pressures of the nations in which you have wandered. This is a sublime mercy from the Lord, for He has granted you such abundant freedom in these realms that you may now take the first step toward your belated repentance. Consider this a great consolation, and you will find relief for your tribulations in a refuge so certain and sure. For here you may come to terms with your soul, and be unafraid that pressures will remove it from His Law, as has happened in other kingdoms.

In addition to all these public salvations, the Lord has employed many secret ones with you, which you cannot understand;[162] for since your merit is little, He communicates His secrets to you in obscure terms.

Now I will fully answer the doubts concerning the Holy Land which you have expressed in your lament. You have said that the Lord ought to restore her former fertility, since in her insensibility, she had [not] sinned against Him. You speak to your own disadvantage, and through your great suffering and the excessive pain of your wounds. Know for certain that the great fertility of the Holy Land was turned to aridity for good reason.

From the beginning, when the Lord of the heavens created the world and gave all nations their possessions and portions in it, the Holy Land fell to you, Israel, as your portion and inheritance. And all the blessings, great and small, which He bestowed upon her more generously than on the other lands in the world were on account of the [chosen] inhabitants who were to enjoy her delights. Like a mother eager to see her beloved son, the land waited in the hands of the Canaanites, the Hittites and the other nations, until you, its rightful owner, should come to claim her. Then she would sit you tenderly on her lap and give you the sweet milk of her abundant breasts, as she did on your arrival from Egypt. But now she sees her children so distant, roaming the world in exile, sad and cloaked in anguish and thraldom's garb, while she is in captivity and bound to the hands of strange peoples. Why should this disconsolate mother dress in joy? Grief is her natural garb.

And further, the Lord expressly did not want the Holy Land to be fertile for any other people, or for strange nations to enjoy the delights of which you were deprived. And as if He had given her a rational soul to discern, and the five senses He gives human beings to perceive, He desired her to show sadness at your absence, to feel the oppressive burdens of her own captivity and yours, and to disown and maltreat the strangers who possessed her and who were unworthy of her excellent fruits, the choicest in all the world. We have witnessed this in the case of the heathens who were imported by Shalmaneser and Esarhaddon, the kings of Assyria, when it was emptied of your brethren, the Ten Tribes. Lions came out of the woods to attack these people, and dismembered and devoured them in the very midst of their homes.

Do you see what little cause you have to say what you did? For there is much reason for you to thank the Lord for His kindness. Until this day He has not given any of your blessings to another people, both in order not to defile the holiness which these blessings contain, and in order not to grieve you by putting them in the unworthy hands of others.

YCABO: You have truly illumined the eyes of my understanding with your lofty and noble arguments, and now I see with what ingratitude we have requited the Lord. We have dwelt on the travails we suffer, and disregarded and overlooked the benefits we receive. More precisely, we have been inattentive to our blessings. Thus have we justified the low estate into which we have been put and rejected heaven's meager recognition of our affliction. Beyond a doubt, if my children carefully considered your words, many would not chafe at their punishment and would feel the burdens of captivity less. Still, if I may return to this subject in order to complete it: although I recognize that the blessings you have related are excellent ways to assuage my sorrow and ease the anguish of my affliction, they have not been adequate to stop them altogether, which is what I now so badly need. Indeed, my misfortunes appear to be everlasting and boundless.

Look! Did you not console me in the past, when I lost the ten brethren who were taken into captivity by Sennacherib and Shalmaneser, that the Lord would not abandon Israel forever or pass over to another people? Then, though so many ages have gone by since that time, why have my tribulations not found a complete remedy and full cure? I fear that my continued defiance and my refusal to repent may have revoked that judgment, and that the Lord has now abandoned and forgotten me:[163] "We faint, we will come no more unto Him" (Jer. 2.31). And were you to explain that just as the captivities which I suffered under the Egyptians and Babylonians came to an end, the one in which I now find myself will end, you would not be making a satisfactory comparison. The Egyptian captivity lasted two hundred and ten years, or four hundred and thirty according to the sages, and the Babylonian only seventy, while this captivity has endured for a thousand and three hundred years.[164] And while the nations that had mastery over me in the past were speedily destroyed, their memory uprooted from the world and consumed because they followed erroneous beliefs and laws—those in whose captivity I now suffer do not meet a similar fate. In fact, their dominion upon the earth has long continued; ages and aeons have passed and my neck still bears their heavy yoke. Thus I must ask you for a sign, by which I may recognize that the Lord has not yet forsaken me or passed over to another nation, and that He is still my God as He used to be, so that I may again pacify my anxious and troubled spirit, which is daily exposed to such long tribulations. I beg you not to consider my question importunate.

ZICAREO: The Lord now sends you the following answer:[165] "Just as it is impossible for Me to have made a covenant with the day and night that day and night should cease in their proper time, so is it impossible for Me to reject the seed of Jacob and of David My servant." "And from his seed I shall take princes over the seed of Abraham, Isaac and Jacob, and I will return their captivity and have compassion upon them" (Jer. 33.20-21, 26). "Fear not, for you are Israel, My servant, and you Jacob, whom I have chosen, are the seed of Abraham, My friend. I have taken you from the ends of the earth and have called you from its heights and said to you, you shall be My servant. I have chosen you; I will never cast you away. Fear not, for I am with you. Do not look to any side, for I am your God, who strengthens you and gives you help, and I make you shine with the right hand of My righteousness" (Isa. 41.8-10). "Can a woman perchance forget her suckling child, and not have compassion on the son of her womb? (Certainly not), and even though she forget him, I will never forget you, O Israel" (Isa. 49.15).

Thus, O brother, take courage, for Israel and Judah will not be left orphaned of their God, the Lord of Hosts, the Holy One of Israel, though they fill the earth with iniquities (Jer. 51.5).

Reflect upon the marvelous words of this message which the Lord sends you. See the extent of His infinite love, which He has bestowed upon you; how liberally does He cleanse your stains and clear all the doubts that you have expressed, and can ever imagine.

Reflect on the sweep of human history, so that you see more clearly how this message is being fulfilled in your days. What other people has ever received signs by which it may recognize that the Lord is walking in its midst and that heaven favors it, as you have? Who among the nations now can bring fire down from heaven when it is needed, or cross rivers with a cloak, or stop rain or bring it with a word, as Elijah did? Who can revive the dead, or sweeten bitter waters, or make the sterile earth fertile, as Elisha did? Who can see the glory of the Lord, as Ezekiel did? Who can prophesy the future, like Isaiah and the rest of the divine company of the prophets? What prince today, regardless of his earthly wealth, does the Most High assure that he will emerge victorious from battle, as He assured David? When David asked, "Shall I go against the Philistines? Will You perchance deliver them into my hand?", He answered him, "Go, for I will certainly deliver them into your power and you will conquer them" (II Sam. 5.19). Is there now any holy man on earth among the nations who can assure kings of victory in wars, as the man of the Lord assured Ahab, though he was a wicked king of Israel? When Ben-hadad, the king of Syria, accompanied by thirty and two kings, attacked Ahab, the holy man, speaking for the Lord, told Ahab, "Have you seen this huge multitude? Well, I shall deliver it into your hand today" (I Kings 20.1, 13).

Certainly, as far as we know, there is no people in the world that has attained these blessings in the past except Israel, nor is there any other that enjoys them at the present time. Degraded and crushed though you are, blessings come to the world because of you, as Micah says, and you alone receive heaven's favors. These words bear witness to it: "The remnant of Jacob shall be in the midst of many peoples, as dew from the Lord, as rain upon the earth" (Mic. 5.6). And observe that he did not say "Israel," which is an epithet of the righteous, but "Jacob," which means in the state of sinner,[166] your present condition as you move among the nations. Thus the spiritual blessings you lost were acquired by no other, nor does anyone possess the Holy Land and the terrestrial blessings it had when it was in your power. Rather the world receives benefit from your existence.

Rely upon the Lord more than you have done in the past, and endeavor earnestly to do what is right. And fear not, O Israel, for He who gave Elijah the skill to make rain fall on the arid ground, and Elisha the power to restore the souls of the dead, and other great worthies and prophets the ability to perform so many miracles, still lives and walks with you. He will shower acts of compassion and mercy upon you. He will lift the oblivion which hides the Ten Tribes and raise from their low estate the others who wander through the world. And though this time be de- layed, wait, for the promise He made to your fathers will certainly be fulfilled, though you have no merits. The Lord promised it in these words: "Not for you will I do this, O house of Israel, but for the sake of My holy name, which is profaned among the nations where you go" (Ezek. 36.22).

YCABO: O Lord on high, whose lovingkindness extends beyond the heavens and covers the whole earth like a speck, when will the hour of my liberation arrive? O brothers, the impression which your arguments made on my soul is certainly profound; I am certain that you are mes- sengers from God. But to calm my spirit completely, I must ask you one further question. Perchance, can you let me know when this mercy you speak of will take effect and when the misfortunes I presently suffer will have an end?

NUMEO: We shall not be able to give the answer you desire to your very important question. People who have sought to learn the answer offer various lengthy explanations. We shall give you another, the most plausible we have,[167] and one that has been attained through study. It is this:

The most reliable of all the prophets who foresaw the history of Israel was our teacher, Moses. As you well know, after Moses prophesied exactly how our misfortunes would occur one after the other, he con- cluded: "The Lord will scatter you among all peoples from one end of the earth even to the other end of the earth; and there you shall serve other gods which you have not known, you or your fathers, etc.[168] And among these nations you shall have no rest and there shall be no repose for the sole of your foot, but the Lord will give you there a constant restlessness of heart, sunken eyes and sadness of soul, and your life shall dangle on a thin thread before you. You shall be afraid by night and by day and shall have no assurance of your life. Rather in the morning you shall say, 'O would it were already night,' and when you find yourself in night you shall say, 'O would it were already morning,' because of the great fear of your heart and the strange cruelties which you shall see them perpetrating against you with your own eyes" (Deut. 28.64-67).

With this calamity, Moses puts an end to all the curses and to the chapter.[169] And then he begins again: "And when all these things are come upon you, you shall turn your heart, there among the nations and consider the state in which you are and why so many misfortunes befall you, and you shall repent. With this, God's mercy will descend upon you and He will gather you from all the peoples whither He scattered you, etc." (Deut. 30.1-3).

YCABO: I confess to you that things have happened in this way, but what is the implication of your words?

NUMEO: This is an obvious proof! These were the last curses uttered by Moses. You have already suffered all the others, and lately you have suffered these in the Inquisition of Spain and Portugal; these countries are called the end of the earth (as indeed they are), the place where Moses said these curses would be fulfilled. This means that you have run the entire gauntlet of misfortunes, and have reached the end of your tribulations. And since there is no further province for you to go to, your wandering will now end; you will begin to turn your face and your heart toward the ancient lands of your yearning, from which you were banished so long ago, and there you will make penance for your sins.

You can see for yourself that your children are now returning there. Not only from all corners of Europe, but also from other parts of the world, a larger number has assembled there now than ever before in the past. The ancients were unable to attain this proof, as were we, for we find ourselves living it in experience, which is the mirror where truths are clearly seen.

YCABO: What you tell me contents my soul. Perhaps it is because the effects of the prophecy have been so precisely fulfilled in our hardships in Spain and Portugal. It almost appears that the prophecy is applied with greatest certainty in these misfortunes, for since they are at the end of the earth, Spain and Portugal fit and fulfill the entire prophecy exactly.

Now that I have shown you all my wounds, and you have anointed them with such precious salves, I entreat you to cure them completely with detailed news, if you bring any, of my full recovery. When will that desired hour arrive? What blessings shall I possess that will bring me all this boon? They should be at least as clear to the world and to me as the Lord's present blessings are obscure. And please, brothers, do not withhold your names from me, so that I may be fully satisfied, though good medicine may be received from any hand.

FINAL AND DIVINE CONSOLATION,
WITH ALL THE PROPHECIES OF THE BLESSINGS
WHICH ISRAEL AWAITS AS A TRUE REMEDY
AND FULL SATISFACTION FOR ALL ITS MISFORTUNES

NUMEO: Hear new marvels, O Israel, since you have now banished your false opinions. "For the day of the Lord is *now* near upon all the nations: as they have done unto you, so shall it be done unto them" (Obad. 15). Wash your heart with waters of joy that no mark be left of the sadness which formerly filled it. Spread out the wings of your five senses, which are now shriveled, and open wide the doors of your afflicted soul, the port where all your sorrows disembarked; and great hosts of joy will enter by land, and mighty fleets of contentment by sea. For the news which I bring you is from the Fountain whence true and certain news flows, and where the medicine was prepared for you even before you received your wound, as these words of Jeremiah [sic] witness: "Before she conceived, she brought forth, and before her pain came upon her, she was delivered of a male child" (Isa. 66.7).[170]

And since we do not desire to prolong your suffering, but wish you to give credence to our prophetic arguments, know that I am the prophet Nahum, and this companion of mine is Zechariah. We have been sent to you by God's command: Zechariah to remind you of the blessings and satisfactions you have received to compensate for your misfortunes; and I to console you in them. Before we arrived here, we completed the greatest journey ever taken, for we passed through all the worlds of heaven as we descended to this world of earth, and then we quickly circled the earth and visited your children who are scattered all over it. And from all worlds we bring you very special and good tidings regarding your hopes.

The farthest circle is the circle of [the last] heaven. Its grandeur encompasses and contains all the other heavens, and the force of its revolution governs all the heavenly stars and their orbits from East to West. There the three patriarchs sit, and the choicest seat is occupied by Abraham. He has charge of opening the gates of the treasury of life to admit the happy pilgrims of the Law, those who by their own speculation, without the help of parents or any other means whatever, understand the First Cause and proclaim His Law and doctrine throughout the world.[171]

Jacob, our immediate ancestor, is followed by a greater number, for he rules over all the rest of Israel's host. And though all are dressed in one color, their clothing varies in style and character. Some are attired in zeal and jealousy for God's service; among these Phinehas occupies the first position.[172] Others are covered with the Law and learning, to which they had devoted their days on earth below, and of these the seventy elders and the founders of the Talmud have the richest crowns of all.[173]

Of the kings of Israel and Judah, David is seated on the most exalted throne, and Hezekiah and Josiah are very near him.

In the choir of prophets, Moses occupies the choicest seat. At his left is Samuel,[174] and all the rest of the host are round about, aglow with the lofty spirit of prophecy. And Moses' brother Aaron is prince over all the priests.

Envy has no place in any of these blessed companies when one person sees his neighbor's advantageous position, but all live in great gladness and rejoice in their full lot. Their faces and the eyes of their understanding are all blissfully intent upon the Good Supreme, and continuous praise of God is on their lips. Once each day they ask for your perpetual remission, O Israel. The force of their petition has helped your entreaties and your cries to gain admittance to heaven.

The cries which you uttered in the Fifth Age[175] (when the majority of your children went into captivity in Assyria, and the rest to Babylonia) rose to the first heaven, where the moon has its abode. And those of the Sixth Age (in which the people were so harshly purged with the destruc' tion of the Second Temple by Titus) rose further to the second circle, which is known as the heaven of Mercury. And your outcries from the afflictions of this Seventh Age (which began at that time and is still with us) took various and lofty flights.

First, your laments and shouts of pain when you were subjected to cruelties at your sad arrival in Rome penetrated from the second to the third heaven, the heaven of Venus.[176] Afterwards, your pitiful cries from the mortal wounds you received on your tired body throughout Italy, moved from the third to the fourth circle. This is the abode of the planet Sun, the greatest of all the luminaries, whose mass is a hundred and seventy times greater than the earth's. Your shouts amidst your mis' fortunes in France sped from the fourth to the fifth heaven, the heaven of Mars. Your groans at England's bitter punishments ascended from the fifth heaven to the sixth, that of Jupiter. The groans which left your soul during your precipitous falls in harsh and arrogant Germany rose from the sixth heaven to the seventh, that of Saturn. And the pitiful exclama' tions which you have uttered until now from the countless misfortunes you have suffered in Spain rose from the seventh heaven to the eighth, that of the twelve signs of the zodiac. Finally, your shouts at the time of the recent burnings and tribulations in Portugal flew from the eighth to the ninth circle, the circle of the seven stars, and here was where we left this great host.[177]

The Lord most high has seen that in these punishments which you have received, you have begun to attain the final stage of your preparation for redemption. Therefore His divine justice, to begin your remission, would now inform you of the vengeance which, for your sake, He is first determined to take on your enemies for what they have made you suffer.

CHAP. {sic} CONCERNING VENGEANCES

"Come now, you nations, and hear, and you peoples be attentive. Let the earth hear and all that is therein, the globe and all its plants. For the Lord's anger is coming against all the nations, and His fury against all their hosts. With curses He has offered them up and delivered them to sacrifice and slaughter that their slain might be cast out and a pestilential stench rise from their bodies, and the mountains drip with their blood. And all the host of heaven shall wax rotten, and the heavens shall be rolled together as a scroll of a book is rolled and all their host shall fall down as the leaves fall from the vine and fig tree. For My sword has drunk its fill in the heavens; behold, it shall come down upon Edom and upon the people for whom I prepared My vengeance. The sword of the Lord is filled with blood and has been made fat with fatness, with the blood of lambs and goats and with the fat of the kidneys of rams. For the Lord has a sacrifice in Bozrah and a great slaughter in the land of Edom. And the unicorns and bulls, *who are their princes and nobles*, shall come down with their people, and the land shall be watered with their blood, and the dust will be made fat with their fatness. For the Lord has a day of vengeance, a year of recompense for Zion to be avenged of its enemies. And the streams shall be turned into pitch and their dust into brimstone, and their land shall be burning pitch, whose fire shall not be quenched either by night or by day, and whose smoke shall rise for ever. From generation to generation it shall lay waste, and there shall be no one to pass through it for ever and ever. For the pelican, *an animal of Egypt*, and the beaver shall possess it; the owl and raven shall dwell therein. And the Lord shall stretch over it the line of emptiness. Its nobles will call but there shall be no kingdom there, and all its princes shall be turned to naught. Thorns shall grow in its palaces; nettles and holm-leaves shall be its ornaments. It shall be converted into a habitation of dragons and a hall for ostriches' young. There they will find the spirit of the frightful howler, and the satyr, *an animal in human form*, shall cry to his fellow. There the shriek-owl shall seek refuge and shall find it and the vulture shall make a nest and bring forth and in its shadow brood her eggs *and take out her young in great pain*. The kites shall likewise be gathered there, each one with its companion. Learn then from the book of the Lord and read, for not one of all these things shall fail. Nor shall any one of these animals lack its companion here because of the desolation and abandonment of the place. For the Lord's lips commanded it to be so and the breath of His spirit has gathered them. They cast lots for them, and by His hand He divided this lodging unto them. So that creatures such as these shall possess *Bozrah* and the *land of Edom* forever as an inheritance; from generation to generation they shall dwell therein" (Isa. 34.1-17).

"And though you, Edom, soar as high as the eagle and set your nest among the stars, I will throw you down from there by force" (Obad. 4).

"And on that day, says the Lord, I will destroy your wise men and discernment from the mountain of Esau. And on account of the violence which you committed unto your brother Jacob, you shall be injured and forever cut off from the earth" (Obad. 8-10). Thus "I will turn Bozrah into a desolation, a dishonor, a destruction and a curse, and all its cities shall be wastes perpetually" (Jer. 49.13). "I will wrap My arrows in blood and My sword shall devour flesh, for the blood of the slain *of the children of Israel and for the sake of its captives.*" "And the blood of His servants shall be avenged and the Lord will take vengeance on His adversaries" (Deut. 32.41-42), as He favors His land and His people. Therefore the Lord says "concerning all My neighbors who mistreat and defile My heritage which I possess with hereditary right, *which is My people Israel*" (from Jer. 12.10): "I will pluck them up from off their land and will pluck up the house of Judah from among them" (Jer.

12.14). "For as you who belong to My holy mountain have drunk, says the Lord, so also shall all the nations drink bitterness. They shall drink and swallow at the same time and shall become as though they had never been" (Obad. 16).

Thus is the manner of vengeance which the Lord shall perform for you by His hand. But in order that you may glory against those who have gloried and still glory in burning and destroying you, and that they may pay by the measure which they meted out to you,[178] the Lord says: "The house of Jacob shall be a fire, and the house of Joseph a flame, and the house of Edom shall be stubble, and they shall be kindled therein and it shall be burned, and there shall be nothing remaining from the house of Esau, for thus says A[donay]"[179] (Obad. 18).

This is the first present which our Lord is now sending to you as a recompense for the infinite misfortunes which you have suffered at the hands of Edom and all the other nations in the world. Take courage therefore, for the scales with which the Lord repays each one for his works are the same. Now you, Zicareo, tell your message also, for I have for the time being finished mine.

ZICAREO: "Woe unto the shepherds of the nations that destroy and rout the sheep of My pasture, *which is Israel,* says the Lord, shepherds that feed My people niggardly. You have destroyed My flock, and I will therefore visit upon you the evil of your thoughts. And I will gather the remnants of My flock from all the countries where I have driven them and will bring them back to their luxuriant pastures which they used to have, that they may visibly grow and multiply. And I will set up over them shepherds who will feed them *with tender care* so that they no longer need fear *the wolves and evil animals;* nor shall they be dismayed *when they feed, as they now are.* And there shall not be anything for them to desire, *because of the great abundance which they shall have.*" Thus, "a time shall come, says the Lord, when I will raise up a righteous shoot of David who will reign and govern wisely. He shall execute justice and righteousness in the land. In his days Judah shall be saved and Israel, and they shall dwell safely *in their lands,* and this shall be the name whereby he shall be called, 'The Lord our righteousness.' " Then "it shall no more be said, 'As the Lord lives, that brought forth the children of Israel out of the land of Egypt,' but, 'As the Lord lives, that brought them up from the land of the north and from all the countries where He had driven them.' *Thus I shall bring back the captives of My people Israel and Judah* to the land which I gave to their fathers and they shall possess it" (Jer. 23.1-4, 5-6, 7-8).

BLESSINGS FOR THE PEOPLE

NUMEO: Go no further, Zicareo. Let me console this shepherd, for since my name is Nahum, it behooves me to do this, and what I forget you will remind me of.

"The spirit of the Lord is upon me, for He has anointed me to announce good tidings to the gentle and to heal the wounds of the broken-hearted and to proclaim liberty to the captives, a release to the bound and sight to the blind; and to proclaim the year which is pleasing to the Lord and the day of vengeance of our God; to comfort all those who mourn for Zion with a rich ornament for ashes, the oil of joy for mourn-ing, the mantle of praise for the heavy spirit, and to call them trees of righteousness, the plant of the Lord prepared that He may be glorified through it. And they shall build the wastes of old and raise up the former desolations and shall rebuild the destroyed cities and people the places that have been deserts for many ages. And there shall be among you strangers to feed your flock, and these shall be your shepherds and vinedressers. But you shall be called priests of the Lord, and ministers of our God shall be your name. *And you shall not be occupied in vile things*; rather you shall eat the wealth of the nations and you shall delight in their splendor. Thus for the punishment you suffered, you will receive a double reward and you shall be joyous forever, for I the Lord, a lover of righteousness, hate robbery in sacrifice.[180] *I shall restore con-stancy to the service of your children*, and I shall make an everlasting covenant with them *in the midst of the peoples*, and all who see them then shall acknowledge that it is the seed which the Lord has blessed" (Isa. 61.1-9), just as they now mark them as cursed by their sin.

BLESSINGS ON JERUSALEM AND THE HOLY LAND

ZICAREO: You tell me to keep silent, Numeo, but "for Zion's sake I shall not be silent and for Jerusalem's sake I shall not cease until her triumph appear as brightness and her salvation blaze like fiery torches. And the nations shall see your salvation and all the kings of the world your glory, *O Jerusalem*. And you shall be called a new name, which the Lord's lips shall mark out. And you shall be a crown of grandeur in the hand of the Most High and a royal diadem in the power of your God. You shall no more be termed 'Forsaken,' neither shall your land be reproached any more with the grievous name of 'Desolate.' But they shall call you 'He[f]zi-bah' ('In-Whom-The-Lord-Put-His-Pleasure-And-Love') because He favors you. And your land shall be accompanied by its Husband. And as a young man weds a virgin, so shall your sons espouse you, and as the bridegroom rejoices with his bride, so shall your God rejoice over you. And upon your walls, O Jerusalem, I shall then set watchmen and guards perpetually, who shall not fail day or night nor hold their peace: 'O you *who are returning* to remember the Lord with penitence, cease not. *Importune Him with your righteousness and en-treaties* until He restore and make Jerusalem a praise in the earth'" (Isa. 62.1-7).

YCABO: These words which my unworthy ears hear are heavenly. It indeed seems that this is a message from heaven since, like an excellent medicine, it has destroyed all the poison I have swallowed. But since I have received so much benefit from your coming, brethren, I beg you not to deny your medicine to my remaining doubt. Tell me, since the Lord wishes to grant me such lofty mercies, how can I receive a blessing so immense? No part of my body is prepared to hold it, unless its essence be changed, for the matter I am now composed of is not fit for so divine a form. How can my turbulent spirit, inured to the constraint of such long ills and woes, stop its continuous fluttering caused by my tribula- tions? And can I don a garb of liberty large enough to cover the marks made on my body by my long and extended captivity? Can dominion, rule or power come to me as long as I remain a broken servant and afflicted slave, and live in my ancient and abiding lowliness? Truly if God's hand, which is omnipotent, does not fully and completely divest me of the garb of sorrow which I have worn among the nations, and change my outward and inward form from beginning to end, I shall be incapable of holding the blessing of which you speak.

And what shall I say concerning the Holy Land and the divine city of Jerusalem, for which you prophesy the same blessings? The Holy Land is in a state of captivity like my own, inured to strangers' feet and pre- disposed to sterility and desiccation. She has become accustomed to the vain ceremonies and rites of the heathens who have so long possessed her, and almost oblivious of her own children, since they have been away from her longer than anyone can remember. How can she show a festive mood when she beholds them, for she hardly recognizes them as her chil- dren any more? How can she hope to deck herself with herbs and pleasant trees if for so long a time her garb has been thistles and thorns? How can clear waters flow from her arid and sterile desert? Or when divine services are held, how can she show respect and deference after the shameful and profane services to which she has hitherto become accus- tomed? Woe is me! Each one of these things requires a miraculous and supernatural power to be remedied. They all need new souls and new characters for God to impress such new blessings upon them!

CHAP. {sic} HOW FOR ISRAEL'S BENEFIT ITS NATURE AND THAT OF THE HOLY LAND ARE TO BE CHANGED

NUMEO: "The Lord said to me: 'Arise and go to the potter's house, and there I will make you hear My word.' I went to the potter's house and he was doing work on the wheel. One vessel broke in his hand and he immediately made another vessel from it. After I had seen this done, the Lord said to me, 'Do you not perchance believe that just as this potter remade this vessel I can remake you, O house of Israel? For you are in My hand as the clay in the potter's hand'" (Jer. 18.1-6). Certainly it is credible that He who created you from nothing can again remake you from something. Thus the Lord is about to remake you like

242

a broken vessel, O house of Israel, and it shall be in this way, says the Most High:

"That, assembling you from among the nations and gathering you from the countries *where you are scattered* and giving you the land of Israel for your habitation, I shall put a new heart and a new spirit in your inner parts, and I shall remove the heart of stone from your flesh and I shall replace it with a heart of flesh, so that in this garb you may walk in My statutes, keep My judgments and do them; and you shall then *with more reason* be My people and I will be your God" (Ezek. 36.24-28).

"At that time the eyes of the blind shall be illumined and the ears of the deaf shall be opened and the lame man shall leap as a hart and the tongue of the dumb shall sing. Places of waters shall break out in the wilderness and streams in the arid ground, and the barren land shall be like a sea and the dry ground a lusty spring. In the place where serpents dwelt there shall be reeds and rushes, and there shall be a high-way and a road, and it shall be called the Way of Holiness. The unclean shall no longer pass through it. But the Lord will go along the road *with these children of yours so that the ignorant* shall not lose their way. There shall be no lion in it nor assault by a wild beast, but the redeemed shall walk safely and they shall return with joy to Zion. Here everlasting rejoicing shall be upon their heads and great contentment and pleasure shall accompany them continually, and the sighs and sufferings which they now experience shall vanish" (Isa. 35.5-10).

"In the wilderness, *which the Holy Land presently is*, I will set tall and beautiful cedars, fragrant and delicate acacias, the myrtle and the blessed olive. And in the desert place I shall set tall beeches, and lush poplars and a large populace, so that people may see *beyond any doubt* and consider that *only* the power of the Lord has done all this and the Holy One of Israel created it" (Isa. 41.19-20), miraculously in the sight of all the living, and that it is not a counterfeit work or a deceitful remission.

You can now see how our Lord will change you and infuse in you and the land a different nature, that you may receive His new mercies and be fit for the infinite blessing with which He will cover you both. Besides this "the Lord has sworn by His right hand and by the power of His strength, saying, 'I will no more give your corn as food to your enemies, O Holy Land, nor shall strangers drink the wine for which you toiled, but they that have prepared it shall enjoy it and praise the Lord, and they that have gathered it shall drink it in the courts of My sanctuary'" (Isa. 62.8-9). "Wherefore, you shameful in heart, be strong and fear not. Behold, your God will come with vengeance: this is His recompense. He will come *speedily* to you and save you" (Isa. 35.4).

And in such a time the Lord says, "I will show My strength against the peoples and set up My ensign over the kingdoms, and they shall bring you your sons in their arms and shall carry your daughters on their shoulders. And kings shall be their foster-fathers and their queens shall serve them. And they shall bow down to you with their faces to the ground and lick the dust of your feet. Then you shall know *perfectly* that I am A[donay], for I will remove the faces of shame from those who wait for Me, and will fight with him that contends with you and will preserve your children. I will feed your enemies with their own flesh and they shall be drunk with their own blood. And thus all flesh shall come to know that I am the Lord who saves you and your Redeemer, the Mighty One of Jacob" (Isa. 49.22-23, 25-26).

Can you not see, Israel, that the low estate in which you now live and of which you complain will be greatly lifted? Surely you should be satisfied in this regard and praise the Lord for such sublime and signal mercies as are now coming your way.

YCABO: "I will greatly rejoice in the Lord. My soul shall be joyful in my God, for He has clothed me with garments of salvation and enveloped me with wraps of victory. As a bridegroom He will adorn me with grandeur, and like a bride adorned with her jewels will He clothe my ancient motherland. And as the earth throws forth her growth and the garden makes its seed spring forth, so the Lord God will make the righteousness and praise of Israel bloom and spring forth before all the nations *of the world*" (Isa. 61.10-11).

But I beg you, brothers, that you yet console the holy city of Jerusalem with all the other good tidings you may know, for she is fallen on the ground disconsolate and yearning, covered with mourning like a widow.

ZICAREO: "Awake, arise, put on your strength, O Zion. Don the garments of your beauty, O Jerusalem, holy city, for henceforth the uncircumcised and the unclean shall no more come into you. Shake yourself from the dust, arise and sit down in rest, O Jerusalem. Loose the bands of captivity from your neck, O captive daughter of Zion" (Isa. 52.1-2).

And also to you, her children, "thus says the Lord. You were sold for nothing *when the Romans captured you, there being no one who wanted to give money for you*; therefore you shall now be redeemed without money" (Isa. 52.3). "Break forth *the words which you have held back in your breast out of fear of the nations* in praise of your Redeemer, and together with this, rejoice, you *who are now* the solitary places of Jerusalem, for the Lord has bared His holy arm in the sight of all the nations, and all the ends of the earth shall see the salvation of our God. Depart, depart, children of Israel, go out *now* from *among the nations*, and touch no unclean thing. Go forth from their midst. Cleanse yourselves, you who bear the vessels of the Lord" (Isa. 52.9-11).

YCABO: If the Almighty does not take us out with His miracles, and free us as He did in Egypt, what strength is there in us to flee from among the nations? Will we not have to flee from their power by cunning?

ZICAREO: A much more undisturbed and marvelous salvation will this, your second one, be than the first, for "you are not going to leave in haste nor shall you go as fugitives are wont to. For the Lord is the one who will go before you, and the God of Israel shall Himself be gathering your company of people" (Isa. 52.12). "And He will then stop the tears from all faces *of your children, Israel,* and He will remove the reproach of His people from all the earth. And one shall say on that day, 'Lo, this is our God, for whom we have waited. *He has saved us for this blessing.* This is the Lord, for whom we have been waiting *so long.* Let us rejoice and be glad with His salvation' " (Isa. 25.8-9).

BLESSINGS ON JERUSALEM

NUMEO: "Arise, O Jerusalem, shine, for your light is *now coming,* and the glory of the Lord *is beginning* to rise upon you. Behold, darkness shall cover the earth and thick darkness the peoples, but upon you the Lord will arise and His glory will appear upon you. Nations shall come in your light and kings at the brightness which will radiate from you. Turn your eyes round about and see that all these who are coming to you are gathering together. Your sons shall come from afar and your daughters shall be greatly favored. Then you shall see and shall abound in all good. Your heart shall be thrilled and joyous when you possess that great wealth and abundance, such as there is in the sea, and all the wealth of the nations shall flow to you. The abundance of camels shall cover you, and the dromedaries of Midian and Ephah, all will come from Sheba; they shall bring gold and incense as they proclaim great praises to the Lord. All the sheep of Kedar shall be gathered together to you. You shall be served by the rams of Nebaioth and they shall be sacrificed upon the altar of My pleasure. And I will make the house of My grandeur beautiful and fair" (Isa. 60.1-7).

"Who are these that fly like clouds and like doves to their cotes? *They are the scattered children of Israel whom the Lord is gathering together with joyous haste to Jerusalem, their natural and ancient habitation.*[181] For the isles are awaiting Me and the ships of the sea, just as they were at the beginning, to bring your sons from afar, and with them their silver and their gold, in the name of the Lord your God and of the Holy One of Israel, *who is exalting you from your humble estate.* And alien children shall build your walls and their kings shall serve you, for just as I smote you in My wrath, with My pleasure have I had compassion upon you. Your gates shall be open so that they may be shut neither by day nor by night, that through them the wealth of the nations may enter and be brought unto you, and their kings shall deliver it into your power. In short, the nation or kingdom that will not serve you shall perish, and such a nation shall be utterly destroyed. The glory and excellence of Lebanon shall come unto you, the beech, the pine and the box together to adorn the place of My sanctuary, and for Me to make the place of My feet renowned. They shall come bending to you, and all of those who afflicted you shall be desolate and all those who blasphemed you shall throw themselves at your feet. And they shall call you City of the Lord, Zion of the Holy One of Israel.

"And whereas you have been forsaken and hated so that no one passed through you, I will again make you fair perpetually and joyous forever and ever. And you shall suck in the milk of the nations and shall suck the breast of kings and you shall *then truly* know that I am the Lord your Savior and your Redeemer, the Mighty One of Jacob. For brass I will bring gold, and for iron I will bring silver and for wood brass and for stone iron. To those who will have charge of rebuilding you, I shall give peace and to the workers righteousness. Robbery shall no more be heard of in your country or destruction or desolation in your borders. But your walls shall be called Salvation and your gates Praise. The sun shall no longer be your light in the day and the brightness of the moon shall not illumine you, but the Lord Himself shall be your everlasting light and your God your brightness. Your sun shall no longer set nor shall your light hide itself, for the Lord shall be your everlasting light, and the days of your *long* sadness *until now* shall be recompensed. Your people shall all be righteous and shall possess the land forever, the flower of their planting, the work of My hands, wherein I may glory. The smallest shall grow into a thousand and the least into a strong nation. I the Lord will hasten this in its time" (Isa. 60.8-22).[182]

BLESSINGS FOR JERUSALEM AND THE PEOPLE

ZICAREO: O Numeo, you have said a great deal. However, the Lord of hosts is sending him yet another present by my hand, saying: "Extremely great is the concern which I have for Zion, and I am inflamed with great ardor of affection and jealousy for its welfare, and I cannot bear to see it so hapless for so long a time. Therefore let Zion know that I have restored it to My favor, and that I will dwell in the midst of Jerusalem so that it may thenceforth be called Loyal City and the Mountain of the Lord of Hosts, The Holy Mountain. And old and aged men shall yet abide in the broad places of Jerusalem, so old that they shall go leaning on and supported by their staves because of the multitude of their days. And the squares of this city shall be full of boys and girls who will play in them. And although this would seem difficult to the remnants of the Israelitic people which is now living at this time, will it therefore perchance seem difficult to Me, says the Lord of hosts? *Certainly not!* Thus I will bring My people from the west country and from the land of the rising of the sun, and I will bring them to dwell in Jerusalem itself and they shall be My people and I will be their God in truth and righteousness.

"Therefore, thus says the Lord of Hosts: 'Let your hands be strong, you who in these present times hear these words from the lips of the prophets who come from that day when the foundations of the house of

246

the Lord of Hosts were overthrown and from that day when the rebuilding of the Temple was begun. And just as you, O house of Judah and house of Israel, were a curse among the nations, so will I save you that you might be a blessing.' Fear not, but let your hands be strong, for thus says the Lord of Hosts: 'As I purposed to afflict you, when your fathers provoked Me to anger, and I repented not, so on the contrary have I proposed this time to do good unto Jerusalem and to the house of Judah. *And so that this might be speedily confirmed and come*, take this prescription: Speak the truth, every man with his neighbor and execute a judgment of peace in your gates, which will consist in your not doing evil nor any one of you thinking of doing so against his neighbor, and love not a false oath, for all these things are what I hate,' says the Lord. In short, love truth and peace, and it shall come to pass in that good time that ten men out of all the languages of the nations shall take hold of the skirt of the garment of one that is a Jew, saying to him, 'We will go with you, for we have heard that God is with you' " (Zech. 8.1-9, 13-17, 19, 23).

YCABO: Since, brethren, you have given so many and such plentiful consolations to Jerusalem and to the Holy Mountain of Zion, remember the Holy Land once more. Since she presently finds herself alone and childless among the lands of the world, she anxiously awaits comfort and satisfaction from you for this misfortune and the others she suffers. Allay her fears; tell her that the time will come when she will give birth like the other lands, her neighbors; thus can she wipe away the tears from her eyes, and dispel the sadness in which she lives.

BLESSINGS FOR THE HOLY LAND

NUMEO: "Make a rejoicing, you barren one who does not bear, and rejoice with songs, you who do not travail, for more shall be your children, desolate one, than those of the married wife, says the Lord. Let the place of your tents be large, and stretch forth well and without mourning the curtains of your pavilions. Lengthen your cords as much as you desire and fasten them with your nails, for in this way shall you spread abroad both on the right hand and on the left *with a great blast of joy.* And your seed shall possess countless nations and the desolate cities shall be reinhabited. Fear not, for you shall not be ashamed, neither shall you be dishonored or blush with shame. Rather, *with the abundant blessing,* you shall forget the confusion and reproach of your youth, and the dishonor of your widowhood you shall remember no more, for your husband is your Maker; His name is the Lord of Hosts, your Redeemer, the Holy One of Israel; the God of the whole earth shall He be called. The Lord will call you as a wife forsaken and grieved in spirit, and as a wife of youth who has been rejected, says your God. For a small moment have I forsaken you, but with great compassion will I take you back.

For a moment I was angry and hid My face from you, but with ever-lasting kindness will I have compassion upon you, says the Lord God, your Redeemer. And this shall be like the waters of Noah unto Me, for I swore that they would return no more to overflow the earth. So have I sworn not to be wroth with you any more nor chastise you. For the mountains will leave their place and move from their location and the hills will move their heads[183] before My kindness abandon you or before I move the covenant of My peace from you, says the Lord most high who is about to have compassion upon you.

"Hear, hear, you poor darling, beset with tempests and storms and bereft of consolation. *I will throw down your false stones to the ground* and will lay your foundations with sapphires. Your windows will I make of crystal and your gates of carbuncle stone and your ends and borders of the most perfect and excellent stones. In short, all your children shall be taught of the Lord and He shall be their teacher, and they shall enjoy great peace. And you shall be established with righteousness and shall be far removed from violence, for no one will employ it against you; for you shall not be afraid nor shall fear overtake you from afar. Consider henceforth and behold that if a multitude of people gather together against you at any time, it shall nevertheless be without Me; so that whosoever gathers against you in this manner shall fall" (Isa. 54.1-15).

Here, Israel, you can see how the Lord will compensate your Holy Land—now so poor that your children do not wish to live there because of its wretchedness, which is greater than that of all the other lands in the world—for all its degradation and shame with double prosperity and great glory.

CONSOLATION FOR THE LAND

ZICAREO: Since you did not remember to announce this additional blessing for the Holy Land, Numeo, "O you mountains of Israel, hear the word of the Lord, who says as follows to the mountains and the hills and the rivers and the valleys, to the destroyed and desolate places and forsaken cities that were prey and spoil for all the other nations round about. Therefore the Lord God says thus: 'Surely in the fire of My jealousy have I spoken against all Edom, who took My land unto them-selves as a possession with the joy of all their heart, and with disdain of soul *on seeing Israel beaten.*' Therefore, prophesy concerning the land of Israel and say unto the mountains and the valleys, streams and hills: 'Thus says the Lord God: In My jealousy and in My wrath have I spoken when you suffered the injury received from the nations. There-fore I have lifted up My hand so that the nations that are round about you might also suffer your same affront. But you, O mountains of Israel, shall produce your trees and yield your fruit for My Israelite people to eat' " (Ezek. 36.4-8).

YCABO: O Lord, and when shall it be?

ZICAREO: This is about to come, "for I am coming to you, O mountains of Israel, and I shall look out for you. You shall be tilled and sown, and I will multiply men on you, those of all the house of Israel. And these shall inhabit the *new* cities *which are to be built* and the places which are now destroyed, which shall be restored. And I will multiply upon you men and beasts and both shall be fruitful. And I will settle you *on your ancient residences* and will perform greater benefits for you than I did before, at the beginning. And thus you shall know that I am the Lord who will bring men upon you, who will be My people Israel; they will occupy you, and you shall be their inheritance and shall not forsake them any more. And as for what they now say unto you, 'You, holy land, are a devourer of men and have been a maker of orphans of your own nation'; at that time you shall not devour them, nor shall I consent for you to hear this reproach henceforth from the nations or suffer this disgrace any more from the peoples *or make your children orphans*, says the Lord God" (Ezek. 36.8-15).

BLESSINGS FOR ISRAEL

NUMEO: If you, Zicareo, remembered the joyous message to give the Holy Land, I cannot keep silent this other good news for its people: "I, I, the Lord will search for My sheep and will seek them out *with great diligence*, as a shepherd searches out his flock on the day when he happens to be among his scattered sheep. So will I seek out My sheep and deliver them from all places where they are scattered in the day of cloud and thick darkness. And I will bring them out from the peoples; I will gather them from the countries *of the world* and I will bring them into their own land. And I will feed them upon the mountains of Israel, by the streams, and in all the *best* dwelling-places of the land. In good pastures shall I feed them, and on the *hills and in the lush valleys* of Israel shall their resting place be. There they shall lie down and they shall feed in fat pastures, the pastures of the mountains of Israel. I will feed My sheep and I will make them to lie down *in rest*, says the Lord God. The sick one I will strengthen and the fat and unduly strong one I will repress, and I will feed them in justice" (Ezek. 34.11-16).

"And I will guard all My sheep that they no longer suffer being carried away, and I will judge between cattle and cattle. And I will raise over them a shepherd to feed them: My servant David, he shall feed them, and he shall be their shepherd. And I the Lord will be their God and My servant David prince among them. I the Lord have spoken this. And I will make with them a covenant of peace, and I will cause every evil beast to cease from the land that they may dwell safely in the desert and sleep without fear in the woods. I will surround them with blessing upon My holy hill, and I will cause the rain to come in its season, and showers such as these shall be blessed. And the tree shall then yield its fruit and the earth her produce, and they shall be safe in their land. And they shall know that I am the Lord *when they see this and* when I break the chains of their yoke and deliver them out of the hands *and power* of those who *now* hold them subjected in servitude. They shall no longer be a prey to the nations nor shall the beast of the earth devour them, but they shall dwell safely and none shall make them afraid. Finally, I will raise up unto them a plant of marvelous fame, and they shall no longer be consumed by hunger in the land nor shall they bear this shame of the nations. And they shall know that I the Lord their God am with them and these are My people, the house of Israel, says the Lord God. You, My sheep, the sheep of My pasture, are men and I am the Lord your God" (Ezek. 34.22-31).

CONSOLATION FOR THE PEOPLE

ZICAREO: The Lord spoke also to me, saying: "O son of man, when the house of Israel dwelt in their own land, they defiled it with their *evil* way and with their works. Their way before Me was as the uncleanliness of a woman with her impurity. And I poured out My fury and wrath upon them for the blood which they shed in the land, which they further-more defiled with their idols. Wherefore I scattered them among the nations and they are *now* dispersed among the countries: according to their ways and according to their doings have I judged them. And when they had come among the nations *where they strove to enter with their evil works*, they there profaned My holy name in being a cause for people to say of them with scorn, pointing at them with a finger, 'These are the Lord's people and they are gone forth out of His land.' But *now* I *have* had pity for My holy name, which the house of Israel profaned among the nations where they came. Therefore say unto the house of Israel: 'Not for your sake am I doing this, O house of Israel, says the Lord, but for the sake of My holy name, which you have defiled among the nations whither you have come. Wherefore I will sanctify My great name, which is profaned among the nations, which you have profaned *with them*, so that the nations may know that I am the Lord God when I shall be sancti-fied in you before *your* eyes.'

"I will take you from the nations and gather you from all the countries and bring you into your own land. And I will sprinkle clean waters upon you and will cleanse you from all your uncleanliness, and from all your idolatries will I purify you. And I will give you in addition a new heart, and a new spirit will I put within you. And I will take away the stony heart out of your flesh and I will give you a heart of flesh. And I will put My spirit within you, and make you walk in My statutes, and you shall keep My ordinances and do them. And you shall *then* dwell in the land which I gave to your fathers *in ancient days*, and there you shall be My people and I will be your God. For I will save you from all your filthiness. And I will call for the corn: I will multiply it and send no famine among you. I will further multiply the fruit of the trees and the produce of the field so that you may no longer suffer the reproach of famine among the nations. And you shall then remember your evil ways and your past doings, which were not good. Not for your sake am I doing this, says the Lord God, be this known unto you; be ashamed of your ways, O house of Israel.

"For on the day when I cleanse you from all your iniquities I will make the cities to be inhabited and the devastated places to be rebuilt and the land that was destroyed to be tilled, since it was a desolation in the sight of all those that passed by. And the passers-by shall say at that time, 'This land that was devastated has become like a garden of delight and the desolate, destroyed and ruined cities are now fortified and inhabited.' And then the nations that are left round about you shall know that I the Lord have built the ruined places and planted what was desolate. I the Lord have spoken and will do it.

"And yet for this will I be concerned for the house of Israel, to do a kindness unto them; namely, I will increase them with men like sheep, I mean holy sheep, as sheep of Jerusalem in festive seasons. And the waste cities shall be filled with these human sheep and they shall know that I am the Lord" (Ezek. 36.16-38).

BLESSINGS FOR THE PEOPLE OF ISRAEL AND JUDAH

NUMEO: You have spoken at length, Zicareo, and I do not wish you to surpass me. Then in addition, O Israel, hear more divine arguments from my lips, inspired by the prophetic spirit.

"The days will come, says the Lord, when I will gather the captives of My people Israel and of Judah and will bring them again to the land that I gave to their fathers, and they shall possess it.

"And these are the words which the Lord spoke to them: We have heard a sound of the sword, trembling and not peace.[184] Ask now, I entreat you, and see whether a man can bear a child, for I saw a very strong man put his hands on his loins as a woman who is in travail, and the faces of all turned ashen. Alas! for this day is great, such that there is none other like it, and it is a time of affliction for Jacob himself, but out of it, however, shall he be saved *and free*.

"And it shall come to pass on that day, says the Lord of Hosts, that I will break their yoke from off your neck, O *Jacob*, and I will loosen your bands with which you are tied, and I will bring it about that strangers no longer subject you with servitude, but your children shall serve their Lord God and David their king, whom I will raise up unto them.

"Therefore My servant, Jacob, fear not, says the Lord, neither be dismayed, Israel. For I will save you from afar and your seed from the land where you are held captive. And Jacob shall return to his land and rest, and he shall be at ease and secure, and none shall make him afraid, since I am with you, says the Lord, to save you. And I will make a full end of all the nations where I have cast you, but I will not make a full end of you. Rather I will correct you in measure but in no way will I make an end of you. Though your rupture is incurable and your wound is grievous, there is none to judge your cause or to bind up the wound, nor do you have the means to heal it. All your lovers have forgotten you and seek you not. For I have wounded you with the wound of an enemy, and given you a cruel punishment for the magnitude of your iniquity, because your sins were increased *above your good works*. Why do you cry at your trouble and hardship? You felt your pain greatly because of the abundance of your iniquity, and because your sins were greatly increased have I done all this to you. But in short, all those who devour you and all your enemies shall be devoured, and in addition they shall also go into captivity; those who carry you off shall be carried off and those that spoil you I shall make a spoil. I will cover the mark of your wound and will heal you of your sores, says the Lord.

"In truth they have called you 'Forsaken,' saying, 'As for Jerusalem, no one loves her any more or asks for her.' Then see what the Lord says regarding this: 'I will return the captivity of Jacob's tents and have compassion upon his dwelling-places. The city of Jerusalem shall be builded upon its hill where it used to be, and the palace shall stand upon its place, and out of them shall proceed praise and the voice of the merry. I will multiply them and they shall not be diminished. I will make them honored and they shall never be abject. Their children shall be as at the beginning and their congregation shall go straight before Me. I will punish all those who afflict Israel. And from it itself shall a magnificent captain come and the one that will bear rule over it shall proceed from its midst.[185] I will call him nigh and he shall approach Me, whosoever offers his heart to approach Me, says the Lord. You shall be My people and I will be your God' " (Jer. 30.3-22). Therefore, Israel, wait for such blessing and in the end of days you will understand what this is to be.

"And at that time, says the Lord, I will be God to all the families of Israel and they shall be My people, because the people that were left from the slaughter of the sword found favor in the wilderness. I will yet build you and you shall be built, O virgin of Israel. You shall yet be adorned with your timbrels; you shall go forth in the dance of those who make merry and rejoice. You shall yet plant vineyards on the mountains of Samaria. A time shall come when the watchmen on the mountain of Ephraim shall call out, 'Arise, let us go to Zion, unto the Lord our God.' For thus does He say: 'Rejoice with gladness for Jacob's sake and *sing psalms in Jerusalem*, in the capital *and chief city* of the nations. Proclaim, praise and say, O Lord, save Your people, the remnant of Israel.' The Lord answers you: 'Behold I am bringing them from the north country

252

and will gather them from the sides of the earth. Among them there shall be together the blind, the lame, the pregnant woman and the woman who has borne; a great company shall they return here. With weeping *did they go forth; with favors* will I bring them back. I will guide them to the rivers of waters *of learning of My holy Law,* and in a straight path so that they might not stumble, for I am a father unto Israel; Ephraim is My first born.'[186]

"Hear the word of the Lord, you nations, and proclaim it in the islands which are far away: He who had scattered Israel will gather him. He will keep him just like a shepherd his flock. For the Lord freed Jacob when he came with all his wealth from Laban's house, and He delivered him from the hand of Esau, who was more powerful than he *in a manner showing that He is now about to do the same for His children by freeing them from the power of this enemy, and from all the others whose forces prevail over Jacob's*" (Jer. 31.1-11).

"The days shall come, says the Lord, when I will sow the house of Israel and of Judah with the seed of men and with the seed of beasts. And it shall *then* come to pass that as I have watched over them to uproot them, destroy them, overthrow them, ruin them and bring them low, so will I watch over them to build and plant them, says the Lord God. In these times they shall no longer say, 'The fathers have eaten sour grapes and the children's teeth were set on edge,' but every one shall die for his own iniquity, and whoever eats the sour grape, his teeth alone shall be set on edge" (Jer. 31.27-30).

YCABO: The superabundant blessing which you offer my present wretchedness puts a fear in me of losing it at that time, just as has happened in the past. And there is no doubt that since the Lord will immediately execute the penalty for my sin, as He has done until now, I shall quickly be ruined; and if He leaves me with my present evil inclina- tion, I shall not last long in His service and in my good fortune. As I see it, this is incredible. I beg you, brother, to enlighten me on this point.

CONSUMMATE BLESSING ON ALL

NUMEO: "Fear this not, O blessed people, for a time will come, says the Lord, that I will make a new covenant with the house of Israel and of Judah, not according to the covenant which I made with their fathers at the time when I took them out of the land of Egypt. They broke this covenant of Mine, and I showed Myself to be their Lord *in the punish- ment which I gave them.* But at that time I will put My law in their inward parts and will write it on their hearts: I will be their God and they shall be My people. And no one shall any longer teach his neighbor *the fear of the Lord* nor shall any man say to his brother, 'Know the Lord,' for they shall all know Me from the least of them to the greatest of them. For I will be kind to [them in] their iniquities and I will not remember their sins any more" (Jer. 31.31-34). Thus even though they be sinners they shall be redeemed.

"This *illimitable* Lord further says, He who gave the sun for a light by day and the moon and the array of the stars for a light by night, who makes the waves of the roaring sea thunder and crash, the Lord of Hosts is His name: 'If these laws are removed from My sight and cease— *which is impossible, since I determined this from the beginning*—the seed of Israel shall also cease from being a nation before Me forever. And if the heavens above can be measured and the foundations of the earth which are beneath searched out, I will also cast off all the seed of Israel for what they have done,' says the Lord. And the time is now approach- ing when the city shall be built to the Lord from the tower of Hananel to the gate of the corner; then the measuring line shall go to the hill of Gareb[187] and shall turn to Goah. And the whole valley of the dead bodies and of the ashes and all the fields unto the brook Kidron unto the corner of the gate of the horses eastward shall be something holy unto the Lord and shall not be cut off, destroyed or demolished any more forever and ever" (Jer. 31.35-40).

SUBLIME AND MARVELOUS MANNERS OF CONSOLATION FOR ISRAEL

ZICAREO: To this doubt which Ycabo raised I also wish to answer what I have been commanded: "I, I, *who am always one and the same*, says the Lord, will blot out and destroy your transgressions, and I shall do this for My own sake, and I will remember your sins no more" (Isa. 43.25).

And furthermore the Lord who created you and formed you again says unto you: "Fear not, for I have redeemed you; I have called you by your name that you might be Mine and that when you pass through the waters, I might be there with you; that when you go through the rivers you might not be drowned and when you walk through the fire you might not be burned or the flame kindle upon you. For I am the Lord your God, the Holy One of Israel, your Savior. All sorts of nations have I blotted out and rejected for you and all sorts of peoples have I forsaken on your behalf. Therefore, fear not, for I am with you. I will bring your seed from the east and from the west will I gather you. I will say to the north, 'Give up,' and to the south, 'Keep not back.' 'Bring My sons from lands afar and My daughters from the ends *of the globe* of the earth.' Whosoever calls by My name—I have created him, I have adorned him and made him for My glory (Isa. 43.1-7). I am the Lord, הוא [188] is My name, and My glory I will not give to another nor My praise to images" (Isa. 42.8).

"The former things are come to pass; I declare new things and make them manifest to you before they spring forth (Isa. 42.9): I will pour waters upon the thirsty thing[189] and rivers upon the dry ground. I will pour My spirit upon your seed and My blessing upon your offspring. And your children, Israel, shall grow as if they were among the grass and as willows by the watercourses" (Isa. 44.3-4).

"The Lord, the King of Israel and its Avenger, the Lord of Hosts says: 'I am the first, I am the last, and without Me there is no God. For who is like unto Me? Certainly no one. The fashioners of images are all vain and even the most excellent of them profit not, and they themselves bear testimony to this, for they see not and know not. Therefore those who follow them and worship them shall be ashamed" (Isa. 44.6-9).

"Remember this, Jacob and Israel, for you are My servant, whom I adorned to be My servant, you, O Israel. And so that you may no longer be forgotten by Me I shall blot out—and you consider as blotted out— your blunders and lies (though they are thick as clouds) and your sins as a cloud. Return unto Me, for I have redeemed you" (Isa. 44.21-22).

"Look to Me and be saved, all the ends of the earth, for I am *the true* God and there is no other. By Myself I have sworn. The righteous word has gone forth from My mouth and shall not come back (Isa. 45.22-23). And all the makers of idols shall be ashamed and reproached, but Israel shall be saved in the Lord by an everlasting salvation. It shall not be ashamed at the true time, nor shall it suffer shame any more for ever and ever. Thus says the Lord, creator of the heavens and of the earth, the God who formed the earth and made it and prepared it. I created it not to be destroyed, but formed it to be inhabited. I the Lord and none else say it and shall do it. And I have not spoken this in secret or in any dark place of the earth, nor have I said to the seed of Jacob without cause and great reason: 'Seek Me,' for I am the Lord who speaks right- eousness and am the declarer of things which are right. Therefore draw near and come to the Lord your God. Draw near unto Him, you children of Israel who have escaped from the nations" (Isa. 45.16-20).[190]

BLESSINGS FOR ISRAEL, ADMONISHING IT TO ENTER INTO REPENTANCE

NUMEO: "Return, O Israel, unto the Lord your God, for you have stumbled in iniquity. *At least* take words with you and with them convert to the Lord and say unto Him, 'O Lord, remove from us all iniquity and take the good which there may be in us, and instead of a sacrifice of bullocks take as payment the speech of our lips.' *And with this alone uttered from the heart and with truth, says the Most High, I will heal their adversity.* And I will love them most liberally, for My wrath is already removed from them. And I will be unto Israel as dew, and he shall blossom like the lily and cast forth his roots like Lebanon. *His chastisements shall be turned from ill to good,* and his grandeur shall be like the olive tree and his fragrance like that of incense. And certainly they who dwell beneath the shadow of the Lord *shall return and they shall come to life again* like corn and shall blossom like the vine, and their memory shall be as the wine of Lebanon" (Hos. 14.2-8).

"And then My people Israel shall never be ashamed, and you will *patently* observe that I the Lord will *then* be walking in your midst and that I am *and have always been* the Lord your God and no other, and My people *thenceforth* shall not suffer shame forever" (Joel 2.26-27).

"And it will become customary for Me to pour My spirit upon all flesh and your sons and your daughters shall prophesy. And your old men shall dream dreams and your young men shall see visions. And upon My manservants and My maidservants I will pour out My spirit in these days, and I will show prodigious things in the heaven and in the earth, blood and fire and pillars of cloud. The sun shall be turned into darkness and the moon into blood before that great and terrible day of the Lord comes. And whosoever shall invoke the name of the Lord shall be free, for on Mount Zion and in Jerusalem there shall be salvation for the remnant of Israel, whom the Lord is calling" (Joel 3.1-5).

YCABO: The Lord promises such liberal blessings for my limited merit that I dare to ask you whether this salvation will be extended to the dead of Israel, so many of whom lie beneath the earth, for they perished with the hope of seeing these promises of the Lord fulfilled. Tell me, on your honor, brothers, if you know this.

CHAP. HOW ALL THE DEAD OF ISRAEL ARE TO REVIVE

NUMEO: By these arguments relating to your doubt which I reviewed with the Lord, you will see how His mercy has been extended toward you even to this point:

"The hand of the Lord came upon me and He carried me out in a spirit and set me down in the midst of an open field which was full of bones. And He made me pass round about them, and there was a very great multitude of bones on the surface of that plain, and they were extremely dry. When I had done this, He said to me, 'Son of man, does it seem to you perchance that these bones will live?' I answered, 'Lord God, You know.' He again spoke unto me, 'Then prophesy over these bones and say unto them: Dry bones, hear the word of the Lord, who says thus: I will infuse breath into you and you shall live. I will lay sinews upon you and will dress you with flesh and cover you with skin and put a soul into you and you shall live, and you shall know that I am the Lord.' I prophesied as I was commanded, and as I prophesied a noise came up and immediately thereafter a commotion, and the bones came together, bone to bone. And I waited, and presently I saw sinews upon them. Then flesh came up, which was covered above with skin, but there was, however, no breath in them.

"Then He said to me, 'Prophesy unto the breath, prophesy to the son of man and say to the breath: Thus says the Lord God: Come, O breath, from the four directions and blow upon these slain that they may live.' I prophesied as He had commanded me and the breath came into them, and they lived and stood upon their feet, an exceedingly mighty and great host. *When they had risen and I was contemplating the nature of such a great miracle,* the Lord said to me: 'Son of man, these bones are the whole house of Israel, who say, Our bones are dried up; our hope is lost; we are clean cut off. Therefore prophesy and say unto them: Thus says the Lord God: I will open your graves and bring you out of them, O My people, and I will bring you into the land of Israel. And you shall then know perfectly that I am the Lord when I open your graves and bring you out from where you are buried, O My people. And I will put My spirit in you and you shall live and I will settle you in your own land and you shall know that I am the Lord who has spoken and shall perform it' " (Ezek. 37.1-14).

YCABO: This, I believe, exceeds beyond any comparison all the other favors which I hope to receive from God's hand, and with it many doubts are satisfied which troubled me and burdened my thought. Now since He has put this seal to all my hopes and blessings, like a person who walks without fear and takes his steps with confidence, I must still ask you this remaining question. At the time of the First Temple I recall that the Lord, because of Solomon's sin, divided our kingdom into two parts. Of ten tribes, which were called Israel, He made an independent king-dom, and the other two tribes were separated and given the name of Judah. Because of this division, there were always continuous wars and differences between them. In this good time which we are awaiting, will there perchance be any kind of change in these kingdoms?

CHAP. [sic] HOW THERE WILL BE A SINGLE KING OVER ISRAEL AND JUDAH

NUMEO: Now you will know the answer through the words which I reviewed with the Lord concerning this. "He spoke to me again and said: 'And you, son of man, take one stick and write upon it [for Judah and for the children of Israel, his companions. And take another stick and write upon it][191] for Joseph, the tree of Ephraim and all the house of Israel, his companions. And join them one to the other, that they may be one stick and be united in your hand. And when the children of your people shall say to you: Explain to us what this is, say unto them: Thus says the Lord God. I will take the tree of Joseph, which is in the hand of Ephraim and the tribe of Israel his companions, and I will put them on the tree of Judah, and make of them a single tree, and they shall be one in My hand. For I will take the children of Israel from among the nations where they were cast, and will gather them from all sides and bring them into their own land. And I will make them one nation in the land and upon the mountains of Israel and one king only shall be over all of them, and they shall no more be two nations as they were, neither shall they be divided any more into two kingdoms, nor shall they any more defile themselves with their idols or with their abominations with which they sinned. And I will cleanse them, and they shall be My people and I will be their God. And My servant David shall be their king, and one shepherd shall be over all of them. They shall walk in My ordinances and observe My statutes, and I will cause them to dwell in the land which I gave to My servant Jacob, in which your fathers dwelt. And they shall dwell therein, they [and their children] and their children's children forever and ever, and David My servant shall be their prince forever. And I will make with them a covenant of peace; it shall be an everlasting covenant with them. And I will establish them and multiply them, and I will set My sanctuary in their midst forever. And My dwelling place shall be among them, and I will be their God and they shall be My people. And the nations shall know that I am the Lord, the Sanctifier of Israel, when My sanctuary shall be in their midst forever and ever' " (Ezek. 37.15-28).

THE GREAT AND MOST NOTABLE VENGEANCE AGAINST THE NATIONS IN THE NAME OF GOG AND MAGOG

ZICAREO: And when, in addition to all this, Israel, you once more find yourself at rest in your Holy Land, with such great safety that you need not have walls in the cities or gates in your houses, so that the Lord may complete a full vengeance against all the nations by whom you were abused, and, in so doing, make clear that He is the true Lord of the entire universe and you are His intimate people, hear this message:

"Thus says the Lord God: 'I am coming against you, O Gog, prince and chief of Meshech and Tubal. I will gather you together, and *I will wound you with six wounds*. I will take you out from the sides of the north and I will bring you upon the mountains of Israel. You shall fall, and all your bands and your peoples who are with you. To the flocks of birds and winged animals and beasts of the field have I now determined to deliver you for their food. You shall fall upon the face of the earth, for I have spoken it, says the Lord God.

" 'And I will cast a fire on Magog and upon all those who dwell safely in the islands, and they shall know that I am the Lord. And I will make known My holy name in the midst of My people Israel, and the nations shall know that I am the Lord, the Holy One in Israel. Behold, it has come, and thus has it been done. This is the day of which I have spoken, says the Lord. They that dwell in the cities of Israel shall go forth and shall set fire to and burn the weapons, shields, spears, bows, arrows, slings and halberds for seven years, and they shall bring no wood from the thicket nor shall they cut it out of the forests to burn, but they shall light the fire with weapons and they shall spoil and take prey from those by whom they were robbed, says the Lord God.

" 'And on that day I will give Gog a burial place in the land of Israel, which shall be in the valley by which one passes through to the east by way of the sea. So pestiferous shall this slaughter be that it will make those who pass by hold their noses. There they shall bury Gog and all his host, and they shall call it the valley of Hamon-Gog. And the house of Israel shall be giving these burial for a period of seven months that they may cleanse the land (Ezek. 39.1-12).

" 'This day on which I shall be glorified they shall keep as celebrated and solemn, says the Lord God. And I will set My glory in the nations and all of them shall see My judgment, *that you manifest* My power which I have put to work against them. And the house of Israel shall know *in truth* that I am the Lord their God from that day forward. And the nations shall also know that the house of Israel went into captivity because of its own iniquities, and because they broke faith with Me have I hidden My face from them and delivered them into the power of their enemies *until now*. Thus they have had a recompense according to their iniquity.'

"But furthermore the Lord now says: 'I will bring back the captivity of Jacob and will have compassion upon the whole house of Israel, and I will be jealous for My holy name—since they *bore* their shame and the sin which they committed against Me—at the time when they shall dwell safely in their land, and there shall be none to make them afraid. This shall take place when I have brought them back from the peoples and gathered them out of their enemies' lands and am sanctified in them in the sight of the many nations. And they shall know that I am the Lord their God when they see that I had scattered them among the nations and then regathered them to their own land. Thus at that time I will not leave any one of them in a foreign land, neither will I hide My face any more from them, now that I have poured out My spirit upon the house of Israel,' says the Lord" (Ezek. 39.17, 21-29).

YCABO: As long as these blessings are held back from me I cannot help but fear the enemies who pursue me daily with new temptations, to remove the port from me and lengthen my voyage. Wherefore "awake, awake, put on Your strength, O arm of the Lord. Awake now as You were wont to in times past, *now and ever more in my favor*. Are You perchance not the one who afflicted and killed the ferocious dragon, *the king of Egypt*? Are You not the same one who dried up the sea and the waters of the deep and immense abyss, and made a road in the greatest depths for the redeemed to pass over" (Isa. 51.9-10)?[192] Then come to our help in a like manner in this prolonged captivity of ours, O God.

BLESSING FOR THE ISRAELITIC PEOPLE

NUMEO: Wait, Israel, for "I, even I am the one who comforts you, the Most High says to you. And you, who are you that you should fear mortal man or the son of man, and forget the Lord that made you—who stretched forth the heavens and laid the foundations of the earth? *Do not deceive yourself* and do not be afraid, *for he who afflicts you will not last forever*; rather he shall quickly disappear, and when he has been thrown into the pits his memory will end. But I, the Lord your God, stir up the sea that its waves beat violently, and the Lord of Hosts is His[193] name. I have put My holy word in your mouth, O Israel, and I will cover you with the shadow of My hand, to plant the heavens and to lay the foundation of the earth and to say in Zion, My people are you, Israel" (Isa. 51.12-16). Therefore fear not, for your "former afflictions *shall be* forgotten and *shall be* hidden from My eyes" (Isa. 65.16).

"Take heed, for I am about to create new heavens and a new earth, and of the old things there shall be no recollection, neither shall they come into mind. *But rather your children shall rejoice, seeing their oppressors vanished and a new nation arisen and a new world*, which I will create, and with these they shall live joyously forever. And likewise I will build Jerusalem so that she be joy itself and her people contentment. And I will delight with Jerusalem and rejoice in My people, and there shall no longer be heard in her a voice of weeping or a voice of crying. And from then on there shall no longer be anyone, young or old in age, who will not fill out his days, for the young shall die at the age of a hundred years, and whosoever sins at this age shall be accursed. They shall build houses and inhabit them. They shall plant vineyards and eat their fruit. They shall not build and others inhabit, *as they did in the time of the First and Second Temple*, nor shall they plant and another afterwards eat *the fruit*. And the days of My people shall be as the days of the tree, and the works of their hands shall endure like My chosen ones. They shall not labor in vain nor shall they bring forth with perturbation.[194] In short, it will be a seed of the blessed of our Lord and their shoot and offspring will be just like them.

"At such a time as this, before they call I will answer them,[195] and before they speak I will hear them. The wolf and the lamb shall feed together peacefully, and the lion shall eat straw like the ox, and dust shall be the serpent's food. They shall not hurt nor harm anything in all the holy mountain, says the Lord" (Isa. 65.17-25), for I shall restore to them some of the compassionate and gentle nature which was separated from them before sin perverted the first good inclination which I granted all things in their creation.[196]

ZICAREO: Remember, O Israel, that until your salvation comes, travails may effect a change in you and alter this divine disposition at which you have now arrived. Wherefore the Lord commands you to be advised to keep unshaken trust in Him in all your misfortunes (Isa. 30.15), because He wishes the hour to arrive in which His liberal compassion will reach you, and this is one of the gates by which it comes forth to visit the world, as I have already told you.[197] Do not become dejected, for those who ridicule your hopes shall find themselves confused and ridiculed.

YCABO: "I will wait for the Lord. I will trust in the God of my salvation. He will hear me. Rejoice not against me, you, my enemy *Bozrah*
because I have fallen, for I will arise *with the Lord's favor*, and though
I sit in darkness, He will give me light there, for He is my light. I will
bear His indignation with patience, for I have erred against Him, until
He renders a favorable decision in my case and judges my cause, and
brings me forth to the light *from the darkness where I am at present*, and
then I shall behold His righteousness. I shall also see my enemy *Bozrah*
covered with dishonor and shame, she who now asks me mockingly:
'Where is your God? *Why does He not save you from your perils and
from my hands?*' *But I trust in the Lord of Hosts that* my eyes shall see
her trodden down as the mire in the streets" (Mic. 7.7-10).

"Who is like unto You, O God, who pardons iniquity and passes by
the *hideous* sin of the remnant of Your heritage, Israel? *Therefore, you
enemies of mine, do not glory over me*, for the Lord my God does not
hold back His anger forever; rather He delights greatly in dealing kindly.
He will again have compassion upon us *who are so dejected*. He will
subdue our iniquities *with the force of His lovingkindness*. And You,
O Lord, will cast all the sins of Israel into the depths of the sea. You will
fulfill the oath which You promised to Jacob and Your goodness to
Abraham, which You swore to our fathers from days of old" (Mic.
7.18-20).

BLESSINGS FOR ISRAEL

NUMEO: Since you have attained such a state of hope which, like
Abraham's faith, is considered righteousness before the Lord (Gen. 15.6),
"Hearken to me, you that follow after this righteousness, and seek the
Lord, *as a final conclusion and culmination of all you have heard so far.*
Look to the rock from which you were hewn and the pit of the lake from
which you were digged. Look to Abraham, your father, and to Sarah,
that bore you. Just as when he was one and alone I called him and en-
riched him and multiplied him, says the Lord, so am I[198] *about to* comfort
Zion and all its desolations and to convert its wilderness into the like of
paradise. And I shall remake and beautify its solitude like the Garden
of Eden,[199] the delightsome garden of the Lord. Gladness and joy and
voices of melody shall be found continually in Jerusalem.

"Therefore, look toward Me, O My People, and you, My populace,
give ear unto Me, for instruction shall go forth from Me and I will show
My judgment in the light of all peoples. My favor is now near. My
salvation has *already* gone forth, and My powers shall judge the people.
Lift up your eyes to heaven, and look upon the earth beneath, for these
heavens shall vanish like smoke, and the earth shall perish with age like
a garment, and they that dwell in it shall die in the same way, but My
salvation shall last forever.

"*Therefore*, hearken unto Me, you that know righteousness, O My people, who hold My Law in your hearts: Fear not the affront of mortal man, and let not your spirit be dismayed because of their reproaches *and persecutions*, for the moth shall eat them up like a garment and the worm shall eat them like wool. But My favor shall last forever and My salvation, *which I shall establish in you, Israel*, will remain unshaken forever and ever" (Isa. 51.1-8).

But if it should enter your imagination that something might inter' vene to disturb this, let these prophetic words be an answer to such a doubt:

"Just as the rain or snow comes down from heaven and does not return to it without accomplishing its task: rather it waters the earth and makes it fructify and produce, to give seed to the sower and bread to eat; so shall be this *good* word of Mine and *all the blessing which you have heard thus far*, for since it has already left My mouth, it shall not return to Me void, but shall accomplish everything that I want it to do and shall make *you, Israel*, to whom I sent it, prosper" (Isa. 55.10-11).

And since this is so, "Sing unto the Lord a new verse and proclaim His praise to the end of the earth" (Isa. 42.10).

NUMEO: [*sic*] It is late, let us retire.

ZICAREO: What do you think, brother Ycabo, of the fresh and sweet arguments which Numeo has given you? Of a truth they were divine.

YCABO: Nor were yours of any less importance. I trust in the infinite and omnipotent Lord that these and the other messages come to pass quickly.

ZICAREO: I desire it.

YCABO: And I await it.

NUMEO: And I consider it certain.

ZICAREO: Brother Ycabo, so that this little trip may be more pleasant for us, I beg you begin some sweet song like those which your ancient shepherdesses sang on the hills of Zion as they watched their cattle. You must still remember them well, for many of them were compiled by the son of Jesse.

NUMEO: You have spoken very well, Zicareo. Let Israel leave happily since he entered sad.

YCABO: Who can refuse what you bid?

ZICAREO: Begin then.

PSALM CXXVI

YCABO:

When our Lord will deign return
Our Zion to her ancient fame
Our boon shall seem well-nigh unreal
A dream dreamt all day long.

But once we kindle our memory's flame
And our promised pardon learn,
Our mouths shall ring with laughter's peal,
Our tongues with joy of song.

Through the nations then it shall be told,
"Great marvels hath God for Jews wrought."
Indeed we shall all in echo say,
"What plenteous favors the Lord hath done!"

With these, though saddened and distraught
By troubles suffered from of old,
In joy we shall return, and gay,
With victory and full praise won.

So doubt not that our Lord will make
A change for Zion's captive state,
As He doth bless parched trees with rain.
And those who tearfully their seeds now sow,

At last shall reap in pleasure great:
Though teardrops mark the sower's wake,
In bliss shall he come back again,
His sheaves in arms, with song aglow.

THE END, PRAISE BE TO GOD.

APPENDICES, NOTES, AND BIBLIOGRAPHY

APPENDIX A

Translations and Studies of the

CONSOLAÇAM ̀AS TRIBULAÇOENS DE ISRAEL

A full translation of the *Consolaçam as tribulaçoens de Israel* has never previously been published in any language. Meyer Kayserling's promise of a German translation did not materialize.[1] Julius Steinschneider likewise promised a full German translation of the *Consolaçam*, but published only a few random passages in translation, which appeared in his general study of Usque's book and which were prepared for him by Paul Zunker.[2] Joaquim Mendes dos Remedios asserted[3] that he had heard of an English translation in preparation, and Moses Gaster de- clared[4] that he possessed the manuscript of an English translation by E. H. Lindo, from which he claimed he selected the brief excerpts he published in a Jewish review.[5]

In 1949 Elias Lipiner published a Yiddish translation of several passages of the first and second Dialogues of the *Consolaçam* and a con- siderable portion of the third in a praiseworthy effort to bring Usque's work back within the purview of Jewish readers.[6] Several years earlier we hear of a partial translation of the *Consolaçam* into English by Gerson Gelbart, which, unfortunately, has remained in manuscript and which the present translator has not been privileged to see.[7]

The need has long been recognized for an accurate, modern translation of the entire *Consolaçam*.[8] The lack of such a translation has been in large measure responsible for the limited attention Jewish scholarship has given to Usque's work. Doubtlessly the most inclusive study on Usque to date is Abraham Neuman's essay, which first appeared in 1946.[9] Steinschneider's lengthy article, published in 1893, does not represent that scholar at his best.[10]

One problem of the *Consolaçam*, that of its medieval sources, has received a modicum of attention. This has been due not to a direct interest in the work, but rather to the fact that the *Consolaçam* contains numerous passages which are paralleled in Ibn Verga's *Shevet Yehuda* and copied by Joseph Ha-Kohen into his *Emek Ha-Bakha*. The relation- ships between these passages have been investigated by the partisans of Ibn Verga and Ha-Kohen. Studies by Graetz,[11] Loeb,[12] Baer[13] and others[14] have delved deeply into the problem of the common sources, but even here they have hardly done justice to the *Consolaçam*.

Aside from these studies, the only mentions of the *Consolaçam* are to be found in bibliographical or encyclopedia articles, which copy greatly from each other and rely heavily on the general studies available to them. The better known of the bibliographers, Bartoloccio,[15] Barbosa Machado,[16] Antonio,[17] Ribeiro dos Santos,[18] Wolf,[19] Rodriguez de Castro,[20] de Rossi,[21] da Silva,[22] Fürst,[23] Kayserling,[24] and King Emanuel[25] either fail to mention Samuel Usque or say very little about him and the *Consolaçam*, while the better encyclopedia articles, such as those by Meyer Kayserling,[26] Moritz Freier,[27] and Ezriel Schochet,[28] evidence the same lack of originality and acceptance of cliches. Of a much higher tone than all of these works is the still eminently valuable note by Graetz on the three Usques, which appeared in the appendix to the ninth volume of his monumental history, and which, though subject to challenge, is worthy of lasting respect.

APPENDIX B

A study of the sources that a historian uses is as valuable for an understanding of his contribution as it is a fascinating quest. But in the case of the author of the *Consolaçam*, the research assumes a special urgency, for so infinitesmally little has emerged about Samuel Usque's life that his work remains the only quarry from which one may hope to extract substantial data on his elusive personality. Fully applicable in Usque's case is a paraphrase of Sancho Panza's demand: "Show me with whom you associate, and I'll tell you who you are."

Usque, as we have seen, was an apologete as much as he was a historian. In the elaboration of his thesis he was interested in utilizing historical accounts that were familiar to his audience, and he felt no qualms about the indiscriminate employment of traditional texts, provided they strengthened his message. Both source analysis and critical reappraisal were foreign to his purpose. As an original historian, Usque contributed but little—a mere thirteen chapters in the historical section of Dialogue III. The rest of his lengthy message was built on the data, the concepts, and often the very words of others.

These sources therefore hold the key to the mystery of Samuel Usque's readings, to the nature and content of his education, to the scope of his knowledge, and in some measure at least, to his identity. Yet an investigation of these sources, far from being a routine task, is fraught with countless dangers. It is not the readily discernible ultimate provenance of his material that obstructs success, but the inextricably complicated dilemma of intermediate sources. An original document or quotation may reach a given author through a labyrinth of intermediate works, whose detection is well-nigh impossible. This is especially true in Usque's case, for in the troubled era when he lived, numerous works were lost in the Jews' wanderings or burned in the Inquisition's pyres or simply buried in archives throughout Europe.[1] This sober realization tempers any hope for complete accuracy in discovering the sources of the *Consolaçam*. Yet, handicaps and reservations notwithstanding, an investigation of these literary fountains reveals astounding information about the life and character of Samuel Usque.

Once again the casual reader of the *Consolaçam* may be deceived by its Prologue, where he is assured that all sources are faithfully cited in the margins of the book:

I have . . . proposed to relate the tribulations and hardships which have befallen our people and the causes which led to each disaster. I have culled them, indeed not without some toil and trouble, from various highly accredited authors, as can be seen in the margins, and from the most recent works which contain the eye-witness accounts of our elder contemporaries.[2]

While Usque does list the titles of some books in the margins, these citations are far from accurate and are frustratingly incomplete.[3] One may well ask: Was Usque's partial revelation of these books another of his discreet acts? Was his promise implying completeness intended to distract the reader, or perhaps a censor, from his most intimate sources, whose discovery might have endangered him or others, or revealed his identity, if his name were a pseudonym? Were the sources he did disclose intended to emphasize certain aspects of his knowledge and to minimize others? What prompted him to cite some so meticulously and so jealously to conceal the others? A study of the sources of the *Consolaçam* supplies the answers to some of these questions.

1. THE BIBLE

First among Usque's references was the Bible, which provided him with the historical content of Dialogue I and the theological framework for his entire work. He copied faithfully from the biblical narratives. He omitted sections not germane to his thesis and he separated the synchronized account of the kings of Israel and Judah.[4] In the theological sections, however, he took great liberties, inserting comments and paraphrastic explanations in order to make the words of ancient prophets and sages ring with contemporaneity.[5] Usque's masterly use of the Bible suggests that, like the learned clerics of his day, Usque could quote the Scriptures from memory.[6] The occasional incorrect citations of biblical chapters[7] and at times of books[8] can be explained as memory lapses, since they would surely have been avoided if Usque had had the Bible before him.[9]

The Book of Deuteronomy and the writings of the early prophets exerted a strong influence on the *Consolaçam*.[10] From them was derived the leit-motif of sin and punishment that pervades Usque's writing. And from the section beginning with Deuteronomy 28, the so-called *Parasha Tohahot* (the Section of Rebukes), came a preponderant number of all the prophetic pronouncements of doom found in the *Consolaçam*. This statistic, as will be seen, assumes an additional significance in the determination of another major source of the *Consolaçam*.[11]

2. JOSEPHUS OR YOSIPPON?

In dealing with the period from Ezra to the Bar Kokhba revolt, Usque relied heavily on a source cited as "Jocefo" (or in a variant spelling),[12] and "*Jocefo das estorias judaicas.*"[13] Was it the original Josephus to which Usque returned? If so, he would be the first Renaissance Jew to eschew the pseudo-Josephus or *Yosippon* which passed for the original throughout the later Middle Ages. But such was not the case. A comparison of all the texts involved reveals that Usque, far from discarding the *Yosippon*, followed it slavishly throughout his second dialogue and in part of the first. Which of the different versions of the *Yosippon* he utilized is difficult to determine, for of the various early editions available to him (Mantua, *a*.1480; Constantinople, 1510; Worms, 1529; Basel, 1541), not one contains all the *Yosippon* material found in the *Consolaçam*.[14] Usque appears to have relied most heavily on the Mantua princeps. He seems to have supplemented this with the 1529 edition, prepared by the famous editor and polemic, Sebastian Münster. Münster's inclusion of anti-Jewish tracts in the same volume with the *Yosippon* could hardly have failed to whet Usque's interest and ire.[15]

However, in the long narrative of Israel's tribulations found in Dialogue I, there are not only excerpts from the *Yosippon*, but some accounts which are traceable only to the original Josephus.[16] Amazingly, Usque thus utilized Josephus and at least two versions of the *Yosippon* without exhibiting an awareness of the distinction between the original and the apocryphal works. His then must be the honor of rediscovering Josephus for the Jews. But like Columbus, Usque in his discovery believed he was in familiar lands rather than in a different world.

3. THE CLASSICS

Even more fascinating information is revealed as one approaches the historical sources cited for occasional incidents in Dialogues I and II. Usque, for example, mentions Plutarch in connection with Emperor Octavian's judicial murders;[17] yet neither this incident nor any other concerning the Roman emperors as narrated by Usque is paralleled in detail or even in sequence in Plutarch's *Parallel Lives*.

Usque also cites Lucan's *Civil War* (the so-called *Pharsalia*)[18] when he deals with the war between Caesar and Pompey,[19] and immediately thereafter, Ovid's *Metamorphoses*, when he comes to Caesar's death;[20] yet the accounts of both Lucan and Ovid are totally disparate from Usque's, and it becomes apparent that Usque's citations are merely comparative references which suggested themselves to him as he was composing the *Consolaçam*.

Then, on three occasions, Usque cites a chronicle of Roman emperors.[21] It may have been the famous medieval *Chronicle of Emperors and Popes* by Martin of Troppau (Oppaviensis), which Usque utilizes in Dialogue III.[22] But Usque specifies neither this nor any other chronicle, and his treatment of the emperors is too general to permit any identification.

A solution to this enigma may be found in the proposed solution of another. One marginal notation, appearing opposite the account of the massacre of the Cyprian Jews, bears the notation "Bion."[23] In the Gothic print of the first edition this could understandably have been an error for "Dion," and might have referred to the popular *Roman History* of Dio(nis) Cassius, which parallels Usque not only on this point but throughout most of his account of the emperors![24]

Most interesting, however, is Usque's marginal reference to Berosus' *Chaldaica*, found three times in the section entitled "Origin of Idolatry." Since Berosus' work disappeared in ancient times, Usque could not possibly have consulted it.[25] He may have learned of it and its contents in scant references such as are found in Vitruvius, Pliny and Seneca; and he may have studied the fragments of Berosus imbedded in Eusebius' *Chronicle*[26] or Josephus' *Antiquities* or his *Apology for the Jews (Against Apion)*,[27] but none of these works could have provided Usque with his account.

One famous work, restored to vogue in the sixteenth century, did contain the material from which Usque might have synthesized his brief history of idolatry, and it even affords striking similarities with the *Consolaçam* in numerous other details. This work was Augustine's *City of God*.[28] In it can be discovered the accounts of the strange rites and deities that fill Usque's section on idolatry.[29] In it also can be found a condemnation of Romulus and his wicked retinue;[30] a diatribe against the obscenities of Roman idolatry;[31] and the thesis that Rome was destroyed by God for her sins, particularly that of pride, and that the Goths were but instruments of the divine will.[32] Above all, the deep religious spirit of the *City of God*, its zealous endeavor to demonstrate God's concern for a particular faith, its stress on God's prescience, immutability and control of history,[33] its theology and its concern with the two Jerusalems are reflected repeatedly and splendidly in the pages of the *Consolaçam*.[34]

What conclusions are therefore to be drawn from Usque's citation of classical works, not one of which actually served him as a primary source? It appears that these citations were specious, and calculated to impress the reader with Usque's broad classical knowledge. Indeed, the very dedication of the *Consolaçam* opens with an allusion to Socrates,[35] as if to announce to all skeptical readers that this work was not a hackneyed reiteration of medieval thinking but the fresh investigation of a mind disciplined by the learning of the Renaissance.

Even more than in these random citations, the *Consolaçam* displays Usque's knowledge of classical literature in its parallel of Ovid's description of the Golden Age,[36] and above all in the refreshing pastoral language and scenery, which derive ultimately from the bucolic literature of Greece and Rome.

4. CONTEMPORARY LITERATURE

If, as it appears likely, Usque consulted Augustine's *City of God*, his reluctance to cite it in a work dedicated to a defense of Judaism would be understandable. With similar discretion he foregoes references to the New Testament[37] and even to the controversial works of Philo,[38] though traces of both are detectable in the *Consolaçam*. It is apparent that Usque was at home not only in these works but in the entire corpus of apologetical and polemical literature in which they played so vital a role. While he appears to have relied most heavily on a single anti-Jewish work, the *Fortalitium Fidei*,[39] his knowledge of the overall currents of contemporary anti-Jewish polemics is patent throughout his work.

The Renaissance influence is reflected in the *Consolaçam*, as we have seen, in Usque's attraction to bucolic literature, the new historiography, and the utilization of the vernacular. It is manifest as well in two other areas. One was Neoplatonic thought, which was pervading the cultural circles in Italy in the decades when Usque lived there and where he conceived his work. In the *Consolaçam* God appears as the First Cause, and the paragon of perfect love, and the heavens, with their twelve zodiacal signs and seven spheres, move in musical harmony, precisely as they did in other works reflecting Neoplatonic thought.[40] It is a noteworthy coincidence that Usque's few Neoplatonic allusions appear in the famous *Dialogues of Love (Dialoghi d'amore)*, composed by Leone Ebreo, the son of Isaac Abravanel, around the year 1535, and famous from the moment of its initial publication.[41]

The second area of Renaissance influence included the exotic literature of travel, which piqued men's minds with new curiosity now that the Portuguese had reopened the East and the Spaniards had discovered the West. The *Consolaçam* contains excerpts from two of the most famous geographical works of Usque's day. One of these, which is cited as the "Ytinerario" and dated with the Hebrew years 5270 (1510) and 5274 (1514), turns out to be not a Hebrew work, but the popular *Itinerary* of Ludovico di Varthema, composed in Italian.[42] From it Usque copied verbatim almost all the passages dealing with the strange religious rites and customs of the African and Asian aborigines.[43] One cannot determine why Usque chose to cite Varthema's dates in Hebrew (and to add a full decade to them, despite Varthema's frequent mention of his dates). Usque's verbatim copying of a geographical text rules out any reliance on memory. Perhaps Usque was misled by a later edition of the *Itinerary*, or perhaps he confused it with the much later date of another book of travel he consulted.

While the only geographical literature Usque cited was the *Itinerary*, several sentences in Usque's section on Asia and Africa are not to be found in Varthema's work. They are, however, present almost verbatim in an equally renowned book, which first appeared in 1550 and was already famous before the *Consolaçam* went to press. This was *The*

History and Description of Africa, probably composed in Arabic by a Moorish convert to Christianity who is known to posterity as Leo Africanus.[44]

The discovery of these two famous sources confirms an important insight into Usque's method. Like a skillful preacher seeking convincing and current examples to prove the point of his sermon, Usque was quick to grasp upon those aspects of all literature known to his readers which would confirm and corroborate his thesis.

5. RABBINIC LITERATURE

As eager as Usque appears to disclose his classical sources, so reluctant was he to reveal the origin of his numerous allusions to rabbinic literature. He certainly utilized the liturgy,[45] particularly the Passover Haggadah.[46] He was acquainted with rabbinic thought on such basic theological problems as the nature of the soul,[47] resurrection,[48] retribution,[49] and immortality.[50] He quoted the rabbinic concepts of measure for measure,[51] the saving grace of ancestral merit[52] and the vicarious atoning power of saintly worthies.[53] He was aware of the role played in polemics by the account of the binding of Isaac (Gen. 22).[54] He named the Messianic precursors mentioned by the rabbis[55] and reproduced their picture of the Garden of Eden.[56] He frequently alluded to the legends found in the Midrash,[57] particularly those referring to the miracles of the First Temple and the captivity of the Ten Tribes[58] beyond the nebulous "dark hills" or "Caspian mountains."[59] These legends,[60] as well as Usque's strong Messianism and even his concept of the transmigration of souls, played a vital role in the kabbalistic circles of Safed.[61] Yet nowhere did Usque volunteer a source reference for any of these. Indeed, he cited rabbinic sources only twice—both on the same folio—once from the Babylonian Talmud, where he incorrectly named the passage, and once correctly from Lamentations Rabba.[62]

Significantly, these passages include no legal (halakhic) material. The absence of halakha and the inaccuracy of the one talmudic citation in the *Consolaçam* make it impossible for us to assume that Usque was learned in Jewish law, the area on which rabbinic reputations depended. And when we consider that Usque's allusions to rabbinic literature were limited in scope and widely known, it becomes impossible to conclude that he had acquired a deep knowledge of rabbinic lore. On the contrary, these considerations lead to a suspicion that Usque did not consult original rabbinic texts, but obtained his material from an intermediate source. Such a suspicion is justified by the discovery that a single author, the towering literary figure of the age in which Usque lived, not only utilized all the rabbinic allusions which are to be found in the *Consolaçam*, but the entire philosophy which pervades it and even the periodization of history which it employs. This author was Isaac Abravanel.

6. USQUE AND ISAAC ABRAVANEL

Perhaps more than any other man, Don Isaac Abravanel epitomized the Iberian Jew of the late fifteenth and early sixteenth centuries. In him were reflected the pride and loyalty of Sephardic Jewry, the heights of knowledge and dignity they scaled, and the tragedy of their decline. More keenly than most of his ill-fated generation, Abravanel had experienced the pain of wandering, from Spain to Portugal, from Portugal to Spain, from Spain to Italy, and there from one city to another until death gave him rest in Venice in the year 1508.[63] Wherever he went he re-established his ties with princes and kings, rebuilt his repeatedly confiscated fortune, and hoped in vain that disaster would not strike him again. It is highly probable that in painting the literary portrait of his protagonist, Ycabo, Usque was thinking of none other than Isaac Abravanel.

Abravanel's relationship to the writings of Samuel Usque lies not so much in his brilliant biblical commentaries—though Usque displays an acquaintance with their contents—nor in many areas of his philosophical contributions. It lies primarily in three major areas of his writings and thought—in his Messianic writings, his philosophy of Jewish history, and his abortive history, whose manuscript never saw the light of day.

In Italy, Abravanel completed his Messianic trilogy, comprising the titles *Mayyenei ha-Yeshuah* (*Wells of Salvation*), *Mashmia Yeshuah* (*Announcer of Salvation*) and *Yeshuot Meshiho* (*Salvations of His Anointed*). In these books he presented his unique views on Jewish Messianism, which distinguish him as an original thinker and which are reflected in their entirety, along with other aspects of Abravanel's unique philosophy, in the work of Samuel Usque.

It was Isaac Abravanel who provided Usque with his concept of an unchangeable Deity, who rules history with a determinable Law and whose love and covenant for Israel were everlasting.[64] From him came the Ptolemaic cosmography that is found in the *Consolaçam*.[65] From him also came the unwavering trust in the Bible as a historical source and as a reflection of the truth of prophetic prediction,[66] and the stress on the Deuteronomic view of sin and punishment.[67] Of all the medieval and early Renaissance Jewish philosophers, Abravanel alone revived the biblical ideal of a theocratic state and condemned Israel's longing for a monarchy as an example of assimilative tendencies.[68] And this view is carried over into the *Consolaçam*. Usque also adopted Abravanel's keen interest in Judeo-Christian polemics, his inspired defense of Judaism as God's chosen faith,[69] his insistence that the Second Temple was inferior to the First and hence not the Messianic Shrine,[70] his venom toward the religion of Israel's foes,[71] his identification of these enemies with those mentioned in the Bible,[72] and an identical anticipatory gloating over Israel's revenge, assured by the prophets.[73] Usque's rabbinic legends, including his stress on the miracles in the First Temple[74] and the Ten

Tribes[75] and his utilization of angelic messengers as spokesmen of a particular phase of God's will,[76] all derive from Abravanel. From him also Usque borrowed the strong mystical atmosphere which pervades his work. It contains the concept of the transmigration of souls,[77] the calculations of the pre-Messianic era,[78] the interpretation of Daniel 7 to demonstrate the disintegration of Christianity and the imminence of the millennium,[79] the identification of Gog and Magog with Christianity and Islam, and the entire spirit of contemporaneity which guides Usque's quotation of the Messianic prophecies of the Bible.[80]

And above all, it was almost certainly Abravanel's unfinished historical work, the *Yemot Olam*, dealing with the history of the Jews from biblical times and colored by Abravanel's theology, which provided Usque with the idea and the framework for the *Consolaçam*. The *Yemot Olam*, begun in 1495 but never completed, was to contain a running account of Jewish suffering and persecution "from the day Adam was born until the present time."[81] The purpose of this work, which was never published and which is no longer extant, appears to have been apologetic. Through it Abravanel hoped to give reassurance and comfort to his Jewish brethren whose century of suffering had reached its nadir in their heartbreaking flight from the Iberian Peninsula.[82] "In this work," says a recent biographer, "Abravanel wanted to present a general survey of Jewish history, analyze the impact of the world's history upon that of the Jewish people, and demonstrate the indestructibility of the Jews by their ability to weather any storm and survive any persecution."[83]

Equally striking is the fact that both Usque and Abravanel were moved to pen their works by the physical and spiritual enervation of their people and their exposure to the Christian polemicists' devastating interpretations of their lot.[84] The reinterpretation of Israel's history, found identically in both authors, their stress on God's process of special election which culminated in the seed of Jacob,[85] and their conscious attempt to demonstrate the reliability of Jewish Messianic tradition,[86] all stem from the same life situation which confronted Jew and Marrano in the sixteenth century.

Indeed, the only major difference in approach between Usque and Abravanel lies in the latter's attempt, despite his theoretical pronouncements to the contrary, to fix the Messianic year in 1503 and 1535.[87] The dismal failure of such attempts by Abravanel and other calculators and the noxious appearance of self-styled Messiahs to fulfill these predictions were sufficient to warn Usque against repeating such a mistake. He was content to stress the immediacy of the Messianic era without hazarding a guess as to the year of its arrival.

It was doubtlessly from the writings of Abravanel, which reflect not only a vast knowledge of rabbinics, but a thorough grounding in Arabic, Greek and Latin literature that Usque realized the necessity of displaying the knowledge of humanistic studies which is evident in his quotations from Plato and citations of Latin authors. It is also not surprising that one of the works which influenced the thought of Abravanel was Augustine's *City of God*, which has already been identified as a possible source of the *Consolaçam*. It may even have been Usque's hope that his book might excite among Protestant thinkers, who shared with him an abiding faith in the verities of the Bible and in an imminent millennium, some measure of the interest which had been aroused by the writings of Abravanel.

The import of the discovery of this link between Usque and Abravanel cannot be exaggerated. With it the role of Samuel Usque as a creative historian is diminished and subordinated to the greater genius of Isaac Abravanel. At the same time the brilliance of Usque's contribution appears with greater clarity. For not only did Samuel Usque carry to fruition Abravanel's dreams of a theologically oriented history of the Jews, but he also presented this history in such an appealing, artistic and popular form that it could reach and move an audience of far greater scope than any of Abravanel's works in their original Hebrew or in their Latin translations. It is regrettable that the loss of Abravanel's *Yemot Olam* renders impossible any comparison with the *Consolaçam* to determine the extent to which Usque copied directly from this work or utilized it as a base on which to construct his own historical writing. Yet because the *Yemot Olam* was neither completed nor published, because it therefore remained relatively obscure even by comparison with the *Consolaçam*, we must grant to Samuel Usque the honor of introducing into Jewish historiography the ideology and the method found in Abravanel's work. It was Abravanel's genius which had conceived both the thought and the approach; it was Usque's genius which recognized their potential and applied their possibilities with such creative power.

Once Abravanel's thorough influence on the *Consolaçam* has been established, one has achieved an important clue to aid in the solution of the complex and intriguing problem of historical sources afforded by the third Dialogue of Usque's work.

7. THE HISTORICAL SOURCES OF DIALOGUE III

Chapters 1-24 of Dialogue III are derived from two major sources, Alfonso de Spina's vitriolic *Fortalitium Fidei* and a hitherto unidentified source cited enigmatically as *L. I. E. B.* or *Li. Eb.*[88] This elusive abbreviation, suggesting Usque's intention to disclose its identity to only part of his audience, whets a historian's desire to decipher the letters, especially since this source appears to have been utilized by the author of the *Shevet Yehuda*.[89] The task is by no means easy, for it involves a separation of the *L. I. E. B.* from the various other literary strata with which it is connected in these chapters of the *Consolaçam*. The stratum of the *Fortalitium Fidei* offers no obstacle, since it is easily checked against the original. Usque cites it in thirteen chapters by various abbreviations (chapters 1-7, 10, 13, 19, 20, 22, 23),[90] and carelessly omits it in another (15). Perhaps here the note was misplaced, for another chapter (20) which cites Spina could not possibly have been derived from him. Such errors need not be surprising: there are likewise numerous errors in the citation of page and folio of the *Fortalitium Fidei*.[91]

Only two chapters (2 and 5) are wholly derived from Spina; the others contain additional elements which may belong to the *L. I. E. B.* in whole or in part. In those chapters where no source other than *L. I. E. B.* is cited, the remaining material may reasonably be attributed to it. But where additional sources are listed, it is necessary first to remove their strata. Usque cites a total of nine apparently secondary sources, eight once and another four times. Of the nine, six are written out in full or nearly in full. Four refer to Christian works: *Cor. de España* (chapter 10); *Coron. dos empera. e dos papas* (19); *Vicencio manho no espelho das ystorias* (5); *Estorias de san dinis de Frãça* (10). Two, similarly written out, are Jewish sources: *R. Leui ben gersõ e outros* (10) and *R. abrahão leui no liro de Cabbala* (24). The remaining three are puzzling abbreviations: *Cor. Ym.* (12); *A. F. 154* (5) and *U. M.* (7, 8, 18, 20).

A scrutiny of these sources reveals amazing facts. The *Crónica de España*,[92] the *Speculum historialis* of Vincent of Beauvais[93] and the *Chronicon imperatorum paparumque*[94] were all utilized and cited by Spina in the *Fortalitium Fidei* and copied over into the *Consolaçam* by Usque without any evidence of his having consulted them directly. Though each of the chapters in Usque's work where these sources appear contains material not found in Spina, none of this is traceable to the secondary sources in question and hence must be attributed to the *L. I. E. B.* In this regard, the *Chronicle of Emperors and Popes* is particularly interesting. Like this work and unlike the *Crónica de España*, Spina inserts an unusual sentence concerning Mohammed in an account dealing with Sisebut: "*huio tempore nephandus Mahomet ab hyspania fugit.*"[95] This sentence is structurally and stylistically parallel to the Chronicle's statement "*Hoc tempore Magumet princeps Sarracenorum movitur.*"[96] The meaning to be sure is not identical, but a misreading by Spina of "*movitur*" for "*moritur*" and his natural Hispanic identification of "*Sarracenorum*" with the Moors could account for his unusual insertion. Usque copies this statement verbatim from Spina in Chapter 1, and had he read either the *Chronicle of Emperors and Popes* or the *Chronicle of Spain* he would certainly have avoided it.

Later in Dialogue III, after the historical chapters, Usque again cites the *Crónica de España*, from which he apparently excerpted another sentence, this one dealing with Sisebut's death.[97] While this may or may not have represented a direct borrowing, it is certain that in his historical chapters he did not utilize this work.

The account from the "*Estorias de san dinis de Frãça*" was not taken from the *Fortalitium Fidei*. Ultimately it derives from the *Chroniques de Saint Denis*, a famous medieval French rendering of Rogard's *Gesta Philippi Augusti*.[98] But a comparison with both French and Latin accounts reveals Usque's text to be only a brief summary of these chronicles; it does not exhibit the same faithfulness in copying as Usque manifests in the case of the *Fortalitium Fidei* and includes details not found in the chronicles which betray a distinctively Jewish point of view. Among these are the king's allocation of Jewish wealth for his building projects; a quotation from Gersonides; a paragraph imputing the Christians' hostility toward the Jews to their desire to proselytize among them, and a long introductory section which could hardly have derived from a Christian account. These anomalies could all be explained by the hypothesis that Usque did not utilize the French account directly but borrowed from a Jewish source that had incorporated it. This source would of course be the *L. I. E. B.* If this were the case, it would help clarify the unusual translation of *Chroniques* by *Estorias* rather than the more suitable *Crónicas* which Usque did not hesitate to employ with other Christian sources. If Usque were copying from a Hebrew text, where *Chroniques* would be translated by *Divre ha-Yamim*, his rendering of these words by *Estorias* would be understandable.

The hypothesis that the *Chroniques* came to Usque by way of an intermediate Hebrew text would be buttressed by a study of Usque's citation of Gersonides (*R. leui ben gersõ e outros*) in the same chapter. All that is taken from Gersonides amounts to a few words describing the Jews expelled from France as "a people whose number was twice that which left Egypt." This partial, almost proverbial statement, is extracted from a larger comment,[99] all of which could have profitably fit within the framework of the *Consolaçam*. This, plus the more striking fact that Gersonides' remarks are made to refer not to the expulsion of 1183, but anachronistically to that of 1306,[100] militate against Usque's having consulted them directly.

The words "*e outros*" help substantiate this position, for Usque cites no authors besides Gersonides. Again it appears likely that this title was borrowed from Usque's major Jewish source, the *L. I. E. B.*, which must have contained quotations from Shem Tob ben Joseph Falaquera (1225—after 1290),[101] Estori Parhi (ca. 1282-1350)[102] or other authors who commented on the Jews' expulsion from France in 1306.

A similar conclusion may be drawn regarding Usque's reference to "Rabenu Moses bar Maimon" in Chapter 4. Here he deals with Maimonides' flight to Egypt (1165) and his subsequent *Epistle to the Yemenites* (1171) as events contemporaneous with the rest of the chapter, dated 1190. Neither this brief mention nor the confusion of the dates evinces a deep knowledge of Maimonides; but they can be explained as derived from a secondary source.

Similarly, any direct utilization by Usque of Ibn Daud must be ruled out. Usque parallels the *Sefer Ha-Kabbalah* in only an insignificant portion of Chapter 24.[103] Besides, for Ibn Daud's correct dating of 4827 (1066)[104] Usque substitutes the impossible 5248 (1488), a change which cannot be attributed to a mere textual misreading;[105] for Usque also changes Ibn Daud's Moorish setting to a Christian one, apparently unaware that Granada remained in Moorish hands until 1492![106] It seems certain that Usque's knowledge of Ibn Daud was indirect. While it would be unfair to impute such errors to the unknown *L. I. E. B.*, it may be that this work, like the *Shevet Yehuda* and unlike the *Consolaçam*, was not concerned with chronology and it therefore juxtaposed undated the account of Jewish persecutions in Granada by the Moors in Joseph Ha-Levi's time and similar persecutions after the Christian conquest, and that this accounts for Usque's confusion. The parallel narrative in the *Shevet Yehuda* (Section 5) is superior to Usque's, but this does not prove that *L. I. E. B.*, the common source of both authors, contained the correct version[107] and that all errors are ascribable to Usque. In this instance, Usque's and Verga's narratives are so dissimilar that only a remote common source could be posited.[108] Indeed, Verga, following Ibn Daud, makes Ha-Levi the center of this account; in Usque, his life occupies a place of incidental importance. The near identity of the accounts in the *Shevet Yehuda* and the *Sefer Ha-Kabbalah* seem to argue for a direct utilization by Verga of Ibn Daud rather than the *L. I. E. B.*

This hypothesis regarding the *L. I. E. B.* remains intact after an examination of those minor sources which are abbreviated beyond ready identification. The *Cor. Ym.* of Chapter 12 has tenaciously resisted a satisfactory explanation. Heinrich Graetz would read it "Coronica de Yngraterra," forgetting that *Ym.* could hardly be a likely Portuguese abbreviation for *Yngraterra*; or perhaps he assumed a printing error.[109] He would consider these words as a generic reference to an English chronicle, the *Chronicle of Florence of Worms*, which recounts the conversion to Judaism of the predicant friar Robert of Reading, out of love for a Jewish maiden, and the vengeance taken through the queen by the other Dominican monks.[110] The first paragraph of Usque's narrative Graetz would trace to a seemingly parallel account in the *Zikhron Ha-Shemadot* of Prophiat Duran (Efodi).[111] But we have of Efodi what corresponds to only several lines in Usque. There is no reason to suppose on this basis that any of his narratives was as long as Graetz would assume for Usque's twelfth chapter. Graetz may well have discovered the ultimate source of Usque's account, but Usque's proximate source remains shrouded in darkness.

But there can be little doubt that this source was a Jewish text. The viewpoint of the narrative is distinctly Jewish. The errors in dating this account by both Usque and Verga point to a misreading of a Hebrew date.[112] The confusion of events, which asserts that the incidents of Robert of Reading (1275 CE) and the charge of counterfeiting (1278) are the immediate causes of the exile of 1290, is a further characteristic of Usque's Jewish source.[113] It thus appears that a Jewish text, not identifiable as Efodi's, was the source from which Usque drew his account. This text would be the L. I. E. B.

There is thus ample circumstantial evidence to argue for Usque's having consulted only two major works, the *Fortalitium Fidei* and the *L. I. E. B.* and having copied from one or the other of these major sources all source references to secondary works.

The two remaining abbreviations turn out to be something other than source references. The *A. F. 154* appearing in one of the two chapters which is taken wholly from Spina, in all likelihood represents an error for A(no) 4954.[114] Similar marginal references to the year are found nine times in the historical material of the third Dialogue. The interchange of F and 4 is a common error, and the substitution of the digit 1 for a 9 is not surprising, when it is considered that of all the errors in page references of the *Fortalitium Fidei*, the most egregious was the substitution of a 1 for a 9 in the source of Chapter 13. Elsewhere the 1 is substituted for other digits in the work.[115] The Hebrew year 4954 (C.E. 1193-1194) would be the approximate date of Usque's account. The *Gesta Philippi Augusti*, the original source of Spina, gives the date as 1192.[116]

The U. M. appears four times, always in connection with the *L. I. E. B.*,[117] and the suggestion has been made that it is to be read "*um manuscrito*" indicating that the *L. I. E. B.* was available to Usque in manuscript form.[118] Aside from the unlikelihood of any abbreviation in Portuguese conserving the indefinite article, the question could be raised as to why it was cited only four times in connection with the *L. I. E. B.*

Some light is thrown on this problem by a scanning of the *Shevet Yehuda* for accounts parallel to those in which Usque adds U. M. The results are interesting: two of Usque's narratives (7 and 9) are not found in Verga at all. One (Chapter 18) is so different from Verga's (21) that divergent original accounts must be posited. On the other hand, the fourth (18) is beautifully paralleled in Verga (43), and these two accounts show the least textual deviation of any of those which are traceable to the common source. In view of this data, the reading "*último manuscrito*" appears a more plausible explanation for the letters U. M., especially since, as will be shown, the existence of more than one copy of *L. I. E. B.* must be stipulated for those cases where the diver-gence of Usque and Verga from an obvious common source would otherwise be too difficult to explain.

It thus appears that the *L. I. E. B.* can be separated from the rest of the historical material of Chapters 1-24 by removing from it the stratum of the *Fortalitium Fidei*. Written from a distinctly Jewish point of view, it manifests a deep concern for the sufferings and dangers of the Jews. In it are contained the references to Maimonides, Ibn Daud and Gersonides cited by Usque. And while the *L. I. E. B.*'s dependence upon Christian sources is apparent, its utilization of them is characterized by a vagueness, a condensation of details and a confusion of incidents, such as those in Chapter 12, or those in Chapter 21, where the account of the persecutions of 1391 coalesces with the trying events two decades later.[119]

The *L. I. E. B.* is cited seventeen times in Chapters 1-24.[120] It is omitted in Chapter 15 (derived partly also from the *Fortalitium Fidei*, which is likewise not mentioned) and 19 (where the *Fortalitium Fidei* is recorded) as well as in 14 and 16 which appear to belong entirely to it.[121] Chapter 14 manifests the characteristic viewpoint, selectivity, compression and factual confusion found in *L. I. E. B.*[122] Similarly Chapter 16's patently late, muddled, and infelicitous fusion of original Spanish and French accounts of the incidents described point to its Jewish origin.[123]

The identity of the *L. I. E. B.* has intrigued scholars of the *Shevet Yehuda*, for though this work does not cite its sources, its parallel to many of Usque's accounts indicates that Verga used it, or a source related to it, in at least seventeen of his sections.[124] A study of the parallel passages has inspired the formulation of three basic hypotheses aimed at identifying the *L. I. E. B.*

1) In 1875 Graetz proposed that *L. I. E. B.* signified *Libro Ebraico* ("a Hebrew book") and referred to the *Zikhron Ha-Shemadot* by Prophiat Duran.[125] Of Duran's book, no longer extant, only several quotations are preserved—all in Abravanel's *Yeshuot Meshiho*.[126] All are parallel to material in Usque and Verga. On the basis of these texts Graetz assumed the total lost work of Efodi to be the *L. I. E. B.*

2) In 1888 Isidore Loeb, writing on Joseph Ha-Cohen, deciphered the letters to read "Liber Iehuda Ebn (sic) Berga (sic)."[127] Struck by the similarities between Usque 16 and Verga 6 and especially by those in Usque 8 and Verga 31, he said:

It therefore seems impossible for one of the two writers not to have copied the other, and since the compilation of the Shevet Yehuda *was already begun in Spain, one can admit that if Usque didn't have a printed copy of the work (the first edition being perhaps later than that of Usque's work), he could have seen a manuscript copy of it.*[128]

To the objection that Verga's work might have appeared in print later than Usque's, he affirmed:

It appears certain to us that the Shevet Yehuda *was redacted in its present form before Usque's work.*[129]

He failed to justify the unusual "Ebn" and explained the substitution of B for V in Verga as due to the identical pronunciation and frequent interchange of these letters in Spanish.[130]

3) In 1923 Fritz Baer, studying Verga's sources,[131] observed that

the various parallels between Usque and Verga revealed different degrees of relationship to a common source, with now Usque and now Verga appearing to possess the correct version. On the basis of tenuous stylistic evidence,[132] Baer refuted both Graetz and Loeb but left the problem of *L. I. E. B.*'s identity unsolved.[133] He could even have refuted them more convincingly.

Of these two, Loeb's was the weaker argument. His contention that the *Shevet Yehuda* was begun in Spain and was available to Usque in printed or manuscript form cannot be corroborated. It is further weakened by Baer's sound argument that the entire *Shevet Yehuda* is the product of the sixteenth century and the pen of a Solomon ibn Verga, whose relationship to the supposed author of the *Shevet Yehuda* is unknown, and who utilized the more renowned name of Judah ibn Verga to lend authority to his own composition.[134] Loeb's insistence on the interchangeability of Spanish B and V is miscarried, for this was not true of proper names, especially those of noble families like the Vergas. Besides, the name Verga appears with a *Vav* in the *Shevet Yehuda*, not a *Bet*,[135] and if Usque were transcribing this spelling into either Spanish or Portuguese it is inconceivable for him to have utilized anything but a V.

Besides, there are striking dissimilarities in Usque and Verga. As Loeb realized later, in Usque 20—Verga 21, 24 and 25, Usque has the clearer and superior version.[136] The differences between Usque 24 and Verga 5 (relative to Joseph Ha-Levi) are not explainable from Verga's text.[137] And Usque's account of Sisebut's persecution (1) so completely differs from Verga's (9) that different sources must be posited. These examples suffice to discount the claim that *L. I. E. B.* was the *Shevet Yehuda*. In addition, at least ten chapters of the *Consolaçam* containing *L. I. E. B.* material find no parallel in Verga.[138] It is inconceivable for a source to possess less material than its derivative. Clearly, the *L. I. E. B.* was not the *Shevet Yehuda*. Both Usque and Verga consulted the *L. I. E. B.* but apparently possessed different versions of the text.

Graetz's hypothesis is refutable by a simple study of chronology. The dates of Efodi's birth and death are uncertain. It is known that in 1391 he was sufficiently mature to assume a position as tutor in the Crescas family. After 1413 nothing further is heard from him and he is assumed to have died in 1415.[139]

Yet the *L. I. E. B.* includes material beyond the fifteenth century. The date 1488 found in Chapter 24 might have been occasioned by Usque's error rather than late composition by the author of *L. I. E. B.*, but there can be no doubt that the *L. I. E. B.* excerpts in Chapter 22 belong in the second half of the fifteenth century. This chapter is dated 1215, but Usque's otherwise strict adherence to chronology and Hebrew dating of chapters suggests 4255 and this is confirmed by the date 1455 in the corresponding account of the *Fortalitium Fidei*, which likewise was consulted for this chapter. Chapter 22 then represents one account later than Efodi.

Indeed, contrary to Graetz's assertion,[140] Efodi probably did not write the narrative on which Chapter 21 (dated 1390) is based.[141] This chapter's fusion of the account of the 1391 persecutions with that of Vicente Ferrer's missionary activity two decades later points to an author who was not a contemporary of the events described but who wrote sufficiently later for the two catastrophes to have blended in the haze of popular memory. Besides, both Usque and Verga list Aragon as a scene of persecutions, while Efodi, writing in his *Maaseh Efod*,[142] specifically states that Aragon remained free from persecutions. Further-more, the narrative in question commits a gross anachronism when it identifies the king of Portugal in 1390 as King Edward (Duarte)—who did not mount the throne until 1433, long after the assumed date of Efodi's death.[143]

Thus, unless the unlikely and unsubstantiatable assumption is made that Efodi was still living after 1455, it must be concluded that the *L. I. E. B.* was composed by someone other than and later than him. Yet Efodi's influence on the *L. I. E. B.* is undeniable.

But the problem of the identity of *L. I. E. B.* remains. Graetz's suggestion of *Livro Ebraico* is weak, for while the title is possible on the basis of the form *Li. Eb.*, he overlooked the form *L. I. E. B.*: I and B would hardly have been capitalized if they represented nothing more than the second letter of a common noun. And if one of these abbreviations is inaccurate, it would probably be the *Li. Eb.*, for this occurs only in Chapters 10 and following, which is the section where the greatest amount of error is discernible in the citation of other literary sources. In addition, since Usque cited other Hebrew words by their specific name, the utilization of a *L. I. E. B.* to indicate simply "*Livro Ebraico*" would have been meaningless.

That the *L. I. E. B.* was a Hebrew book is beyond doubt.[144] Aside from the *Consolaçam*, there is not a single major Jewish historical work of the medieval or Renaissance periods written in a language other than Hebrew. Many of the errors in Usque and Verga are attributable or traceable to an original Hebrew source. Francisco Cantera Burgos objects to Baer's positing of a Hebrew chronicle as the basis for Usque III, 16-Verga 6, on the ground that the common source utilized by the two Jewish authors evidences syntactical constructions peculiar to Latin and the Romance languages.[145] Rather than an argument for a non-Hebraic source, as Cantera would suppose, this merely indicates that the Hebrew narrative depended heavily on Christian writings, either in Latin or in one or more of the Romance languages, a fact which we have already observed.

The date when *L. I. E. B.* was composed cannot be determined with certainty. Since 1488 is suspect, 1455 (Chapter 22) becomes the *terminus a quo.* The *terminus ad quem* is more difficult. At first glance, the *L. I. E. B.* would seem to have been completed prior to 1492, for no subsequent work devoted to the calamities of the Jews could have avoided mentioning those of 1492 and the years following. But the possibility remains that the *L. I. E. B.* was composed in whole or in part after 1492 but for some reason remained incomplete. In this case, the date of composition could be extended far into the sixteenth century.

Likewise uncertain is the place where the *L. I. E. B.* was composed. Its interest in Spanish history, its relationship to Efodi and its direct influence on only Usque and Verga point to an Iberian origin, and its failure to mention Portugal limits it to Spain. Thus if the work were completed prior to 1492, the place of composition can safely be assumed to have been Spain. After 1492, it might have been composed in Portugal, Italy or even the Ottoman Empire, but in any case it was composed by someone who was close to the soil and history of Spain. The latter possibility would also offer an explanation as to the place where Usque and Verga, writing after the expulsion, might have consulted it.

These data and circumstantial conclusions stress the problem of the identification of *L. I. E. B.* in all its complexity and present the limitations within which the solution must be found. They thus serve as a reliable base and point of departure for the construction of a more plausible hypothesis than has hitherto been possible.

8. THE L. I. E. B. AND ABRAVANEL

All evidence presently available points to an identification of the *L. I. E. B.* with Isaac Abravanel's historical chronicle, the *Yemot Olam*. The few facts known about Abravanel's work—its contents, its existence only in manuscript form and the fullness of its narrative—produce an amazing similarity to the *L. I. E. B.*[146] And when one adds to this Abravanel's foremost position in the philosophy of Jewish history during his epoch, his crucial role in the preservation of Efodi's chronicle,[147] and above all his pervasive influence on every aspect of the thought and structure of the *Consolaçam*,[148] the identification of *L. I. E. B.* with the *Yemot Olam* appears most plausible. Such an identification would also explain the mystery of why Abravanel nowhere mentions the *L. I. E. B.*, though his high position in government circles and his keen interest in Jewish historiography could not have allowed a work of such import, and circulating in at least two different versions, to have escaped his attention. Besides, the fact that the *L. I. E. B.* appears to have found echoes only in the *Consolaçam* and the *Shevet Yehuda* can best be explained by the close ties of friendship with the Abravanel family enjoyed both by Usque and the Vergas.[149]

To be sure, the letters *L. I. E. B.* cannot be made to yield the name of Isaac Abravanel or the title of his book. But they could well represent the famous name of Isaac's oldest son, Judah Leon Abravanel, author of the *Dialoghi di amore*, and known in the Christian world as Leon(e) (H)Ebreo. *L. I. E. B.* can be deciphered in Portuguese as L(EON) I(EHUDA) EB(REO).

In addition to writing his great classic of Neoplatonic thought, Judah was also a devoted student of his father's, and a gifted Hebrew poet, some of his compositions appearing as prefaces to his father's works.[150] In this close relationship of father and son may lie the clue to the appearance of the letters *L. I. E. B.* Exactly how the name of Leon Ebreo might have been linked to the *Yemot Olam* no one can tell. Judah may have prefaced an introductory poem to his father's work, and Usque, in ignorance, may have ascribed the work to him.[151] Perhaps the title page of the *Yemot Olam* was lost, and a poem bearing Judah's name was the first item to greet the reader. Perhaps on Isaac's death the manuscript fell into Judah's possession and was then associated with him. Or perhaps Isaac's name was abbreviated by the Hebrew letter *Yod*, which Usque could easily have assumed to mean "Yehuda" at a time when the renown of the author of the *Dialoghi* both as a writer and as the personal physician of the Great Captain, Gonzalo Fernández de Córdova, was still freshly etched in the popular memory.[152]

That the *L. I. E. B.* was obtained directly from Judah was unlikely. Judah died in 1535, when Usque, in all probability, had not yet begun his composition. Besides, if it were obtained from Judah, it cannot be assumed that he failed to indicate the correct author. But for Usque to have consulted this manuscript in the rich library of his friend, Samuel Abravanel, without further investigation of its authorship, would be a most plausible explanation!

To be sure, the possibility remains that Judah himself penned the *L. I. E. B.*, though there is little evidence to support such a contention. Aside from his poetic piece, the *Teluna al Ha-Zeman*, which deals primarily with contemporary history, nothing is known about Judah as a historian. Yet one fact, in Chapter 50 of the *Shevet Yehuda*, cannot be overlooked. There we read of a work by Judah Abravanel, called the *Parasha Tohahot* and presumably based on Deuteronomy 28, which recounts tribulations suffered by the Jews in the expulsions from Spain and Portugal, at the time of Fray Vicente (Ferrer) "and others."[153] The unexpected appearance of Judah's name (Yehuda) has led some amazed scholars to pronounce it a misreading for Isaac (Yitzhak),[154] but in so doing they overlooked the fact that the section in question in Isaac Abravanel's Pentateuchal Commentary makes nothing more than a summary mention of calamities and fails to give any details regarding Fray Vicente Ferrer or any other persecutions.[155] There is thus a likelihood that the author of the *Parasha Tohahot* in question is Judah. If this were true, Judah's claim to the authorship of the *L. I. E. B.* might somewhat be strengthened, but it could still hardly destroy the more substantial hypothesis that Isaac Abravanel was the author of the *L. I. E. B.*

Numerous possibilities thus lead to the conclusion that *L. I. E. B.* stands for L(eon) I(ehuda) EB(reo), and that the work in question was the *Yemot Olam*.

The order of the names Leon and Yehuda in the abbreviation should not be surprising. The name Judah Leon Abravanel is indeed more common. In this instance, however, the name Leon, famous outside Jewish circles, is an insertion, added for greater identification. Likewise, when presenting the name Leon Ebreo to an audience with Jewish interests, the name Judah is a similar insertion and correctly follows the name Leon.

That Usque utilized the name "Iehuda" is not inconsistent with his practice of inserting Hebrew names and terms which would be known to his public. That he chose the name Leon Ebreo to Jehuda Abravanel is also understandable. Writing as he did at a time when the former appellation was at its zenith, he preferred to identify his source with the current and famous name of this outstanding literary figure of the sixteenth century.

NOTES

INTRODUCTION

CHAPTER I

[1] H. V. Livermore, A History of Portugal (Cambridge, Eng., 1947), pp. 186 ff.

[2] See A. Farinelli, Marrano: Storia di un vituperio (Geneva, 1925). For other satirical names heaped upon the New Christians, see C. Roth, A History of the Marranos (Philadelphia, 1932), pp. 27 f.

[3] The history of Spanish Jewry in this chapter is based largely on the following works: J. Amador de los Ríos, Estudios históricos, políticos y literarios sobre los judíos de España (Madrid, 1848); idem, Historia política, social y religiosa de los judíos de España y Portugal II and III (Madrid, 1875-1876); R. Altamira y Crevea, Historia de España, II (Madrid, 1928); F. Baer, Toledot ha-Yehudim biSefarad ha-Notzrit (Tel Aviv, 1959); and C. Roth, op. cit.

[4] The famous contemporary Green Book of Aragon (Libro verde de Aragón) lists the Jewish ancestry of the most famous New Christians of the era. Since one of King Ferdinand of Aragon's maternal great-grandmothers was a Jewess, the New Christians were even accused of a plot to take over the throne. Cf. Amador de los Ríos, Historia, III, p. 12; H. C. Lea, A History of the Inquisition in Spain, I (New York, 1906), p. 120.

[5] J. Amador de los Ríos, Historia, III, pp. 113 ff.; idem, Estudios, pp. 129-130: Hasta entonces se habían dirigido no obstante, todos los tiros contra los que permanecían contumaces en negar la venida del Mesías: aun en medio de las rebeliones y matanzas se habían respetado las vidas y las haciendas de los que abrazaban el cristianismo. La persecución presentada ya otro aspecto: hasta entonces se había aborrecido al incrédulo: ya se odiaba el descendiente de Judá, por el mero hecho de serlo. Hasta entonces se habían prodigado honores y mercedes a los que abjuraban del judaísmo: ya se les miraba con recelo, se sospechaba de su sinceridad y se les armaban asechanzas.

[6] The first major work known to contain these charges is Fray Alonso de Spina's Fortalitium Fidei, which was completed in 1458 or 1459. Cf. below p. 9. During the entire first half of the fifteenth century there are few instances in the literature of Spain where the religious zeal or sincerity of the converts is questioned: the governmental and Inquisitional documents affirming Marrano insincerity prior to the middle of the fifteenth century were for the most part framed after that date. On this entire problem, see E. Rivkin, "The Utilization of non-Jewish Sources for the Reconstruction of Jewish History," Jewish Quarterly Review (New Series), XLVIII (1957-1958), pp. 189 ff.

[7] Perhaps the most important of these were: 1) the defense of Fray Alonso de

Oropesa, who in 1465 finished a work entitled *Lumen ad revelationem gentium et gloriam plebis tuae Israel*, whose purpose was "to remove from the converts the reproach and opprobrium with which wicked (Old) Christians were seeking to crush and destroy them." Cf. P. José de' Sigüenza, *Historia de la orden de San Jerónimo*, part II, book 3, chap. 18, in *Nueva biblioteca de autores españoles*, VIII, p. 370 (Madrid, 1907); and 2) the defense by Cardinal Juan de Torquemada, entitled *Tractatus contra madianitas et ismaelitas* (ed. Burgos, 1957). For a list of the various defenses of the Marranos, see the introduction—tendentious but valuable—to Torquemada's pamphlet, by Nicolás López Martínez and Vicente Proaño Gil.

Indeed, as late as 1488, the famous book *Alboraique*, which questions the sincerity of the New Christians of Toledo, Murcia and all Extremadura and Andalusia, asserts that among the *conversos* of Old Castile, Leon and Zamora, "there are found hardly any heretics." See text in I. Loeb, "Polémistes chrétiens et juifs en France et en Espagne" in *Revue des études juives*, XVIII (1889), p. 241. Cf. A. Castro, *La realidad histórica de España* (Mexico, 1954), p. 446, n. 6. In addition, testimony given in the early Spanish *autos da fé* shows that the New Christians "chose Christianity to die an easier death [*i.e.*, than the one to which they were subject by renouncing it and affirming Judaism], and they died with a cross in their hands." [A. Neuman, *The Jews in Spain*, I, (Philadelphia, 1942), p. 59.] Thus, while the Marranos as a whole might not have been more sincere Christians than the rest of the social class to which they belonged, they were certainly not sincere Jews.

[8] H. Lea, *op. cit.*, p. 121; Neuman, *op. cit.*, II, p. 270.

[9] For a contemporary picture of the wretchedness of the converts, see the poem "A D. Alonso de Aguilar cuando la destrucción de los conversos de Córdoba," by Antón de Montoro, which may have been addressed to King Ferdinand. A. de Montoro, *Cancionero*, ed. by E. Cotarelo y Mori (Madrid, 1900), pp. 80 ff. and 333 f.

[10] H. C. Lea, *op. cit.*, I, pp. 130 ff.

[11] *Ibid.* Cf. A. de Castro, *A History of Religious Intolerance* (London, 1853), pp. 23 ff.

[12] For Portuguese Jewish history, see M. Kayserling, *Geschichte der Juden in Portugal* (Leipzig, 1867); J. Mendes dos Remédios, *Os judeos em Portugal*, 2 vols. (Coimbra, 1895, 1928); J. D'Azevedo, *História dos christãos novos portugueses* (Lisbon, 1921), and C. Roth, *op. cit.* On the general background, see D. Peres et al., *História de Portugal*, 8 vols. (Barcelos, 1928-1938); J. Ameal, *História de Portugal* (Porto, 1940), and J. Oliveira Martins, *História de Portugal* (Porto, 1886). Good one volume English summaries are H. M. Stephens, *Portugal* (in *The Story of the Nations*) (New York and London, 1893) and H. V. Livermore, *A History of Portugal* (Cambridge, Eng., 1947).

[13] W. Prescott, *History of the Reign of Ferdinand and Isabella the Catholic*, II (Philadelphia, 1872), p. 356.

[14] For the most detailed account of this period, see A. Herculano, *Da origem e estabelecimento da Inquisição em Portugal*, 3 vols. (Lisbon, 1855-1859), and the partial English translation by John C. Branner, *History of the Origin and Establishment of the Inquisition in Portugal* (Stanford, Cal.; 1926). Cf. also A. Baião, *A Inquisição em Portugal e no Brasil* (Lisbon, 1921).

Emanuel had apparently sent overtures to Rome as early as 1515 regarding the introduction of an Inquisition, but nothing came of them. See Herculano, *op. cit.*, Eng. trans., p. 272. On the flight of the Marranos, see H. Graetz, *Geschichte der Juden* (Leipzig, 1877), pp. 543 ff.

[15] Cf. A. H. Silver, *A History of Messianic Speculation in Israel* (New York, 1927), *passim*.

[16] The predicament of the Marranos in the early fifteenth century led to the rise of Messianic expectations among them. See F. Fernández y González, "El

mesianismo israelita en la península ibérica durante la primera mitad del siglo XVI," in *Revista de España*, XVIII (1871), pp. 406 ff.

[17] J. D'Azevedo, *op. cit.*, pp. 92, 487.

[18] C. Roth, *op. cit.*, p. 147.

[19] Cf. J. D'Azevedo, *op. cit.*, pp. 91-92, the "Processo do Desembargador Gil Vaz Bugalho," *ibid.*, pp. 447-450.

[20] M. Kayserling, *op. cit.*, p. 230.

[21] See A. L. Williams, *Adversus Judaeos: A Bird's Eye View of Christian Apologiae until the Renaissance* (Cambridge, Eng., 1935), *passim*; "Controverses avec les juifs" in A. Vacant, E. Mangenot and E. Amann, *Dictionnaire de théologie catholique*, VIII, part 2, (Paris, 1925), cols. 1870-1914; F. Pérez Castro, "Ojeada rápida a la literatura polémica anti-judía" in his edition of *El manuscrito apologético de Alfonso de Zamora* (Madrid, 1950), pp. xciv-ci. The claim that the Church was the New Israel appears in the earliest strata of anti-Jewish polemics. See Marcel Simon, *Verus Israel: Études sur les relations entre chrétiens et juifs dans l'empire romain, 135-425* (Paris, 1948), pp. 87 ff. On the length of the Diaspora, cf. J. Parkes; "Church and Synagogue in the Middle Ages" in *The Transactions of the Jewish Historical Society of England*, XVI (London, 1952), p. 29 and A. Williams, *op. cit.*, pp. 252, 273 and *passim*.

[22] The entire corpus of Portuguese anti-Jewish polemical literature before the forced conversion of 1497 included only four major works, all relatively mild in tone. One of these, the *Ajuda da fé*, though based on the virulent writings of the Spanish apostate, Gerónimo de Santa Fe, even manifests an effort to delete the Spaniard's most baneful passages. See the introduction to João de Barros' *Diálogo evangélico sobre os artigos da fé contra o Talmud dos Judeus* by I. S. Révah (Lisbon, 1950), pp. xv ff.

[23] *Ibid.*

[24] These are the editions of Strassburg (n.d., *ca.* 1471); Basel (n.d., *ca.* 1475); Nuremberg (1485, 1494, 1525); Lyons (1487, 1511). Cf. Vacant-Magenot-Ammon, *op. cit.*, col. 1893. Cf. F. da Mareto, "Spina, Alfonso Lopez de," *Enciclopedia Cattolica*, XI, col. 1122. J. Amador de los Ríos, *Estudios*, p. 435, mentions four editions (Nuremberg, 1485 and 1494; Lyons, 1511 and 1525).

[25] Spina has erroneously been considered a Jew. Cf. M. Jost, *Geschichte des Judenthums und seiner Secten*, III (Leipzig, 1859), p. 96; H. Graetz, *op. cit.*, VIII, pp. 228 ff. Spina's first edition appeared anonymously, but the book has been almost universally attributed to him. Cf. P. Robinson, "Alfonso de Spina," in *The Catholic Encyclopedia*, XIV, p. 216.

[26] *Consolaçam*, p. 39.

[27] *Ibid.*, p. 38.

[28] See M. Menéndez y Pelayo, *Orígenes de la novela in Nueva biblioteca de autores españoles*, I (Madrid, 1905), pp. ccxi ff. The influence of the pastoral genre in the Renaissance, apparent already in Boccaccio's *Ameto*, reached its zenith precisely at the time Samuel Usque was composing his *Consolaçam*. See E. H. Wilkins, *A History of Italian Literature* (Cambridge, Mass., 1954), p. 169. This was due in no small measure to Giacomo Sannazaro's lyric novel, the *Arcadia*, which profoundly stimulated the flourishing of pastoral poetry and prose from the moment of its publication in 1504. See M. Scherillo, ed. *L'Arcadia di Jacobo Sannazaro* (Turin, 1888), p. ccxii; and J. B. Fletcher, *Literature of the Italian Renaissance* (New York, 1934), p. 167. The favor with which the *Arcadia* was received and the vogue of the pastoral genre in general lay to some extent in the fact that the pastoral represented a reaction to an era ridden with war and bloodshed. See H. A. Rennert, *The Spanish Pastoral Romances* (Philadelphia, 1912), p. 14. The pastoral of course was literature of escape, not only from arms and warfare, but from the turmoil and insecurity of the bustling urban centers, and their new and often disillusioning ways of

life. See E. Baret, *De l'Amadis de Gaule et de son influence sur les moeurs et la littérature au XVIe et au XVIIe siècle* (Paris, 1873), *passim*. From Italy, the pastoral genre was transplanted into the Iberian Peninsula. A Spanish translation of the *Arcadia* appeared in Toledo in 1547 and a second in 1549. Two decades before, the influence of the Italian pastoral was already inspiring the most outstanding peninsular poets of the epoch, Garcilaso de la Vega, Gutierre de Cetina and Francisco de Figueroa in Spain, Francisco Sa de Miranda, Diego Bernardes and later Francisco de Camoens himself in Portugal. By the time of Usque, the pastoral enjoyed a prime rank among the major literary genres. See F. Torraca, *Gl'imitatori stranieri di Jacopo Sannazaro* (Rome, 1882), pp. 7 ff.; J. Hurtado and A. González-Palencia, *Historia de la literatura española* (Madrid, 1949), pp. 265 ff.; A. F. G. Bell, *Portuguese Literature* (Oxford, 1922), pp. 132 ff. Cf. Castonnet Desfosses, *La Pastorale en Portugal* (Paris, 1882), *passim*. The attempt of Elias Lipiner, *Bei die Teichn von Portugal* (Yiddish) (Buenos Aires, 1949), p. 32, to demonstrate that the pastoral setting in Usque is Jewish is not quite correct. Usque's subject matter contained elements lending themselves to a pastoral framework, but the framework itself is a product of the Renaissance.

[29] I. R. Hirzl, *Der Dialog* (Leipzig, 1895), pp. 385 ff.
[30] J. W. Thompson, *A History of Historical Writing*, I (New York, 1942), pp. 520 ff.; cf. P. Polman, *L'élément historique dans la controverse religieuse du XVIe siècle* (Gembloux, 1932), a basic work in this field, though its major concern is the tracing of the utilization of history by the Protestant and the Catholic Reformations.
[31] Cf. E. Schaefer, *Luther als Kirchenhistoriker* (Gutersloh, 1897), pp. 10, 14, 19, 83 ff.; cf. O. Scheel, *Martin Luther. Vom Katholizismus zur Reforma-tion*, 2 vols. (Tübingen, 1916, 1917).
[32] Cf. J. Thompson, *op. cit.*, pp. 527 f.
[33] P. Polman, *op. cit.*, pp. 281 ff.; pp. 465 ff.
[34] M. Kayserling, *Biblioteca española-portugueza-judaica* (Strassbourg, 1890), pp. xii-xiii.
[35] *Consolaçam*, Prologue, p. 40.
[36] Cf. A. F. G. Bell, *op. cit.*, p. 18: "Of those writing in Latin, one collection alone, the *Corpus Illustrium Poetarum Lusitanorum qui latine scripserunt* (Lisbon, 1745) is 8 vols., and Domingo García Pérez' *Catálogo Razonado* (Madrid, 1890) contains over 600 names of Portuguese authors who wrote in Spanish."
The renowned Spanish Protestant Alfonso de Valdés wrote in his brilliant apology of the Spanish tongue, the *Diálogo de la lengua*, that it was considered a "*gentileza y galanía*" to speak Spanish in Italy. *Diálogo de la lengua* (Madrid, 1928), p. 4. The Pole in Cervantes' *Persiles y Sigismunda* described Spain as "*centro de los estrangeros y madre común de las naciones*," ed. Schevill and Bonilla, II (Madrid, 1913), p. 63.
The significance of Spanish is attested to by the Ferrara Bible (1554): ... quesimos todavia tomar este trabajo tan ageno de nuestras fuerças viendo que la biblia se halla en todas las lenguas y que solamente falta en la Española siendo tan copiosa y usada en la major parte de la Europa y en algunas provincias fuera della. . . .

CHAPTER II

[1] The name Usque is not found before the middle of the sixteenth century. At that time it appears as the surname of three great figures of the Marrano literary circle of Ferrara. See below, p. 14. It is not contained in any document originating in Spain and Portugal nor is it ever found among the names of distinguished Jewish or Marrano families. The *Catálogo dos portu-guezes christãos-novos que se hião declarar judios a Italia* by Fernando de Goes

Loureiro, in which we would certainly expect to find his name, is unfortunately not available. See D. Barbosa Machado, *Bibliotheca Lusitana*, II (Lisbon, 1747), p. 27. Cf. M. Kayserling, "Samuel Usque," in *The Jewish Encyclopedia*, XII, p. 387a. Balletti (*Gli ebrei e gli estensi*, Emilia, 1930, p. 88), speaking of Abraham Usque, makes the unusual statement "*Abraham da Uesca di Zamorra* [!], *perciò noto col nome di Usque*," but fails to substantiate or cite sources for the hypothesis that the Usques originated in Zamora. Huesca at this time was the seat of a large Jewish population and had experienced violent anti-Semitic outbreaks since the massacres of 1391. Cf. I. Baer, *Die Juden im christlichen Spanien*, I (Berlin, 1929), p. 686, and A. Castro, *op. cit.*, p. 479.

The name Usque does not appear in Hebrew characters in the *Consolaçam*. It is written אוסקי by Gedaliah ibn Yahia in his *Shalshelet ha-Kabbalah* (Warsaw, 1877), pp. 151 and 153. The spelling עושקי reflects no reliable source. It is found in J. Bartoloccio, *Bibliotheca Magna Rabbinica*, I (Rome, 1675), p. 49, with reference to Abraham Usque. More acceptable is the spelling אושקי found in J. Rodríguez de Castro, *Biblioteca española*, I (Madrid, 1781), p. 566, col. 2; S. P. Rabinowitz, *Motzoei Golah* (Warsaw, 1894), p. 287 and *passim*; E. Schochet in the article on Usque in the *Hebrew Encyclopedia*, II (Jerusalem, 1950), p. 335 and elsewhere. The name "Ibn Usque" often appears. J. Fürst, *Bibliotheca Judaica*, III (Leipzig, 1863), p. 465; David Amram, *The Makers of Hebrew Books in Italy* (Philadelphia, 1909), p. 283. Isaac Da Costa (*Israel en de Volken* [Haarlem, 1873]) asserted that the name Samuel Usque was an anagram for Manuel Gomes. This view was accepted by J. Teixeira Rego, *Estudos e controvérsias, Segunda série* (Porto, 1931), p. 63.

Portuguese Marranos as a rule preserved a Hebrew name alongside the Christian name they bore in Portugal. Once they left, they usually shed their Marrano name and reverted to or adopted a Hebrew name. Thus Gracia Mendes Nasi's name in Portugal was Beatriz de Luna; that of Amatus Lusitanus was João Rodrigues (de Castelobranco); that of Joseph Nasi was João Migues, that of Abraham Usque was Duarte Pinhel, etc.

[2] *Consolaçam*, Prologue, p. 40, below.

[3] This would mean that Usque was in his early thirties when he left Portugal and fifty-five when the *Consolaçam* was published (1553).

[4] *Consolaçam*, Prologue, p. 40.

[5] Usque's erudition is to be inferred from the sources which he utilized, the literary forms which he had mastered and the philosophical and ideological currents which his work reveals.

[6] I. Aboab, *Nomologia* (Amsterdam, 1629), p. 304, where the author of the *Consolaçam* is called "Rabi Abraham (!) Usque." On the basis of this statement, Mendes dos Remédios called Samuel a "*pobre e perseguido rabino*" when he escaped from Portugal. J. Mendes dos Remédios, Introduction to the *Consolaçam*, p. xl. (*Os Judeos*, II, p. 350.)

It should be noted that Usque's acquaintance with the Talmud, though apparent, is not deep. Statements like that of Joseph Rodríguez de Castro, *Biblioteca española*, I, p. 566, col. 2, that Usque "*se hizo célebre entre los suyos por su instrucción en Talmud*," a judgment copied almost verbatim by Mendes dos Remédios, ed. *Consolaçam*, Prologue, p. xiv and *Os Judeos*, II, p. 338, is based on no evidence. On the possibility that Usque's talmudic knowledge may be second-hand, cf. Appendix B, below, pp. 274 ff.

[7] M. Kayserling, *Geschichte der Juden in Portugal*, pp. 136, 141.

[8] Cf. Abraham Saba, in *Tseror Hakesef*, quoted in S. P. Rabinowitz, *op. cit.*, pp. 33-34 n.

והנה בהיותי בפורטוגאל מגרוש קסטיליא עלה בדעתי לפרש חמש מגלות ופרשתי

אותם, ואז חרה אף (ה') בעמי בגירוש שני מפורטוגאל, והנחתי כל הספרים

ושמתי עצתי להביא עמי ללישבון פירוש התורה שחברתי בפורטוגאל עם פירוש
המגלות, ופירוש מסכת אבות עם חבור הכסף שחברתי בימי נעורי, ובהגיע
ללישבון באו אלי אנשי יהודה ואמרו לי שעבר קול במחנה, שמי שמוציא ספר
אזר דתו להמית, ומיד הלכתי וטמנתי אותם תחת זית אחד. ‎(Italics mine).

[9] A. Neuman, "Samuel Usque: Marrano Historian," in *To Dr. R(osenbach)* (Philadelphia, 1946), p. 181.

[10] Cf. T. Braga, *História da Universidade de Coimbra nas suas relações com a instrucção pública portugueza*, I (Lisbon, 1892), pp. 449 ff.

[11] This aspect of Marrano life and the psychological conflicts it engendered are captured with intuitive brilliance and artistic imagination by A. A. Kabak in his Hebrew trilogy, *Shelomo Molcho*.

[12] Roth is of the opinion that the earlier chapters of the third dialogue of the *Consolaçam* are likewise autobiographical: "An attentive reading of the text makes it seem probable (the point has, I think, never been noted before) that the work contains a good deal of autobiographical material, the author's personal experiences being treated apparently as typical. It seems pretty certain, for example, that in his own peregrinations he followed the path of exile which he depicted with such feeling. Thus he presumably fled from Portugal to England, where perhaps he arrived in 1531; he mentions indeed the display of traitors' heads on London Bridge as though he had seen it with his own eyes. He then went on by way of Flanders and Germany and through Switzerland, giving a particularly vivid description of the fugitives' sufferings in the Alpine passes. Arrived in Italy, he settled first in Milan and then in Ferrara, being one of the victims of the expulsion in 1551, of which he speaks with exceptional warmth." C. Roth, *The House of Nasi: Doña Gracia* (Philadelphia, 1947), p. 200, n. 14.

[13] C. Roth, *The History of the Jews of Italy* (Philadelphia, 1946), p. 189.

[14] If these cities were on Usque's itinerary, the fact that he mentions distinguished men like Dr. Moses Hamon in his chapter on Constantinople or Manuel Bichacho in his chapter on Ferrara does not necessarily imply a direct acquaintance with them. (Dialogue III, pp. 211, 214.)

[15] *Consolaçam*, Dialogue III, p. 212.

[16] S. Schechter, "Safed," in *Studies in Judaism*, Second Series (Philadelphia, 1908), p. 228.

[17] Ed. Constantinople, 1577, f. 5b-6b. The *Kol Mevasser*, printed with the *Maase bet David bime' malkhut Paras*, begins on f. 5b of this volume.

[18] *Consolaçam*, p. 213. Yet soon thereafter, the Jews (or many of them) were expelled from Ferrara. See Dialogue III, ch. 36.

[19] Cf. M. Kayserling, "Usque, Abraham" in *Jewish Encyclopedia*, XII, p. 387a, and C. Roth, "The Marrano Press at Ferrara," *The Modern Language Review*, XXXVIII (1943), pp. 307 ff.

[20] M. Kayserling, "Usque, Solomon," *loc. cit.*, p. 388a. The identification of Solomon Usque with Duarte Gómez, the trusted agent of the firm of Gracia Mendes (Nasi) is based on a misunderstanding. Cf. C. Roth, "Salusque Lusitano" in *Jewish Quarterly Review* (NS), XXXIV (1943-1944), pp. 65-85.

[21] J. C. Wolf, *Bibliotheca Hebraea*, III (Hamburg, 1727), p. 1071; G. B. De Rossi, *De typographia hebraeo-Ferrariensi* (Parma, 1780), p. 64; J. Amador de los Ríos, *Estudios*, p. 496; M. Kayserling, *Sephardim*, p. 140; *idem*, "Samuel Usque," *loc. cit.*, p. 387; J. Steinschneider, "Zur Geschichte jüdischer Martyrologien (R. Samuel Usque's 'Trost Israels in seinen Trübsalen')," in *Festschrift zum X. Stiftungsfest des Akademischen Vereins für jüdische Geschichte und Literatur an der kgl. Friedrich-Wilhelms-Universität zu Berlin* (Berlin, 1893), p. 30; D. Amram, *op. cit.*, p. 283; A. Neuman, *op. cit.*, p. 180.

[22] I. Da Costa, *op. cit.*, p. 378; M. Kayserling, *Biblioteca española-portugueza-judaica* (Strasbourg, 1890), p. 107; J. L. D'Azevedo, *História dos christãos*

novos portugueses, p. 365; Rabinowitz makes Solomon a brother of Abraham and Samuel: op. cit., pp. 286 ff.

[23] A. Neuman, op. cit., pp. 180, 185 and especially 186; S. P. Rabinowitz, op. cit., p. 288.

[24] A. Pesaro, Memorie storiche sulla communità israelitica ferrarese (Ferrara, 1878), p. 23: C. Roth, op. cit., p. 311, claims that Solomon was Abraham's son but says nothing of Samuel's relationship to Abraham. Cf. also Roth, "Salusque Lusitano," op. cit., p. 77. The claim of this relationship is based on evidence which is entirely circumstantial.

[25] Cf. "Usque, Samuel" (author not listed) in Universal Jewish Encyclopedia (New York, 1943), p. 384a, based on M. Freier, Jüdisches Lexicon, V, p. 1147.

[26] I. Aboab, Nomologia (Amsterdam, 1629), p. 304 and J. Mendes dos Remédios later the editor of the Consolaçam (!) in Os judeos em Portugal, I, p. 299.

[27] Cf. U. Cassuto, "Un ignoto capitolo di storia ebraica," in Judaica, Festschrift zu Hermann Cohens siebzigstem Geburtstage (Berlin, 1912), p. 396. Some of the confusion may have been caused by the fact that Abraham's father's name is known to have been Solomon. Cf. C. Roth, op. cit., p. 313. One scholar, after discovering a document relating to Gracia Nasi in which a certain Samuel is sent on a business trip to the Aegean island of Naxos, even goes so far as to identify him with the author of the Consolaçam. See A. Galante, "Deux nouveaux documents sur Dona Gracia Nassy," in Revue des études juives, LXV (1913), pp. 151-154. The pertinent passage of the document in question, written at Gracia's order, reads as follows in translation: Ainsi, j'ai ordonné que, lorsque son représentant Samuel ira chez vous, vous déployiez vos efforts pour faire payer à la personne qui a vendu aux habitants de Naxos les marchandises pillées par les pirates, et qui a pris l'engagement de s'acquitter de cette dette, la somme qu'elle doit encore. Tâche de remettre à son représentant la somme que tu encaisseras. Ibid., p. 154.

[28] C. Roth, The House of Nasi: Doña Gracia, p. 60. Fleeing with her was her daughter Reyna.

[29] Ibid., pp. 400-404, 474.

[30] Consolaçam, Dialogue III, p. 230.

[31] Cf. K. J. Holzknecht, Literary Patronage in the Middle Ages (Philadelphia, 1923), which also covers the Italian Renaissance, pp. 57-58.

[32] The Ferrara Bible left Abraham Usque's press in 1554 in two versions, identical except for the dedication (the one version, the so-called Jewish version, dedicated to the Duke of Ferrara, the other, the so-called Christian version, to Doña Gracia); the colophon (the one version naming Duarte Pinhel as editor and Jeronimo de Vargas [Español] as bearer of the costs, the other naming Abrahã [sic] Usque as editor and Yom Tob Atias for the costs); the translation of the sensitive passage in Isaiah 7.14; the Christian and Jewish dates; and the appearance of a list of Haftara readings in the so-called Jewish version. Cf. C. Roth, Doña Gracia, pp. 73 f.

[33] Consolaçam, Prologue, p. 37.

[34] Cf. ibid., Dialogue III, pp. 230 f.; and Prologue, loc. cit.: "and I desire . . . to show myself in some small way grateful for the largesse I have received from your generous hand."

[35] Dialogue III, pp. 209 f. M. Kayserling, Geschichte der Juden in Portugal, pp. 264 ff.; H. Graetz, op. cit., IX, pp. 37 and 327 ff.; C. Roth, The History of the Jews of Italy, p. 189.

[36] M. Kayserling, Die jüdischen Frauen (Leipzig, 1879), pp. 77 ff.; I. Aboab, op. cit., p. 304. C. Roth, The House of Nasi: Doña Gracia, pp. 66 f.

[37] The great Portuguese Marrano physician Amatus Lusitanus (João Rodrigues· de Castelobranco) seems to have frequented their circle, and David Reubeni is known to have aroused their interest and to have received a handsome

gift from them. E. Lipiner, *op. cit.*, p. 178. S. P. Rabinowitz, *op. cit.*, p. 133 f. Cf. Maximiano Lemos, *Amato Lusitano: A sua vida e a sua obra* (Porto, 1907), pp. 81-83.

[38] *Consolaçam*, Dialogue III, p. 210.

[39] See Appendix B, p. 285 above.

[40] C. Roth, *The House of Nasi: Doña Gracia*, p. 200, n. 10, claims that Doña Gracia had already left Ferrara in 1551, before the appearance of the *Consolaçam*, and that the *Consolaçam* and the Ferrara Bible "were obviously prepared for the press while she was still at hand." This is certainly possible. It would mean that the thirty-seventh historical chapter, dealing with the desecration of the synagogue at Pesaro, was composed nearly two years later than the rest of the work and was appended to it just before the *Consolaçam* left the press. Whether Usque fled Ferrara in 1551 is conjectural.

[41] Cf. above n. 17. See also M. Kayserling, "Usque, Samuel," *op. cit.*, p. 387b; J. Mendes dos Remédios, ed. *Consolaçam,* Introduction, p. xvii (*Os Judeos, II,* p. 339); C. Roth, "The Marrano Press," p. 316.

CHAPTER III

[1] Prologue, p. 39.

[2] Usque changes many of the biblical verses he quotes. A simple omission, addition or explanatory clause helps to adjust them to the contemporary situation. In the concluding section of Dialogue III the changes, particularly the additions, become increasingly bolder. In this section I have italicized the most significant of these alterations. The poem which concludes Dialogue III, though not italicized, is a paraphrase of Psalm 126.

[3] Pp. 44 f.

[4] P. 56.

[5] On Esau and Edom (used interchangeably to denote Christianity) see E. G. Hirsch, "Esau," in *The Jewish Encyclopedia*, V, pp. 206-208 and M. Seligsohn, "Edom, Idumea," *ibid.*, pp. 40-41. The Talmud already applies these names to the Roman Empire, and they then came to mean the Christian faith which spread through it. *Ibid.*, p. 41. During the Middle Ages Christian censors were careful to expunge references to Edom or Esau from Jewish books, and Jewish authors often substituted other names for these. Cf. W. Popper, *The Censorship of Hebrew Books* (New York, 1899), pp. 58, 59, 80, 86, 87.

   On Ishmael, cf., R. Gottheil, "Abraham in Mohammedan Legend," in *The Jewish Encyclopedia*, I, pp. 87 ff. (containing a fine bibliography), and H. Hirschfeld, "Ishmael in Arabic Literature," *ibid.*, VI, p. 648.

[6] P. 79.

[7] P. 105. Cf. p. 104: "Thus your healthy flesh was not cut off, nor was any creature punished with death or exile who had not first, with his own hands, made the sword that cut him and prepared the snare into which he fell."

[8] Pp. 83 f.

[9] P. 84.

[10] P. 87.

[11] *Ibid.*

[12] P. 102.

[13] P. 89.

[14] P. 90.

[15] P. 91.

[16] P. 106.

[17] *Ibid.*

[18] P. 123.

[19] Pp. 151 f.

[20] P. 153.

[21] The theme of *"where are they now?"* (*Ubi Sunt?*) was very common in

Iberian literature during the fifteenth century and was brilliantly utilized by Jorge Manrique in his celebrated *Couplets* (*Coplas*) written at the death of his father, a composition which remained a favorite well into the sixteenth century. Cf. A. Krause, *Jorge Manrique and the Cult of Death in the Cuatrocientos* (Berkeley, 1937), *passim*.

[22] P. 115. Thus Sabinus (p. 59), Shishak (p. 57), Nebuchadnezzar (pp. 113 f.) and Titus (p. 139) are regarded as surrogates of God. Cf. also p. 63. The Jews' sins (personified!) are considered as having been responsible for the coming of oppressors (pp. 139, 159, 213, 224 and *passim*).

[23] P. 159.

[24] P. 213. Cf. p. 178: "But in truth these misfortunes come to me from a much higher source."

[25] See p. 204 (ch. 28), esp. the use of the quotation from Deut. 28.64 f. and (p. 236): "It almost appears that the prophecy is applied with greatest certainty in this misfortune, for since they are at the end of the earth, Spain and Portugal fit and fulfill the entire prophecy exactly." Cf. I. Abravanel, *Commentary to the Pentateuch* (Jerusalem, 1956) to Deut. 28, p. 6b, col. 2.

[26] P. 215. Cf. p. 259.

[27] P. 38.

[28] P. 231.

[29] Cf. the interesting parallel in Machiavelli: "It is not unknown to me how many have been and are of opinion that worldly events are so governed by fortune and by God, that men cannot by their prudence change them. . . . *This opinion has been more held in our day, from the great changes that have been seen, and are daily seen, beyond every human conjecture*" (Italics mine). *The Prince* (New York, 1954), p. 131.

[30] P. 220.

[31] P. 222.

[32] *Ibid.*

[33] P. 223.

[34] P. 228.

[35] P. 229. For other cases where Usque unexpectedly stops at a critical point in a discussion, lamely apologizes to the reader and allows him to proceed by *inference* to an obvious conclusion, see pp. 87, 159, 162, and 222.

[36] P. 229.

[37] *Ibid.* For clarity and emphasis, I have reversed these two sentences of Usque's.

[38] P. 231.

[39] Pp. 231 f., and corresponding note.

[40] P. 232.

[41] P. 236.

[42] P. 237.

[43] P. 248.

[44] As indicated above (n. 2), I have italicized the most significant additions and some changes. It has, however, been impossible to indicate the omissions and the paraphrases which are equally significant. The reader should compare Usque's text with the Bible to appreciate all the nuances of his message.

[45] P. 224.

[46] P. 226.

[47] P. 234.

[48] P. 244.

[49] P. 255.

[50] P. 180. Cf. p. 260.

[51] P. 190.

[52] Pp. 255, 261.

[53] P. 260. Cf. p. 244, where, paraphrasing Isaiah, he urges the New Christians still in unfriendly lands to depart from them.

[54] P. 260.
[55] *Ibid.*
[56] P. 261.
[57] P. 262.
[58] P. 260.
[59] *Ibid.*
[60] P. 261.

CHAPTER IV

[1] *Consolaçam*, Prologue, p. 40.
[2] The Library of the Hebrew Union College-Jewish Institute of Religion, Cincinnati Campus, possesses a copy of all three editions of the *Consolaçam*.
[3] Heinrich Graetz (*op. cit.*, vol. IX, p. 544) incorrectly asserts that the date belonged to the secular year 1552, and this error is copied by Lipiner and others. September 7, 1552 belonged to the Hebrew year 5312 (the year 5313 began on September 19). Thursday, September 7, 1553 fell during the closing days of the Hebrew year 5313; Rosh Hashanah 5314 fell on Saturday, September 9, 1553. Cf. E. Mahler, *Handbuch der jüdischen Chronologie* (Leipzig, 1916), pp. 578-579.
[4] *Emek ha-Bakha* (Cracow, 1895), *passim*. *Shalshelet ha-Kabbalah* (Warsaw, 1887), pp. 151 (twice) and 153.
[5] L. Wolf, *Essays in Jewish History* (London, 1934), pp. 85 ff., esp. 88 f.
[6] *Processo 1449—Inquisition of Lisbon* (Arquivo Nacional da Torre da Tomba). These documents, collected by Lucien Wolf, were published after Wolf's death by Cecil Roth in *Miscellanies of the Jewish Historical Society of England* (London, 1935), pp. 32-56, under the title "The Case of Thomas Fernandes before the Lisbon Inquisition." The quotation above is found on p. 47.
[7] *Ibid.*, pp. 48 f.
[8] S. Dubnow, *Divre Yeme Am Olam*, VI (Tel Aviv, 1948), p. 53.
[9] F. H. Reusch, *Die Indices Librorum Prohibitorum des sechzehnten Jahrhunderts* (Stuttgart, 1886), *passim*. Lipner's contention (*op. cit.*, p. 14) that the *Consolaçam* was "immediately placed on all Indexes" is unaccompanied by scholarly support. For an earlier parallel claim, cf. *infra*, n. 19. On the rise of censorship, cf. H. C. Lea, *Chapters from the Religious History of Spain* (Philadelphia, 1890), esp. pp. 56 ff.
[10] For Holland during this period, cf. P. Geyl, *The Revolt of the Netherlands, 1555-1609* (London, 1932), and C. V. Wedgwood, *William the Silent* (New Haven, 1944).
[11] For the role of the Marranos, cf. J. S. da Silva Rosa, *Geschiednis der Portugeesche Joden te Amsterdam* (Amsterdam, 1925); I. Prins, *De Vestiging der Marranen in Noord-Nederland in de XVIe eeuw* (Amsterdam, 1927); C. Roth, *A History of the Marranos*, pp. 236 ff.; and H. Bloom, *The Economic Activities of the Jews of Amsterdam in the Seventeenth and Eighteenth Centuries* (Williamsport, Pa., 1937), pp. 1 ff.
[12] Cf. H. Bloom, *op. cit.*, pp. 7, 19 f.
[13] J. Mendes dos Remédios, ed., *Consolaçam*, pp. xxi ff.; *Os judeos em Portugal*, II, pp. 342 ff.
[14] It may be as Roth suggests, that the editors of the Amsterdam edition mistakenly read "a 7 de Setembro" of the first edition as "27 de Setembro," the "a" being somewhat indistinct. C. Roth, "The Marrano Press at Ferrara," *loc. cit.*, p. 313.
[15] The Ferrara edition measures 116 mm x 67 mm, the Amsterdam edition 125 mm x 72 mm. Each edition averages 28 lines with 30 letters per line. Cf. J. Mendes dos Remédios, ed., *Consolaçam*, xxxvii, *Os judeos*, II, p. 349.

[16] The title page of the Amsterdam edition begins thus: CONSOLACAM (sic)/ AS TRI/BVLACOENS (sic)/DE YSRAEL/ COMPOSTO POR SAMVEL VSQVE. It lists the place as "Ferrare" and carries a lattice-type emblem which contrasts strikingly with Abraham Usque's armillary sphere as it appears in the first edition of the Consolaçam. The name of the Amsterdam printer is not known.

[17] G. B. De Rossi, De Typographia Hebraeo-Ferrariensi, p. 65. Many bibliophiles never suspected the existence of two editions, and for want of having seen them, often considered the Amsterdam edition to be the authentic one. J. Mendes dos Remédios, ed., Consolaçam, pp. xxxvi ff.; Os judeos, II, p. 349 ff.

[18] Ibid., ed., Consolaçam, pp. xlii-xliii; Os judeos, II, p. 352.

[19] M. Kayserling, Biblioteca española-portugueza-judaica, passim.

[20] P. 903. Cf. F. H. Reusch, op. cit., II, part 1, p. 50, and J. Wolf, Bibliotheca Hebraea, III, (Hamburg, 1727), p. 1075. Cf. De Rossi's correction in De Typographia, p. 65.

[21] J. Wolf, op. cit., III, p. 1072 implies the existence of a Spanish edition, but adds that he has never seen it or found it cited. A. Ribeiro dos Santos, Memórias da literatura portuguesa, II (Lisbon, 1792), p. 407, n., makes a similar inference without Wolf's added reservation. Isaac da Costa goes so far as to state that Usque first published his work in Portuguese and then in Spanish, and that both versions were speedily included in the Index. Op. cit., p. 378. Cf. also J. Mendes dos Remédios, ed., Consolaçam, p. xxv, n. (1); Os judeos, II, p. 343, n. (1).

[22] This is doubtlessly the source of Ribeiro dos Santo's citation of the same Hebrew title. J. Mendes dos Remédios, ed., Consolaçam, pp. xxi-xxii; Os judeos, II, p. 342. Mendes dos Remédios, ibid., p. 344 indicates that Usque's work is known among the Jews by the title "Nehama al Telaoth Yisrael," without realizing that this merely represents a rendering into Hebrew of the words Consolaçam as tribulaçoens de Israel. This translated title appears, for example, in works like K. Schulman, Toledot Hakhme Israel, IV (Vilna, 1878), p. 191. A Hebrew title is also posited, perhaps independently, by Inocêncio Francisco da Silva, Dicionário bibliográfico portuguez, VII (Lisbon, 1862), pp. 196 f. The Portuguese title Consolaçam [sic] tribulaçoens [sic] de Israel is rendered Nehama l'Tzarot Israel by I. Zinberg, Toledot Sifrut Yisrael, II (Tel Aviv, 1956), p. 272.

[23] J. Mendes dos Remédios, ed., Consolaçam, Notes, pp. 3-4.

[24] See E. Lipiner, op. cit., pp. 28 ff. Most ingenious, however, is J. Texeiro Rego's attempt to discover in the name Bernaldim Ribeiro an anagram for Judah Abravanel. See J. Teixeira Rego, Estudos e controvérsias, Segunda Serie (Porto, 1931), p. 63.

[25] M. Kayserling, Biblioteca española-portugueza-judaica, p. 115.

[26] Cf. above, Preface, p. viii. The three parts of the Consolaçam were published separately, with separate folio numeration for each volume.

[27] F. de Figueiredo, História da literatura classica, I (Lisbon, 1922), p. 297 Cr. ibid., pp. 300-303. Idem., História literaria de Portugal (Coimbra, 1944), pp. 171, 174; J. Mendes dos Remédios, História da literatura portuguesa (Coimbra, 1930), p. 188; H. Cidade, Lições sobre a cultura e a literatura portuguesas (Coimbra, 1933), pp. 169-171; G. C. Rossi, Storia della Letteratura Portoghese (Florence, 1953), p. 89; A. J. Saraiva and O. Lopes, História da literatura portuguesa (Porto, 1956), pp. 200-202. Cf. J. D'Azevedo, História dos cristãos novos portugueses, p. 365. In the middle of the nineteenth century Jose da Fonseca, in his Prosas Selectas ou Escolha dos melhores logares dos auctores portuguezes antiguos e modernos (Paris, 1837), saw fit to include a selection from Dialogue I of the Consolaçam. This selection, found on pages 163-171, includes the sections entitled "Pastoral Life," "Hunt of Conies and Hares," and "Hunt of Stags [and Herons]." Inocêncio Francisco da Silva,

loc. cit., indicated that he had also included a selection from the *Consolaçam* in his *Pequena chrestomathia portugueza*. I have, unfortunately, not been able to see this book.

DEDICATION & PROLOGUE

[1] That is, the Jews. In Portugal the Jews and Marranos were known as "the nation," or "people of the nation." Elsewhere in Europe Usque's countrymen were referred to as "The Portuguese." Cf. n. 16 below.

[2] That is, the present volume.

[3] This is the first of numerous metaphors in the original which must be translated freely into English. The original, translated literally, reads: "For since you began to show your light, even the tiniest infants of this people have begun to imbibe this truth; in their bones your name and happy memory will forever be engraved."

[4] That is, in the Iberian Peninsula (Spain and Portugal).

[5] The plants are the Marranos. The darkness is the gloom that palls their lives in Spain and Portugal.

[6] Gracia's daughter, Reyna, lived with her mother at Antwerp, Venice and Constantinople. There she was married to her cousin, João Miguez, or Joseph Nasi, Duke of Naxos. After Joseph's death, she devoted a large part of her fortune to Jewish learning.

[7] The statement is actually Usque's, possibly based on a combination of statements in Plato's *Philebus* (ed. B. Jowett, New York, 1937), pp. 375 f.; *Laws*, V (p. 500), and perhaps *The Republic*, X (p. 861).

[8] That is, they remain Christians.

[9] This is one of Usque's major themes. See my Introduction above, pp. 9 f.

[10] See Appendix B, p. 270.

[11] Usque is referring to the prophecies of the Bible, favorable and unfavorable to Israel, all of which were considered to be the word of God.

[12] That is, the entire people of Israel. Usque likes to speak of Jacob as the head of the body of Israel and of the people of Israel as limbs of the body. Using pastoral metaphors, he often allows Ycabo the shepherd to call the children of Israel his lambs and sheep.

[13] That is, Jacob is known as Israel. See Gen. 32.29.

[14] In Hebrew the letters would be the same. יַעֲקֹב would become עַיְקֹב (Ycabo).

[15] I Sam. 4.21 ff. Eli's grandson was named Ichabod.

[16] Usque calls them "the Portuguese," a term commonly used in European circles outside of the Iberian Peninsula to refer to the Portuguese New Christians during the age in which Usque lived. Cf. Dialogue III, n. 118.

[17] That is, Usque is speaking primarily to the Portuguese Marranos.

DIALOGUE I

[1] Usque has in mind the spices, ivory and other valuable commodities which Portuguese sailors were bringing from the East.

[2] That is, because of the wealth brought into it from all other continents.

[3] This is one of the numerous mixed metaphors found in the *Consolaçam*.

[4] That is, the Holy Land.

[5] Usque is fond of describing the Holy Land, the Jewish people and other worthies as stately birds.

[6] Usque will discuss these events below. See below, p. 55. This took place during the reign of Alexander Jannaeus.

[7] See below, p. 55.

[8] See below, pp. 56 ff.

[9] See below, pp. 64 f.

[10] See below, p. 63.

[11] Note that by synecdoche, Jacob stands for all Israel.

[12] See above, n. 12 to Usque's Prologue.

[13] Yranio is also mentioned (in the form Yronio) at the end of Dialogue II (see p. 164). A note in the margin of Usque's text identifies Yranio as the prophet Isaiah.

[14] See Josephus, *Antiquities*, I. 1, 3, Abravanel and the rabbinic commentaries to Gen. 2.10-14. The reference is to Mesopotamia.

[15] Inhabitants of the western littoral region of equatorial Africa. This region had been in the limelight in Portugal since the beginning of the era of the African discoveries.

[16] The Tartars (or Tatars) were descendants of the Mongol invaders who swept across Asia Minor and Europe in the thirteenth century. In Usque's day they dwelt in large numbers in Asia Minor.

[17] Cf. II Kings 2.11. The place of Elijah's abode is not mentioned.

[18] That of loss or injury to his flock.

[19] This idea, as old as Plato, is found in the Stoics, Philo, Christianity and Neoplatonism. Usque's exact source, if any, is therefore difficult to determine. See W. Windelband, *A History of Philosophy*, vol. I (Chicago, 1901), pp. 229 ff.

[20] Gen. 27.

[21] *Ibid.*, 29.

[22] *Ibid.*, 31.

[23] *Ibid.*, 32-33.

[24] *Ibid.*, 30, 35.16 ff.

[25] See I Kings 9.28.

[26] The sacred plant among the Greeks, with which the victors in the Pythian games were crowned. It became the symbol of victory among both Greeks and Romans.

[27] A shepherd's cap worn as a protection against the sun.

[28] Gen. 18.16 ff. On Usque's view of sin and punishment, see Dialogue III, pp. 224 ff.

[29] Gen. 22. In the Middle Ages, influenced by Christian doctrine, the Akedah, the story of Isaac's readiness to be sacrificed for God's will, became the Jewish expression of vicarious atonement for future generations. The phrase "a sacrifice without blemish" goes back to the New Testament, I Peter 1.19.

[30] Mal. 1.2-3.

[31] Gen. 46.5 ff.; Ex. 1.1-5.

[32] Ex. 1.8 ff.

[33] The expression seems to be derived from the Passover *Haggadah* (ed. E. D. Goldschmidt, New York, 1953, pp. 48 ff.) rather than from the Bible. Cf. Pesaḥim X.5.

[34] Ex. 14.29.

[35] *Ibid.*, 13.20-22.

[36] *Ibid.*, 17.6.

[37] *Ibid.*, 16.14 ff. Rabbinic tradition calls it angel's food. See the rabbinic commentators to Ps. 78.25. The Midrash to Ps. 78.4 states that the manna was called the food of angels because the Israelites who ate it became as mighty as angels. The Talmud (Yoma 75a-b) attributes marvelous qualities to the manna and relates that when it descended it was accompanied by precious stones and also by cosmetics for women!

[38] Ex. 16.13.

[39] Deut. 32.7, into which the rabbis read an allusion to the future life. Cf. Rashi, *ad. loc.*

[40] Josh. 24.11.

[41] Ex. 3.8; 3.17 and *passim*.

[42] Gen. 28.17.

[43] This spot is identified in the Midrash with the site of the Temple. The

stone on which Jacob rested was said to have been Eben Shetiyah, the foundation stone at the center of the sanctuary. *Pirke Rabbi Eliezer*, XXXV. Cf. Rashi on Gen. 28.18. The concept that the terrestrial sanctuary is placed opposite the celestial one is widespread and ancient. Cf. *J. Berakhot*, V. 8c; *Genesis Rabba* (Vilna ed.) LV. 7. Cf. Yalkut to Gen. S. 101 and Ta'anit 16a.

[44] According to the Midrash, Adam's sons sacrificed on the spot where the altar was to be erected in Jerusalem. *Genesis Rabba* XXII.5; cf. *Pirke Rabbi Eliezer* (ed. Warsaw, 1852), XXXI. After his expulsion from Paradise, Adam is said to have come to Mount Moriah. *Pirke Rabbi Eliezer*, XX; *Targum Jonathan* to Gen. 3.23. Cf. I. Abravanel, *Commentary on the Pentateuch, ad. loc.*, and Appendix B.

[45] I Kings 6.2.

[46] For a description of the Temple, see I Kings 6 and I. Abravanel, *Commentary on the Early Prophets, ad. loc.* Usque appears also to have relied on Josephus' description in *Antiquities*, VIII, 5. Corinthian architecture is mentioned in VIII. 5, 2, but the idea of Corinthian bronze seems to have come from *The Jewish War*, V.3, 3. The insertion of Corinth appears to be an anachronism based on Herod's temple. See S. Krauss, "Corinth," *Jewish Encyclopedia*, IV, p. 278.

[47] I. Abravanel, *loc. cit.* Cf. also Philo, *Questions and Answers on Exodus*, II, 92; *On the Life of Moses*, II, 87. The designation "Babylonian" does not, however, appear here.

[48] I. Abravanel, *loc. cit.*; cf. also Philo, *Questions . . . on Exodus*, II, 85; *On Mating with the Preliminary Studies*, 116-118; *On the Life of Moses*, II, 84-88.

[49] I. Abravanel, *loc. cit.*; cf. also Philo, *Questions . . . on Exodus*, II, 78, 104; *On the Special Laws*, I, 296-298.

[50] I. Abravanel, *loc. cit.*; cf. also Philo, *On the Special Laws*, II, 161, and Lev. 24.5 ff.

[51] Cf. Philo, *Questions . . . on Exodus*, II, 71. This passage, however, does not number the essences. It is not found in Abravanel.

[52] Philo, *On the Life of Moses*, II, 74-76. Cf. Ex. 25. I. Abravanel, *loc. cit.* (p. 518, col. 1) avers that Solomon's temple differed from the pattern given to Moses.

[53] I Kings 8.27.

[54] I. Abravanel, *loc. cit.*

[55] Zech. 3.7, and rabbinic commentators *ad. loc.*

[56] Ezek. 34.10 ff.; Ps. 23.1.

[57] Prov. 3.18.

[58] Note how Usque shifts his metaphors. The sages were previously called shepherds.

[59] I Sam. 25.29. The phrase is well known. Cf. *Targum* and rabbinic commentaries, *ad. loc.* It is also found in the Midrash and Talmud.

[60] Cf. Ḥagigah 12b, where the concept of heavenly treasuries is linked to that of the souls of the righteous.

[61] See n. 19 above.

[62] I Kings 17.6. The ravens were considered messengers of God. See I Kings 17.4 and Kimhi, *ad. loc.*

[63] Berakhot 17a.

[64] Based on Eccl. 7.1. Death for the righteous is considered to be a release from the "Ayin Harah." *Genesis Rabba* IX. Though dead, they continue to live (Berakhot 18a). Resurrection is reserved for the righteous alone (Ta'anit 7a; *Genesis Rabba* XIII.6).

[65] Usque here is thinking of the celestial and terrestrial Jerusalem. On the celestial Jerusalem, cf. n. 43 above.

[66] I Kings 19.12.

[67] The idea of the planetary spheres was widespread during the Middle Ages

and the Renaissance, as was the concept of the harmony of the spheres. The latter developed out of an analogy first drawn by the Pythagoreans between the harmony in the motion of the heavenly bodies and the harmony in music. See W. Windelband, *op. cit.*, p. 45.

[68] Cf. the Sanctification (*Kedushah*) for the Additional Service of the Sephardic ritual. Cf. *Siddur Otsar ha-Tefilot*, I (New York, 1946), pp. 728 f.

[69] That is, the Garden of Eden.

[70] Cf. the Passover *Haggadah, ed. cit.*, p. 36.

[71] Num. 24.5.

[72] The Urim and Thummin were objects connected with the high priests' breastplate (Ex. 28.30), but probably originally connected with or serving as an oracle. On its cessation with the destruction of the Temple, see Sotah 9.12, Yoma 21b, J. Kiddushin 65b. Most of these miracles are enumerated in I. Abravanel, *Commentary on the Early Prophets*, to I Kings 8.

[73] This reference seems to be to the stream that was said to have begun the Holy of Holies and in which the ritually impure were cleansed. Cf. Yoma 77b-78a.

[74] Num. 19.2 ff.; cf. M. Parah.

[75] See Judg. 6.21, I Kings 18.38. Such a fire was regarded in rabbinic literature as having continued throughout the period of the First Temple but as having irrevocably ceased with its destruction. See Yoma 21b.

[76] Abot 5.6; Yoma 21b.

[77] The injunction against using tools is found in Ex. 20.22. The insect Shamir was a legendary creature, depicted as a worm which was endowed with the ability of cutting through stones on which it was placed. Sotah IX.12; Tosefta Sotah XV.1. Cf. Abot V.6; Pesaḥim 54a; Sifre, Deut. CCLV.

[78] According to the Mishnah (Yoma 6.8) it was a thread of crimson wool, tied to the door of the sanctuary in accordance with the rite prescribed in Lev. 16. The thread miraculously turned white to indicate the remission of Israel's sins. The implication that it changed to many colors is an exaggeration on Usque's part.

[79] Cf. Isa. 40.7; Job 14.2. In the New Testament it is found in James 1.10-11; I Peter 1.24. Cf. the High Holy Day Liturgy, Yom Kippur, musaf, *Unthane Tokef*, H. Adler, ed., *Service of the Synagogue, Day of Atonement*, II (New York, 1908), p. 150.

[80] Ezek. 20.13; Hos. 6.7.

[81] Jer. 2.13; 17.13.

[82] Hos. 13.15.

[83] There are really thirty-three, as can be seen below. The twelve occasions on which foreign enemies hurt the Jews are to be found in paragraphs 1 to 7. A marginal note, however, states "six occasions before the period of the [Hebrew] kings; then [persecutions by] Shishak, Assyria, Nebuchadnezzar, Antiochus, Pompey [and] Titus."

[84] The numeration of these sections is my own. Sections 1-4 contain material which will be found later in Dialogue I; sections 5-13 contain material which Usque will discuss in their historical sequence in Dialogue II. See Dialogue II, n. 1.

[85] Cf. below, pp. 70 ff.

[86] Josh. 23.7-16 and Judg. 2.6 ff.

[87] I Kings 14.25 f.; II Chron. 12.9 f.

[88] Ex. 12.35 f.

[89] II Kings 17.6; 18.11.

[90] *Ibid.*, 24 f.

[91] Cf. above, Introduction, p. 18.

[92] Jer. 25.12.

[93] Ezra 1.2.

[94] Josephus, *The Jewish War*, I. 1, 1 ff.; *Antiquities*, XII. 5, 3 ff.

[95] *Yosippon* (ed. Günzburg, Berditchev, 1896-1913), cols. 193-195; *The Jewish War*, I. 4, 2; *Antiquities*, XIII. 13.
[96] They believed that their continued ministrations would avert further calamities for the Israelites.
[97] *Yosippon*, cols. 221-222.
[98] *Ibid.*, col. 259 (cf. col. 274). By this act he blemished Hyrcanus and thereby disqualified him from the pontificate.
[99] *The Jewish War*, I. 19, 2; *Antiquities*, XV. 5, 2. The interpretation is Usque's.
[100] Cf. I Sam. 8.5 ff. Note how Usque continues to interpret history in the light of Israel's defection from the will of God.
[101] *The Jewish War*, I. 33, 2; *Antiquities*, XVII. 6, 2. Those "who drew sustenance from the full breasts of the Divine Law" were scholars who were urged by two illustrious teachers, Judas, son of Sepphoraeus, and Mattathiah (Matthias), son of Margalus, to avenge God by destroying the images and eagle that Herod had erected.
[102] *Yosippon*, col. 354.
[103] Ycabo is addressing the people of Israel.
[104] *The Jewish War*, II. 3, 2 ff.; *Antiquities*, XVII. 10, 1 f.
[105] *The Jewish War*, II. 4, 2.
[106] *Ibid.*, III. 2-IV. 2.
[107] *Ibid.*, III. 7, 32. However, those slain on Mt. Gerizim were not fugitives from Galilee but Samaritans (67 C.E.).
[108] *Ibid.*, III. 7, 21.
[109] *Yosippon*, cols. 357, 361.
[110] *The Jewish War*, II. 12, 1.
[111] *Ibid.*, II. 18, 1.
[112] *Yosippon*, cols. 375-376.
[113] *Ibid.*, cols. 376-380.
[114] *The Jewish War*, II. 18, 7 f. Josephus lists 50,000 slain.
[115] *Ibid.*, II. 20, 2. Josephus lists 10,500 victims.
[116] *Ibid.*, III. 2, 3.
[117] An ancient district of Asia, south of the Caspian Sea and bounded on the east by the river Oxus. It is mentioned in Strabo, Xenophon and frequently in pastoral literature of the Renaissance.
[118] *The Jewish War*, III. 10, 10. Josephus lists 6,500 dead.
[119] *Ibid.*, IV. 2, 5. Josephus lists 6,000 slain.
[120] *Ibid.*, IV. 5, 1-4; 6, 1. Hananiah, Joshua and Zachariah were opponents of the Zealots. Niger was a military hero who gained fame for his prowess against the Romans at the battle of Ascalon (III. 2 ff.). *Ibid.*, II, 19-20.
[121] *Ibid.*, IV. 7, 2.
[122] *Yosippon*, cols. 421-422. Cf. Josephus, *The Jewish War*, IV. 7, 4.
[123] *The Jewish War*, IV. 8, 2 ff. Cf. *Yosippon*, col. 427.
[124] *Yosippon*, cols. 443 ff. By "holiness" Usque clearly means "God" or the *Shekhinah*, God's Manifest Presence. He seems to overlook the fact that, according to rabbinic tradition, the *Shekhinah* did not visit the Second Temple.
[125] *Ibid.*, cols. 495-498.
[126] The eagle is the symbol of Rome; the "innermost and forbidden part" is the Temple's Sanctum Sanctorum.
[127] *The Jewish War*, VI. 4, 5-5, 2.
[128] That is, the terrestrial and the spiritual (Satan).
[129] The allusion is difficult. The phoenix, considered the immortal bird, becomes a symbol of immortal life and resurrection in both rabbinic and Christian literature. Cf. L. Ginzberg, *Legends of the Jews*, V (Philadelphia, 1910), p. 51, n. 151. Usque appears to be calling the Temple the source of eternal life. In addition, when the Temple was rebuilt, it "revived" like the phoenix.

[130] The Temple was the body that housed the *Shekhinah* (the spirit of God) on earth.

[131] This idea is as early as the Bible: Ezek. 22.30; Ps. 106.23.

[132] *The Jewish War*, VII. 3, 4.

[133] *Ibid.*, VII. 6, 1 and 5.

[134] *Ibid.*, VII. 8, 1 ff.

[135] *Ibid.*, VII. 10, 1.

[136] *Ibid.*, VI. 9, 2; VII. 2, 1.

[137] Isa. 3.16 ff.

[138] Cf. above, n. 4.

[139] Cf. above, n. 91.

[140] *The Jewish War*, VI. 8, 3; VII. 5, 5.

[141] *Ibid.*, VII. 5, 6.

[142] This defective title is found in the original.

[143] That is, the Temple.

[144] Josh. 24.21-24, 31.

[145] Ex. 1.6, 8.

[146] Judg. 3.5-7. Usque's eagerness to insert the name of the goddess Astarte (Ashtarot) whom the Bible often mentions together with Baal [Judg. 2.13; 10.6; I Sam. 7.4, 12.10] makes him overlook the fact that the Bible here reads "Asherot."

[147] Josh. 24.21.

[148] Note that Usque believes that Aram and Naharaim are different places and that the Hebrews were deported by Cushan-Rishathaim and then by subsequent oppressors.

[149] Judg. 3.8-31.

[150] *Ibid.*, 4.1-5, 21.

[151] *Ibid.*, 6.25-40.

[152] *Ibid.*, ch. 7.

[153] *Ibid.*, 8.22 f.

[154] *Ibid.*, 8.33.

[155] *Ibid.*, 9.1-5.

[156] *Ibid.*, 9.50 ff.

[157] *Ibid.*, 10.1-8.

[158] *Ibid.*, 11.9 ff.

[159] *Ibid.*, 12.8-10; 13-15. Usque omits Elon the Zebulonite, who judged ten years.

[160] *Ibid.*, 13.1.

[161] *Ibid.*, 15.15-16. The Bible says that Samson used "a new jawbone of an ass."

[162] *Ibid.*, 16.1-20.

[163] *Ibid.*, 19.2 ff.

[164] *Ibid.*, 19.29. According to the Bible, the Levite divided her into twelve pieces.

[165] *Ibid.*, 20.1 ff.

[166] I Sam. 4.18. Cf. Usque's Prologue, p. 40, and n. 15.

[167] *Ibid.*, 5.1-11.

[168] *Ibid.*, 6.1-12.

[169] Gen. 25.27. Ishmael and Esau may, as they did in subsequent Jewish tradition, refer respectively to Islam and Christianity.

[170] This section deals only with the kings of the United Monarchy. It is immediately followed by a survey of the Northern Kingdom (Israel) from Jeroboam I to the Assyrian captivity. Usque, although relying entirely on the biblical account, separates the history of Judah from that of Israel and places it later.

[171] I Sam. 8.11 ff.

[172] *Ibid.*, 8.5.

[173] *Ibid.*, 9.2, 10.
[174] *Ibid.*, 14.32.
[175] *Ibid.*, 13.8 ff.
[176] *Ibid.*, 15.9.
[177] *Ibid.*, 31.4.
[178] *Ibid.*, 17.4 ff.
[179] II Sam. 23.17; I Chron. 11.19.
[180] II Sam. 12 and 13 and I. Abravanel's commentary, *ad. loc.*
[181] II Sam. 11 and 12.
[182] II Sam. 13.30-19.9.
[183] *Ibid.*, 24.1.
[184] *Ibid.*, vv. 12-15.
[185] I Kings 1-7.
[186] *Ibid.*, 11.1 ff.
[187] *Ibid.*, 11.29-33.
[188] *Ibid.*, 13.4.
[189] *Ibid.*, 15.25-31.
[190] *Ibid.*, 15.33-16.5.
[191] *Ibid.*, 16.8-20.
[192] *Ibid.*, 16.21-31.
[193] *Ibid.*, 21.1 ff.
[194] *Ibid.*, 17.1 ff.
[195] II Kings 2.11.
[196] I Kings 18.20-40.
[197] *Ibid.*, 21.19 ff.; 22.29-38.
[198] II Kings 10.1-11.
[199] *Ibid.*, 6.28 f.
[200] *Ibid.*, 6.8-23.
[201] *Ibid.*, 10.18-30.
[202] The wheel was a symbol of fortune or misfortune.
[203] II Kings 12.18.
[204] See Appendix B, p. 274.
[205] II Kings 13.5.
[206] Ycabo's complaint is that Israel failed to regard its previous sufferings as divine visitations for its sins.
[207] II Kings 14.14.
[208] *Ibid.*, 13.14-21.
[209] *Ibid.*, 14.23.
[210] *Ibid.*, 15.8-10. Jehu was Zechariah's great-great grandfather (Jehu—Jehoahaz—Joash—Jeroboam II—Zechariah).
[211] *Ibid.*, 15.14 ff.
[212] *Ibid.*, 16-27. Regarding Pekah, who actually reigned two years (*ca.* 737-736), Usque follows the biblical account, which states he reigned twenty.
[213] See n. 5, above.
[214] II Kings 15.29. The king was Tiglath-pileser IV (745-727). The Bible mentions only six cities "and Galilee." Perhaps Usque counted Galilee as one city and Abel-beth-maacah as three.
[215] The incident is not mentioned in the Bible.
[216] II Kings 15.30; 17.1 ff.
[217] II Kings 18.9 ff.
[218] That is, the Holy Land. The Holy Land is considered by Jewish tradition to be the center of the earth; Jerusalem is located in the center of Palestine and the Temple in the center of Jerusalem. Cf. L. Ginzberg, *op. cit.*, V, p. 14, n. 39 and p. 19, n. 55.
[219] Usque means the Northern Kingdom (Israel) only.
[220] Cf. Ps. 137.1.
[221] II Kings 17.6.

[222] Cf. below, p. 273.

[223] II Kings 17.24 ff.

[224] Usque does not include Zimri or Jehu in this group. Jehu perhaps because of his zeal for God in the destruction of the priests of Baal. (II Kings 10.18-30.) Zimri is mentioned later in this section.

[225] That is, as long as the people sacrificed in the Temple, they still merited some protection from God.

[226] In the original there is a confusion of persons. Usque, apparently forgetting that Ycabo represents the people Israel, has him say of the people (the *ligeiro veado e mudauel povo*): *O qual saydo que era de suas casinhas e abrigo, desatinado teu fauor, abreuoute de agoas,* etc.

[227] That is, the Holy Land.

[228] A sign of mourning.

[229] Lam. 1.1.

[230] Isa. 54.5; Jer. 3.20; Hos. 2.18.

[231] This seems to be based on an account such as the one of *Midrash Wa-Yosha* in J. D. Eisenstein's *Otzar Midrashim,* I (New York, 1956), pp. 148 f. Cf. Yalkut to Exodus, 234.

[232] Jer. 3.20.

[233] Cf. the statements by Ginzberg, *op. cit.,* V, pp. 150-151 on the prominence of this theme.

[234] This detail is unusual. We would expect mention of the mountain(s) in the district of Ararat. Cf., however, Josephus, *Antiquities,* I. 3, 5 f. who speaks of "the place of descent" and, incidentally, quotes Nicholas of Damascus, who calls it Baris.

[235] Gen. 9.22. Josephus, *Antiquities,* I. 6, 3. On Ham as a sorcerer, cf. Clement of Rome, *Recognitiones,* I. 30 and IV. 28-29.

[236] So writes Usque. Cf. Josephus, *Antiquities,* I. 6, 2.

[237] Usque's source, or Usque himself, combines the names and functions of mythological characters. To trace these, see a work like A. Harper, *A Dictionary of Classical Antiquities,* and the bibliographies cited there. In this and the following notes some details will be given to enable the reader to follow the text.

Saturn, originally a mythical king of Italy, who was credited with the introduction of agriculture and civilized life in general, was later identified with Cronus, the god of time, and Baal.

[238] The relation of Asshur to Nimrod is not given in the Bible (Gen. 10.8-11). Furthermore, it is Josephus (*Antiquities,* I. 4, 2) who ascribes the building of the tower of Babel to Nimrod.

[239] The derivation seems to have been invented by Usque on the basis of *Antiquities,* I. 6, 4.

[240] Sabazius was a Thracian and Phrygian dying and resurrecting deity, often identified with Baal, representing the flourishing and dying cycle of nature.

[241] Not Tethys, but Ceres. The term "Tithea" appears to be a Hebraism, from a word like ציץ or ציצה to express the qualities attributed to Ceres.

[242] Josephus, *Antiquities,* I. 3, 9.

[243] Noah here is identified with Saturn (with whom the Romans in turn identified Chronus).

[244] On the worship of Noah (and his identification with Bel, Baal Pe'or and Bel-Zebub), cf. Abravanel, *Commentary to the Pentateuch,* Parasha Noah, p. 33b, col. 2.

[245] Celo means heaven; Arithia is a derivation from the Hebrew *Eretz,* or earth.

[246] It is interesting that Gedaliah ibn Yahia borrows this section almost verbatim from Usque. *Shalshelet ha-Kabbala* (Amsterdam, 1679), p. 75.

[247] Gen. 9.20.

[248] Usque uses the Hebrew word. יין is the Hebrew word for "wine."

[249] *Yosippon*, cols. 19-27.

[250] *Ibid.*, cols. 29-33. The ultimate source is the apocryphal addition to Daniel, known as "Bel and the Dragon."

[251] Isa. 46.1.

[252] *Ibid.*; Ps. 115.7.

[253] See above, p. 21.

[254] Isa. 40.19.

[255] *Ibid.*, 63.6; Ezek. 22.20; Ps. 78.49; Isa. 13.9.

[256] See below, p. 220.

[257] Jer. 31.15.

[258] Deut. 28.29; Job 5.14.

[259] That is, the good inclination or the *Yetzer ha-Tov* of rabbinic tradition.

[260] Isa. 40.1.

[261] *Ibid.*, 55.8 f.

[262] Ex. 32.

[263] Cf. above, pp. 70 ff.

[264] Cf. above, *ibid.* Usque, of course, enumerates five instances.

[265] I Kings 20.1 ff. Usque again exaggerates in the last sentence. It was Ben-hadad's servants, not his allies, who came to kneel before Ahab (*ibid.*, vv. 31 ff.).

[266] II Kings 7.6-7.

[267] That is, the ten lost tribes. See p. 79 above.

[268] The word "Assyria" is added by Usque.

[269] That is, which of the harbingers of the Messianic kingdom. The Talmud (Sukkah 52b) lists four distinguished personages commonly mentioned as Messiahs or Messianic precursors—Messiah, son of David, Messiah, son of Joseph, Elijah, and the priest of justice (Melchizedek?). The Messiah ben Ephraim is often included, and is mentioned by Usque (Dialogue III, ed. Mendes dos Remédios f. 70a margin). For practical purposes the Messiah of Ephraim and the Messiah of Joseph are identical. See L. Ginzberg, *Eine unbekannte jüdische Sekte*, I (New York, 1922), p. 339.

[270] The word for chapter appears abbreviated in the original.

[271] That is, as divine retribution.

[272] I Kings 14.25 ff.; II Chron. 12.2 ff.

[273] I Kings 12.1 ff.; 14.21 ff.; 15.1-8.

[274] *Ibid.*, 15.9 ff.

[275] *Ibid.*, 15.24; 22.2 ff.

[276] II Kings 8.16 ff.

[277] *Ibid.*, 8.25-9.23.

[278] *Ibid.*, 11.1-16.

[279] That is, with Jacob (Israel).

[280] II Kings 11.17 ff.

[281] *Ibid.*, 12.

[282] *Ibid.*, 14.1 ff. Amaziah, however, ruled for twenty-nine years, according to the Bible. Note Usque's explanation for the king's violent death.

[283] II Kings 15.1-7.

[284] Sin and virtue are both depicted as wheels. The wheel is one of Usque's favorite symbols. Cf. p. 77.

[285] II Kings 15.37.

[286] *Ibid.*, 18.13. Cf. *Numbers Rabba* XVI. 25 and Appendix B, nn. 58 and 60. Usque seems to have confused a later invasion, by Sennacherib, king of Assyria, with the Syrian Rezin's attack. See II Kings 18.13, which event took place in the days of Ahaz's son, Hezekiah; or possibly, it may refer to the Arameans' (Syrians') defeat of Judah in the days of Ahaz (II Chron. 28.4 ff.).

[287] II Kings 16.

[288] *Ibid.*, 18.1 ff.

[289] That is, Satan. The term Azazel comes from Lev. 16.10. The Azazel, the

atonement scapegoat, became in rabbinic literature the symbol of impurity. In the Book of Enoch (chs. 8, 13) Azazel is represented as the leader of the rebellious angels. Azazel is also depicted as a seducer of men and women (Yalkut to Gen. 44,38b). It was Origen, however, who made the identification of Azazel with Satan (*Against Celsus*, VI, 43).

[290] II Kings 19.35 ff. Cf. II Chron. 32.20 ff. Sennacherib was slain by two sons of his, Adrammelech and Sarezer.

[291] II Kings 20.1 ff.

[292] II Kings 20.16 ff.

[293] *Ibid.*, 21.1 ff.

[294] *Ibid.*, 21.19 ff.

[295] *Ibid.*, 22.1 ff.

[296] "Judah" seems to mean "Israel and Judah."

[297] II Kings 23.29.

[298] *Ibid.*, 23.31-33.

[299] *Ibid.*, 23.34 ff.; II Chron. 36.5 ff. Usque collates and confuses these two accounts.

[300] II Kings 24.1-17.

[301] Cf. above, n. 130.

[302] II Kings 25.1-12.

[303] *Ibid.*, 25.27 ff. Jehoiachin's release from prison occurred not at the end of the captivity, but in the thirty-seventh year.

[304] That is, in Judah.

[305] Omitted are Asa, Jehoshaphat, Jehoash, Amaziah, Azariah, Jotham, Josiah. These are the Judean kings whom the Bible calls righteous and whom Usque calls "eight plants which bore healthful and choice fruit." Cf. below, p. 106.

[306] The reference here is to the translation of the *Shekhinah* to heaven. Cf. above, nn. 129 and 130.

[307] Cf. above, n. 12 to Usque's Introduction.

[308] See n. 286 above.

[309] Job 3.6.

[310] That is, the light of the Temple in Jerusalem.

[311] See Yoma 9b, and my Introduction above, p. 18.

[312] Cf. below, Dialogue II, pp. 115 f.

[313] Isa. 9.20.

[314] *Ibid.*, 10.15.

[315] Ps. 44.23; Isa. 53.7.

[316] Job 3.20.

[317] *Ibid.*, 3.11 ff.

[318] *Ibid.*, 10.7 ff.; 14.1 ff.

[319] That is, the terrestrial and celestial.

[320] The idea of God's having created the world with a single word may have come from rabbinic literature (cf. *Mekhilta, Beshalakh*, section 10), from Philo's *Logos* or the corresponding term in the New Testament (John 1.1). See also Abot V. 1, where God is said to have created the world with ten words.

[321] See *Targum* Jonathan to Ex. 14.21.

[322] Ex. 15.8.

[323] *Ibid.*, 17.6.

[324] Yoma 73a-b; I. Abravanel, *Commentary on the Early Prophets*, to I Kings 8.

[325] Cf. above, p. 59.

[326] Cf. above, pp. 58, 62, 63.

[327] This probably refers to the slaughter at Engaddi. Cf. above, *ibid.*

[328] Jer. 30.12.

[329] Ezek. 1.

[330] Dan., *passim*, esp. ch. 7. The third animal in the Bible account is most likely a type of leopard.

[331] This seems to be written in the spirit of Job's lament.

[332] Usque correctly writes "*hum thau*": the *Tav* in the Hebrew script of Ezekiel's time was written *x*.

[333] Jer. 25.11 f.; 29.10.

[334] Usque is referring to the fact that the Jews returned from the Babylonian captivity and were not lost like the Ten Tribes of Israel.

DIALOGUE II

Preliminary Note

In this chapter Usque relied heavily upon the *Yosippon*, or Pseudo-Josephus. Its historical facts—names, dates, explanations—as can be seen by even a cursory comparison with the authentic Josephus, are extremely inaccurate, and it cloaks them in numerous legends culled from various sources. It is impossible to devote space in these notes to the lengthy discussion of the problems and errors inherent in Usque's source: these belong more properly in an annotated translation of the *Yosippon* itself. Such a translation is presently being prepared under my super-vision. It will, however, be helpful to the reader to be aware of the dates of some of the epochal events in the period covered by Dialogue II. These are:

539 B.C.E.	The Persians under Cyrus capture Babylon and permit the Jews to return to the Holy Land.
520-515 B.C.E.	The Second Temple is constructed.
Mid 5th century	The Return under Ezra.
331 B.C.E.	Beginning of the Greek era in the Holy Land, as Alexander the Great passes through it.
323 B.C.E.	Death of Alexander the Great.
305-285 B.C.E.	Ptolemy I of Egypt: The Greek translation of Scrip-ture (the Septuagint).
168 B.C.E.	The Antiochian persecution and the Maccabean revolt.
165 B.C.E.	The rededication of the Temple.
160 B.C.E.	The death of Judah Maccabee.
142 B.C.E.	The death of Jonathan.
142-135 B.C.E.	The ethnarchate of Simon Maccabee.
135-104 B.C.E.	The rule of John Hyrcan(us).
104-103 B.C.E.	The reign of Aristobulus.
103-76 B.C.E.	The reign of Alexander (Jannai).
76-67 B.C.E.	The reign of Salome Alexandra.
67 B.C.E.	Civil War between Hyrcanus and Aristobulus.
39 B.C.E.	Herod named king. Reigns 37-4 B.C.E.
4 B.C.E.-41 C.E.	Partition of Herod's kingdom; rule of Archelaus, Antipas and Philip; rule of procurators in Judea; rise of Agrippa.
41-44 C.E.	Agrippa I.
50-100 C.E.	Agrippa II.
66-73 C.E.	The War with Rome. Temple destroyed 70 C.E.
115-116 C.E.	Jews of Cyrene, Cyprus and Egypt revolt.
132-135 C.E.	The Bar Kokhba Rebellion.

[1] II Kings 25.27 ff.; Jer. 52.31.

[2] Dan. 5.1 ff.

[3] *Yosippon*, cols. 15 f. Cf. Josephus, *Antiquities*, X. 11, 2, and Dan. 5.1-28.

[4] That is, Aramaic. Usque's text omits the expression "he weighed" at this point, but explains it below.

[5] Dan. 5.25-28.

[6] Jer. 29.10 ff. The captivity is that of Babylonia.

[7] Usque writes "Nebuchadnezzar." The *Yosippon* does not mention Nebuchad-

nezzar. Could Usque's confusion have resulted from a recollection of Josephus' *Antiquities*, X. 10, 3 ff. or from Dan. 2.4, where Daniel interprets Nebuchadnezzar's dreams?

[8] *Yosippon*, col. 17.
[9] *Ibid.*, col. 18.
[10] *Ibid.* Cf. Isa. 13.17; Jer. 50.29 ff., 51.6 and 24.
[11] That is, his rule over Babylonia.
[12] Ezra 1.11.
[13] *Yosippon*, col. 28. Cf. *Antiquities*, XI. 1, 1 ff.
[14] Ezra 3.10-13. Usque's text is corrupt. He speaks of the *choro alegre* of the old timers, but the sense of the passage forces us to translate *choro triste*.
[15] Ezra 4.5.
[16] *Ibid.*, 6, 14 f.
[17] *Ibid.*, 7.
[18] Neh. 4.
[19] Cf. Dialogue I, n. 5.
[20] Neh. 8.
[21] Note the mixed metaphor. Ycabo represents the entire people. He was slain and resurrected, that is, some of the people were slain and others arose in their place.
[22] Isa. 10.5.
[23] *Ibid.*, 13.17-18.
[24] *Ibid.*, 13.19.
[25] Note Usque's felt need to explain the word "satyrs."
[26] Isa. 14.14.
[27] Ps. 113.9. The woman is, of course, the Holy Land.
[28] Isa. 17.14.
[29] I. Abravanel, *Commentary on the Early Prophets*, p. 526a (to I Kings 8). See also Dialogue I, p. 55.
[30] Abot 5.5; Yoma 21b.
[31] That is, it was forbidden to use ordinary fire.
[32] *Yosippon*, cols. 48 f. Cf. II Maccabees 2.4-5.
[33] *Ibid.*, cols. 63 f. Cf. *Antiquities*, XI. 8, 2.
[34] *Yosippon*, cols. 111 f. Cf. *Antiquities*, XII. 1 ff.
[35] *Yosippon*, col. 122.
[36] This is the translation known as the Septuagint. Usque's account is based on the *Yosippon*, ed. S. Münster (Worms, 1529). For this study I have used the Basel, 1559 edition. See pp. 5-8 and Appendix B, p. 271.
[37] Actually the words "I went down there" are not found in the Bible. In the form *va-ered* ("I went down") the numerical value of the Hebrew letters would total approximately 210 (211 to be exact). However, the only biblical parallel available is Deut. 26.5, where the third person, *va-yered* (numerical value 220) is found.
[38] Azariah de' Rossi, in his *Me'or 'Enayim* (Vilna, 1866), p. 130, borrows this explanation from the *Yosippon*. See also A. Geiger, *Judaism and its History* (New York, 1911), p. 147 f.: "Among the prohibited animals, the 'hare' is mentioned. Now, the Hebrew term would have required the word 'lagos' in the Greek version; but as the royal family was called the 'family of the Lagi,' the mention of this name in the law of the Jews would have given offense. They changed it and adopted a word which signifies 'hairy-footed,' 'thick-footed,' a word which they coined to avoid offense. Asses were used only by the lower classes for riding; but in Holy Writ they are mentioned as being often employed for riding in general; for this reason, the translators would not use the term, for fear to excite scorn and derision."
[39] In this section, Usque's text incorrectly reads "Seleucus" instead of "Ptolemy." Usque creates the impression that these Jews had been residing in Egypt for centuries, perhaps since Jacob's time.

[40] *Yosippon*, ed. Günzburg, col. 123. Cf. *Antiquities*, XII. 2, 8.

[41] Note how Usque continues to regard Israel's oppressions as brought on by his sins.

[42] *Yosippon*, *loc. cit*. Cf. *Antiquities*, XII. 4, 11 ff.

[43] *Yosippon*, col. 124.

[44] *Ibid*.

[45] *Ibid*., col. 125.

[46] That is, they would destroy their lives and lose their opportunity for life eternal.

[47] *Yosippon*, cols. 125 f. The statement "O Lord, now I recognize that You love me since You have led me to fulfill the precept 'You shall love the Lord with all your soul,'" derives ultimately from the account of Rabbi Akiba's martyrdom in Berakhot 61b.

[48] Usque's text appears to be defective. It says: "*porque afliges nossas almas que tu nos nam deste nem criaste?*"

[49] That is, by dying without breaking the laws of his faith.

[50] *Yosippon*, cols. 126-132.

[51] That is, the coming of Antiochus, the martyrdom of Eleazar, and that of Hannah and her seven sons.

[52] The idea that the suffering of the righteous atones for the sins of the community is found frequently in rabbinic literature. Cf. *Ex. Rabba* XLIII.6; Sanhedrin 39a. The expression "a pure lamb without blemish" derives from the New Testament, I Peter 1.19.

[53] *Yosippon*, col. 132 ff. Cf. Josephus, *Antiquities*, XII. 6, 1, and *The Jewish War*, I. 1, 3. Mattathiah was a priest of the sons of Joarib, but not the High Priest.

[54] *Yosippon*, col. 133.

[55] *Ibid*., col. 134.

[56] *Ibid*., col. 134 f. Antiochus and his followers, though Syrian Greeks, regarded themselves as successors of Alexander the Great, who came from Macedonia, and they are therefore referred to as "Macedonians." Cf. II Maccabees 8.20.

[57] *Yosippon*, col. 142. Cf. *Antiquities*, XII. 7, 6; *The Jewish War*, I. 1, 4.

[58] *Yosippon*, col. 143. Cf. *Antiquities*, XII. 8, 4.

[59] *Yosippon*, col. 148.

[60] *Ibid*., cols. 152 f.

[61] *Ibid*., col. 156.

[62] *Ibid*., cols. 157 f. Cf. *Antiquities*, XII. 9, 4.

[63] *Yosippon*, cols. 163-5. Cf. *Antiquities*, XII. 11, 2.

[64] *Yosippon*, cols. 165-167. Cf. *Antiquities*, XIII. 1 ff.; *The Jewish War*, I. 2, 1.

[65] *Yosippon*, col. 167. Cf. *Antiquities*, XIII. 7, 4. Ptolemy was really Simon's son-in-law.

[66] *Yosippon*, cols. 167-170; cf. *Antiquities*, XIII. 8, 1.

[67] That is, Pharisees.

[68] *Yosippon*, cols. 177 f. Cf. *Antiquities*, XIII. 10, 6.

[69] *Yosippon*, col. 178.

[70] *Ibid*., cols. 178 f.

[71] *Ibid*.

[72] That is, he chose not to be both High Priest and king.

[73] *Yosippon*, cols. 180-186. Cf. *Antiquities*, XIII. 11, 1 ff.; *The Jewish War*, I. 3, 1 ff.

[74] *Yosippon*, cols. 186-188. Cf. *Antiquities*, XIII. 12, 2; *The Jewish War*, I. 4, 2.

[75] *Yosippon*, cols. 188 f.

[76] *Ibid*., col. 193. Cf. *Antiquities*, XIII. 13, 5.

[77] That is, the Pharisees.

[78] Demetrius came from the Seleucid empire and was forced to return to Syria, not to Greece.

[79] Usque's sources speak of eight hundred Pharisees. *Yosippon*, cols. 194 f. Cf. *Antiquities*, XIII. 14, 2.

[80] *Yosippon*, cols. 196 f. Cf. *Antiquities*, XIII. 15, 5 ff.

[81] *Yosippon*, cols. 197-204. Cf. *Antiquities*, XIII. 16, 1 ff.; *The Jewish War*, I. 5, 1 ff.

[82] *Yosippon*, cols. 204-206. Cf. *Antiquities*, XIV. 1, 2; *The Jewish War*, I. 6, 1.

[83] This account of Antipater's origin is legendary. Cf. the account in *Antiquities*, XIV. 1, 3, which is doubtless also a legend.

[84] *Yosippon*, cols. 206-209.

[85] *Ibid.*, cols. 209-211. Cf. *Antiquities*, XIV. 2, 1.

[86] *Yosippon*, cols. 212 f. Cf. *Antiquities*, XIV. 3, 1 ff.; *The Jewish War*, I. 7, 1 ff.

[87] *Yosippon*, cols. 219-223.

[88] *Ibid.*, col. 231.

[89] *Ibid.*, cols. 232 f. Cf. *Antiquities*, XIV. 7, 4; *The Jewish War*, I. 9, 1.

[90] *Yosippon*, cols. 237-246. Cf. *Antiquities*, XIV. 11, 3; *The Jewish War*, I. 11, 4.

[91] *Yosippon*, cols. 253-257. Cf. *Antiquities*, XIV. 13, 5 ff.; *The Jewish War*, I. 13, 1 ff. Usque omitted an important section of the *Yosippon* at this point.

[92] *Yosippon*, cols. 259, 274. He would be physically blemished and ineligible to continue in the High Priesthood.

[93] *Yosippon*, cols. 257-259. Cf. *Antiquities*, XIV. 14, 3; *The Jewish War*, I. 14, 3.

[94] *Yosippon*, cols. 259-268.

[95] Ycabo here is speaking as a contemporary of Usque. See my Introduction, p. 19 above.

[96] Babylonia.

[97] *Yosippon*, cols. 269-273. Cf. *Antiquities*, XV. 2, 3 ff.

[98] *Yosippon*, cols. 274-277. Cf. *Antiquities*, XV. 3, 1 ff.

[99] *Yosippon*, col. 277. Usque misread the *Yosippon* here. It was Herod who rallied at Alexandria.

[100] *Ibid.*, cols. 277-280. Cf. *Antiquities*, XV. 3. The word "offspring" refers to Herod's children by other wives.

[101] *Yosippon*, cols. 289-296.

[102] *Yosippon*, col. 297.

[103] *Ibid.* Cf. *Antiquities*, XV. 10, 1; XVI. 1, 2; *The Jewish War*, I. 23, 1 ff.

[104] *Yosippon*, cols. 304-311. Cf. *Antiquities*, XV. 11, 1 ff., and the Mishna Middot. Usque's description contains several original details.

[105] *Yosippon*, cols. 311-316. Cf. *Antiquities*, XVI. 3, 3.

[106] *Yosippon*, cols. 316-320. Cf. *Antiquities*, XVI. 8, 1 ff.

[107] *Yosippon*, cols. 324 f. Cf. *Antiquities*, XVI. 11, 4 ff.; *The Jewish War*, I. 27, 4 ff.

[108] This theological note, as well as others dealing with sin, the Adversary, and the divine guidance of history, are interpolated by Usque in his version of the *Yosippon* accounts. See above, pp. 22 ff.

[109] *Yosippon*, cols. 325 f. Cf. *Antiquities*, XVII. 1, 1; *The Jewish War*, I. 28, 2.

[110] Usque writes the Portuguese word for "parents."

[111] *Yosippon*, cols. 328-347. Cf. *Antiquities*, XVII. 1 ff.; *The Jewish War*, I. 30 ff.

[112] *Yosippon*, cols. 328-351. Cf. *Antiquities*, XVII. 6 f.; *The Jewish War*, I. 33.

[113] This was forbidden by the religious law.

[114] *Yosippon*, cols. 356 f. Cf. the Münster edition of the *Yosippon*, pp. 189 f. Cf. also *Antiquities*, XVII. 9 ff.; *The Jewish War*, II. 1 ff.

[115] This was a double offense against the religious law.
[116] *Yosippon*, col. 361. The Rabbi Johanan whom Usque has in mind is not the High Priest, but rather John the Baptist, as the *Yosippon* carefully states. See. Matt. 14.3-12; Mark 6.17 ff.; Luke 3.19 f. On the belief that John the Baptist was of priestly stock, see Luke 1.5 ff. Cf. *Antiquities*, XVIII. 5. Antipas called himself Herod.
[117] *Yosippon*, col. 361. Cf. *Antiquities*, XVIII. 6; *The Jewish War*, II. 9 ff.
[118] *Yosippon*, col. 364.
[119] *Ibid.*, col. 366. The text confuses Agrippa I with Agrippa II.
[120] This is, of course, the Temple.
[121] *Yosippon*, col. 367.
[122] *Ibid.*, cols. 367-373.
[123] Really the upper city. As Josephus explains (*The Jewish War*, II. 17, 5) "the seditious part had the lower city and the temple in their power."
[124] See my Introduction, pp. 18 ff., and n. 108 above.
[125] *Yosippon*, cols. 373-375. Cf. *The Jewish War*, II. 17 ff.
[126] *Yosippon*, cols. 375-379. The Simon here was Simon son of Saul and is not to be confused with Simon of Giora. Cf. below, p. 142.
[127] *Yosippon*, cols. 380-382.
[128] That is, as a signal for attack.
[129] *Ibid.*, cols. 384 f.
[130] *Ibid.*, col. 386. Cf. *The Jewish War*, III. 1 ff.
[131] *Yosippon, loc. cit.*
[132] The name Halah is the result of a misunderstanding of the Hebrew text which speaks of ארץ נפתלי והלאה *Yosippon*, col. 387. Usque was doubt-lessly thinking of the Halah in II Kings 17.6 and 18.11. The treasures spoken of were in Taricheae. See *The Jewish War*, II. 20, 5 ff. and cf. *Yosippon*, col. 389.
[133] *Yosippon*, col. 389.
[134] *Ibid.*, cols. 390-394.
[135] *Ibid.*, cols. 394-415. Cf. *The Jewish War*, III. 8, 1 ff.
[136] *Yosippon*, col. 416. Cf. *The Jewish War*, III. 9 f. (The *Yosippon* reads "Acco".)
[137] *Yosippon*, col. 417.
[138] *Ibid.*, cols. 417-419. Cf. *The Jewish War*, IV. 1 f.
[139] *Yosippon*, col. 419.
[140] *Ibid.*, cols. 419 f.
[141] *Yosippon*, ed. Münster, p. 217.
[142] *Ibid.* Josephus (*The Jewish War*, IV. 3, 8) calls him Phannias, son of Samuel.
[143] That is, the non-Jews.
[144] There were several cities so named, after Seleucus Nicator, who founded the Seleucid dynasty. The Seleucia mentioned here was no doubt Seleucia Pieria, located in Syria.
[145] *Yosippon*, ed. Münster, pp. 218 f. Cf. *The Jewish War*, IV. 4 ff.
[146] *Yosippon*, ed. Münster, pp. 219 f.
[147] *Ibid.*, pp. 220 f.
[148] *Ibid.*, pp. 221 f.
[149] *Yosippon*, ed. Günsburg, col. 421.
[150] The text of the *Consolaçam* incorrectly says "Titus."
[151] *Ibid.*, cols. 421 f.
[152] *Ibid.*, cols. 423-429. Cf. *The Jewish War*, IV. 9 f.
[153] *Yosippon*, ed. Münster, p. 225. This text says it was Vespasian, not Titus, who smote Agrippa. From Usque one almost gets the impression that Josephus smote the king!
[154] *Ibid.*, col. 429.
[155] *Yosippon*, col. 430. Cf. *The Jewish War*, V. 1 ff. Note Usque's desire to create the impression, here and below, that Rome was innocent and was

merely acting as God's instrument in the punishment of Israel. Later, however, he does include Rome among the nations destroyed for gloating over Israel's misfortune.

[156] *Yosippon*, cols. 431 f.

[157] *Ibid.*, cols. 438-440.

[158] *Ibid.*, cols. 440-451. Cf. *The Jewish War*, V. 7 ff.

[159] *Yosippon*, col. 455.

[160] *Ibid.*, cols. 473 f.

[161] *Ibid.*, col. 474.

[162] *Ibid.*, cols. 481 f.

[163] *Ibid.*, col. 482. Cf. *ibid.*, col. 522. The Sicarii (so-called because they carried daggers) were part of a group who wanted to expel the Romans from the Holy Land by force.

[164] *Yosippon*, cols. 482-492.

[165] *Ibid.* Cf. *The Jewish War*, V. 13, 7.

[166] *Yosippon*, cols. 495 f.

[167] *Ibid.*, cols. 496 f.

[168] *Ibid.*, cols. 497 f.

[169] Cf. nn. 41 and 155 above.

[170] *Yosippon*, cols. 500-502. Cf. *The Jewish War*, VI. 1, 1 ff.

[171] *Yosippon*, col. 503.

[172] *Ibid.*, cols. 503-508.

[173] *Ibid.*, cols. 508-510. Cf. n. 169 above.

[174] *Yosippon*, col. 508.

[175] *Ibid.*, cols. 510 f. Note Usque's attempt to make this situation resemble that of the ancient Hebrews' Eisodus into Egypt by his mention of the land of Goshen. Titus had actually sent them to Gophna, about twelve miles north of Jerusalem. See *The Jewish War*, VI. 2, 2.

[176] *Yosippon*, col. 512. Arustius is not mentioned here. He is mentioned in the Venice edition. See the Jerusalem, 1957, edition of this text, p. 374.

[177] *Yosippon*, cols. 513 f.

[178] *Yosippon*, cols. 516-519. Cf. *The Jewish War*, VI. 3 ff.

[179] *Yosippon*, cols. 519-522.

[180] *Ibid.*, cols. 524-526.

[181] *Ibid.*, col. 529.

[182] *Ibid.*, cols. 526 f.

[183] This seems to reflect a deliberate change by Usque of the story of the priests whom Titus refused to spare, a story which occurs at this point of the *Yosippon* (col. 530).

[184] *Yosippon*, col. 531.

[185] *Ibid.*, cols. 531 f. Cf. *Yosippon*, ed. Münster, p. 272.

[186] *Yosippon*, ed. Münster, p. 273. Cf. *The Jewish War*, VI. 9, 3.

[187] *Yosippon*, ed. Münster, pp. 274 f. Cf. *The Jewish War*, VII. 8 f. Eleazar was besieged not by Titus, but by Flavius Silva.

[188] Actually the Bar Kokhba rebellion aroused Jews throughout the Holy Land. Bethar, besieged for three and a half years by the Romans (132-135), was the site of the Jews' final and most heroic defense.

[189] Cf. *Yosippon*, ed. Münster, pp. 286 f., and pp. 398 ff. This account, however, does not carry the name Bar Kokhba. The margin of Usque's text bears the notation "Book of Sanhedrin, in the chapter which begins 'At three seasons' (he seems to have in mind Sanhedrin 93b, in the section 'Portion' [*Perek Helek*]; cf. also Ta'anit 31a, where Bethar is mentioned) and in the book 'Lamentations Rabba.'" On these citations, see Appendix B, pp. 274, 277 ff.

[190] Bar Kokhba (?). The reference is not clear.

[191] The original has the word for "stain."

[192] The Syrtis is one of two quicksands of the northern coast of Africa.

[193] Note how Usque keeps returning to the theme of idolatry and the zeal of the Israelites for their faith.

[194] *Yosippon*, cols. 61 f. Cf. *Antiquities*, XI. 8, 5. The numeration of the paragraphs is mine.

[195] *Yosippon*, cols. 118-121.

[196] See I Kings 19.11.

[197] Ibid., cols. 134 f. Cf. *Antiquities*, XII. 6, 1 ff.

[198] Ibid., cols. 139 f.

[199] Nicanor was not a son of Antiochus, though the *Yosippon* states so.

[200] That is, Seleucids here and below, in sections 7 and 8. See n. 56 above.

[201] *Yosippon*, cols. 141 f.

[202] Ibid., col. 143. Cf. *Antiquities*, XII. 8, 6.

[203] *Yosippon*, cols. 144-147. Cf. *Antiquities*, XII. 9, 2 ff.

[204] *Yosippon*, cols. 153 f.

[205] *Yosippon*, cols. 155-157. Cf. *Antiquities*, XII. 8, 1 ff.

[206] *Yosippon*, cols. 161-163. Cf. *Antiquities*, XII. 10, 5.

[207] *Yosippon*, cols. 170-175. Cf. *Antiquities*, XIII. 9 f.

[208] *Yosippon*, cols. 175 f. Cf. *Antiquities, loc. cit.*

[209] *Yosippon*, cols. 186-192, esp. cols. 191 f. Cf. *Antiquities*, XIII. 13, 1 ff.

[210] *Yosippon*, col. 192.

[211] Note a parallel in Dialogue I, p. 87 above.

[212] Usque is saying that God was prepared to give the Israelites a chance to mend their ways by forgiving their sins and their internecine hatreds; at the same time the praeternatural light warned them of the possibility that the Temple, the source of their protection, might some day be destroyed.

[213] *Yosippon*, cols. 527-529.

[214] See my Introduction, p. 24 above.

[215] See Appendix B, p. 272.

[216] Pompey was married to Julius Caesar's daughter, Julia.

[217] See Appendix B, p. 272.

[218] Cf. Dialogue I, p. 87, and my Introduction, p. 26.

DIALOGUE III

[1] Read 4377 (617). Sisebut reigned from 612 to 620. In Dialogue III, Usque, following his Hebrew source, generally gives the Hebrew year in his chapter headings. See Appendix B, p. 280. Usque provides a date, generally the Hebrew date, for some chapters. Whenever he does, I usually give the corresponding date of the Common Era in brackets. I do not do so in those cases where the date given by Usque is manifestly erroneous.

[2] That is, the Visigoths, who began conquering the Iberian Peninsula in the early fifth century and ruled it until the Moorish conquest at the beginning of the eighth.

[3] Actually it was Catholic Christianity that had recently become the religion of the court, when King Reccared embraced it in 587. The Visigoths had previously been Arian Christians.

[4] So states the *Fortalitium Fidei*! Mohammed fled in 622, but it was from Mecca to Medina.

[5] Actually Witiza did not ascend the throne until 701.

[6] Note Usque's interpretation of the biblical verse, where God is the subject.

[7] This date, apparently carried over from Chapter 1 above, is erroneous. The *Fortalitium Fidei* (Lyons, 1511, f. 185b) relates these events in connection with the expulsion of the Jews from France in 1306. Henry VII was Emperor from 1308 to 1313.

[8] Apparently only these ten or twelve were actively involved and not the "many Christians" who, according to the beginning of this account, were envious of the Jews.

[9] Literally "as it says here," that is, in the *Fortalitium Fidei*.

[10] The corresponding account in the *Fortalitium Fidei* is dated 714.

[11] That is, the faults of the nations. Cf. Isa. 53.4.

[11a] The original reads "Medina Talbi."

[12] The Portuguese reads "*abrahão de la capa.*"

[13] The date 4950 (1190) is found in the margin at this point. If this chronology is correct the edict of the Moorish kings in 1190 could hardly have resulted from the events of 1163. Usque may well have telescoped two separate accounts dealing with the Moors' persecution of the Jews.

[14] The *Iggeret Teman*. Usque actually calls it "The Letter to the South." It was written in response to a request for advice by Jacob al-Fayumi, a leading Jew of Yemen, who was distressed by the troubles faced by the Jews of his land.

[15] Usque does not assign a date to this chapter. In the margin, however, an unusual notation appears—A.F. 154, which may be a printer's error for Anno 4954 (Year 1194). Such errors involving numbers are frequent in the *Consolaçam*. See Appendix B, p. 281.

[16] Tabara (Thabara) is the same as Zamora.

[17] Usque does not make clear whether this word refers to location or importance.

[18] Usque uses the Hebrew term "Targum."

[19] The lack of clarity here results from Usque's loose syntax.

[20] God's name was thought to possess hidden powers which could be unleashed when properly pronounced. Traditionally in Judaism the name יהוה is pronounced not as written but Adonay (אדני).

[21] That is, the Diaspora. The Prince of the Captivity was the Exilarch.

[22] The *Iggeret Teman* contains no mention of David Alroy; neither does any other work of Maimonides carry this account. Reference to Maimonides in connection with this narrative is also made by Ibn Verga (*Schevet Yehuda, ed. cit.*, pp. 76 f.). Usque and Verga apparently borrowed from an identical account. See Appendix B, below, pp. 282 ff.

[23] Usque places this story between two others dated 4924 (1164) and 4943 (1183), respectively. However the *Fortalitium Fidei* bears the correct date of 1420.

   In both Spina and Usque there is a conjunction of two separate accounts, the charge of ritual murder, which is the subject of their narratives, and the more famous case of the charge of host desecration in 1420. The charge of host desecration is dated 1420; the public burning of the Jews took place on March 12, 1421.

[24] The *Fortalitium Fidei* is responsible for the erroneous detail "*imperante Friderico imperatore.*" Frederick III was born in 1415 but did not begin to rule until 1440. Frederick II, born in 1194, was monarch from 1196 to 1250.

[25] That is, the burning of three hundred innocent Jews.

[26] Philip (II) Augustus ruled and extended the Capetian domains from 1180 to 1223.

[27] Usque is fond of portraying Jacob with wings. See above, Dialogue I, n. 5.

[28] Here the margin cites Levi ben Gerson (Gersonides). See his commentary to Lev. 26.38 and Appendix B, p. 279.

[29] That is, Paris.

[30] Note how this chapter parallels the situation of the Marranos.

[31] Umberto Cassuto shows that this account refers to the persecution of the Jews in 1290, and that the year 5000 given by Usque is a round figure. See his article "Un ignoto capitolo di storia ebraica," in *Festschrift zu Hermann Cohens siebzigstem Geburtstage* (Berlin, 1912), pp. 389 ff.

[32] Charles I. His son, who appears later in the account, was Charles II.

[33] Usque simply says "they would be saved." Note the parallel to the situation of the converts in Spain and Portugal.

[34] The date is wrong. It should be 5050 (1290). See Appendix B, pp. 280, 330.

[35] That is, the Diaspora.

[36] This is a metaphor. It does not refer to specifically Jewish attire.

[37] That is, cutting off precious metal from coins, thereby debasing their value.

[38] In his German translation of the *Emek ha-Bakha* (Leipzig, 1858), Max Wiener, commenting on Ha-Cohen's mention of the *eretz norti*, taken from Usque, identifies Norti with Northumbria.

[39] Usque says "their entrails."

[40] The correct date is 1290. Usque regards these events as having transpired around the time of the date of chapter 12.

[41] Henry III (1207-1272) was succeeded by his son, Edward I (1239-1307).

[42] Usque, thinking in terms of his own theology, makes the Christians confess that a sin has occasioned their troubles.

[43] Usque is referring to the Reformation in England, which can be said to have begun under Henry in 1534.

[44] Note Usque's personification of the sins, rather than the things sinned against. Later in this chapter, he again personifies sin, this time as a demon.

[45] Note how Usque uses the details in the Book of Jonah. Jonah had sinned, but was a righteous man when compared to the sailors of the ship on which he was traveling. Similarly the Jews of England, though sinners themselves, were righteous, according to Usque, when compared to their non-Jewish neighbors.

[46] However, the Bible reads: "But they know not the thoughts of the Lord[!], neither understand they His counsel."

[47] For a discussion of the date of this chapter and the event to which it refers, see Appendix B, pp. 282, 331.

[48] Usque's text reads "Teuthonie forkim." Isidore Loeb suggests that the town involved is Foreheim (in Bavaria). See *Joseph Haccohen et les chroniquers juifs* (Paris, 1888), p. 40.

[49] This chapter relates the famous Shepherds' Rebellion of 1320.

[50] Granada, the last territory ruled by the Moors in Spain, was not overcome by the Christians until early 1492.

[51] See Appendix B, p. 282. The word *meltsar* is the Hebrew word for "steward." Usque apparently borrowed this name from his Hebrew source.

[52] That is, believing the danger past.

[53] Usque or his source was confused here. Toulouse and Bigorre are located in separate provinces. Perhaps the reference is to the general region between these towns.

[54] One of the fast days in the traditional Jewish calendar. It commemorates the breaking down of the walls of Jerusalem by Nebuchadnezzar.

[55] The correct name and identity of this sister of the Pope have not been determined. H. Gross, "Zur Geschichte der Juden in Arles," *Monatsschrift für Geschichte und Wissenschaft des Judentums*, XXVIII (Krotoshin, 1879), p. 545, suggests that this Sancha was the daughter of James I of Majorca. The Pope in question is John XXII (Pope, 1316-1334).

[56] Both Usque and Verga (section 14) call him Robert; Joseph Ha-Cohen (sections 61 and 62) calls him Frederick.

[57] The spirit of desolation mentioned in the Bible (Lev. 16) and in rabbinic literature. Here the term is the equivalent of "devil." Cf. Dialogue I, n. 289.

[58] This is the narrative of the well-known Lepers' Rebellion.

[59] Note Usque's personification of the sins and cf. n. 44 above.

[60] See Dialogue II, n. 52.

[61] This is an error for 5106 (1346). The *Fortalitium Fidei* dates this account 1345.

[62] There is no province by this name. As Loeb (*op. cit.*, p. 43) correctly points out, this is the result of a misreading by Usque of the following passage in *Fortalitium Fidei*:

> *Compertum est in Alemania quod Iudei intoxicassent omnes fontes et puteos ut occiderent omnes xpristianos dicte provincie. Torti enim aliqui eorum id confessi fuerunt esse verum.*

[63] Cf. n. 59 above.

[64] The account, however, may represent an attempt to place the expulsion of 1306 (5066) in a later era. For a discussion of this expulsion, see I. Loeb, "Les expulsions des Juifs de France au XIVe siècle," in the *Graetz Jubelschrift* (Breslau, 1877), p. 44 ff.

[65] Literally "to acquire new feathers." Cf. n. 27 above.

[66] Philip IV, "The Fair" (ruled 1285-1314). Usque's identification, however, is not accurate. Philip IV was the son of Philip III and the *grandson* of Louis IX. Louis IX in turn was the grandson of Philip Augustus.

[67] The ninth of Ab commemorates the destruction of the Temple in Jerusalem in the year 70 C.E. Many other tragic events in Jewish history, including the destruction of the First Temple in 586 B.C.E., were said to have occurred on that day.

[68] That is, with Jewish converts to Christianity.

[69] Note how Usque presses the parallel to the Marranos of his own era.

[70] Usque is referring to all Protestant groups.

[71] John II (reigned 1350-1364); Charles V (reigned 1364-1380); Charles VI (reigned 1380-1422). The date 5140 (1380) appears in the margin.

[72] Usque, of course, means that many of the Jews were killed. His difficulty in expressing himself clearly at this point arises from his identification of Jacob with the entire people Israel.

[73] See above, n. 6.

[74] This is an error for 5150 (1390).

[75] The name Alvaro de Luna appears erroneously here. It was Pedro de Luna (1328-1422 or 1423) who was elected Pope by the cardinals at Avignon in 1394. Alvaro de Luna, the Constable of Castile, Grand Master of Santiago and a favorite of John II of Castile, lived more than a generation later (d. 1453).

[76] Innocent VII (1336-1406) was Pope from 1404 to 1406.

[77] Vincent Ferrer (1350-1419) was the private chaplain and confessor of Pedro de Luna. He was a gifted orator and used his abilities in conversionist activities among the Jews. He was responsible for the conversion of many distinguished Jews to Christianity, among them Rabbi Solomon Levi of Burgos, who came to be known as Paul of Burgos.

[78] Ferdinand of Antequera (1373-1416), who ruled Aragon for two years as Ferdinand I, was offered the crown of Castile at the death of his brother Henry III in 1406. He declined, and instead acted as co-regent for the infant John II with Catherine, the widow of Henry III.

[79] According to the lexicographer Sebastián de Covarrubias, writing in 1611, *confeso* means "one who is descended from parents who were Jewish or converted to Christianity." The more common term is *converso*, and Covarrubias uses the two words interchangeably.

[80] These laws were promulgated in Valladolid in 1412.

[81] Read 5215 (1455).

[82] The location described and the identity of the man are difficult to determine. The *Fortalitium Fidei* gives the name of the place as "Almanca." In the section of Spina's book which corresponds to Usque's Chapter 7, Tabara is a city in Castile, in the territory of Louis of Almanca. Cf. n. 16 above. Joseph Ha-Cohen's *Emek ha-Bakha* follows Usque and calls the place "Salamanca."

It seems certain that the place is not Salamanca even if the Almanca of the

Fortalitium Fidei is an error for the city of that name. At most, the Almanca or Salamanca would be a family name or a reference to the personal or family origin of the Louis described.

[83] The date must be that of the plot to poison the bishop, the second of the two episodes narrated. It cannot refer to the episode in the reign of John II, for he died in 1454.

[84] King Henry III, known as El Doliente (the Sufferer), died at the age of twenty-seven in December, 1406. He had ascended the throne in 1390.

[85] Usque uses the term *escolas* (like the German *Schulen*) to designate the "houses of study" or the synagogues.

[86] Actually the events of this chapter took place in 1066 and not in 1488. The confusion results in all probability from the failure of Usque's source to provide a date for this narrative and its juxtaposition of this narrative to others occurring much later. Joseph was the son of the famous Samuel the Nagid. See Appendix B, pp. 279 f.

[87] This is the date of the chapter as a whole. Later in the chapter there are marginal notations giving the date of the entry of the Inquisition in Spain (5248-1488 [sic]) and the date of the Expulsion of the Jews (5252-1492). The Inquisition actually began to function in 1480.

[88] See n. 79 above.

[89] Cf. Ps. 90.5 f.

[90] That is, the Inquisition.

[91] Portuguese coins originally of gold and later silver, and bearing the figure of a cross. They were worth roughly the equivalent of a Spanish ducat or one-seventh of an English pound sterling.

[92] Jewish writers have offered various estimates of the number of refugees entering Portugal. See I. Loeb, "Le nombre des Juifs de Castille et d'Espagne au moyen âge," in *Revue des études juives*, XIV (1887), pp. 173 ff.

[93] The island was not St. Thomas in the West Indies, which had as yet not been discovered and which was never in the possession of the Portuguese, but São Thomé, off the West African coast. It was "colonized and became the principal base for trade on the Niger-Cameroons coast from about 1493." J. D. Fage, *An Atlas of African History* (Bungay, Suffolk, 1958), p. 27. See also C. Roth, *A History of the Marranos*, pp. 55 and 382, and, before him, Mendes dos Remedios, *Os Judeos de Portugal*, vol. I, p. 274, as well as the Portuguese chroniclers. On Usque's exaggerations, see J. L. D'Azevedo, *Historia dos christãos novos portugueses* (Lisbon, 1921), p. 24.

[94] Cf. n. 39 above.

[95] Interestingly the subsequent verses of Psalm 44 are found at the end of the following chapter. Usque's application of this Psalm to the situation of the New Christians is unmistakable.

[96] John II died on October 25, 1495, and was succeeded by Emanuel I, called "the Fortunate," who reigned until 1521.

[97] Usque's text reads "*morresem morte natural e perdesem as fazendas por ysso.*"

[98] *Os Estãos* was the name of a palace which became the seat of the Inquisition in Portugal.

[99] Usque employs the Hebrew transliteration *taleciod*.

[100] That is, their Judaism.

[101] What Usque means is that the terrestrial king decided to persecute the Jews. The Jews deserved to be punished because of their sins against God, who moved the king to inflict the punishment.

[102] That is, the Inquisition.

[103] This thought is not completed.

[104] Jean de la Foix was apparently one of the officials in Milan, perhaps even a member of the ruling family, the Visconti.

[105] For the possible dates of the events of this chapter, see above, p. 13 and n. 13.

[106] In the margin this family is identified as "The house of the Abravanels."

[107] The margin reads "His honor (O señor) Don Samuel Abravanel."

[108] The margin reads "Her honor (a señora) Dona Benvenida Abravanela [sic]."

[109] See n. 44 above.

[110] The margin correctly dates these events in 5301 (1541).

[111] The Portuguese reads "*por mais fraco e debil lugar.*"

[112] The margin identifies this Jew as Moses Hamon, who was the personal physician of Emperor Suleiman II and a powerful figure at the Ottoman court.

[113] The name given to cities with impressive Jewish populations and culture.

[114] Although the exact allusion is not clear, Usque appears to be referring to scholars and sages.

[115] On this famous incident, see I. Broydé, "Salonica," in *The Jewish Encyclopedia*, X, pp. 658 f.

[116] The date should be 5306 (1546). By Germany, of course, Usque means the Holy Roman Empire.

[117] That is, the covenant solemnized by circumcision (cf. Ex. 4.25).

[118] Usque's account is the primary, perhaps the only, source of information about the banishment of 1551. Judging from Usque's panegyric upon Ferrara (pp. 230 f. below), it did not last long. Note that Usque refers to the Portuguese New Christians as Hebrews (or Jews).

[119] The most easterly and largest of the Swiss cantons.

[120] Usque says "the Portuguese," as the New Christians were frequently called outside of Portugal.

[121] The margin names this Jew—"Manuel Bichacho."

[122] Usque transliterates the Hebrew word, *cefer.* He uses the singular, though the context calls for the plural, "scrolls," which I have used. Later in this narrative, Usque writes *tĕffilyn* (phylacteries), *mappot* (mantles) and *echal* (ark).

[123] This word is used ironically.

[124] The Portuguese reads "*rõcando passa a noute de hum sono.*"

[125] Usque seems to be alluding to the pioneers in Portugal's far-flung empire, and even more likely, to those in the New World.

[126] Note the unusual metaphor, which is repeated below, p. 228.

[127] Literally, *señor da natureza de todo o criado.* Cf. Num. 27.16.

[128] That is, the four traditional elements of the ancient and medieval world—earth, air, fire and water. Usque here attempts to relate the various types of suffering of the Israelites in Europe to each of these elements. The allusions are to chapters 1-37 of Dialogue III.

[129] This term, current as late as the middle of the seventeenth century, was generally used to refer not so much to a particular body of water as to the aggregate of the waters that cover the earth.

[130] Ycabo seems to forget that Joseph is his son.

[131] Usque equates Asshur with Ninus, who along with Semiramis, are the mythical founders of the Assyrian empire. According to one account, Semiramis succeeded in imprisoning and executing the king in order to obtain royal power for herself. Cf. Dialogue I, p. 85.

[132] See Dialogue I, pp. 86 f.

[133] This is Gaius Caligula. See Dialogue II, p. 137.

[134] Cf. Tacitus, *Annals*, Book XIV, chs. 1-9. Tacitus says that Nero's mother, Agrippina, tried to incite her son to incest and that Nero had her murdered, "but as to whether Nero surveyed the breathless body of his mother, and applauded its beauty; there are those who have affirmed it, and those who deny it" (ch. 9).

[135] Arabia Deserta is the classical name given to the arid regions in the Northern and Western parts of the Arabian Peninsula. Classical authors divided the peninsula into Arabia Felix (the Southern region); Arabia Petraea (the Northwest); and Arabia Deserta.

[136] Usque copied these data and the data which follow from Ludovico di Varthema's *Itinerario*. The passages involved can be found in the edition of Alberto Bacchi Della Lega (Bologna, 1885), pp. 19 ff., 55 f., 79 f., 87 ff., 101 ff., 128 ff., 133 ff., 216 f., 218 f.

[137] Here Usque relied on Leo Africanus' *Della descrittione dell' Africa*. The passages involved can be found in G. B. Ramusio's *Delle navigationi et viaggi*, I (Venice, 1563), folios 1b ff. and 12a ff.

[138] Cf. Isa. 63.16. This revealing statement attests to the animosity shown by Jews to their New Christian brethren.

[139] That is, in the Book of Lamentations, traditionally attributed to Jeremiah.

[140] In the Middle Ages and early Renaissance phlebotomies were commonly used by surgeons (and barber-surgeons) in their therapy. See C. C. Mettler, *History of Medicine* (Philadelphia, 1947), pp. 839 ff.

[141] At this point the margin refers the reader to Hos. 6. See Hos. 6.7 ff.

[142] Gen. 17.1.

[143] Sanhedrin X.1. The proof-text from Isaiah which follows implies that since God once made this promise, it will be fulfilled.

[144] Cf. Philo, *Allegorical Interpretation of Genesis*, III, sections 15 ff.

[145] *Ibid.* Cf. also Gen. 28.12 and the corresponding rabbinic commentaries.

[146] The reference to metempsychosis and the secret doctrines of the Kabbalists seem to have been learned by Usque in Safed. See my Introduction, p. 27, and Appendix B, p. 274.

[147] See above, n. 126.

[148] Note the parallel to Num. 22.22 ff. Actually, Prince Alphonse (Affonso) had died in 1491; the Jewish children were sent to São Thomé in 1493. It did not take long, however, for the Marrano mind to confuse the dates and make the latter event the cause of the former. Cf. the anonymous *Apologia em abono dos christãos cognominados novos deste reyno de Portugal, dedicada a santidade de Urbano VIII, Pontifice Supremo* (1624), cited by J. Mendes dos Remédios, *Os Judeos*, I, pp. 275 f.

[149] The marginal note mentions the enemy "Manuel, Duke of Aveiro, son of Prince Ferdinand." The reference is to Emanuel I, who succeeded John in 1495.

[150] Usque says "*sangue ytaliano*" by synecdoche.

[151] See n. 5 to Usque's first Dialogue. The reference here is to the New Christians who have escaped from Portugal and Spain.

[152] Cf. Ex. 2.4.

[153] Judith, chs. 8-16. The margin reads "The righteous Dona [sic] Gracia Nasci [sic]."

[154] That is, the Inquisition.

[155] See above, Dialogue III, ch. 36, and n. 118.

[156] Usque says "*seu braço douro*."

[157] See n. 15 to Usque's Introduction. Below, Usque also pictures Duke Hercules of Este as possessing wings.

[158] The city is Ferrara. The man, of course, is Duke Hercules.

[159] This is another favorite metaphor of Usque's. See Dialogue II, p. 115, and Dialogue III, p. 180. The heavy cloak is the faith of Christianity; the natural garb refers to Judaism.

[160] This is another example of Usque's mixed metaphors.

[161] That is, revert to Judaism.

[162] See my Introduction, p. 27, and n. 146 to Dialogue III.

[163] Cf. Dialogue I, pp. 83 f.

[164] Cf. Ex. 12.40 and the rabbinic commentaries. Usque's 1300 years is a

round number; he counts from the destruction of the Temple (70 C.E.) or, more likely, from the Bar Kokhba revolt (135 C.E.).

[165] In this and subsequent sections Usque has added many words and phrases to the biblical text to give it a ring of contemporaneity. I have underlined the most interesting of these additions, as well as a few representative alterations by Usque of the biblical text.

[166] See Philo, *On Dreams*, I, sections 159-170, and *On the Change of Names*, sections 81 ff.

[167] Here Usque is referring to the answers given by mystics, whom he mentions in his prologue as having sought to identify biblical prophecy with specific events, particularly those in Usque's own time.

[168] The "etc." here is Usque's.

[169] The chapter actually does not end here, but continues for two additional verses. Usque means that this is the chapter's last major point on the subject.

[170] The Fountain is God or heaven; the "she" refers to the earth, or the Holy Land, or perhaps the people Israel.

[171] Usque appears to be alluding to some of the New Christians who have reverted to Judaism.

[172] The margin at this point reads "All of this is divine service, but it was achieved in different ways."

[173] Cf. the Talmud, Berakhot 17a.

[174] Cf. Ps. 99.6.

[175] The margin reads "The Fifth Age is reckoned from the time of the building of the First Temple until its destruction, which was 497 years." Below it reads: "Sixth Age, from the rebuilding of the Temple to its destruction, which was 428 [years]."

[176] Usque follows the Ptolemaic system, according to which the planets revolved in small circles or spheres around the earth. Venus was the third in the sequence of "planets." The sequence was: Moon, Mercury, Venus, Sun, Mars, Jupiter and Saturn.

[177] That is, the host of laments.

[178] This is a frequent theme in rabbinic literature. See, for example, Sanhedrin 90a.

[179] Usque uses the abbreviation for the Hebrew reading of God's name. This was common Marrano usage. See also n. 20 and p. 244. Note that in Usque's time "Edom" and "Esau" were used to refer to Christendom.

[180] This may be an allusion to the Inquisition.

[181] The margin reads "This is now taking place in part with the arrival [of Jews] from Portugal."

[182] The margin reads "It was not this way in the Second Temple; rather they built with their weapons in hand."

[183] This metaphor is Usque's.

[184] At this point the margin reads "The Messiah of the tribe of Ephraim." The period of unbearable suffering (the *hevle ha-Mashiah*) heralds the Messianic era.

[185] Here the margin reads "Messiah."

[186] Here the margin reads "This can now be seen in the arrival of [Jews from Portugal] to Turkey."

[187] Usque says "Garel."

[188] Usque's text carries the Hebrew.

[189] So Usque writes.

[190] Note again how in all these biblical quotations Usque is addressing himself to the situation of the New Christians.

[191] The words "For Judah . . . write upon it" were omitted from the Portuguese text. This was clearly a printer's error.

[192] The margin refers the reader to Jer. 29. The allusion is doubtlessly to God's promise in Jer. 29.10 to bring His people back from captivity after

"seventy years be accomplished." On the association of the dragon (Rahab) with Pharaoh and Egypt, see the Targum and rabbinic commentaries, *ad. loc.*

[193] Note the confusion of persons. It is God who is speaking.

[194] The margin reads "There will not be a blemished child of either sex."

[195] The margin reads "answering before hearing as repayment for 'we shall do and we shall hear' which Israel said in the desert." Cf. Ex. 24.7.

[196] The margin refers the reader to Gen. 1 and the refrain "And God saw that it was good."

[197] See above Dialogue I, p. 91.

[198] Usque writes "He" for God at this point.

[199] Here Usque transliterates the Hebrew "*Ganheden.*"

APPENDIX A

[1] S. Rabinowitz, *Motzoei Golah* (Warsaw, 1894), p. 308, n. 1.

[2] J. Steinschneider, "Zur Geschichte jüdischer Martyrologien (R. Samuel Usque's 'Trost Israels in seinen Trübsalen')," in *Festschrift zum X. Stiftungsfest des Akademischen Vereins für jüdische Geschichte und Literatur an der kgl. Friedrich-Wilhelms-Universität zu Berlin* (Berlin, 1893), pp. 24-77.

[3] Ed. *Consolaçam*, n. 4.

[4] M. Gaster, "Abravanel's Literary Work," in *Isaac Abravanel: Six Lectures*, edited by J. B. Trend and H. Loewe (Cambridge, Eng., 1937), p. 68, n. 2.

[5] M. Gaster, "Samuel Usque, Consolations for the Troubles of Israel," *The Jewish Forum*, XIII, pp. 367-374.

[6] The work was published in Buenos Aires, 1949.

[7] A. Neuman, "Samuel Usque: Marrano Historian of the Sixteenth Century," in *To Doctor R.: Essays Here Collected and Published in Honor of the Seventieth Birthday of Dr. A. S. W. Rosenbach* (1946), pp. 180-203. An announcement of the publication of a photographic reproduction of Gelbart's manuscript has recently been made by the Bloch Publishing Company of New York.

[8] A. Neuman, *op. cit.*, p. 117: "A complete translation of the *Consolaçam* into one of the present world languages, preferably English—and, most of all, also into the living Hebrew of today—should not be long delayed." Cf. also H. N. Bialik, *Letters* (Hebrew), IV (Tel Aviv, 1938), pp. 66 f.

[9] A. Neuman, *op. cit.*

[10] J. Steinschneider, *op. cit.*

[11] H. Graetz, *Geschichte*, VIII (Leipzig, 1873), n. 1, pp. 393-399. "*Efodi oder Profiat Duran als historischer Schriftsteller und seine Schriften.*"

[12] I. Loeb, "Comparaison d'Usque et de l'Emek habbakha," in *Revue des études juives*, XVI (1888), pp. 212-223; *idem, Josef Haccohen et les chroniquers juifs* (Paris, 1888).

[13] F. Baer, *Untersuchungen über Quellen und Komposition des Schevet Jehuda* (Berlin, 1923).

[14] Cf. Appendix B, p. 277.

[15] I. Bartoloccio, *Bibliotheca Magna Rabbinica*, I (Rome, 1675), p. 49; II (Rome, 1678), p. 19. Bartoloccio deals with only Abraham Usque.

[16] D. Barbosa Machado, *Bibliotheca Lusitana*, III (Lisbon, 1762), p. 672.

[17] N. Antonio, *Bibliotheca Hispana Nova*, II (Madrid, 1788), p. 275.

[18] A. Ribeiro dos Santos, *Memórias da literatura portuguesa*, II (Lisbon, 1790), p. 406.

[19] J. C. Wolf, *Bibliotheca Hebraea*, III (Hamburg, 1727), pp. 1071 ff.

[20] J. Rodríguez de Castro, *Biblioteca española*, VII, pp. 536 ff.

[21] G. B. de Rossi, *De typographia hebraeo-ferrariensi commentarius historicus* (Parma, 1800), p. 64; *Biblioteca Judaica Antichristiana*, p. 125; *Historisches Wörterbuch der jüdischen Schriftsteller und ihrer Werke* (translation of *Dizionario storico degli autori Ebrei e delle loro opere* by C. H. Hamberger)

(Leipzig, 1839), pp. 324 f. Cf. *idem, Della vana aspettazione degli ebrei* (Parma, 1773), pp. 41 f.

[22] I. Da Silva, *Dicionário bibliográfico portuguez*, VII (Lisbon, 1862), pp. 196 f.

[23] J. Fürst, *Bibliotheca Judaica*, III (Leipzig, 1863), p. 465.

[24] M. Kayserling, *Biblioteca española-portugueza-judaica* (Strassburg, 1890), p. 107.

[25] El Rey D. Manuel, *Livros antigos portugueses*, II (Cambridge, Eng., 1935), pp. 303-379.

[26] M. Kayserling, "Samuel Usque," in *The Jewish Encyclopedia*, XII, pp. 387b-388a.

[27] M. Freier, "Usque," in *Jüdisches Lexicon*, V (1930), p. 1147a. This article forms the basis of the article "Samuel Usque" (no author given) in the *Universal Jewish Encyclopedia*, X (1943), p. 384a.

[28] E. Schochet, "Usque, Shemuel" in *The Hebrew Encyclopedia* (in Hebrew), II (1950), p. 335a.

APPENDIX B

[1] Cf. I. Aboab, *op. cit.*, pp. 220-221: *y ansi auia en España muchos libros manuscriptos de rarissima perficion: . . . Despues que los Reyes don Fernando de Castilla, y don Manuel de Portugal, nos desterraron de sus Estados, todos los libros que auia se esparzieron, segun que sus dueños fueron habitar por diuersas partes del mundo.*

[2] *Consolaçam*, Prologue, p. 39.

[3] Usque's marginal notations have invariably misled scholars into an acceptance of the works cited as his true sources. So v. g., Mendes dos Remedios, ed. *Consolaçam*, Notas, p. 7. The problem of Samuel Usque's sources has hitherto attracted little attention. Most attention has been given to one source of Dialogue III which seems to have been consulted also by the author of the *Shevet Yehuda* and is therefore of interest to students of this work. See below, pp. 277 ff.

[4] *Consolaçam*, Dialogue I, pp. 74 ff.

[5] The most striking examples of this procedure are to be found in the concluding section of Dialogue III. All such significant paraphrases and additions in this section have been italicized in the translation.

[6] B. Smalley, *The Study of the Bible in the Middle Ages* (Oxford, 1941), pp. ix ff.

[7] Cf. the following cases (the folio references are to Mendes dos Remedios' edition) (1) Dialogue I, f. 13a (Jer. 1; read Jer. 9); (2) *ibid.*, 13b (Jer. 4; read Jer. 5); (3) *ibid.*, 14a (Mic. 1; read Mic. 3); (4) *ibid.*, 15b (Is. 9; read Is. 1); (5) *ibid.*, 17a (Jer. 4; read Jer. 5); (6) *ibid.*, 17b (Jer. 5; read Jer. 34); (7) *ibid.*, (Hos. 13; read Hos. 10 and 14); (8) *ibid.*, 21a (Ezek. 20; read Ezek. 17); (9) *ibid.*, 22b (Jer. 16; read Jer. 22, 26); (10) *ibid.*, (Deut. 23; read Deut. 28); (11) *ibid.*, 24a (Judg. 6; read Judg. 4); (12) *ibid.*, 26a (Gen. 21; read Gen. 25); (13) *ibid.*, 34a (Jer. 13; read Jer. 3); (14) *ibid.*, 40b (Jer. 24; read Jer. 23); (15) *ibid.*, 52a (Ezek. 9; read Ezek. 8); (16) Dialogue II 3a (2 Ezra 7; read [1] Ezra 6-7); (17) *ibid.*, 6b (Ex. 18; read Ex. 12); (18) *ibid.*, 43b (Is. 14; read Is. 51); (19) Dialogue III 4b (Jer. 17; read Jer. 24); (20) *ibid.*, 15a (Ps. 108; read Ps. 109); (21) *ibid.*, 15b (Ezek. 5.2; read Ezek. 5.12); (22) *ibid.*, 19a (Jer. 11; read Jer. 12); (23) *ibid.*, 20b (Jer. 9.9, 13; read Jer. 18); (24) *ibid.*, 27a (Jer. 1; read Jer. 2); (25) *ibid.*, 30b (Jer. 7; read Jer. 18); (26) *ibid.*, 33b (Jer. 15; read Jer. 17); (27) *ibid.*, 33b (Jer. 22; read Jer. 23); (28) *ibid.*, 34b (Jer. 15; read Jer. 17); (29) *ibid.*, 47b (Gen. 2.15; read Gen. 2.17); (30) *ibid.*, 48b (Is. 43, 44; read Is. 44); (31) *ibid.*, (Hos. 1; read Hos. 2.1); (32) *ibid.*, 50a (Jer. 1; read Jer. 30); (33) *ibid.*, 63a (Ezek. 1; read Ezek. 36); (34) *ibid.*, 71b (Jer. 30;

read Jer. 32); (35) *ibid.*, 77a (Mic. 8; read Mic. 7); (36) *ibid.*, 78b (Is. 44; read Is. 42).

An interesting feature is that nine or one-fourth of these errors involve the digit 1, (nos. 1, 3, 4, 13, 21, 24, 31, 32, 33). This factor, to all appearances insignificant, assumes considerable importance in the determination of Usque's major unknown source. Cf. below, n. 8.

[8] Cf. the following cases: (1) Dial. I f. 8b (Hos. 6; read 1 Kings 6); (2) Dial. I f. 11a (Deut. 33; read Nu. 24); (3) Dial. I f. 13a (Jer. 39; read Is. 39); (4) *ibid.*, 16b (Ezek. 22; read Is. 9); (5) *ibid.*, 17a (Jer. 4; read Is. 3); (6) *ibid.*, 18a (Is. 13; read Jer. 9); (7) *ibid.*, 23b (Jer. 31; read Josh. 24); (8) Dial. III f. 19a (Ps. 108; read Ezek. 7); (9) *ibid.*, 31b (Ezek. 44; read Ps. 44); (10) *ibid.*, 45b (Amos 10; read Hos. 10); (11) *ibid.*, 49b (Exod. 4; read Deut. 4); (12) *ibid.*, 58b (Jer. 69; read Is. 66).

In a number of cases biblical books mentioned in the margin are not alluded to or quoted in the body of the text. Thus, v. g., Dial. I, 13b (Ezek. 7); *ibid.*, 18a (Jer. 16); Dial. III, 47b (Is. 45); *ibid.*, (Is. [?] 4); *ibid.*, 56a (Dan. 5). These errors can be explained by the hypothesis that Usque worked from memory, though the printer may have been responsible for some or many of them.

[9] There is in addition one case (Dialogue I, f. 12b) where the text correctly cites Micah while the corresponding marginal note refers to Isaiah. There are other curious citations in the *Consolaçam*. Thus in Dialogue II, f. 3a and 3b Usque refers to Nehemiah as Second Ezra, while elsewhere (*ibid.*, f. 3a) he cites Nehemiah 2 L(ivro) 4. On another occasion he cites Nehemiah, chapter 4 correctly. Then again, there are the cases of the unusual references to the second book of Kings, in Dialogue I, ff. 30a, 30b, 43a. In the first and last of these instances the chapter citations are inaccurate. Dial. I, 30a reads 4 R. 17.18 and should read 2 Ki. 15; 17. The citation on f. 43a reads "Sanch. [Sennacherib] 4 R. 7" but should read 2 Ki. 18.13. The citation on f. 30b correctly reads 4 R. (i.e., 2 Ki.) 17, 18, 19. The references to Second Ezra and to Fourth Kings are not sufficient or sufficiently accurate to warrant any conclusions regarding the relationship of Usque to the Catholic version of the Bible.

[10] Cf. for example, the extent of the utilization of Deuteronomy from the notes to the translation of Dialogue III, chaps. 1-37.

[11] Cf. below, pp. 275 ff.

[12] *Consolaçam*, Dialogue II, ff. 13a, 26a, 36b, 37b.

[13] *Consolaçam*, Dialogue I, f. 36a; Dialogue II, ff. 4b-5a. In two other instances, Josephus is cited only by a reference to the correct book and chapter of his *Antiquities* (Dialogue II, ff. 12a-b; f. 13b).

[14] For this study I have utilized the edition of David Günzberg (Berditchev, 1896-1913), based on the princeps of Mantua, 1480. This edition has the convenience of having each page divided into two columns and is numbered by columns. I have also used the Münster version (ed. Basel, 1559).

On the *Yosippon*, cf. I. Baer, "Sefer Yosippon Ha-Ivri," in *Sefer Dinaburg* (Jerusalem, 1949), pp. 178-205; A. Neuman, "Josippon: History and Pietism," in *Landmarks and Goals*, pp. 1-34; *idem*, "Josippon and the Apocrypha," *ibid.*, pp. 35-59; L. Wallach, *Quellenkritische Studien zum hebräischen Josippon* (Breslau, 1939); *idem*, "Yosippon and the Alexander Romance," in *Jewish Quarterly Review* (New Series), XXXVII (1947), 407-422; A. Neuman, "A Note on John the Baptist and Jesus in the Josippon," in *Hebrew Union College Annual*, XXIII, Part 2 (1950-51), pp. 137-149.

[15] Viktor Hantzsch, *Sebastian Münster: Leben Werk, wissenschaftlichle Bedeutung* (Leipzig, 1898).

[16] These include nos. 5, 9, 11, 12, 13, 15, 19, 20, 21, 22, 23, 24, 25, 30, 31, 32, 33 and perhaps 27, for a total of 17, possibly 18, out of 29 passages (nos. 5-33) dealing with the Second Temple. It is interesting to note that

translations of Josephus into Spanish were published in Barcelona (1482), Seville (1492), Madrid (1536), and Lisbon (n.d.; 1500 ?).

[17] *Consolaçam*, Dialogue II, f. 41a. The notation "Conforme a Plutarcho" appears in the Ferrara edition, f. 151b, and in the Amsterdam edition, f. 152a, but was omitted from the modern Portuguese edition of Mendes dos Remédios.

[18] The title *Pharsalia* is actually inappropriate for the book as a whole, inasmuch as it refers primarily to the events described in Book VII. Cf. Lucan, ed. J. D. Duff (London, 1928), p. 10.

[19] *Consolaçam*, Dialogue II, f. 40b; Lucan, *Civil War*, Book 7.

[20] *Ibid.*, f. 41a. Ovid, *Metamorphoses*, I, verse 201. Usque's treatment of Caesar's death is in no way like that of Ovid, who refers to Caesar's death only incidentally and stresses his translation to heaven, a fact totally omitted by Usque.

[21] *Ibid.*, ff. 34b (Coroni-/ca dos/ empera/dores/ roma-/nos.); 35a (Coro./ dos em/ pe. Ro-/ma.); 42b (Empe-/rado-/res. Roma/nos.).

[22] Cf. below, n. 94.

[23] *Consolaçam*, Dialogue II, 34b.

[24] Dio Cassius's history, however, does not go beyond Alexander Severus (222-235). Dio Cassius includes the remark found in the *Consolaçam* (Dialogue III, f. 43a-b) and perhaps ultimately in Tacitus' *Annals*, Book 14 (ch. 1-9), to the effect that Nero bared the body of his mother.

[25] J. Thompson, *op. cit.*, I, pp. 47, 12 f. E. Havet, *Mémoire sur Bérose et Manéthon* (Paris, 1873), pp. 1-5. Cf. also pp. 9, 10 and *passim*.

[26] Cf. *Eusebii Pamphili: Chronicon Bipartitum*, ed. J. B. Aucher (Venice, 1818), part I, pp. 10, 16-58. Cf. also pp. 62-71.

[27] E. Havet, *op. cit.*, pp. 4-5, Book I, ch. 3, paragraph 6.

[28] For this study I have used the translation of R. H. Barrow. Cf. also J. Figgis, *The Political Aspects of St. Augustine's "City of God"* (London, 1921), *passim*.

[29] *Consolaçam*, Dialogue I, pp. 84 ff. *City of God*, I, pp. 141 f., 277 ff., 282, 286; II, pp. 109 ff., 218-220.

[30] *Consolaçam*, Dialogue III, p. 219; *City of God*, I, pp. 95 f., 140.

[31] *Consolaçam*, Dialogue III, p. 220; *City of God*, I, p. 53.

[32] *Consolaçam*, Dialogue II, p. 162; *City of God*, pp. 135 ff., 145 f.

[33] *Consolaçam, passim*, esp. Dialogue III, pp. 232 ff.; *City of God*, I, pp. 79 ff., 177 ff., 500 ff. Cf. *ibid.*, pp. 459 ff.; II, pp. 333 ff.

[34] *Consolaçam*, Dialogue I, nn. 43, 44 and 65; *City of God*, I, pp. 436 ff.; II, pp. 47 ff., 326 ff., 377, 540-545.

[35] *Consolaçam*, Prologue, p. 38 and n. 7. Cf. also Dialogue I, n. 19.

[36] *Metamorphoses*, I, verses 89-112; *Consolaçam*, Dialogue I, pp. 46 ff.

[37] See, for example, Dialogue I, nn. 29, 79; Dialogue II, n. 52.

[38] Cf. Dialogue I, nn. 47-52; Dialogue III, nn. 144, 166. It is difficult to determine the extent of Usque's direct use of the Apocrypha, largely because most of his references to the Apocrypha are to be found in *Yosippon*. His mention of Judith (Dialogue III, p. 230) is doubtlessly the product of general knowledge rather than research.

[39] Cf. my Introduction, p. 9 and below, pp. 277 ff.

[40] For examples in Usque, cf. Dialogue I, ff. 7b, 8b-9a (the speculative ideal), Dialogue III, f. 45a (the mind Divine diffused through the spheres) and Dialogue I, ff. 7a, 26, 31a and *passim* (God as First Cause and parallel concepts). On this subject, see N. Robb, *Neoplatonism of the Italian Renaissance* (London, 1925), *passim*.

[41] L. Hebraeus, *The Philosophy of Love (Dialoghi d'Amore)*, tr. by F. Friedeberg-Seeley and J. Barnes with an introduction by C. Roth (London, 1937), p. 107. On Leon Hebreo, cf. C. Gebhardt, *Leone Ebreo, Dialoghi d'Amore* (Heidelberg, 1929).

[42] L. Varthema, *Itinerario*, ed. Alberto Bacchi Della Lega (Bologna, 1885), *passim*. An excellent English translation under the auspices of the Hakluyt Society was prepared by John Winter Jones in 1863. The voyage took place between 1502 and 1508.

The fame of the *Itinerario* is attested to by the sixteenth-century translations made of it into Latin (1510, 1511); German (1515, 1516, 1518, 1548); Spanish (1520, 1523, 1570, 1576); French (1556); Dutch (1563); and English (1577), in addition to the many subsequent publications of the book in various languages. Cf. Jones' translation, introduction, p. xviii. It is also interesting to note that Varthema, an Italian gentleman, was eventually knighted by the Portuguese! (*Ibid.*, p. xvii.) On editions and bibliography of Varthema, see Pietro Amat di San Filippo, *Bibliografia dei viaggiatori italiani* (Rome, 1874), pp. 43 ff.

[43] Cf. *Consolaçam*, Dialogue III, pp. 220 f. and n. 136.

[44] Cf. *ibid.*, Dialogue III, n. 137. The Italian text of Leo Africanus is published in Gio. Battista Ramusio's *Delle Navigationi et viaggi*, I (Venice, 1563), ff. 1-95. The work was translated into English in 1600 by John Pory and re-edited by Robert Brown for the Hakluyt Society (London, 1896, 2 vols.).

[45] *Consolaçam*, Dialogue I, nn. 68, 79. That Usque knew Hebrew is evidenced not only by his utilization of the *Yosippon* and other Hebrew texts, but also by his not infrequent inclusion of Hebrew words—particularly though not exclusively for ritual objects—within the body of his text. Thus, for example, the word *Tamares* ("palm trees") in Dialogue I, f. 1a; *Mana* (which he explains as "angelic food") in I, 8; *Gan-Eden*, I, 11a margin; *Yayin* (written in Hebrew characters), I, 36a; *Adar*, II, 3a; *Berid* (covenant), II, 7b; *Sucod*, II, 14a; *ululab*, *ibid.*; *Scivan* (i.e., *Sivan*), II, 30b; *Cahal*, *Quehilot*, III, 6b, 17b, 18a, 21b; *Tamuz*, III, 18a; *Ab*, III, 21b; *Taleciod* (prayer-shawls), III, 30a; *Cefer*, III, 39a; *Echal*, *ibid.*; *Téffilym*, *ibid.*; *Mappoth*, *ibid.*; *Ganheden*, III, 78a; the inclusion of the word *Hu* written in Hebrew in the quotation of a biblical verse, III, 72b, and the Portuguese expression *Talhar pauto*, in III, 62a, which appears to be the literal translation of the Hebrew *likhrot brit*. It is interesting that Usque finds it necessary to explain *mana* and *cefer*. Cf. also III, 7b for the Portuguese verb *heremar*, appearing in the form *heremareño* and derived from the Hebrew *herem*.

[46] *Ibid.*, Dialogue I, nn. 33, 70.

[47] Dialogue I, pp. 46, 53. Cf. n. 48 and 50 below.

[48] See Dialogue II, p. 121; Dialogue III, p. 256.

[49] *Ibid.*, *passim*; Dialogue II, n. 155 and Dialogue III, n. 101. Cf. my introduction, chapter 3, n. 7.

[50] *Ibid.*, Dialogue I, nn. 39, 60, 64.

[51] *Ibid.*, *passim*, especially Dialogue III, pp. 224 f., 240.

[52] *Ibid.*, Dialogue I, n. 204, pp. 77 and 106; Dialogue III, p. 187.

[53] *Ibid.*, Dialogue I, pp. 96, 106; Dialogue II, p. 123.

[54] *Ibid.*, Dialogue I, n. 29.

[55] Cf. Dialogue I, n. 269, Dialogue III, nn. 184 f. and ed. Mendes dos Remedios, Dialogue III, f. 70a margin.

[56] *Ibid.*, Dialogue I, pp. 46 ff. and 54 f.

[57] References to mishnaic and talmudic literature include Dialogue I, nn. 33, 37, 43, 44, 55, 60, 63-65, 72-78, 129, 231, 259, 286, 289, 311, 321; Dialogue II, nn. 52, 189; Dialogue III, nn. 67, 143, 164, 173, 178.

[58] Dialogue I, nn. 267, 286.

[59] *Ibid.*, and n. 60 below.

[60] On the problem of the Ten Tribes, cf. M. Lewin, *Wo wären die "zehn Stämme Israels" zu suchen?* (Pressburg, 1901), esp. pp. 11-14 and nn. 31-36. The phrase "dark hills" is found clearly in the Targum to Jer. 13.16, and even more clearly in the Targum's translation of *ture k'valah* for the simple

harah of I Chr. 5.26. Cf. also *Zohar*, s.v. *Behaalothekha*, vol. III, p. 149a.

For this and other locations suggested for the Ten Tribes, cf. A. Neubauer, "Where Are the Ten Tribes?" in the *Jewish Quarterly Review*, I (1889), pp. 14-28; 95-114; 185-201; 408-423.

[61] Dialogue III, pp. 231 f. and my Introduction, p. 27.

[62] Dialogue II, ed. Mendes dos Remédios, f. 33a-b.

[63] On the life and thought of Abravanel, cf. J. Sarachek, *Don Isaac Abravanel*; *Isaac Abravanel: Six Lectures* (by Paul Goodman, I. G. Llubera, M. Gaster, L. Rabinowitz, L. Strauss and A. R. Milburn) edited by J. B. Trend and H. Loewe (New York, 1938); J. Guttmann, *Die Religions-philosophischen Lehren des Isaak Abravanel* (Breslau, 1916), but especially the recent thorough and scholarly work by B. Netanyahu, *Don Isaac Abravanel: Statesman and Philosopher* (Philadelphia, 1953), which served me as a guide to most of Abravanel's writings dealing with Usque, and to whose perceptive analysis and thorough documentation I owe most of my discoveries regarding the relationship of Abravanel and Usque. Therefore, it is to this book, wherever possible, rather than to Abravanel's original work, that I refer the reader.

[64] B. Netanyahu, *op. cit.*, pp. 131, 134, 144, 148. On his concept of the universe, cf. *ibid.*, pp. 109 ff.

[65] B. Netanyahu, pp. 108 ff.

[66] B. Netanyahu, pp. 121, 144.

[67] B. Netanyahu, pp. 136 ff.

[68] B. Netanyahu, pp. 180, 190 ff.

[69] B. Netanyahu, p. 239.

[70] B. Netanyahu, pp. 205-209. Cf. *ibid.*, pp. 145 and 316.

[71] B. Netanyahu, pp. 233 f.

[72] B. Netanyahu, pp. 233 f.

[73] B. Netanyahu, p. 226.

[74] Cf. Dialogue I, nn. 72-78 and *passim*.

[75] B. Netanyahu, *op. cit.*, pp. 229, 238.

[76] B. Netanyahu, p. 110.

[77] B. Netanyahu, p. 117.

[78] B. Netanyahu, p. 133. Cf. *ibid.*, p. 252.

[79] B. Netanyahu, pp. 237, 244, 212 ff. On the nature of the millennium, cf. *ibid.*, pp. 145, 207.

[80] B. Netanyahu, p. 228.

[81] The work is first mentioned by Abravanel in the introduction to his *Commentary to the Book of Kings* (Leipzig, 1686), f. 190a, col. 2.

[82] I. Abravanel, *Mayyene ha-Yeshuah* (Ferrara, 1551), f. 21b.

[83] B. Netanyahu, *op. cit.*, p. 65.

[84] B. Netanyahu, *op. cit.*, pp. 201 ff.

[85] B. Netanyahu, *op. cit.*, p. 143.

[86] B. Netanyahu, *op. cit.*, pp. 203 f. On the practical import of the Messianic belief in Abravanel, cf. *ibid.*, pp. 199 ff.

[87] B. Netanyahu, *op. cit.*, p. 235. The final possible date conceived by Abravanel for the Messiah's arrival was 1573 (*ibid.*).

[88] Unless otherwise noted, the abbreviation L. I. E. B. in this study will refer to material listed under the abbreviation Li. Eb. as well.

[89] Cf. below, pp. 282 f.

[90] Cited as For. fi. (chs. 1, 19); For. f. (chs. 4, 5, 6); For. F. (ch. 7); For. (chs. 2, 3); F.F. (chs. 10, 13, 19, 20, 22, 23); F.f. (ch. 13). In addition, Usque cites the number of the book of the *Fortalitium Fidei*, which is always the third. This notation, however, is not made consistently. Appearing as "3 L." (*tercer livro*) it is omitted on five occasions (chs. 2, 4, 19, 20, 23), while in chapter one, there is a lower case "l" followed by a meaningless "f" and indicating what is surely a printer's error.

[91] Most of these stem from Usque's listing of the recto of the following leaf

when his account begins on a verso in Spina's book. Thus chapter 3 is taken from *Fortalitium Fidei* 185v, not 186 as quoted; chapter 5 from 186v, not 187; chapter 7 from 189v, not 190 and chapter 22 from 190v, not 191. In the citation of chapter 13 there is a more serious error: though listed as deriving from folio 211 of the *Fortalitium Fidei*, the narrative is really taken from f. 219.

Moreover, some folio references are omitted entirely; thus chapter 2, where the correct folio is 216v; chapter 19, where it is 187v and chapter 23, where it is 190r.

[92] *Primera Crónica General (Crónica de España)*, ed. R. Menéndez Pidal, in *Nueva biblioteca de autores españoles*, V, p. 268; A. de Spina, *op. cit.*, f. 220v; Usque, Dialogue III, chapter 1.

[93] The account is taken from Book 20, chapter 29.

[94] This popular compendium of papal and imperial history by Martin of Troppau (Oppaviensis), goes no further, however, than the year 1277, the year before its author's death; and though numerous continuations were attempted, none that is extant reaches the period of Clement VI, and the year 1345, where Spina places his account. Whether Spina or his source committed a gross error here or whether he utilized some now unknown chronicle that continued or was modeled after the famous work of Martin of Troppau cannot be determined, but this is of little significance as far as Usque is concerned. Cf. L. Weiland, in the introduction to his edition of the chronicle in *Monumenta Germaniae Historica, Scriptores*, XXII (Hanover, 1872), p. 377.

[95] *Ibid.*, f. 220v.

[96] *Op. cit.*, p. 457.

[97] *Crónica de España*, ed. *cit.*, p. 272; Usque, Dialogue III, p. 228.

[98] J. de Ghellinck, *L'essor de la littérature latine au XIIe siècle*, II (Paris, 1946), p. 136. Rigord's work is edited in Bouquet's *Recueil des historiens des Gaules et de la France*, XVII (Paris, 1821), pp. 1-62, by Michel-Jean-Joseph Brial; cf. J. Thompson, *op. cit.*, pp. 271 f.

[99] The passage is taken from Gersonides' comment to Leviticus 26.38, and not, as Verga recalls, to Numbers 23.10. Cf. *Sefer Kehilot Moshe*, f. 194b: and *Shevet Yehuda*, no. 21, ed. Baer and Schochet (Jerusalem, 1947), p. 69. Francisco Cantera-Burgos, in his translation of the *Shevet Yehuda (La vara de Judá)* (Granada, 1927), p. 128, n. 2, gives the reference as Numbers 22.10.

[100] H. Graetz, *op. cit.*, VII, p. 265.

[101] Falaquera may have composed the well-known apology for Maimonides' *Guide* promulgated by a number of French rabbis after 1290. It was published in the Pressburg 1838 edition of Abba Mari of Lunel's *Minḥat Kenaot*, pp. 182-185. Cf. S. Munk, *Mélanges de philosophie juive et arabe* (Paris, 1857), p. 495. See also *Minḥat Kenaot*, p. 179 (no. 100) for a contemporary description of the expulsion, along the lines Falaquera might have written.

[102] *Caftor vo-Ferah* (ed. Jerusalem, 1946), p. 18.

[103] *Sefer ha-Kabbalah*, ed. Neubauer, in *Medieval Jewish Chronicles*, I (Oxford, 1887), p. 73; Usque, Dialogue III, p. 197.

[104] I. Loeb, *Josef Haccohen et les chroniquers juifs* (Paris, 1888), p. 44; M. Steinschneider, *Polemische und apologetische Literatur*, (Leipzig, 1877), pp. 138-140, who puts Samuel's death in 1055.

[105] *Op. cit.*, p. 44.

[106] R. Altamira y Crevea, *op. cit.*, II, pp. 372 ff. During the war with Granada, the Jews of Christian Spain were invaluable assets to the crown, and their indispensability brought them not only royal protection but also the ignoring of grave royal ordinances which had been issued against them early in the 1480's. *Ibid.*, p. 379. Usque's error was clearly seen as early as 1629, when Isaac Aboab wrote in his *Nomología*, p. 272:
Ioseph ha-Leui . . . el qual fue matado en Granada, con otros muchos

Iudios en el año de quatro mil y ochocientos y veynte y quatro, en nueve del mez de Tebet; como traen Areabad en su libro de la Cabalá; Abraham Zachuto en el suyo de las Genealogias, Guedaliah Yahia en su Cadena de la Cabalá; y Iehudá Abenbergue en su Sebet Iehudá. Por donde se vé, que el Vsque, en su Consolacion de Israel, no aduirtió á contar la muerte deste ilustre varon, en su justo tiempo, pues dize, que sucedió en el año de cinco mil y doziẽtos y quarenta y ocho de la creacion, en que ay de diferencia quatrocientos y veyntiquatro años: que causa no pequeño espanto, en vn hombre dotado de buenas letras humanas, y versado en las historias, como el era: y tanto mas que alega con el mismo Areabad, que lo trae como auemos dicho en el tiempo de los Reyes Moros que entonces dominauan a Granada, y el Vsque lo pone en tiempo de Christianos; los quales no ganaron a Granada hasta el año de mil y quatrocientos y nouenta y dos de nuestra cuenta. De manera que, aun que el desastrado sucesso del Nagid Ioseph ha-Leui, vuiera sido en el año de cinco mil y dozientos y quarenta y ocho, como el quiere, no pudo ser en tiempo de Christianos, sino de Moros como auemos dicho.

[107] Cf. I. Loeb, op. cit., p. 44.

[108] That the presence of narratives about a given event or subject in the *Shevet Yehuda* and in the *Consolaçam* does not necessarily imply a common source is seen most clearly in a comparison of Usque's first chapter with the ninth account in Verga. See below, p. 283.

[109] H. Graetz, op. cit., VIII, p. 381.

[110] B. Abrahams, *The Expulsion of the Jews from England in 1290* (Oxford, 1895), p. 63.

[111] Op. cit., VII, p. 463 ff.

[112] The original account doubtlessly bore the date 5050 (1290). Verga's date of 5020 (1260) reveals a mistaken reading of the final Hebrew letter of the original as *Kaph* instead of a *Nun*. Usque, on the other hand, misread the same letter as *Beth*, and dated his account 5002 (1242). See Graetz, op. cit., VIII, p. 385.

[113] See below, p. 282.

[114] Similar marginal references to the Hebrew year are found nine times elsewhere in the historical material of the third Dialogue, and on numerous other occasions throughout the book. They are present in the margins of chapters 4, 20, 25 (twice), 28, 29, 30, 32 and 34. References with the word "Ano(s)" followed by the Hebrew year appear frequently in the chapter heading, v. g., chapters 11, 15, and 20.

[115] Elsewhere, in the heading of chapter 22, a 1 is again the erroneous substitution, this time for a 5. In Mendes dos Remédios' edition of the *Consolaçam*, chapter 35 bears the date 1306, an obvious error for 5306. The error, however, was committed by Mendes, and is found neither in the edition of 1553 nor in that of 1597.

[116] Ed. cit., p. 36.

[117] It is found in the margins of chapters 7, 9, 18 and 20.

[118] E. Lipiner, op. cit., p. 101, n. 2 and p. 147, n. 5.

[119] A Jewish account is the only work extant which fuses these events. It is the *Iggeret Musar* by Solomon Alami. The narrative is found on page 22 of the Jellinek edition (Leipzig, 1854).

[120] It is written L. I. E. B. before chapter 10 (Chaps. 1, 3, 4, 6, 7, 8 and 9) and Li. Eb. thereafter. Chaps. 11, 12, 17 and 20 cite it as l.Eb.; 13, 21, 22 and 24 list it as Li.Eb.

[121] The omission of this notation in chapters 14 and 16 is not a criterion for the postulation of a different source, as Baer emphatically states. H. Baer, *Untersuchungen über Quellen und Komposition des Schebet Jehuda* (Berlin, 1923), pp. 32-34, 37. Verga's claim that he took his sixth account (which parallels Usque's sixteenth chapter) from a Spanish chronicle is false, as is

his claim that his twentieth account derives from a German chronicle. Baer, *op. cit.*, p. 20. Graetz, *op. cit.*, VIII, p. 466, though asserting that Efodi was the common source used by Usque 16 and Verga 6, accepts Verga's statement at face value. Baer's statement concerning the *L. I. E. B.* that "sie findet sich auch bei Stücken, die U(sque) ganz und gar dem Fortalitium Fidei entnommen hat" (*op. cit.*, p. 37), cannot be substantiated.

[122] Baer's statement that "Die Quelle von Kap. 14, *gewiss kein hebräische, ist ebenfalls noch nicht nachgewiesen*" (*op. cit.*, p. 38, italics mine) cannot be accepted.

Chapter 14 of Usque's third Dialogue bears the title "Flanders." It is preceded by two accounts dealing with the expulsion of the Jews from England. Although chapter 14 is not dated, chapter 12 bears the incorrect date of 5002 (1242) (see above, n. 12). It is clear that Usque intended this date for both accounts. Chapter 15 is dated 5022 (1262). On the basis of the position of chapter 14, Loeb, *op. cit.*, p. 40, makes the assumption that it is to be dated around 1260. This assumption, however, is based on the incorrect premise that Usque, who strove for chronological sequence, utilized correct dates in all cases. An examination of the dates given or inferable on the basis of position in chapters 2, 5 and 9 as well as 12 and 13 gives indisputable evidence that this was not so.

Nor does Loeb have any right to assume, on the basis of the unusually scant and vague data of the chapter, that it is historically accurate throughout. There is, in effect, no record of any host-desecration in Flanders at this time. See J. Corblet, *Histoire dogmatique et archéologique du sacrement de l'Eucharistie* (Paris, n.d.) esp. II, pp. 556-588; R. de Fleury, "La messe," in *Études Archéologiques*, IV (1889), pp. 21-40; R. De Sarachaga, *Les collections d'histoire et d'art du musée eucharistique de Paray-le-Monial* (Paris, n.d.), containing a valuable bibliography of the *Monographies sur les hosties de miracles*; H. Leclercq, "Host," in *Catholic Encyclopedia*, VII, pp. 489-493; D. Chwolson, *Die Blutanklage und sonstige mittelalterliche Beschuldigungen der Juden* (Frankfort a.M., 1901), pp. 4 ff. Cf. H. Strack, *The Jew and Human Sacrifice* (New York, 1911), etc.

These facts, coupled with the extremely general nature of Usque's account, point to a confusion in a *Jewish* source he utilized rather than a direct utilization by him of a Christian account.

In view of the fact that the remaining thirty-six chapters in the section of the *Consolaçam* under consideration deal with exemplary events in Jewish history, the account in chapter 14 must similarly describe a signal occurrence. The most sensational charge of host desecration, and the only one worthy of note in that general area during the Middle Ages was the Brussels libel of 1370, which continued to inflame the rabble in Usque's day and up to the end of the nineteenth century, and of which there exists a fifteenth century Flemish account. See D. Liber, *Le faux miracle du saint sacrement* (Brussels, 1874), p. 153. It is likely this was the libel resumed in Usque's Jewish source, with errors in detail not dissimilar to those observable elsewhere in *L. I. E. B.*

Gelbart's suggestion, quoted by Neuman, *op. cit.*, p. 132, that "Brussels" be understood for "Flanders" in Usque's text is valid, provided it is clear that Usque and doubtlessly his source had Flanders and not Brussels in mind when composing their narratives. Of course, I assume here that Gelbart's proposal is based on a hypothesis similar to the one outlined above and that he would have agreed that the original narrative referred to the libel of 1370.

All of this information further emphasizes the unlikelihood of a direct utilization by Usque of a Christian account.

[123] Baer, *op. cit.*, pp. 2 ff.

[124] The parallel sections are as follows: Usque 4 and Verga 30; U 8 and V 31; U 11 and V 19; U 12 and V 18, 20; U 16 and V 6; U 17 and V 14, 39;

U 18, V 43; U 19 and V 26; U 20 and V 21, 24, 25; U 21 and V 27, 46, 48, 49.

[125] Op. cit., VIII, pp. 393 ff. The spelling "Libro" is Graetz's.

[126] Ed. Carlsruhe (?), 1828, f. 30b. (Iyyun 2, Pereḳ 2, toward the end).

[127] Op. cit., p. 102.

[128] Ibid., p. 38. See also ibid., p. 42. Loeb's inexplicable election to render L. I. E. B. in Latin pays no attention to the rudiments of Latin syntax, which would require the proper nouns in the genitive.

[129] Ibid., p. 102.

[130] Ibid.

[131] Op. cit. This hypothesis was first posited by Umberto Cassuto in 1912, with respect to a single set of parallels—Usque 11 and Verga 19. "Un ignoto capitolo di storia ebraica," in Judaica (Festschrift für H. Cohen) (Berlin, 1912), pp. 399 ff.

[132] An internal approach such as Baer's is limited by many external factors. These include imperfect recollections or exaggerations of the sources by the authors, who did not always have the source texts before them when they wrote, printing errors, coincidences, popular moulds of expression of given ideas or narratives which do not necessarily indicate a traceable or common literary source, etc. A lack of scientific devices to gauge these areas circumscribes the value of conclusions based on internal evidence alone.

[133] Though on one occasion he insists, probably correctly, that the common source was written in Hebrew (op. cit., p. 13) he casts doubt on the possibility that Usque utilized it directly.

Zumal es zweifelhaft ist, ob U(sque) imstande war, eine hebräische Chronik zu benutzen, oder ob er sich nicht bereits einer portugiesischen oder anders-sprachigen Übersetzung der ihm mit V(erga) jedenfalls gemeinsamen Quelle bedient hat (ibid., p. 37).

[134] Op. cit., pp. 61 ff.

[135] Loeb, op. cit., p. 102, claims the name Verga was written with a B, but adduces no evidence for this statement. Nor was this interchange common in Portuguese. Cf. E. Williams, From Latin to Portuguese (Philadelphia, 1938), p. 59.

[136] I. Loeb, "Les expulsions des Juifs de France au XIVe siècle," in Graetz-Jubelschrift (Breslau, 1887), pp. 44 f.

[137] Cf. above pp. 279 f.

[138] These include Chaps. 1, 3, 6, 7, 9, 10, 13 and 22, where L. I. E. B. is listed as a source and Chaps. 15 and 19, where the indication of the presence of L. I. E. B. has been erroneously omitted.

[139] S. Gronemann, De Profiatii Durani Vita ac Studiis (Breslau, 1869), pp. 5-15.

[140] Op. cit., VIII, p. 397.

[141] Usque's chapter bears the date 5850, an obvious misprint for 5150.

[142] Maaseh Efod, p. 14. Here Efodi states:

ומי יודע אם הצלת קהילות ארגון אשר הם העקר שנמלט מגלות ספרד היתה לרוב שקידתם על התפילה ולקום בלילי אשמורות להתחנן לה' בתחנונים.

[143] Op. cit., VIII, p. 127, n. 1. Graetz himself noticed this error, but failed to draw any conclusions from it.

[144] Cf. above, pp. 180 ff.

[145] Op. cit., p. 11.

[146] Cf. Mayyene Ha-Yeshuah (Ferrara, 1551), f. 21b.

[147] See n. 126 above.

[148] Cf. above, pp. 275 ff.

[149] Cf. above, pp. 15 f. Abravanel's influence on Verga, while not as pervasive as on Usque, was nevertheless not inconsiderable, and Verga manifests a direct acquaintance with several of Isaac's works. In addition, he appears in two

chapters of Verga's book. In chap. 51, there is a direct quotation from the introduction to his commentary on the Book of Kings, while chapter 7 includes a fictitious conversation concerning the Hebrew word *Nokhri* and the biblical prohibition of usury, in which there enters "a noble of the sons of Abravanel who had come from Seville, his native city."

[150] Three of these, the introductory poems to *Rosh Amanah, Naḥlat Abot* and *Zevaḥ Pesaḥ* appeared in 1509. The fourth, a comparatively lengthy encomium of Isaac Abravanel, introducing the commentary to the Prophets, appeared in 1520. N. Slouschz, *Poésies hebraiques de don Jehuda Abravanel* (Lisbon, 1928), p. 3.

[151] It is likely that Judah wrote works in Hebrew other than those presently extant. For these see B. Zimmels, *Leo Hebraeus* (Leipzig, 1886), pp. 49 ff.

[152] *Ibid.*, pp. 3 f.

[153] *Shevet Yehuda*, ed. Baer, p. 120.

[154] *Ibid.*, p. 207.

[155] *Ibid.* and Abravanel's Commentary *ad loc.*

BIBLIOGRAPHY

ABOAB, ISAAC. Nomologia. *Amsterdam, 1629.*

ABRAHAMS, B. LIONEL. The Expulsion of the Jews from England in 1290. *Oxford, 1895.*

ABRAVANEL, ISAAC. Mayyene Ha-Yeshuah. *Ferrara, 1551.*

————. Perush al-Neviim Rishonim. *Leipzig, 1686 and Jerusalem, 1956.*

————. Perush Ha-Torah. *Jerusalem, 1956.*

————. Yeshuot Meshiḥo. *Carlsruhe, 1828.*

ADLER, HERBERT M. Service of the Synagogue; Day of Atonement. *2 vols., New York, 1908.*

AKRISH, ISAAC. Kol Mevasser. *Constantinople, 1577.*

ALAMI, SOLOMON. Iggeret Musar. *Ed. by Adolf Jellinek, Leipzig, 1854.*

————. Iggeret Musar. *Ed. by A. M. Haberman, Jerusalem, 1946.*

ALFONSO, X. Primera Crónica General (Crónica de España). *Ed. by Ramón Menéndez-Pidal, in* Nueva biblioteca de autores españoles, *Vol. V, Madrid, 1906.*

ALTAMIRA Y CREVEA, RAFAEL. Historia de España. *Vol. II, Madrid, 1928.*

AMADOR DE LOS RÍOS, JOSÉ. Estudios históricos, políticos y literarios sobre los judíos de España. *Madrid, 1848.*

————. Historia social, política y religiosa de los judíos de España y Portugal. *3 vols., Madrid, 1875-1876.*

AMAT DI S. FILIPPO, PIETRO. Bibliografia dei viaggiatori italiani. *Rome, 1874.*

AMEAL, JOÃO. História de Portugal. *Porto, 1940.*

AMRAM, DAVID W. The Makers of Hebrew Books in Italy. *Philadelphia, 1909.*

ANTONIO, NICOLÁS. Bibliotheca Hispana Nova. *2 vols., Madrid, 1783-1788.*

The Apocrypha and Pseudepigrapha of the Old Testament. *Ed. by Robert H. Charles, Oxford, 1913.*

AUGUSTINUS, AURELIUS (ST. AUGUSTINE). The City of God. *Ed. and tr. by Reginald H. Barrow, London, 1950.*

————. Tractatus adversus Judaeos. *Ed. by J. P. Migne,* Patrologia Latina. *Vol. XLII (Augustine, vol. VIII), Paris, 1886, cols. 51-64.*

AZEVEDO, J. LÚCIO D'. A evolucão do sebastianismo. *Lisbon. n.d.*

————. História dos christãos novos portugueses. *Lisbon, 1921.*

The Babylonian Talmud.

BAECK, SAMUEL. "Alami, Solomon." The Jewish Encyclopedia. *Vol. I, New York, 1901, pp. 316-317.*

————. "Apologists." The Jewish Encyclopedia. *Vol. II, New York, 1902, pp. 8-11.*

BAER, FRITZ [ISAAC]. Die Juden im christlichen Spanien. Vol. I, Berlin, 1929.

_____. "Sefer Yosippon Ha-Ivri." Sefer Dinaburg. Jerusalem, 1949, pp. 178-205.

_____. Toledot Ha-Yehudim bi-Sefarad Ha-Notzrit. Tel Aviv, 1959.

_____. Untersuchungen über Quellen und Komposition des Schebet Jehuda. Berlin, 1923.

BAIÃO, ANTÓNIO. A inquisição em Portugal e no Brasil. Lisbon, 1921.

BAINTON, ROLAND H. The Reformation of the Sixteenth Century. Boston, 1952.

BALLETTI, ANDREA. Gli ebrei e gli estensi. Emilia, 1930.

BARBOSA MACHADO, DIOGO. Bibliotheca Lusitana. Vols. II & III, Lisbon, 1747-1752.

BARET, EUGÈNE. De l'Amadis de Gaule et de son influence sur les moeurs et la littérature au XVIe et au XVIIe siècle. Paris, 1873.

BAROJA, JULIO CARO. Los judíos en la España moderna y contem-poránea. 3 vols., Madrid, 1961.

BARROS, JOÃO DE. Diálogo evangélico sobre os artigos da fé contra o Talmud dos Judeus. Ed. by I. S. Révah, Lisbon, 1950.

BARTOLOCCI(O), IULIUS. Bibliotheca Magna Rabbinica. 5 vols., Rome, 1675-1694.

BATAILLON, MARCEL. Érasme et l'Espagne. Paris, 1937.

BELL, AUBREY F. G. Portuguese Literature. Oxford, 1922.

BIALIK, HAYYIM N. Letters (Hebrew), Vol. IV, Tel Aviv, 1938.

BLOOM, HERBERT I. The Economic Activities of the Jews of Amster-dam in the Seventeenth and Eighteenth Centuries. Williamsport (Penna.) 1937.

BRAGA, THEOPHILO. História da Universidade de Coimbra nas suas relações com a instrucção publica portugueza. 4 vols., Lisbon, 1892-1902.

BROSCH, MORITZ. "The Height of the Ottoman Power." Cambridge Modern History. Vol. III, New York, 1905, pp. 104-139.

BURCKHARDT, JAKOB. The Civilization of the Renaissance in Italy. Tr. by S. G. C. Middlemore, London, 1892.

BURY, J. B. "The Ottoman Conquest." Cambridge Modern History. Vol. I, New York, 1903, pp. 67-103.

CASSIUS DIO COCCEIANUS. Dio's Rome. Ed. by Herbert B. Foster, Vol. V (Book 62), Troy (New York), 1905-1906.

CASSUTO, UMBERTO. "Un ignoto capitolo di storia ebraica." Judaica, Fest-schrift zu Hermann Cohens siebzigstem Geburtstage. Berlin, 1912, pp. 389-404.

CASTONNET DESFOSSES. La Pastorale en Portugal. Paris, 1882.

CASTRO, AMÉRICO. La realidad histórica de España. Mexico, 1954.

CASTRO Y ROSSI, ADOLFO DE. A History of Religious Intolerance in Spain. London, 1853.

THE CATHOLIC ENCYCLOPEDIA.

CERVANTES, MIGUEL DE. Persiles y Sigismunda. Ed. by Adolfo Bonilla and Rudolfo Schevill, Madrid, 1913.

CHAPMAN, CHARLES E. A History of Spain. New York, 1931.

CHWOLSON, DANIEL. Die Blutanklage und sonstige mittelalterliche Beschuldigungen der Juden. Frankfurt a M., 1901.

CIDADE, HERNANI. Lições sôbre a cultura e a literatura portuguesas. Coimbra, 1933.

CLEMENT (OF ROME). Homiliae. Ed. by J.P. Migne, Patrologia Graeca. Vol. II, Paris, 1886, cols. 19-468.

_____. Recognitiones. Ed. by J.P. Migne, Patrologia Graeca. Vol. I, Paris, 1886, cols. 1201-1454.

COHEN, MARTIN A. Studies in the Sources of Samuel Usque's Consolaçam as Tribulaçoens de Israel. Hebrew Union College-Jewish Institute of Religion Rabbinic Dissertation, 1957 (unpublished).

CORBLET, J. Histoire dogmatique et archéologique du sacrément de l'Eucharistie. Vol. II, Paris, n.d.

COSTA, ISAAC DA. Israël en de Volken. Haarlem, 1873.

Dictionnaire de théologie catholique.

DUBNOW, SIMON. Divre Yeme Am Olam. Vol. VI, Tel Aviv, 1948.

DURAN, PROPHIAT. Maaseh Efod. Ed. by Y.T. Friedlander and J. Kohn, Vienna, 1865.

Enciclopedia Cattolica.

EUSEBIUS PAMPHILIUS. Eusebii Pamphili Chronicon Bipartitum. Ed. by J.B. Aucher, Venice, 1818.

FAGE, J. D. An Atlas of African History, Bungay, Suffolk, 1958.

FARINELLI, ARTURO. Marrano: Storia di un vituperio. Geneva, 1925.

FERNÁNDEZ Y GONZÁLEZ, FRANCISCO. "El mesianismo israelita en la peninsula ibérica durante la primera mitad del siglo XVI." Revista de España. Vol. XVIII, Madrid, 1871, pp. 406ff.

FIGGIS, JOHN N. The Political Aspects of St. Augustine's City of God. London, 1921.

FIGUEIREDO, FIDELINO DE. História da literatura clássica. Vol. I, Lisbon, 1922.

_____. História literária de Portugal. Coimbra, 1944.

FITA, FIDEL. La España Hebrea. 2 vols., Madrid, 1889-1898.

FLETCHER, JEFFERSON B. Literature of the Italian Renaissance. New York, 1934.

FLEURY, ROBERT DE. "La messe." Études Archéologiques. Vol. IV, Paris, 1889, pp. 21-40.

FONSECA, JOSE DA. Prosas Selectas. Paris, 1837.

FRANCO, MOISE. Essai sur l'histoire des israélites de l'empire Ottoman. Paris, 1897.

FREIER, MORITZ. "Usque." Jüdisches Lexicon. Vol. V, Berlin, 1930, p. 1147.

FÜRST, JULIUS. Bibliotheca Judaica. Vol. III, Leipzig, 1863.

GALANTE, ABRAHAM. "Deux nouveaux documents sur Doña Gracia Nassy." Revue des Études Juives. Vol. LXV, Paris, 1913, pp. 151-154.

GASTER, MOSES. "Abravanel's Literary Work." Isaac Abravanel: Six Lectures. Ed. by J.B. Trend and H. Loewe, Cambridge (Eng.), 1937. pp. 39-73.

_____. "Samuel Usque, Consolations for the Troubles of Israel." The Jewish Forum., Vol. XIII, New York, 1930, pp. 367-374.

GEBHARDT, CARL. Leone Ebreo: Dialoghi d'Amore: Hebraeische Gedichte. Heidelberg, 1929.

GEYL, PIETER. The Revolt of the Netherlands 1555-1609. London, 1932.

GHELLINCK, JOSEPH DE. L'essor de la littérature latine au XIIe siècle. 2 vols., Paris, 1946.

GINZBERG, LOUIS. Eine unbekannte jüdische Sekte. New York, 1922.

_____. Legends of the Jews. 7 vols. Philadelphia, 1909-1938.

GOTTHEIL, RICHARD. "Abraham in Mohammedan Legend." The Jewish Encyclopedia. Vol. I, pp. 87-90.

GRAETZ, HEINRICH. Geschichte der Juden. Vols. VII-IX, Leipzig, 1873-1877.

GRAYZEL, SOLOMON. "Abravanel and the End of an Era." Reconstructionist. Vol. III, no. 17, New York, 1937, pp. 7-13.

GRONEMANN, SELIG. De Profiatii Durani vita ac studiis. Breslau, 1869.

GUTTMANN, JULIUS. Die Religions-philosophischen Lehren des Isaak Abravanel. Breslau, 1916.

HA-COHEN, JOSEPH. Emek Ha-Bakha. *Ed. by M. Letteris, Cracow, 1895.*
Haggadah for Passover. *Ed. by Ernst D. Goldschmidt, New York, 1953.*
HANTZSCH, VIKTOR. Sebastian Münster: Leben, Werk, wissenschaft-liche Bedeutung. *Leipzig, 1898.*
Harper's Dictionary of Classical Literature and Antiquities. *Ed. by Harry Thurston Peck, New York, 1896.*
HAVET, ERNEST. Mémoire sur Bérose et Manéthon. *Paris, 1873.*
HERCULANO, ALEXANDRE. História da origem e estabelecimento da Inquisiçao em Portugal. *3 vols., Lisbon, 1855-1859.*
_____. History of the Origin and Establishment of the Inquisition in Portugal. *Tr. by John C. Branner, Stanford University, California, 1926.*
HIRSCH, EMIL G. "Esau." The Jewish Encyclopedia. *Vol. V, New York, 1903, pp. 206-208.*
HIRSCHFELD, HARTWIG. "Ishmael in Arabic Literature." The Jewish Encyclopedia. *Vol. VI, p. 648.*
HIRZL, RUDOLF. Der Dialog. *Leipzig, 1895.*
The Holy Scriptures. *Philadelphia, 1917.*
HOLZKNECHT, KARL J. Literary Patronage in the Middle Ages. *Philadelphia, 1923.*
HURTADO, JUAN AND GONZÁLEZ-PALENCIA, ANGEL. Historia de la literatura española. *Madrid, 1949.*
IBN DAUD, ABRAHAM. Sefer Ha-Kaballah. *In Adolf Neubauer, Medieval Jewish Chronicles. Vol. I, Oxford, 1887, pp. 47-84.*
IBN VERGA, SOLOMON (?). Shevet Yehuda. *Ed. by Fritz Baer with notes by Ezriel Schochet, Jerusalem, 1947.*
_____. Chébet Jehudá (La vara de Judá). *Tr. by Francisco Cantera Burgos, Granada, 1927.*
IBN YAHIA, GEDALIAH. Shalshelet Ha-Kabbalah. *Warsaw, 1877.*
The Jerusalem Talmud. *Krotoshin ed.*
JOSEPH BEN GORION (pseudonym). Sefer Yosippon. *Mantua, 1480 (?); Constantinople, 1510; Worms, 1529; Basel, 1541; Venice, 1544; Basel, 1559 (Münster edition identical with 1541 edition and utilized, because of its superior pagination, for quotation in text above); Berditchev, 1896-1913 (utilized as standard Yosippon in text above).*
JOSEPHUS, FLAVIUS. Works. *Tr. by William Whiston, London, 1895.*
_____. Works. *Tr. by H. St. John Thackeray, 8 vols., London-New York, (1926-1934), The Loeb Classical Library.*
JOST, ISAAC M. Geschichte des Judenthums und seiner Secten. *Vol. III, Leipzig, 1859.*
KAYSERLING, MEYER. Biblioteca española-portugueza-judaica. *Strasbourg, 1890.*
_____. Die jüdischen Frauen. *Leipzig, 1879.*
_____. Geschichte der Juden in Portugal. *Leipzig, 1867.*
_____. "Nasi, Reyna." The Jewish Encyclopedia. *Vol. IX, New York, 1905, p. 174.*
_____. Sephardim: Romanische Poesien der Juden in Spanien. *Leipzig, 1859.*
_____. "Spina, Alfonso de." The Jewish Encyclopedia. *Vol. XI, New York, 1905, p. 510.*
_____. "Usque, Abraham." The Jewish Encyclopedia. *Vol. XII, New York, 1905, p. 387.*
_____. "Usque, Samuel." The Jewish Encyclopedia. *Vol. XII, New York, 1905, pp. 387-388.*
_____. "Usque, Solomon." The Jewish Encyclopedia. *Vol. XII, New York, 1905, p. 388.*
KRAUSE, ANNA. Jorge Manrique and the Cult of Death in the Cuatrocientos. *Berkeley, 1937.*

337

LEA, HENRY C. Chapters from the Religious History of Spain. Philadelphia, 1890.
――――. A History of the Inquisition in Spain. Vol. I, New York, 1906.
LECLERQ, H. "Host." Catholic Encyclopedia. Vol. VII, New York, 1910, pp. 489-493.
LEMOS, MAXIMIANO. Amato Lusitano: A sua vida e a sua obra. Porto, 1907.
LEO AFRICANUS. Delle Navigationi et Viaggi. Ed. by Giovanni Battista Ramusio. Vol. I, Venice, 1563, pp. 1-95.
――――. The History and Description of Africa. Tr. by John Pory (1600) and ed. by Robert Brown, 2 vols., London, 1896.
LEO HEBRAEUS (JUDAH ABRAVANEL). The Philosophy of Love (Dialoghi d'Amore). Tr. by F. Friedeberg-Seeley and J.H. Barnes, Introduction by C. Roth, London, 1937.
LEVI BEN GERSON (GERSONIDES). Commentary to the Pentateuch. Sefer Kehilot Moshe. 4 vols., Amsterdam, 1724-1728.
LEWIN, M. Wo wären die "zehn Stämme Israels" zu suchen? Pressburg, 1901.
LIBER, DOM. Le faux miracle du saint sacrément. Brussels, 1874.
LIPINER, ELIAS. Bei die Teichen von Portugal (Yiddish). Buenos Aires, 1949.
LIVERMORE, HAROLD V. A History of Portugal. Cambridge (Eng.), 1947.
LOEB, ISIDORE. "Comparaison d'Usque et de l'Emek habbakha." Revue des Études Juives. Vol. XVI, Paris, 1888, pp. 212-223.
――――. "La Controverse de 1240 sur le Talmud." Revue des études juives. Vol. I (1880), pp. 247-261; Vol. II (1881), pp. 248-270; Vol. III (1881), pp. 39-57.
――――. "Les expulsions des juifs de France au XIVe siècle." Jubelschrift . . . H. Graetz. Breslau, 1887, pp. 39-56.
――――. Joseph Haccohen et les chroniquers juifs. Paris, 1888.
――――. "Polémistes chrétiens et juifs en France et en Espagne." Revue des études juives. Vol. XVIII (1889), pp. 43-70 and 219-242.
LÓPEZ-MARTÍNEZ, NICOLÁS. Los Judaizantes castellanos y la Inquisición en tiempo de Isabel la Católica. Burgos, 1954.
LUCAN(US), MARCUS ANNAEUS. The Civil War. Tr. by J. D. Duff, London, 1928.
MACHIAVELLI, NICCOLÒ. The Prince. Ed. C. Gauss, New York, 1954.
MAHLER, EDUARD. Handbuch der jüdischen Chronologie. Leipzig, 1916.
MANUEL II, KING OF PORTUGAL. Early Portuguese Books. 3 vols., Cambridge (Eng.), 1929-1935.
MARETO, FELICE DA. "Spina, Alfonso Lopez de." Enciclopedia Cattolica. XI, Vatican City, 1953, col. 1122.
MARK, B., "Cenny Egzemplarz Samuela Usque: 'Consolacam as Tribulacoens de Israel,' " biuletyn zydowskiego instytutu historycznego, II-III (6-7) (Warsaw, 1953), pp. 236-239.
MEKHILTA DE-RABBI ISHMAEL. Ed. by Jacob Z. Lauterbach, 3 vols., Philadelphia, 1933-1935.
MENDES DOS REMÉDIOS, JOAQUIM. "A Consolação às tribulações de Israel." Biblos. Vol. III, Coimbra, 1927, pp. 408-424.
――――. História da literatura portuguesa. Coimbra, 1930.
――――. Os judeos em Portugal. 2 vols., Coimbra, 1895, 1928.
――――. "Os judeos portuguess através dalguns documentos literarios." Biblos. Vol. III, Coimbra, 1927, pp. 237-263.
MENÉNDEZ-PIDAL, RAMON. Manual de gramática histórica española. Madrid, 1925.

338

MENÉNDEZ Y PELAYO, MARCELINO. Historia de los heterodoxos españoles. Vol. III, Santander, 1946-1948.

_____. Orígines de la Novela. Nueva biblioteca de autores españoles. Vol. I, Madrid, 1905.

MERRIMAN, ROGER B. Suleiman the Magnificent, 1520-1566. Cambridge (Mass.), 1944.

METTLER, CECILIA C. History of Medicine. Philadelphia, 1947.

The Midrash Rabbah. Wilna edition.

Midrash Tannaim. Ed. by David Z. Hoffmann, Berlin, 1908-1909.

Midrash Tehillim (Psalms). Ed. by Solomon Buber, Wilna, 1891.

Midrash Wa-Yosha. Ed. by Adolf Jellinek in Bet-Hamidrasch. Vol. I, Vienna, 1853, pp. 35-37.

Minkhat Kenaot (of Abba Mari of Lunel) and other writings. Pressburg, 1838.

The Mishnah.

MONTORO, ANTÓN DE. Cancionero. Madrid, 1900.

MUNK, SOLOMON. Mélanges de philosophie juive et arabe. Paris, 1857.

NETANYAHU, BENZION. Don Isaac Abravanel, Statesman and Philosopher. Philadelphia, 1953.

NEUBAUER, ADOLPH. "Where Are the Ten Tribes?" The Jewish Quarterly Review. Vol. I, London, 1889, pp. 14-28; pp. 95-114; pp. 185-201; pp. 408-423.

NEUMAN, ABRAHAM A. The Jews in Spain. 2 vols., Philadelphia, 1942.

_____. "Josippon and the Apocrypha." Landmarks and Goals. Philadelphia, 1953, pp. 35-59.

_____. "Josippon: History and Pietism." Landmarks and Goals. Philadelphia, 1953, pp. 1-34.

_____. "A Note on John the Baptist and Jesus in the Josippon." Hebrew Union College Annual. Vol. XXIII, Part 2, Cincinnati, 1950-1951, pp. 137-149.

_____. "Samuel Usque: Marrano Historian of the Sixteenth Century." Landmarks and Goals. Philadelphia, 1953.

_____. "Samuel Usque: Marrano Historian of the Sixteenth Century." To Doctor R. Essays . . . Collected and Published in Honor of the Seventieth Birthday of Dr. A. S. W. Rosenbach. Philadelphia, 1946.

OLIVEIRA MARTINS, JOAQUIM PEDRO. História de Portugal. Porto, 1886.

ORIGEN. Contra Celsum. Ed. by J. P. Migne in Patrologia Graeca. Vol. XI (Origen, Vol. I), Paris, 1862, cols. 637-1710.

OVIDIUS NASO, PUBLIUS. Metamorphoses. Tr. by Frank J. Miller, London, 1939.

PARHI, ESTORI. Caftor vo-Ferah. Ed. by Hirsch Edelmann, Berlin, 1852.

PARKES, JAMES A. "Church and Synagogue in the Middle Ages." The Transactions of the Jewish Historical Society of England. Vol. XVI, London, 1952, pp. 25-33.

PENROSE, BOIES. Travel and Discovery in the Renaissance. Cambridge (Mass.), 1952.

PERES, DAMIÃO ET AL. História de Portugal. 8 Vols., Barcelos, 1928-1938.

PÉREZ CASTRO, FEDERICO. "Ojeada rápida a la literatura polémica anti-judía." In his edition of El manuscrito apologético de Alfonso de Zamora. Madrid, 1950, pp. xciv-ci.

PESARO, ABRAMO. Memorie storiche sulla comunità israelitica ferrarese. Ferrara, 1878.

PHILO JUDAEUS. Works. Tr. by F. H. Golson, G. H. Whitaker and R. Marcus, vols. 1-11, Cambridge (Mass.), 1949-1954.

Pirke d'Rabbi Eliezer. Ed. by Samuel Lurie, Warsaw, 1852.

PLATO. The Works of Plato. *Tr. by B. Jowett and selected and ed. by I. Edman, New York, 1928.*

POLMAN, PONTIEN. L'elément historique dans la controverse religieuse du XVIe siècle. *Gembloux, 1932.*

POPPER, WILLIAM. The Censorship of Hebrew Books. *New York, 1899.*

PRESCOTT, WILLIAM H. History of the Reign of Ferdinand and Isabella, the Catholic. *3 vols., Philadelphia, 1872.*

Primera Crónica General (Crónica de España), *edited by Ramón Menéndez Pidal, in* Nueva biblioteca de autores españoles. *Vol. V, Madrid, 1906.*

PRINS, IZAK. De Vestiging der Marranen in Noord-Nederland in de zestiende eeuw. *Amsterdam, 1927.*

RABINOWITZ, SAUL P. Motzoei Golah. *Warsaw, 1894.*

RANKIN, OLIVER S. Jewish Religious Polemic. *Edinburgh, 1956.*

RENNERT, HUGO A. The Spanish Pastoral Romances. *Philadelphia, 1912.*

REUSCH, FRANZ H. Die Indices Librorum prohibitorum des sechzehnten Jahrhunderts. *Stuttgart, 1886.*

RIBEIRO, BERNALDIM. Obras. *Ed. by F. I. Pinheiro, Lisbon, 1852.*

RIBEIRO DOS SANTOS, ANTÓNIO. Memórias da literatura portuguesa. *Vol. II, Lisbon, 1792.*

RIGORD. Gesta Philippi Augusti. *Ed. by Michel-Jean-Joseph Brial in* Recueil des historiens des Gaules et de la France. *Vol. XVII, Paris, 1821, pp. 1-62.*

RIVKIN, ELLIS. *"The Utilization of Non-Jewish Sources for the Reconstruction of Jewish History."* Jewish Quarterly Review *(New Series). Vol. XLVIII, Philadelphia, 1957/1958, pp. 183-203.*

ROBB, NESCA A. Neoplatonism of the Italian Renaissance. *London, 1935.*

ROBINSON, PASCHAL. *"Alfonso de Spina."* The Catholic Encyclopedia. *Vol. XIV, New York, 1912, p. 216.*

RODRÍGUEZ DE CASTRO, JOSEPH. Biblioteca Española, *2 vols., Madrid, 1781-1786.*

ROSANES, SOLOMON. Divre Yeme Israel B'Turgema. *5 vols., Husiatyn, 1907-1937.*

ROSSI, AZARIAH DEI. Me'or Enayim. *Wilna, 1866.*

ROSSI, GIOVANNI BERNARDO DE. Bibliotheca Judaica Antichristiana. *Parma, 1800.*

───────. Della vana aspettazione degli ebrei. *Parma, 1773.*

───────. De typographia Hebraeo-Ferrariensi commentarius historicus. *Parma, 1780.*

───────. Dizionario storico degli autori ebrei e delle loro opere. *2 vols., Parma, 1802.*

───────. Historisches Wörterbuch der Jüdischen Schriftsteller und ihrer Werke *(translation of* Dizionario storico degli autori ebrei e delle loro opere). *Tr. by C. H. Hamberger, Leipzig, 1839.*

ROSSI, GIUSEPPE CARLO. Storia della letteratura portoghese. *Florence, 1953.*

ROTH, CECIL. *"The Case of Thomas Fernandes before the Lisbon Inquisition, 1556. From the Papers of the Late Lucien Wolf."* Miscellanies of the Jewish Historical Society of England. *Vol. II, London, 1935, pp. 32-56.*

───────. The History of the Jews of Italy. *Philadelphia, 1946.*

───────. A History of the Marranos. *Philadelphia, 1932.*

───────. The House of Nasi: The Duke of Naxos. *Philadelphia, 1948.*

───────. The House of Naxos: Doña Gracia. *Philadelphia, 1947.*

───────. *"Joseph Saralvo: A Marrano Martyr at Rome."* Festschrift zu Simon Dubnows siebzigstem Geburtstag. *Berlin, 1930, pp. 180-186.*

_____. "The Marrano Press at Ferrara." MODERN LANGUAGE REVIEW. Vol. XXXVIII, Cambridge (Eng.), 1943, pp. 307-317.

_____. "Salusque Lusitano." JEWISH QUARTERLY REVIEW (New Series). Vol. XXXIV, Philadelphia, 1943-1944, pp. 65-85.

SANNAZARO, JACOPO. L'ARCADIA. Ed. by Michele Scherillo. Turin, 1888.

SARACHAGA, R. DE. LES COLLECTIONS D'HISTOIRE ET D'ART DU MUSÉE EUCHARISTIQUE DE PARAY-LE-MONIAL. Paris, n.d.

SARACHEK, JOSEPH. DON ISAAC ABRAVANEL. New York, 1938.

SARAIVA, ANTÓNIO J. AND LOPES, ÓSCAR. HISTÓRIA DA LITERATURA PORTUGUESA. Porto, 1956.

SCHAEFER, ERNST. LUTHER ALS KIRCHENHISTORIKER. Gutersloh, 1897.

SCHECHTER, SOLOMON. "Safed in the Sixteenth Century." STUDIES IN JUDAISM (Second Series). Vol. II, Philadelphia, 1908, pp. 202-285.

SCHEEL, OTTO. MARTIN LUTHER. VOM KATHOLIZISMUS ZUR REFORMATION. 2 vols., Tübingen, 1916-1917.

SCHOCHET, EZRIEL. "Usque, Samuel." THE HEBREW ENCYCLOPEDIA (Hebrew). Vol. II, Jerusalem, 1950, p. 335.

SCHULMAN, KALMAN. TOLEDOT HAKHME ISRAEL. Vol. IV, Wilna, 1878.

SELIGSOHN, MAX. "Edom, Idumea." THE JEWISH ENCYCLOPEDIA. Vol. V, New York, 1903, pp. 40-41.

THE SEPTUAGINT.

SIDDUR OTSAR HA-TEFILOT (Sefardic). New York, 1946.

SIFRE DEUTERONOMY. Ed. by Meir Friedmann (Ish Shalom), Vienna, 1864.

SIGÜENZA, JOSÉ DE. HISTORIA DE LA ORDEN DE SAN JERÓNIMO, SEGUNDA PARTE. NUEVA BIBLIOTECA DE AUTORES ESPAÑOLES. Vol. VIII, Madrid, 1907.

SILVA, INOCÊNCIO FRANCISCO DA. DICIONÁRIO BIBLIOGRÁFICO PORTU-GUEZ. Vol. VII, Lisbon, 1862.

SILVA ROSA, JACOB SAMUEL DA. GESCHIEDNIS DER PORTUGEESCHE JODEN TE AMSTERDAM, 1593-1925. Amsterdam, 1925.

SILVER, ABBA HILLEL. A HISTORY OF MESSIANIC SPECULATION IN ISRAEL. New York, 1927.

SIMON, MARCEL. VERUS ISRAEL: ETUDES SUR LES RELATIONS ENTRE CHRÉTIENS ET JUIFS DANS L'EMPIRE ROMAIN. Paris, 1948.

SLOUSCHZ, NAHUM. POÉSIES HEBRAIQUES DE DON JEHUDA ABRAVANEL. Lisbon, 1928.

SMALLEY, BERYL. THE STUDY OF THE BIBLE IN THE MIDDLE AGES. Oxford, 1941.

SMITH, PRESERVED. THE AGE OF THE REFORMATION. New York, 1920.

SOLOMON BEN ISAAC OF TROYES (RASHI). COMMENTARY TO THE PENTATEUCH.

SPINA, ALFONSO DE. FORTALITIUM FIDEI. Lyons, 1511.

STEINSCHNEIDER, JULIUS. "Zur Geschichte jüdischer Martyrologien (R. Samuel Usque's 'Trost Israels in seinen Trübsalen')," in FESTSCHRIFT ZUM X. STIFTUNGSFEST DES AKADEMISCHEN VEREINS FÜR JÜDISCHE GESCHICHTE UND LITERATUR AN DER KGL. FRIEDRICH-WILHELMS-UNIVERSITÄT ZU BERLIN, Berlin, 1893, pp. 24-77.

STEINSCHNEIDER, MORITZ. POLEMISCHE UND APOLOGETISCHE LITERATUR. Leipzig, 1877.

STEPHENS, HENRY M. PORTUGAL. In THE STORY OF THE NATIONS. New York and London, 1893.

STRACK, HERMANN L. THE JEW AND HUMAN SACRIFICE. Tr. from the German by H.F.E. Blanchamp, New York, 1911.

SYMONDS, JOHN A. THE RENAISSANCE. Vol. I, New York, 1887.

TACITUS, CORNELIUS. THE ANNALS OF TACITUS. Book 14, ed. by E. C. Woodcock, London, 1939.

TARGUM YERUSHALMI to the Pentateuch.

TEIXEIRA REGO, JOSÉ. Estudos e controvérsias, Segunda Série. Porto, 1931.

THOMPSON, JAMES WESTFALL. A History of Historical Writing. 2 vols., New York, 1942.

TORQUEMADA, JUAN DE. Tractatus contra madianitas et ismaelitas. Ed. by Nicolás López Martínez and Vicente Proaño Gil, Burgos, 1957.

TORRACA, FRANCESCO. Gl' imitatori stranieri di Jacopo Sannazaro. Rome, 1882.

TOSEFTA. Ed. by Moses S. Zuckermandel, Halberstadt, 1881.

TROPPAU, MARTIN OF. Chronica summorum pontificum imperatorum-que. Ed. by Ludovicus Weiland in Monumenta Germaniae Historica, Scriptores. Vol. XXII, Hanover, 1872, pp. 377-475.

USQUE, SAMUEL. Consolaçam as tribulaçoens de Israel. Ferrara, 1553.

————. Consolaçam as tribulaçoens de Israel. Amsterdam, 1597.

————. Consolaçam as tribulaçoens de Israel. ed. Joaquim Mendes dos Remedios, 3 vols., Coimbra, 1906-1908.

VALDÉS, ALFONSO DE. Diálogo de la lengua. Madrid, 1928.

VARTHEMA, LODOVICO DI. Itinerario. Ed. by Alberto Bacchi Della Lega, Bologna, 1885.

————. The Travels of Ludovico di Varthema. Tr. by John Winter Jones, London, 1863.

VERNET, F. "Controverses avec les juifs." A. Vacant, E. Mangenot, and E. Amann, Dictionnaire de théologie catholique. VIII, Part 2, Paris, 1925, cols. 1870-1914.

VINCENT OF BEAUVAIS. Speculum Historialis.

WALLACH, LUITPOLD. Quellenkritische Studien zum hebräischen Josippon. Breslau, 1939.

————. "Yosippon and the Alexander Romance." Jewish Quarterly Review (New Series). Vol. XXXVII, Philadelphia, 1947, pp. 407-422.

WEDGWOOD, CICELY V. William the Silent. New Haven, 1944.

WILDBOLZ, RUDOLF. Der philosophische Dialog als literarisches Kunstwerk. Bern and Stuttgart, 1952.

WILKINS, ERNEST H. A History of Italian Literature. Cambridge (Mass.), 1954.

WILLIAMS, ARTHUR L. Adversus Judaeos: A Bird's Eye View of Christian Apologiae until the Renaissance. Cambridge (Eng.), 1935.

WILLIAMS, EDWIN B. From Latin to Portuguese. Philadelphia, 1938.

WOLF, JOHANN C. Bibliotheca Hebraea. Vols. III and IV, Hamburg, 1727, 1733.

WOLF, LUCIEN. Essays in Jewish History. London, 1934.

YALKUT SHIMONI. Ascribed to Simeon Kara. 3 vols., Salonica, 1521-1527.

ZIMMELS, BERNHARD. Leo Hebraeus: ein jüdische Philosoph der Renaissance. Leipzig, 1886.

ZINBERG, ISRAEL. Toledot Sifrut Yisrael. Vol. II, Tel Aviv, 1956.

THE ZOHAR. 3 vols., Amsterdam, 1715.

[   ]. "Usque, Samuel." Universal Jewish Encyclopedia (based on M. Freier, Jüdisches Lexicon, Vol. V, p. 1147), Vol. X, New York, 1943, p. 384.

SCRIPTURAL INDEX

Dialogues I, II, III

THIS INDEX CONTAINS REFERENCES TO THE HEBREW SCRIPTURES.
THE NUMBERS ON THE RIGHT REFER TO PAGES IN THE TEXT.

INDEX OF PROPER NAMES FOUND IN THE TEXT OF THE CONSOLAÇAM

347

Aristobulus, High Priest, son of Alexandra, 131, 132, 133
Aristobulus, son of Mariamne, 134, 135, 137
Aristobulus, grandson of Herod, 136
Arithia, 86
Ark, 40, 73, 102, 115, 177, 215, 223
Armenia, 130
Artaxerxes, 113
Arustius, 148
Asa, 93, 99, 106
Ascalon, 62, 142
Ashdodites, 113
Ashtoreth, 70, 73, 82
Asia, 43, 44, 85, 161, 217, 220, 221, 227
Asshur, 85, 219
Assochis, 127
Assyria, 57, 78, 79, 83, 85, 88, 89, 90, 95, 100, 105, 113, 163, 232, 238
Athaliah, 94, 98, 99, 105
Athenians, 38
Augustus Caesar, 131, 135
Azariah, 94, 99, 106
Azazel, 95, 100

Baal, 70, 71, 72, 73, 76, 77, 82, 96, 105
Baal-zebub, 76
Baasa, 75, 80, 105
Babel (tower of), 85, 117
Babylon, 58, 85, 97, 106, 114, 115, 161, 224
Babylonia, 95, 98, 100, 111, 112, 113, 114, 115, 151, 152, 163, 216, 238
Bacchides, 125
Bagdad, 174, 175
Balbinus, 162
Bar Cozba, 150, 151
Barak, 71
Barbary, 171, 194
Barbastro, 188
Barcelona, 188, 194
Bathsheba, 74
Bel, 86, 87
Belgas, 66
Belshazzar, 111, 112
Ben-hadad, 77, 234
Benedict (Pope), 194
Benjamin, 72, 75, 93, 98, 100, 105, 106, 113
Berdoa, 221
Bethar, 150
Bethel, 75
Bichacho, Manuel, 214
Bohemia, 212, 213
Bordeaux, 187
Borhan, Joseph, 175

Bozrah, 239, 261
Brahmans, 221
Brazilians, 103
Brother Vincent; see Vincent
Brutus, 160

Caesaria, 138, 139, 142, 143
Cain, 219
Calicut, 221
Caligula, 137, 160, 220; see also Gaius Caesar
Cambay, 220
Canaan, 46, 56, 71, 73
Canaanites, 70, 89, 232
Cappadocia, 136
Captivity, 157
Caracalla, Bassianus Macrinus, 161
Carcassone, 187
Caspian Mountains, 100
Cassius, 160
Castelsarrasin, 187, 188
Castile, 171, 196, 200, 201, 206
Castor, 144
Catalonia, 192
Catherine, Queen Regent of Castile, 196
Celus, 86
Cestius [Gallus], 139
Chabulon, 60, 139
Chaldea, 112
Chaldeans, 58, 85, 86, 87, 97, 112, 225
Champeaux, 177
Chaphton River, 174
Charles V, Emperor (Charles I of Spain), 209
Charles V, king of France, 193
Charles VI, king of France, 193
Chemosh, 75
Chisdai, 171
Christ, 197
Christendom, 169, 193, 196
Christianity, 168, 183, 192, 199, 208, 229
Christians, 168, 169, 171, 172, 173, 179, 182, 183, 185, 191, 192, 193, 194, 195, 197, 198, 200, 202, 203, 205, 206, 207, 213, 221
Cleopatra, 127, 132, 157
Commodus, 161
Condom, 188
confesos, 195, 198, 199
Constantinople, 210
Cordel, 187
Corinth, 51
Court of Segovia, 197
Cumanus, 61

Cushaim, 82
Cushan-Rishathaim, 70, 73, 90
Cyrene, 152
Cyrus, 58, 111, 112, 113, 134, 153

Damascus, 62, 130, 138
Dan, 75, 78
Daniel, 86, 87, 104, 112, 124
Darius I, 86, 111, 112, 113, 153, 154
Darius II, 113
David, 51, 74, 91, 95, 96, 105, 160, 202, 228, 233, 234, 237, 240, 249, 251, 258
Day of Atonement, 115
De Luna, don Alvaro, 194
De la Foix, Jean, 208
Dead Sea, 142
Death, 212
Deborah, 71, 230
December, 111
Delilah, 72
Demetrius, 58, 128
Devil, 187; see also Satan
Diaspora, 40, 174, 175, 218
Diaspora of Castile, 40
Diaspora of Portugal, 215
Didius Julianus, 161
Distorter, 74; see also Satan
Dominican Order, 194, 205
Domitian, 160, 220
Don Alphonse, 229
Dora, 157
Dothan, 77

Easter, 168
Edom, 124, 238, 239, 240, 248
Edomites, 124
Edward, king of Portugal, 194
Egypt, 51, 57, 63, 68, 75, 82, 85, 90, 93, 94, 97, 100, 117, 118, 125, 132, 133, 137, 148, 152, 157, 161, 164, 171, 177, 219, 224, 230, 232, 239, 240, 244, 253, 259
Ehud, son of Gera, 71
Ekron, 76
Elagabalus, 161, 220
Elah, 75, 80, 105
Eleazar, Chief of the Priests, 119, 120, 123, 155
Eleazar, head of the delegation to Ptolemy, 117
Eleazar, son of Abdia, 60
Eleazar, son of Hananiah, 64, 65 (? sic), 138, 143, 150
Eleazar the Maccabean, 124, 125
Eli, 40, 73, 223

Eliakim, 97, 98, 99, 100, 105, 113
Elijah, 53, 54, 76, 234
Elisha, 76, 77, 78, 234
Ellon, 143
El-Mumenin (Emir), 175
Enemy, 74, 77, 81, 83, 93, 95, 118, 129, 142, 167, 171, 183, 185, 187, 188, 189, 192, 209, 213, 225; see also Satan
Engaddi, 63
England, 44, 180, 181, 182, 184, 187, 202, 208, 218, 224, 229, 238
English silver, 56
Ephah, 245
Ephraim, 65, 92, 252, 253, 257
Epicrates, Prince of Macedonia, 157
Esarhaddon, 79, 232
Esau, 51, 73, 141, 239, 240
Essenes, 126
Esther, 190, 230
Ethiopia, 100
Ethiopians, 88, 103
Eupator, 125
Euphrates, (River), 44
Europe, 43, 44, 85, 161, 199, 209, 211, 217, 227, 230, 231, 236
Evil-merodach, 111
Ezra, 113

Faniel, 141
Faruth, 141
Feast of Booths, 133; see also Succoth
Ferdinand, king of Spain, Aragon and Castile, 194, 198, 209, 229
Ferrara, 213, 230
Fifth Age, 237
Flanders, 181, 185, 208, 230, 231
Florus, 137, 138
Foreheim, 185
France, 44, 168, 169, 171, 172, 177, 181, 185, 188, 190, 191, 192, 193, 208, 218, 224, 229, 231, 238
Frederick, 176

Gadara, 142
Gaius Caesar [Caligula], 60, 137, 160, 219; see also Caligula
Galba, 142
Galilee, 60, 127, 131, 140, 153
Gallienus, 220
Gallus, 139, 162; see also Cestius
Gamala, 140
Ganges (River), 44
Garden of Delight, 55
Garden of Eden, 261
Gareb, 254
Gascony, 188
Gaza, 142, 157

Jehoash, king of Israel, 78, 80, 105
Jehoash, king of Judah, 94, 99, 106
Jehoiachin, 97, 98, 100, 105
Jehoiada, 94, 99
Jehoram, king of Israel, 76, 77, 80, 83, 90, 93, 105
Jehoram, king of Judah, 93, 98, 99, 105
Jehoshaphat, 93, 99, 106, 141
Jehu, 76, 77, 78, 93
Jephthah, 72
Jeremiah, 104, 112, 115
Jericho, 124, 133, 151
Jeroboam, 75, 78, 80, 83, 104, 105, 106
Jeroboam II, 78, 80, 105
Jesse, 262
Jeshua, 113
Jewish Senate, 132
Jezebel, 53, 76, 80
Johanan, the Galilean, 140, 141, 142, 143, 145, 147, 149, 150; see also John
Johanan, High Priest, 137, 144
Johanan the Maccabee, 124, 125
John, 64, 140; see also Johanan, the Galilean
John II, of Portugal, 200, 202, 229
John III, of Portugal, 206
John II, king of France, 193
John II, king of Spain, 196
Jonah, 184
Jonathan the Maccabean, 124, 125
Joppa, 60, 124, 132, 140, 142, 156
Jordan, 43, 55, 57, 60, 63, 127, 133, 142
Joseph (biblical), 219, 240, 257
Joseph, husband of Salome, 133, 134
Joseph, son of Antipater, 129
Josephus, son of Dalaeus, 66
Josephus, son of Gorion, 139, 140, 147
Joshua, 56, 62, 70, 223
Josiah, 96, 97, 100, 106, 137
Jotham, 72, 94, 99, 106
Judah, 56, 59, 60, 63, 65, 75, 78, 80, 93, 94, 95, 96, 98, 100, 105, 106, 113, 125, 126, 129, 131, 147, 148, 234, 237, 239, 240, 247, 251, 253, 257
Judah the Maccabee, 124, 126, 155, 156
Judaism, 205, 209, 211, 212, 227, 229, 231
Judea, 57, 63, 68, 128, 130, 131, 139, 142, 150, 153
Judith, 230
Julianus, 161
Julius Caesar, 61, 68, 131, 160
Julius Severus, 153

Juno, 85, 220
Jupiter, 130, 220, 238
Jupiter Belus, 85

Kedar, 245
Kenaz, 71
Kidron, 135, 145, 146, 254

Laban, 253
Lappidoth, 71
Lathyrus, 127, 157
Latin, 131, 134, 229
Lebanon, 67, 255, 256
Lemta, 221
Lent, 168
Lerida, 188, 194
Les Halles, 177
Levi, Rabbi Joseph, 197
Levites, 103, 113
Lisbon, 203, 205
London, 180
London Bridge, 184
Louis of France, 193
Louis of Salamanca, 195
Lucifer, 114
Lutherans, 1u5, 193
Lybia, 221
Lysias, 156
Lysimachus, 157

Maccabees, 123, 124, 129, 132, 133, 134
Macedonia, 118, 124, 154, 155, 156
Macedonians, 124, 155, 156, 158, 159
Magdalene Day, 193
Magog, 258
Malachiah, 147
Malichus, 132
Mallorca, 194
Manasseh, 65, 95, 96, 97, 98, 99, 105, 116, 124, 156
Marcia, 161
Marcus Aurelius, 161
Marcus Cato, 160
Mariamne, 131, 133, i34, 135, 136
Mark Anthony, 132, 133
Mars, 238
Marsan, 187
Masada, 56, 68, 150
Mattathiah the Maccabee, 124, 145, 155
Maximinus, 162
Mayence, 162
Mayer, 196
Mecca, 170
Medes, 57, 79, 111, 112, 114, 159
Media, 174